Broken Bonds

BROKEN BONDS
The Disintegration of Yugoslavia

LENARD J. COHEN

Westview Press
BOULDER • SAN FRANCISCO • OXFORD

Copyright © 1993 by Westview Press, Inc.

Published in 1993 in the United States of America by Westview Press, Inc., 5500 Central Avenue, Boulder, Colorado 80301-2877, and in the United Kingdom by Westview Press, 36 Lonsdale Road, Summertown, Oxford OX2 7EW

Library of Congress Cataloging-in-Publication Data
Cohen, Lenard J.
  Broken bonds: the disintegration of Yugoslavia / by Lenard J. Cohen
    p. cm.
  Includes index.
  ISBN 0-8133-8030-8 — ISBN 0-8133-1854-8 (pbk.)
  1. Yugoslavia—History. 2. Yugoslavia—Ethnic relations.
  I. Title.
DR1282.C64 1993
949.7—dc20   92-44716
                                                                  CIP

Printed and bound in the United States of America

 The paper used in this publication meets the requirements of the American National Standard for Permanence of Paper for Printed Library Materials Z39.48-1984.

10 9 8 7 6 5 4 3

*To future peace and cooperation
among the peoples
of Southeastern Europe*

Contents

9 Yugoslavism's Failure and Future

Tables and Illustrations

Tables

Figures

Maps

Photographs (between pp. 78-79)

Changing of the guard at the "Flower House," the Belgrade mausoleum of Josip Broz Tito

Slobodan Milošević, president of Serbia

Franjo Tudjman, head of the Croatian Democratic Alliance (HDZ), voting in Croatia's first post-World War II multiparty election

Legislative deputies in the Croatian Sabor (legislature) celebrating a proclamation that affirmed Croatia's separate identity as a state

Croatia's President Franjo Tudjman and Slovenia's President Milan Kučan discuss their joint proposal for a confederally organized state

Serbia's first competitive election; mass meeting of opposition party supporters in Belgrade

Opposition party supporters in Belgrade

Police action against anti-Milošević demonstrators in Belgrade

Students protesting in Belgrade against the Milošević regime

Father and son observe federal army tanks assisting the Milošević regime in suppression of the March 1991 protests in Belgrade

Croatian demonstrators attacking federal soldiers in an armored personnel carrier during violent clashes

General Veljko Kadijević, the Yugoslav defense minister

Serbia's President Milošević and President Alija Izetbegović of Bosnia-Hercegovina

Meeting in Belgrade of Croatia's President Tudjman and Serbia's President Milošević

Meeting of the presidents of the Yugoslav republics at Brdo na Kranju to discuss Yugoslavia's future

Photographs (between pp. 206-207)

Slovenian border guards hoist the new flag of an independent Slovenia

Yugoslav federal army soldiers take down the Slovenian flag at a border crossing

Barricade of buses and other vehicles to block federal military forces

Blocked JNA tanks firing during the federal military's invasion of Slovenia

JNA forces retreating under the surveillance of Slovenian Territorial Defense forces

Conversation between Croatia's Stipe Mesić, the last president of the Socialist Federal Republic of Yugoslavia (SFRY), and Ante Marković, the last SFRY prime minister

European Community monitors—the "ice-cream men"—observing hostilities in Croatia

Serbian soldiers marching Croatians out of their village

Refugees from Sarajevo

Residents of Sarajevo digging fresh graves at a Moslem cemetery

President Izetbegović of Bosnia-Hercegovina shaking the hand of President Tudjman of Croatia after signing an agreement

Radovan Karadžić, leader of the Bosnian Serbs, at the United Nations after talks with Cyrus Vance and Lord David Owen

Croatian and Moslem prisoners of war at the Serbian detention camp of Manjača

Croats and Moslems forced to leave an area occupied by Serbian forces in Bosnia

A refugee near Bijeljina in eastern Bosnia

A distraught Moslem woman and her child at a refugee holding center in eastern Bosnia

Armed man with child, a common scene in Bosnia

Hans-Dietrich Genscher, the German foreign minister, with President Franjo Tudjman of Croatia

Canadian peacekeeping troops from the United Nations protection force prepared to deploy at Daruvar, Croatia

An elderly Serbian woman in Kruševac, Serbia, holds an election poster of Milan Panić

Members of a local election board in Belgrade count votes in the race for president of Serbia

Vojislav Šešelj, the ultranationalistic leader of the Serbian Radical Party

Dobroslav Paraga, the ultranationalistic leader of the Croatian Party of Right, at his headquarters

Croatian President Tudjman with other Croatian officials in front of the presidential jet

Serbian-Croatian summit at Geneva

Preface

The twentieth century began, and seems destined to end, with the major South Slav ethnic groups divided among separate Balkan states. Whether such division is a tragedy or a blessing depends on one's vantage point. For many inhabitants and observers of Southeastern Europe, the creation and preservation of a unified "Yugoslav" (i.e., South Slav) state—such as the "First Yugoslavia" (1918-1941) and the "Second Yugoslavia" (1944-1991)—exemplified a natural and desirable arrangement. For others, however, such statehood constituted an artificial phenomenon, speciously conceived and doomed to disintegrate. Unfortunately, contending efforts to either radically engineer or aggressively demolish Yugoslav state cohesion have frequently resulted in grievous suffering for the inhabitants of the Balkan region—a pattern that continues unabated on the threshold of the twenty-first century.

Sharing Rebecca West's view that any excursion into Yugoslavia's complex affairs vividly illustrates how "the past has made the present," I begin this book by revisiting the genesis of the "Yugoslav idea" prior to the creation of the first united South Slav state and also by examining that state's troubled development under both the royalist and communist regimes. In subsequent chapters I discuss the factors that have fostered and impeded the more recent evolution of Yugoslav state and political development, devoting particular attention to the causes and consequences of the Second Yugoslavia's drift toward disintegration in the 1980s and its eventual violent breakup in the early 1990s. In the concluding section of the book I consider the serious difficulties connected with the internationalization of "the Yugoslav crisis" during 1992 and 1993, the savage ethnic and political conflict on the territory of the former Yugoslavia, and also some of the problems facing the successor states to the Yugoslav communist federation.

I would like to express my gratitude to Steve Markovich, Milorad Manojlovic, Primož Južnic, Ljubica Jelušič, Gordana Perc, Marija Nikolic, Ana Davičo, Branka Vujčić, Anita Mahoney, Bill Schuss, and Bob Birtch for various analytical insights, research assistance, and technical help during the preparation of the manuscript. Thanks also to Susan McEachern and Michelle Starika Asakawa of Westview Press for their patience and assistance. Dean Stanley Shapiro and Dean Evan Alderson provided a "road less traveled," and it made all the difference. Helene Michaels, Diane Lesack, Linda Wetzel, Carol Roche, and Margaret Oxnard also provided much appreciated administrative support. Finally, as always, David Jay and Jeanette Vesna make it all worthwhile.

Lenard J. Cohen

Were someone to build them a bridge there, he would do them the greatest service....Nothing could have been more difficult to imagine than such a marvellous structure in this fractured and desolate landscape....But the country could not accept the bridge and the bridge could not accept the country.

—Ivo Andrić, *The Bridge on the Žepa*

1

The Evolution of the Yugoslav Idea: 1830-1980

You cannot understand Yugoslavia without a thorough knowledge of its history even before its official birth in 1918. This, because the reasons for its birth were the same as those for its death.

—Dobrica Ćosić

Just as in earlier centuries the ideas of Croato-Serbian national (linguistic) unity and Yugoslavism grew from common interests in the face of foreign threats...so too did this century's Croato-Serbian conflicts emerge because of different conceptions of Yugoslavism, and especially the contrasting impact of the common Yugoslav state on their national beings.

—Franjo Tudjman

THROUGHOUT THE EXISTENCE of the Yugoslav state from 1918 to 1991, survival against the odds was its quintessential feature. Viewing Yugoslavia's highly diverse regional, religious, and ethnic composition, both foreign and domestic observers typically drew attention to the country's innate fragility or, sometimes less generously, its basic illegitimacy and artificiality. Indeed, convinced that Yugoslavia was doomed to disintegrate, the most hostile commentators plotted to ensure the realization of their prophecy. During the interwar period, for example, Adolf Hitler's hectoring propaganda chief, Joseph Goebbels, described Yugoslavia as "a questionable patchwork of states" whose demise might be hastened if Berlin would "do something with the Croats."[1] Meanwhile, in Rome, Benito Mussolini's son-in-law and foreign minister, Count Galeazzo Ciano, schemed to detach Croatia from Yugoslavia and yearned to organize the Albanians of Kosovo "into a dagger pointed at the side of Belgrade."[2] Having connived to destabilize Yugoslavia for years, the German and Italian fascist regimes eventually collaborated (along with their Hungarian and Bulgarian junior partners) to invade and dismember the young state in March 1941.

Following the bloody resistance struggle and ethnopolitical civil war during World War II, the Yugoslav state was reborn under communist leadership. This new effort at Yugoslav state building soon faced another serious test of survival in 1948 when Joseph Stalin became enraged over Marshal Tito's maverick style and self-confidence. Threatening that he would "shake his little finger and there will be no more Tito," Stalin plotted to have the Yugoslav leader assassinated and subjected the communist political leadership in Belgrade to enormous pressure.[3] The wily Soviet dictator hesitated to invade Yugoslavia, however, thereby allowing Tito and his comrades to weather the storm and remain in power.

Having survived the enmity of the most powerful totalitarian leaders of his time and maintained the cohesion of the Yugoslav state, Tito proceeded to wrap his regime in a mantle of socialist reform and innovation. Precariously situated between the two major world power blocs, the Yugoslav communists searched about for a developmental model that would preserve their one-party and socialist proclivities yet allow them to jettison Stalinism's most egregious facets and selectively incorporate certain useful features and assistance from the Western democracies. What resulted was an eclectic model that theoretically drew upon Marxism's more democratic and humane impulses and also imported various capitalist socioeconomic principles. Initially fashioned as a makeshift alternative to Soviet-type socialism in the wake of the 1948 rift with the USSR, Yugoslavia's regime-sponsored reforms gradually acquired stature as a distinct model of Marxist development. The notion of workers' self-management—which originated with the slogan "Factories to the Workers" and was later recast as a more participatory form of "self-managed socialism"—served as the conceptual basis and label for the Yugoslav reform model.

During the 1950s and 1960s, efforts by the Belgrade regime to construct a less bureaucratized and more democratic variant of socialism won widespread praise both within and outside Eastern Europe. The communist regime took special pride in its management of interethnic relations, proclaiming in 1958 that although "negative manifestations" still existed in this area, the country's socialist system was the guarantee "which assures equality to all peoples and national minorities of Yugoslavia and to each people the right to decide its fate."[4] By early 1973, Edward Kardelj, the principal architect of most major Tito-era reforms, could proudly assert that "self-management had not only demonstrated its economic effectiveness" but also allowed Yugoslavia to "solve democratically most of the contradictions and conflicts that cropped up in society."[5]

At the end of the 1980s, only fifteen years after Kardelj's proud claims, Yugoslav communist leaders again faced a major crisis of survival, regretfully conceding that their country lacked the "elementary rules of behavior in conflict situations which the crisis imposes"[6] and that "priority efforts" must be directed at "raising Yugoslavia's low credibility in the world."[7] During 1990, with the disintegration of the League of Yugoslav Communists (LCY) as a political organization and the advent of competitive elections, Yugoslavia's interregional and interethnic divisions became so pronounced that the country virtually ceased to function as a unified federal state. By the second half of 1991, the Yugoslav state had disintegrated, precipitating military struggles, interethnic violence, and widespread human suffering in several regions of the former country.

What accounted for Yugoslavia's plunge from a seemingly positive to a negative model of socialist reform and intergroup relations? And what measures for recovery were advanced by the country's ethnically and regionally segmented one-party elite? What were the reasons for the eventual abandonment of reform socialism, the elimination of the single-party monopoly, and the disintegration of Yugoslavia as a unified federal state? Why did the noncommunist and born-again or relabeled communist leaders elected to power during the revival of multiparty pluralism in 1990 fail to resolve the crisis through negotiations? And why did they ultimately permit their disagreements to degenerate into interethnic violence and civil war? Can the successor states to Yugoslavia establish stable democratic regimes, overcome their economic difficulties, and find a basis for peaceful cooperation in the Balkan region?

These and other questions are examined in subsequent chapters of this book. It is useful to begin, however, by considering the original motives underlying the creation of the Yugoslav state—both at its point of conception in 1918 and at its second incarnation in 1945—as well as the major problems, achievements, and failures of the country during its relatively short, but troubled, precommunist and communist phases of development.

Yugoslavism Before Yugoslavia

The Nineteenth Century

The modern conception that a single Balkan state should be established by the principal South Slavic (i.e., "Yugoslav") nationalities first achieved prominence in the nineteenth century. Initially such a belief—what was referred to as the "Yugoslav idea" or "Yugoslavism"—was advanced by various Croatian writers who emphasized the common ethnic heritage and linguistic ties among the South Slavs as a basis for their cooperation and eventual political unification. In its early emanation, Croatian inspired Yugoslavism was connected with the so-called Illyrian movement of the 1830s and 1840s, which, drawing upon the impulses toward national awakening generated by the French Revolution, sought to assert the linguistic, ethnic, and territorial rights of the Croats within Hungarian controlled Croatia. Illyrianism actively promoted Croatian cultural renaissance as a first step toward the broader ethnic and political unity of the South Slavs. According to Ljudevit Gaj, the key actor in the Illyrian movement, the Croats and the Serbs were the two major subgroups of the South Slavic or Illyrian nationality, which also included the Slovenes and the Slavic inhabitants of Bosnia, Hercegovina, Montenegro and Bulgaria.[8]

Socially and ethnically, Illyrianism appealed primarily to a narrow portion of the Croatian upper classes but enjoyed little support among the Serbs, Slovenes, or other South Slav peoples. Indeed, Vuk Karadžić, one of the most important Serbian thinkers of the period, although enjoying good personal relations with supporters of the Illyrian idea, worried that the distinctiveness of the Serbian language might be overshadowed by the Illyrian concept.[9] Moreover, although Vuk's own linguistic innovations would facilitate cultural interaction between Serbs and Croats, his argument that the Croats were essentially Serbs, from a linguistic point of view, undercut his role as an advocate of South Slav unity. The ideas of Gaj and his compatriots nevertheless represented a major ideological building block for later efforts to formulate a unifying Yugoslav vision among the varieties of South Slav nationalism taking shape in the Balkan region during this period of time. When Illyrian spokesmen assumed an important role during the revolution of 1848 in the Hapsburg monarchy—which included cooperation between Serbs and Croats in challenging Hungarian rule—they provided an important stimulus to new thinking about South Slav nationalism and unity.

The scope of the original Illyrian idea was substantially expanded during the second half of the nineteenth century by other Croatian intellectuals, such as the liberal Catholic clergymen Bishop Josip Juraj Strossmajer and Franjo Rački, who conceptualized Yugoslavism as a supranational ideology expressing the common origins, cultural ties, and spiritual bonds among the South Slavs. Such bonds would, it was believed, transcend the ethnic, religious, and political divisions separating the individual South Slavic groups—disputes that had been exacerbated during their lengthy subjugation by different external forces and their exposure to contrasting cultural and state traditions (e.g., the Croats and Slovenes living primarily under Austro-Hungarian rule, the Serbs and other South Slavs living mainly under Ottoman tutelage). The Yugoslavism of Strossmajer and Rački, like that of their Illyrian predecessors, represented a rather amorphous striving—at once both romantic and practical—to nurture cultural and political bonds among the closely related South Slav peoples.

Like Gaj, however, Strossmajer and Rački initially made little progress in attracting converts to their ideas outside segments of the Croatian upper strata (i.e., the liberal bourgeoisie, the middle-class intelligentsia, and the liberal Catholic clergy). Obstacles to the vertical dissemination of the Yugoslav idea down through the layers of the Croatian social structure and the lower strata's predominant emotional commitment to its own individual locales, can, to a certain extent, be explained by the educational backwardness of Croatia's agrarian population in the nineteenth century and also its lack of information about other South Slav regions and peoples. Moreover, during the second part of the nineteenth century, proponents of the Yugoslav idea were competing with several other major ideologies, whose adherents sought to mobilize the Croatian masses on the basis of a narrower nationalistic program that contrasted sharply with the transethnic and romantic cultural goals connected with Yugoslavism.[10]

The horizontal spread of the Yugoslav idea to other South Slav nationalities faced similar barriers. For example, the lower social layer of Serbian society lived like the Croats, as a subordinate agricultural stratum within the confines of the oppressive Ottoman imperial system, and also suffered from educational deprivation. Thus, throughout the nineteenth century, it was Serbian nationalism and the Serbs' drive to free themselves from Ottoman control, rather than Illyrianism or Yugoslavism, that preoccupied emergent Serbian elites and their mass peasant constituencies. Members of the Serbian intelligentsia and small ruling circles were by no means unaware of the popularity of the Yugoslav idea in Croatia's upper class, but initially such notions attracted only a small minority of Serbian leaders and thinkers. Focused on their struggle with the Turks, Serbian elites generally saw little benefit in joint political action or South Slav solidarity with the Croats in the Austro-Hungarian empire. Such parochial sentiments were reciprocated by the majority of the Croatian political elite, who were preoccupied with enlarging their own region's autonomy within Austria-Hungary.

The pattern of noncooperation and ethnic distance among South Slav elites was interrupted for a brief period in the mid-1860s when Croatian bishop Strossmajer and the Serbian foreign minister Ilija Garašanin agreed to work for "a Yugoslav state independent from both Austria and Turkey."[11] Motivated primarily by the momentary exigencies of external policy— the Croats wanted Serbia's help against Hungary, and the Serbs sought Croatian assistance against Austria—and with no genuine or deep commitment to Yugoslav ideology on the Serbian side, the agreement was abandoned by the Serbs in less than two years. Among the various issues impeding agreement between Strossmajer and Garašanin was the problem of contending Serbian and Croatian claims to Bosnia-Hercegovina. It is interesting that Garašanin would eventually become renowned not for his Yugoslavism but for formulating writings (which would only become public in 1906) proposing a "Greater Serbia," which would encompass all regions of the Balkans that had large Serbian populations.[12]

The short-lived exercise in Serbian-Croatian elite solidarity in the 1860s revealed not only the relatively weak reception to the Yugoslav idea among the South Slavs, but also the unique character of the relationship between Serbian nationalism and Yugoslavism. Unlike the Croats, who were minority subjects in the Dual Monarchy and were denied the right of self-government, the Serbs were members of a quasi-independent state (after 1817), and although formally still subjects of Turkey, they could see that the achievement of their full independence from Ottoman Turkey was only a matter of time (a goal that was finally achieved in 1878). Unification of all Serbian people in a strong independent state became the paramount goal of the Serbian elite—an achievement that could be realized only by striking a decisive blow at Turkey and by fending off incursions of Austrian power (and to a somewhat lesser extent Russian power) in the Balkans.[13] The Yugoslav idea, and cooperation with other South Slavs, might aid the goal of Serbian unification in specific circumstances, but Serbian nationalism rather than the symbiosis or negotiated integration of the diverse South Slav peoples had first claim on the energies and political passions of the Serbian leaders.

Thus for most Serbs the idea of South Slav unity before World War I was a useful concept only to the extent that it might facilitate and hasten the achievement of Serbia's distinct national and territorial goals. In contrast, those Croats who espoused Yugoslavism sought to achieve some kind of South Slav unity within a federally structured Hapsburg state (based upon the formula of "trialism," which balanced the interests of Austrians, Hungarians, and South Slavs) or, in some cases, an independent South Slav state organized along federal lines.[14] Some Serbs appropriated the Yugoslav idea as a useful means to advance their parochial national strategy, but others were highly suspicious of the concept. Such distrust was largely influenced by the close association of "Yugoslavist" and nationalist ideas in the programs of many Croatian political movements and thinkers and also by the lack of widespread or genuine support for the Yugoslav idea in Croatian elite circles. Moreover, should a unified South Slav state be constituted, the still insecure Serbian elite—that was only partially independent from Turkish rule in the period from 1817 to 1878—hardly relished the prospect of contending with the strong elements of ultranationalism and outright Serbo-phobia prevalent in many sections of the Croat leadership and population. During the nineteenth century, lack of support for the Croatian inspired Yugoslav idea was particularly notable in Serbia's military leadership, one of the major pillars of the fledgling country's political elite. Military leaders were imbued with a deep sense of Serbian history and a dedication to the liberation of territories claimed by Serbia that were still under foreign control.[15]

In addition, elite political culture in Serbia had been shaped in the brutal context of the long Ottoman control of the Balkans and, from roughly 1830 to 1878, in the atmosphere of the more or less benign authoritarian rule wielded by successive Serbian princes functioning under quasi-Ottoman tutelage. As German historian Leopold von Ranke ethnocentrically, but aptly, observed about Serbia in the mid-1830s: "It is remarkable, what ideas are now making their way into this half-Oriental state. These ideas involve the rights and privileges of men...responsibility of ministers; and lastly, that the Prince himself should be amenable to the laws; though it is true, the laws have yet to be framed."[16] Obsessed with the issue of liberating subjugated Serbs, nearly all segments of the Serbian elite—including many of those who flirted with Yugoslavism—had little tolerance for the idea of democratic compromise among the South Slavs. For example, when it came to regions with ethnically mixed populations such as Bosnia-Hercegovina, where Serbs and Croats had advanced sharply conflicting territorial claims, even genuine advocates of the Yugoslav idea could find little common ground.

Thus by the second half of the nineteenth century Serbian elites still had little appreciation of, or experience with, the democratic balancing and compromising of diverse ethnopolitical interests in the kind of federal structures advocated by Croatian and Slovenian adherents of Yugoslavism. Whereas most Croatian Yugoslavists sought a gradually restructured Hapsburg monarchy, giving the Croats, the Slovenes, and the Serbian minority of Austro-Hungary greater autonomy and influence, the citizens of Serbia were interested primarily in the rapid destruction of Hapsburg and Ottoman power in the Balkans and also their own political paramountcy in Southeastern Europe. Thus rather than urging an evolutionary, policentric, and decentralized union of equal South Slav peoples, the Serbian brand of Yugoslavism was revolutionary, centralistic, and Serbo-centric. As Jovan Cvijić, one of Serbia's most prominent intellectuals and a supporter of Yugoslavism, noted with regard to the rise of Serbian nationalist consciousness in the nineteenth century: "Two main ideas were steadily taking root in the minds of the people—the great mission of Serbia and her destined task of destroying the out-of-date powers, Austria and Turkey....The idea of the 'Serbian mission' gradually expanded and it became a Jugoslav mission."[17]

The Early Twentieth Century

Unreconciled ideas about how to realize the idea of Yugoslav unity, as well as both support and opposition to Yugoslavism, came into sharper perspective in the decade prior to World War I. Enthusiasm for South Slav unification remained concentrated in the upper strata of the population, particularly among the intelligentsia, but the expansion of higher and secondary education in the Balkan region broadened the number of individuals engaged in discourse on social and political matters. Increasingly, members of the area's many newly formed youth movements assumed a major role in discussions about the unification of the South Slav peoples. Moreover, within the Hapsburg monarchy, the formation in 1905 of the Serbo-Croat Coalition, an organization of deputies in the Croatian legislature, strengthened solidarity among those political forces dedicated to broadening South Slav cooperation and influence within Austria-Hungary. Some younger Croat leaders also sympathetically entertained the possibility that Serbia could play the role of a kind of Piedmont or Prussia, spearheading the formation of a future state that would unify South Slavs both within and outside the empire. Enthusiasm for the Yugoslav idea appeared to be greatest in Dalmatia, where the mixed Croatian and Serbian population, and the relative distance of both groups from Zagreb and Belgrade (the area was under Austrian rule, unlike the rest of Hungarian-controlled Croatian territories), stimulated support for South Slav cooperation.

Concerned that the spread of Yugoslav ideas would undercut their own control and expansionist plans in the Balkans, Austro-Hungarian authorities suppressed manifestations of South Slav solidarity whenever possible. Thus the notorious Agram (Zagreb) trial of 1909, involving the arrest of several like-minded Serbian and Croatian leaders on charges of treason, was closely linked to the monarchy's formal annexation of Bosnia and Hercegovina in 1908 (the area had already been occupied by Austria-Hungary since 1878). The blatant fabrication of the charges against the defendants, and the obvious bias of the presiding judicial officials, convinced many leaders of the South Slav community as well as foreign observers[18] that reform of the monarchy to accommodate minority ethnic interests was highly unlikely.

Despite increasing support for Yugoslav unity among the South Slav population of the Austro-Hungarian Empire, the majority of Croatian citizens and political activists at the turn of the century still viewed Serbia with suspicion and generally believed that any rhetorical commitment to the Yugoslav idea emanating from Belgrade was a cloak for Serbia's territorial ambitions. Thus the increasingly popular Croatian Peasant Party of Antun and Stjepan Radić, for example, called for greater cooperation among the South Slavs, but such cooperation was to take place within the Hapsburg monarchy. Similarly, support in Slovenia for the Yugoslav idea grew substantially in the last part of the nineteenth and first decade of the twentieth centuries, but the Slovenes also focused on reform of the Dual Monarchy through a trialistic solution which would create a new Slavic third force in Austria-Hungary, rather than on the elimination of the imperial system or direct union of the Slovenes with the Serbian state.[19] By the eve of World War I, however, a minority of Slovenes had become disenchanted with the prospects for Austro-Hungarian reform. For example, Ivan Cankar, one of the most prominent Slovene writers of his time and a maverick member of the Social Democratic Party, argued that enthusiasts of South Slav unity should work for the creation of a Yugoslav republic along federal lines (including linguistic rights for each constituent group).[20]

Many younger Slovenes and Croats active in the radical youth movement were also impressed with Serbian military successes in the Balkan Wars (1912-1913) and grudgingly recognized that Serbian political and military strength might prove to be the essential factor for the achievement of

South Slav unification in Southeastern Europe. Such sentiments were reflected in a manifesto issued by a group of young Slovenian intellectuals in 1913:

> As it is a fact that we Slovenes, Croats and Serbs, constitute a compact linguistic and ethnic group with similar economic conditions, and so indissolubly linked by common fate on a common territory that no one of the three can aspire to a separate future, and in consideration of the fact that among the Slovenes, Croats, and Serbs, the Jugoslav thought is even today strongly developed, we have extended our national sentiments beyond our frontier to the Croats and Serbs....By this we all become members of one united Jugo-slav nation.[21]

Ironically, just when a substantial portion of younger Croatian and Slovenian activists within the Hapsburg monarchy had become more disposed to following the leadership of Serbia, Belgrade's stunning victories in the Balkan Wars, and particularly the euphoria of recovering territory that had been lost to the Serbs for five centuries (such as the Kosovo-Metohija region), impelled most Serbian political leaders to become more aggressive in the pursuit of Serbian national goals. Moreover, many felt that the impressive show of Serbian military power obviated the need for compromise with other South Slav groups, such as the Croats and Slovenes, who were seeking some kind of future Yugoslav federalism. Although the majority of the Serbian elite and masses demonstrated little sympathy for Croatian inspired Yugoslavism, by 1914 many younger Serb activists had become imbued with the romantic notion of South Slav unification. Unfortunately, little practical thought had been devoted to how such unification might be achieved and, even more important, the shape of a future South Slav state. Thus, stirred by a rather incoherent admixture of both Yugoslavism and Greater Serbianism, the extremist fringe of the Serbian youth movement—supported by Gavrilo Princip and his compatriots in the ethnic cauldron of Bosnia-Hercegovina—had become preoccupied with the goal of striking a decisive terrorist blow against Austria-Hungary which was the power viewed as the major impediment to the realization of South Slav unity.

The assassination of Austria's Archduke Franz Ferdinand at Sarajevo by Princip and his accomplices, and the subsequent outbreak of World War I, significantly changed the political prospects for South Slav unification. The onslaught of Austrian hostilities against Serbia pitted the Croats and the Slovenes of the Dual Monarchy against the forces of the Serbian Kingdom, thereby intensifying the extent of interethnic distance and territorial fragmentation that already existed among the major South Slav peoples. Thus the Croats and Slovenes of the monarchy, and even the Serbs under Austro-Hungarian rule, were expected to help defeat Serbia and its allies in the war. At the same time, however, by exposing and exacerbating Austria-Hungary's ethnic, political, and military fragility, the war provided a fresh opportunity for the success of the Yugoslav idea. Whether the Dual Monarchy would remain a unified state or be dismembered as a result of the conflict became the major consideration affecting the future plans of those espousing the cause of South Slav unification.

During World War I the most important nongovernmental advocate of South Slav unity and Austria-Hungary's dismemberment was the Yugoslav Committee, composed mainly of Croatian leaders but also a number of Yugoslav-oriented Serbs and Slovenes. Headed by the Croat Ante Trumbić, the committee—organized in Rome, and later based in London—opposed Greater Serbianism and worked for the establishment of a new South Slav state organized along federal lines. The Yugoslav Committee's predominant Croatian composition, its avowed opposition to Serbian nationalism, as well as its sponsorship of Croatian foreign policy interests (particularly vis-à-vis Italy) made the organization unpopular with the Serbian government which was headed by Nikola Pašić. For its part, Serbia was engaged in a desperate wartime struggle, and although Pašić sought the support of South Slavs in the Hapsburg monarchy, he regarded them as meddlesome allies who might, at best, assist Serbia's national and strategic goals. Thus throughout the war the Yugoslav Committee and Pašić quarreled over the best way to achieve South Slav unity, an idea that had acquired renewed popularity and potential in the Balkan region. When, in July 1917, Pašić and the Committee temporarily worked out a compromise on a joint statement (the so-called Corfu Declaration) endorsing the creation of a South Slav state along democratic and parliamentary lines, the divisive issue of whether such a state would be unitary or federal was deliberately left unclear.[22]

Pašić's attitude concerning the complexities of South Slav unification has long been a source of controversy among historians. Some observers have characterized him as a chauvinist and suggest that his important role in the creation of a South Slav state was an expression of his efforts to ensure the domination of the Serbs over their neighboring ethnic groups. Others, however, emphasize Pašić's genuine commitment to the Yugoslav idea and also to the principles of parliamentary democracy.[23] What is less contentious is that Pašić was an extremely skillful and tactically agile politician who, during the course of World War I, used both the idea of expansive Serbian nationalism and the notion of South

Slav unity to advance Serbia's political interests. Pašić's attitude was also influenced by that of his Western Allies, who, until very near the end of the war, remained committed to the preservation of the Austro-Hungarian monarchy. When it seemed that the monarchy would survive as a result of Allied benevolence, Pašić urged that Serbs be permitted to acquire territories such as Bosnia-Hercegovina, which contained a large Serbian population. If, however, it would be possible to destroy Austria-Hungary altogether, Pašić suggested (as early as September 1914) that he would welcome the union of all the South Slav lands with the Serbian Kingdom.

When the Allies finally opted for self-determination in Europe, and the implied destruction of Austria-Hungary, Pašić had deftly positioned himself to fulfill Serbia's historic "mission": the unification of all Serbs in a single state, with the achievement of a broader Yugoslav state framework in which Serbia would play the major role. In retrospect, the most significant question is really not whether Pašić was an enthusiastic advocate of the Yugoslav idea but rather *what kind* of Yugoslav state he was willing to create and participate in. Thus, the evidence clearly demonstrates that Pašić was willing to support a Yugoslav state under the right circumstances, that is, those in which Serbia's role would be paramount and uncontested. Pašić had no taste for the federal models supported by the Yugoslav Committee, an organization supported by those whom he felt were willing to "weaken and isolate Serbia."[24]

When a breakdown of order in the Hapsburg domains and the threat of an Italian invasion finally led a group of Yugoslav-oriented Croatian and Serbian politicians based in Zagreb to request the Serbian government's leadership in the formation of the South Slav state, Pašić was in a very strong position—as prime minister of a victorious Allied power—to ensure Serbian political hegemony in the new union of different regions and nationalities. Faced with this situation, most Croatian and Slovenian leaders, having been cast adrift by the breakdown of the Hapsburg monarchy and tainted by their wartime association with the Central Powers, had little choice but to prudently "become South Slavs as the lesser evil."[25] After decades of discussions about the subject, a Yugoslav state had finally come into existence. Unfortunately the rather asymmetrical distribution of power among the various ethnic contingents in the new state's founding elite—the Serbs clearly being in a superior position owing to their wartime victory—and the rather uneven popular support for South Slav unity in the general population[26] did not augur well for political stability in the Balkans.

Interwar Yugoslavism

The 1920s and 1930s

The South Slav political union created in 1918—the Kingdom of the Serbs, Croats, and Slovenes—involved the formal amalgamation of highly disparate and historically fragmented territories and peoples. The new state included the previously independent Kingdoms of Serbia and Montenegro (whose full sovereignty was recognized by the Ottoman Empire in 1878); Macedonia, which had been ruled by Turkey up to 1912 and afterward by Serbia; the Austrian-ruled territories of Slovenia and Dalmatia; the Hungarian-governed Vojvodina and Croatia-Slavonia; and Bosnia-Hercegovina, which following centuries of Ottoman control had come under the occupation and administration of the Dual Monarchy in 1878 (and was formally annexed by Vienna in 1908). The new Yugoslav state was multiconfessional, including three large and historically divided religious communities (Eastern Orthodox, 46.7 percent; Roman Catholics, 39.3 percent; and Moslems, 11.2 percent), and was comprised of several different nationalities (e.g., Serbs together with Montenegrins, approximately 42 percent; Croats, 23 percent; Slovenes, 8 percent; Macedonians, 5 percent; the Moslems of Bosnia-Hercegovina and the Sandjak, 5 percent; and Albanians, 4 percent).[27]

Establishing the legitimacy and maintaining the cohesion of a state composed of such varied historical traditions and subcultural groups represented an enormous challenge for the country's political leadership. The idea of a South Slav state had been a prime motive (especially among Croatian and Slovenian participants), inspiring the wartime elite negotiations that resulted in the formation of the new state commitment to the notion of Yugoslavism and the reality of a South Slav state, but it still held only limited attraction for the overwhelming majority of citizens in the ethnically and regionally divided country. "Yugoslavism," as one student of prevailing views during the period observed, "appealed to idealists, but not to those who had to deal with the realities of the South Slav world....South Slav unity or Yugoslavism was at its best...a remote vision."[28] Perhaps the most serious threat to the legitimacy of the new state, however, was the controversy that quickly arose concerning future constitutional arrangements. During constitutional discussions held in 1920 and 1921, for example, Serbian leaders—who were accustomed to a unitary form of government in independent Serbia and were unwilling to forsake the political dominance they wielded in the immediate postwar provisional government—completely rejected initiatives advanced by

Croatian and Slovenian leaders to organize the new state along federal or confederal lines.

Although the most influential Serbian leader, Nikola Pašić, claimed that he was not opposed to a federation in principle, he was unwilling to agree to any arrangement that would divide the country's dispersed Serbs (about 2 million, or roughly 30 percent of whom lived in Vojvodina, Croatia-Slavonia, Dalmatia, and Bosnia-Hercegovina) among different federal units.[29] Believing that a strong centralized state was imperative because of the dangers posed from foreign and domestic subversion, Pašić—as an apt analysis of the constitutional debates suggested—feared "the Croatian and Slovenian spirit, which had acted as a dissolving force in the Austro-Hungarian Monarchy, and he [Pašić] came to the conclusion that if allowed a free course it would disintegrate the Yugoslav state."[30]

Pašić's viewpoint was shared by the vocal leaders of the Serbian minority in Croatia, who became even more aggressive advocates for a highly centralized unitary state. That the regionally popular Croatian Peasant Party, led by Stjepan Radić, refused to participate in the work of the Constituent Assembly assisted Serbian efforts to push through a unitary state model in June 1921, but fueled subsequent Croatian claims that the new state was constitutionally illegitimate. Thus Serbian political forces won a constitutional victory in 1921, but their establishment of a unitary model—though democratically engineered in a freely elected legislative body—would cause irreparable harm to future state unity by seriously alienating the country's two major non-Serb ethnic groups. Indeed, over most of the next seven decades, Croatian and Slovenian protests against various governments and regimes in Belgrade and against the existence of a Yugoslav state would be based in large part on resentment over Serbian refusal to accept a federal system (or after 1944, alleged Serbian manipulation of the spurious one-party federalism established by the communist regime).

According to the constitution adopted in 1921, the new state expressed the political will of the single "three-named Serbo-Croatian-Slovenian people," who allegedly spoke a single "Serbo-Croatian-Slovenian language." Although an ethnic alliance composed of three different "tribes" was theoretically mandated to govern the country, the reality of power and rule was a centralized unitary kingdom, with state authority concentrated in Belgrade. During the first decades of the state's existence, political power was loosely divided between the Karadjordjević dynasty that had previously ruled Serbia and the politicians from the majority Serbian parties that dominated the National Assembly. As a result of this situation, Serbian political forces were able to establish a tight grip over the upper echelons of the state administration, defense forces, and diplomatic corps.[31]

Outside Serbia, the strongest political force in the country was Radić's Croatian Peasant Party, which sought political autonomy for Croatia within some sort of loose federation or confederation. Unfortunately, Radić's outlook (which was similar to that of many of his Croatian and Slovenian compatriots who objected to Serbian centralism) was laced with a strong dose of condescension and cultural disdain regarding his would-be partners in a proposed South Slav federal state. "Our history," Radić explained, "has made us federalists. Our geographical situation, our orientation toward Hungary—a European state—makes us federalists in order not to become dependent on the Balkans which, whatever one may say, is an extension of Asia. Our duty is to Europeanize the Balkans, and not to Balkanize the Croatians and Slovenes—Jugoslavia is a nation only from an external point of view."[32] Meanwhile, the major Slovenian politicians and parties attempted to maximize their own political leverage by maneuvering between the centralist Serbian and the federalist Croatian parties. The same tactic was employed by the Moslems of Bosnia-Hercegovina, a group and territory that was the object of ethnic and irredentist claims from both Zagreb and Belgrade. The smaller South Slavic nationalities such as the Montenegrins and Macedonians, or important non-Slavic peoples such as the Albanians and Hungarians, received no constitutional recognition at all, let alone any *de facto* influence on decisionmaking. Indeed, even the federalist programs of the Croatian and Serbian opposition ignored the ethnic and political aspirations of the smaller South Slav and non-Slav nationalities. Thus, the three-nation monopoly officially directing the new state fell far short of the pan-Yugoslav ideology embraced by earlier generations of Croatian-Slovenian idealists and also managed to offend the several unrecognized "tribal" components within the new kingdom.

Cabinet instability arising from incessant squabbling between the country's ethnic leaders—and especially the dominant Serbian-Croatian conflict—together with the rampant financial corruption in higher political circles sapped the new state's capacity to develop either political legitimacy or the economy, not to mention the "psychological entente" necessary to forge closer bonds among the different South Slav nationalities.[33] Some momentum toward the formation of a Yugoslav identity did take place during the 1920s simply owing to the cohabitation and routine interaction of different South Slav elites and citizens in a unified state, but on balance the countervailing force of disappointment and bitterness regarding overcentralization and ethnic inequalities proved to be far more influential. The general atmosphere of interregional and internationality distrust and recrimination tended to strengthen the respective ethnic loyalties of young people coming to maturity in the new state, and simultaneously eroded any enthusiasm for the "Yugoslav idea."[34] The June 1928 assassination of the Croatian Peasant Party leader, Stjepan Radić, on the floor of the National Assembly (by a Montenegrin deputy belonging to the Serbian-oriented ruling Radical party), underlined the regime's broader failure to achieve interethnic harmony among the principal South Slav peoples. Discussions initiated by King Alexander— who still enjoyed some support among the Croats and Slovenes—about the possibility of the peaceful disassociation of the existing state, or its organization along federal lines, made no headway as a result of opposition from the dominant Serbian parties.

In early 1929, frustrated by his failure to reconcile the competing interests of the country's diverse ethnic groups, King Alexander attempted to forestall centrifugal developments and regain political momentum by imposing dictatorial rule and elaborating new pan-ethnic organizational symbols and structures. In an effort to dilute prior ethnoregional loyalties, for example, the country was renamed the "Kingdom of Yugoslavia" and its traditional territorial units were reorganized and relabeled. The regime also endeavored to cultivate popular attachment to an entirely new syncretic or pan-ethnic notion referred to as "integral-Yugoslav national unitarianism." The rationale for the new notion of Yugoslav identity was explained by King Alexander's handpicked premier, General Petar Živković: "The old traditions and separate flags of the Serbs, Croats, and Slovenes belong to the past. The true Yugoslav acknowledges the national tricolor only and does not know any racial or religious differences among the nation's inhabitants."[35] In keeping with this philosophy, the new constitution adopted in September 1931 strengthened the power of the Crown and central authorities and banned political organizations committed to religious, regional or ethnic goals.

King Alexander's bold departure from the pattern of legislative paralysis and bureaucratic obstruction initially achieved some success (adoption of a uniform legal code was most notable), but the new state-sponsored Yugoslavism proved unable to either transcend the strong ethnic and regional conflicts in the country or legitimize the central government. Although new laws banned traditional party activities and created electoral rules favoring the new government-sponsored National List of Candidates, popular commitment to regionally based ethnic leaders and movements opposed to Alexander and the Serbian-controlled regime continued to flourish. In the undemocratic elections of the 1930s, the major opposition parties from the various regions cooperated as a loose United Opposition bloc challenging the government whereas less moderate opposition ethnic parties such as the radical Croatian Ustasha and the Internal Macedonian Revolutionary Organization (IMRO) preferred more unconventional modes of political participation. The assassination of King Alexander in 1934 by a joint squad of Ustasha and IMRO terrorists revealed the strong undercurrent of ethnic extremism seething beneath the regime's contrived and superficial Yugoslavism.

During the second part of the 1930s, Yugoslavia enjoyed a modicum of stability and some success in pursuing internal and external policies, but the failure by the quasi-authoritarian regime—the post-Alexander regency, operating together with a prime minister (Milan Stojadinović) who looked admiringly on the fascist models proliferating in Europe—to reconcile Serbian-backed centralist notions with Croatian federalist proposals undermined any fundamental improvement in interethnic relations. Cooperation on the part of Slovene and Moslem party leaders with the government increased, but the popular Croatian Peasant party and its leader, Vladko Maček, remained strongly committed to the principles of Croatian national identity and autonomy for Croatia in a reorganized state. Thus Maček was fundamentally Yugoslav oriented, but only if Croatia's sphere of influence in the state was substantially enlarged. It is interesting that Maček's views on reform and federalism were shared by many in the Serbian opposition; indeed, large Serbian crowds warmly received the Croatian leader when he visited Belgrade in 1937. Such incidents—matched earlier by expressions of genuine sadness among many Croats at the news of King Alexander's assassination—demonstrated that there was some popular sympathy for resolving the Serbian-Croatian impasse and for finding a mutually satisfactory model of governance. Still aggrieved, however, by continued Serbian hegemony and the central government's refusal to share power with the provinces, the Croats remained unresponsive to partial schemes of decentralization offered by official Belgrade. Only in August 1939, when a new prime minister, Dragoljub Cvetković, finally presented them with a broad agreement that effectively federalized the country by recognizing Croatian claims to a separate "national unit," enlarging Croatian territory and allowing authorities in Zagreb substantial political autonomy over regional affairs, did Maček and other leading Croatian politicians agree to become actively reinvolved in the country's political system.

MAP 1.1   Kingdom of Yugoslavia, 1929, and 1939-1941

The Accord of 1939 and the Yugoslav "Character"

The regime's recognition of a "Croatian nation" and the new power granted to the Croatians under the so-called "Cvetković-Maček Agreement" of 1939, implied the official departure from the notion of a single "Yugoslav" nation and the centralism mandated by the dictatorial constitution of 1931. It was significant that Croatia gained control over all matters of administration except the military, international trade, and foreign policy. Croatian Peasant party leader Maček also joined the central government as a vice-premier, and the cabinet was reconstituted on its broadest multiparty and multiethnic basis since the creation of the state. The new devolutionary trend had its problems, not least of which was an upsurge of Croatian discrimination against the region's 25 percent Serbian minority.[36] But had the agreement between the central government and Croats been extended to other regions of Yugoslavia (indeed it was rumored that Serbia and Slovenia would soon be granted their own provincial legislatures, just as Croatia), the original aspirations of many pre-1918 Yugoslav oriented forces for a more democratic and federal South Slav state might have come to fruition. Even influential Serbian leaders such as constitutional lawyer and historian Slobodan Jovanović, who worried that because the Croats had been granted too many concessions they would cease to "think about the state as a whole," maintained in early 1940 that hope existed for the "Yugoslav state idea."

> The attempt to use the power of the state to create in as short a time as possible a single Yugoslav nationalism which will stifle Serb and Croat nationalism has not succeeded. But that should not destroy our faith in Yugoslavia. If Yugoslavia as a national idea has met with difficulties in Serb and Croat nationalism, that does not mean it must necessarily encounter the same difficulties as a state idea....We will organize that state so that Serbs and Croats will feel at home, but also open their eyes to the fact that they could find themselves without a home if they cannot live together.[37]

After two decades of bickering and ineffective governance, the Serbian-Croatian Agreement of 1939 was a political deal aimed at power sharing among the country's largest ethnic groups. Although the agreement offered little promise for the smaller and recognized nationalities in Yugoslavia, and had little to do with any spirit of Yugoslavism, it did reflect enhanced prospects for a more decentralized state that would provide greater equity among regional groups. Moreover, there were some signs by the end of the interwar period that a sociopsychological foundation was developing to support such governmental experimentation and restructuring. Admittedly, the bonding or linkage of peoples and regions in either the ethnic or civic sense, remained very limited. However, a good argument could be made that the country's principal groups shared elements of a distinct "Yugoslav spirit" and certain features that constituted a "Yugoslav national character."

For example, in a massive but little-read study published in 1939, Vladimir Dvorniković observed that "Yugoslavs were not yet a 'nation' in the West European and modern sense, one organic and national personality, as are, for example, the English," and conceded the existence of deep divisions among the South Slavs—"from region to region, from tribe to tribe—from village to village!" But Dvorniković also copiously chronicled the mutual features and substantial connections that revealed an: "unconscious feeling of spiritual and ethnic unity among all the Yugoslav regions...a feeling of real ethnic and characterlogical unity remains alive and alongside all the historical and national-political differentiation. All our people felt that something common and they feel it today, from the most differentiated and distinct regions—even when for certain reasons they don't recognize it."[38] Dvorniković described the "feeling of commonality" as a shared notion of what is "ours" among all South Slavs, and of the "totality" of an internally differentiated single Yugoslav "type." This unity was allegedly expressed when Yugoslavs exclaimed that someone is "'our man' that he isn't any longer a Serb or a Croat, nor from this or that tribe, nor this or that religion. Then they are psychologically characterizing themselves as unified, along one or another lines."[39] The basic problem undermining the perceived unity of the Yugoslav peoples, Dvorniković argued, was that the country's scholars and politicians who were addressing the South Slavs searched "only for their differences, confusing themselves, and in the final analysis, failing to provide any trace of some deep synthetic view" that might encompass the whole Yugoslav scene.

Equally unfortunate, in Dvorniković's view, was that alongside the latent but powerful bonds uniting the South Slavs there also existed a strong tendency toward extremism.

> Politically, the Yugoslav man, in his spiritual disposition, is an extremist....A Yugoslav from all provinces and of all varieties, reacts in a political way only if an issue affects the very root of his being, touches his fundamental vital interests of his deepest traditional emotions. Once he has felt the full directness and complexity of an issue inside his own being, he is prepared to commit himself thoroughly to the cause....No difference is made between the conceptual, political, party or personal enemy. In the final analysis, it is either love or hate, friend or foe.[40]

In Dvorniković's scheme, the "stubbornness," "fierceness," "passionate, highly personal, and temperamental outbursts" characteristic of "the deep atavistic Yugoslav psyche" explained an intensity and inconsistency in political life that went beyond the pattern found in most countries.

> The abrupt leaps and turnabouts of our politicians, whether minor or major figures, must be bewildering. But all the acrobatics, running back and forth, or revolving around their own axis, arise from that internal political feverishness and irritable urge to go from one extreme to another which runs over all principles, ethics, and even logic, with the sole aim of keeping afloat and hurting one's main opponent of the moment. "Dictators" turn into fierce democrats, "integrationalists" become advocates of tribal "national individualities" or the other way around, because the main goal continues to be: keep playing your political role.[41]

Dvorniković's interwar analysis suffered from the weaknesses and overgeneralizations typical of national character analyses, as well as the various racial, anthropological, and ethnopsychological theories that heavily influenced his work.[42] But in his exhaustive study he identified some of the fundamental divisions, bonds, and behavioral characteristics that have characterized the South Slavic peoples. Regrettably, Yugoslavia's disintegration and violent wartime experience from 1941 to 1945 fully revealed the population's predilection for political extremism, identified by Dvorniković only a few years earlier (a pattern that would be repeated some fifty years later) and shattered the possibilities inherent in the belated reorganization of the First Yugoslavia on a quasi-federal basis.

Wartime:
Yugoslavism's Failure and Rebirth

The bloody civil war and interethnic violence on the territory of the former Yugoslav state during World War II was a major setback for those seeking cooperation and political unity among the South Slav peoples. The occupation and dismemberment of Yugoslavia by Nazi Germany and its allies initiated a wave of ultranationalism in several regions of the former state as newly installed regional leaders utilized their backing from the Axis powers to implement radical programs of ethnic domination and to settle old ethnic grudges. In the new Independent State of Croatia (which included most of Bosnia-Hercegovina), the Ustashe carried out a ruthless campaign of genocide and terror against Serbs, Jews, and other non-Croats deemed racially or religiously unacceptable. Similar, if less intensive, methods were employed by puppet leaders and occupying forces in Hungarian-controlled Vojvodina, Italian-controlled Kosovo, and Bulgarian-controlled Macedonia.[43] Such brutal policies provoked a strong defensive or reactive ultranationalism on the part of the generally persecuted Serbian population, many of whom became actively involved in the Chetnik guerrilla movement (often guilty of reciprocal atrocities against Croats and Moslems) directed by Serbian military officers loyal to the London based Yugoslav government-in-exile. Because of its close links to the former Serbian-dominated regime in Belgrade and its distance from the reality of the wartime political and military struggle in the Balkans, the exiled government—though multiethnic in composition and "Yugoslav oriented"—was politically disadvantaged in its efforts to shape the future of any resurrected Yugoslav state.

Compared to the ruthless ultranationalist forces, residual spokesmen from the old ruling class, and the brutal occupying forces that dominated the violent wartime political landscape, the leadership of the Communist Party of Yugoslavia (KPJ) initially seemed to offer a sharp contrast. Although during the first two decades of their existence the communists represented only a small underground movement beset by factional struggles, by the late 1930s they had formulated a coherent political program promoting both socioeconomic progress and ethnic equality within the framework of a united and federal Yugoslav state. Led after 1937 by the Croatian communist Josip Broz (later Tito), the KPJ advocated the establishment of a broad-based multiethnic movement that would preserve the unity of the Yugoslav state—an approach reflecting the Popular Front strategy dictated at the time by Stalin and the Communist International. In lockstep with Soviet theory on the "national question," the Yugoslav communists maintained that the creation of a new supranational "universal" culture infused with socialist values was fully compatible with the flourishing of individual "national cultures" in a particular multiethnic country. Such a supranational (Yugoslav) culture bore no resemblance, the communists maintained, to the "integral-Yugoslav" policies of the royalist government in the 1930s because the communist inspired culture would be brought about by organic economic processes and development rather than artificially imposed coercive methods. In his major treatise on the national question first published in 1938, for example, Slovenian communist leader Edward Kardelj optimistically asserted: "The growth of universal culture depends on the consciousness of a universal community, or the common interests of all peoples of all languages. And that consciousness will develop parallel with the development of the means of production with the new forms of the social division of labor, with the progress of socialist societal relations....In that sense we are also speaking of the amalgamation of nations in a universal community."[44] Thus, economic development and the socialization of values espoused by the communists would allegedly provide the key to resolving the ethnic conflict that eluded the interwar regime and its policy of induced Yugoslav nationalism.

The Yugoslav communists' emphasis on ethnic equality and federalism provided them with numerous tactical advantages following the occupation and partition of Yugoslavia. By combining a call for social revolution along traditional Marxist lines with a promise to create separate republican and provincial units for the major nationalities in a new federal state, the communists were able to differentiate themselves from other resistance forces fighting for the reestablishment of the old regime and the various radical ultranationalist forces engaged in violent acts of terror against their neighbors. The communists' sweeping endorsement of equality and federalism was also cast in sufficiently broad terms to satisfy both larger ethnic groups desiring a distinct territorial identity as well as the smaller minorities and previously unrecognized nationalities. As Tito claimed during the war: "The term National Liberation Struggle would be a mere phrase and even a deception if it were not invested with both an all-Yugoslav and national meaning for each people individually....The liberation and emancipation of the Croatians, Slovenes, Serbs, Macedonians, Albanians, Moslems, etc....Therein also lies the essence of the National Liberation War."[45]

Promising a fundamental change in ethnic relations, as well as equal influence for both the larger and smaller ethnic groups, the communists' national program became an important component of their wartime revolutionary struggle. In the heat of war, few communist adherents or members of the Partisan forces had either the time or inclination to dwell on the details or probable operation of the proposed federal state, not to mention whether socialist economic development and the nurturing of socialist values would be able to achieve the eventual "amalgamation of nations in a universal community" as Kardelj had optimistically suggested in 1938. What mattered to the thousands of recruits to Tito's forces was not only that his organization held out a vision of a better future but also that the communists were actively fighting the occupying forces and domestic ultranationalists. Moreover, beyond their programmatic assets the communist movement benefited from having a talented and energetic multiethnic leadership team, an effective clandestine organizational network throughout the country, and the support of enthusiastic young activists, many of whom had acquired military experience during the Spanish Civil War. All these advantages assisted the communists, organized under the banner "Brotherhood and Unity," to attract followers to their movement, particularly thousands of Serbs fleeing from persecution in Croatia, Bosnia-Hercegovina, and Vojvodina. In early 1944 the British government made the cold-blooded decision to concentrate Allied support on Tito's forces and discontinue aid and political backing for the Serbian noncommunist resistance forces led by General Draža Mihailović (linked to the London-based royal government-in-exile). This action ensured that the communists would emerge as the unchallenged victors in the wartime struggle.[46]

As World War II drew to a close, the communists hurriedly endeavored to elaborate the design of their promised future federal state. The communist leadership, having just witnessed an interethnic bloodletting

of staggering proportions, burdened with a crowded and urgent agenda
for the reconstruction of their devastated country, and acting within the
framework of a disciplined and militarized Soviet-style one-party
organization, had little patience for prolonged debate concerning the
contending claims of each ethnic group and region. Because the
communists were preoccupied with consolidating power, their design
of internal borders among the newly formed republics and provinces and
also the treatment of individual ethnic groups, were generally quite
arbitrary and suited to political expediency. Looking back many years
later, Milovan Djilas, one of Tito's closest allies in the wartime communist
struggle, observed that decisions on significant territorial issues were
often made quickly "during a march," without full consideration for all
their nuances and potential consequences.[47]

> We looked on the national question as a very important question, but a
> tactical question, a question of stirring up a revolution, a question of
> mobilizing the national masses. We proceeded from the view that national
> minorities and national ambitions would weaken with the development
> of socialism, and that they are chiefly a product of capitalist
> development....Consequently the borders inside our country didn't play a
> big role....We felt that Yugoslavia would be unified, solid, that one
> needed to respect languages, cultural differences, and all specificities
> which exist, but that they are not essential, and that they can't undermine
> the whole and the vitality of the country, inasmuch as we understood that
> the communists themselves would be unified.[48]

The communists' tactical approach to both the national question and
also territorial issues resulted in a number of decisions that, as is discussed
more fully in later chapters, would eventually become a source of sharp
controversy and violent conflict, and would eventually undermine the
survival of the country. Much to the chagrin of both Croats and Serbs, for
example, Bosnia-Hercegovina, with its heterogeneous population of
Moslems, Serbs, and Croats, was constituted as a separate republic in the
communist federation.[49] Croatia had been given control of substantial
parts of Bosnia-Hercegovina under the 1939 Cvetković-Maček Agreement,
and most Croats viewed the Moslems as Islamicized Croats. Moreover,
many Croats believed that the decision to make the multiethnic region of
Vojvodina a province of the Serbian republic was carried out on the basis
of the very criteria that, if applied fairly across the board, would have
resulted in Croatia receiving much of Bosnia-Hercegovina. Many Croats
were also dissatisfied by the loss of other former Croatian territory, such
as the allocation of Boka Kotorska to Montenegro and the Srem region to

Vojvodina. Meanwhile, the historically distinct Sandjak region, composed of Serbs and Moslem inhabitants, was denied separate standing as a federal unit and was divided between Serbia and Montenegro.[50]

In drawing up the new federation, the communists also faced an especially difficult task with respect to the region of Kosovo-Metohija. The area was the heartland of the medieval Serbian Empire and for centuries Serbs yearned for its liberation. Reintegration with Serbia was not accomplished until 1912. Moreover, in 1945 the area was approximately 70 percent Albanian in ethnic composition, and to make matters worse, the extremely weak communist organization in the area was almost entirely Serbian. By the end of the war, Tito and his colleagues had decided that the area would remain within Yugoslavia (rejecting the desire of some of Kosovo's Albanian communists to unify the area with communist Albania) and under Serbian control. The decision by the new communist government to make Kosovo-Metohija a province within Serbia left the Albanians dissatisfied and opened the door to future difficulties.

MAP 1.2   Yugoslavia as a Federation, 1945-1991

Perhaps the most controversial and potentially troublesome regions, however, were the heavily Serbian inhabited areas of Dalmatia, Lika, Kordun, Banija, Slavonija, and Baranja, whose populations had suffered terrible persecution under the wartime Independent State of Croatia and were now incorporated within the borders of the communist federation's new Croatian republic. Historically these regions had been part of the so-called Austrian military border region that Vienna had settled with ethnic Serbs as a barrier to obstruct the advance of Ottoman forces further into Europe. According to Milovan Djilas, the proposal to form a Serbian autonomous region from such areas was rejected by the communist leadership because of the odd intestine-like shape of such a territorial unit and because of the presence of large numbers of Croats.[51] Forty-five years later, the contentious issue of autonomous status for the Serbs of Croatia would reemerge as a vexing problem for the stability and maintenance of the Yugoslav federation.

Socialist Development and Yugoslavism: Tito's Ambiguous Legacy

Although loudly proclaiming their devotion to ethnic equality, "brotherhood and unity," and also to their newly established federal system (composed of six republics and two provinces), the Yugoslav communist elite that came to power in Belgrade following World War II had no interest in permitting the country's traditional cultural and territorial divisions to become the basis for political pluralism or genuine decentralization.[52] Initially adhering to orthodox interpretations of Marxism-Leninism as elaborated in prevailing Stalinist theory and practice, Yugoslav leaders exuded confidence that their ideologically grounded policies and ambitious postwar program of economic development would eliminate the country's earlier interethnic and interregional problems. Indeed, even after the Tito-Stalin split in 1948 and a wrenching period of ideological reevaluation by the Belgrade regime, various regime strategies for dealing with the "national question" (summarized in Table 1.1) reflected a persistent belief that the maintenance of a single-party and federally structured state (both more or less centralized in practice depending on the particular subperiod of communist rule under consideration), together with economic change, would eventually overcome the country's ethnic conflicts and innate fragility.

In the first several years after World War II, for example, the regime maintained the hope that its centrally planned program of rapid economic

TABLE 1.1   Managing Ethnoregional Diversity in Yugoslavia: Changing Strategies and Institutional Dynamics (1945-1980)

Period	Party Dynamics	Regime's Ethnic Strategy	Federal (State) Dynamics
1945-1952	One-party centralization	Revolutionary fusion ("Partisan Yugoslavism"): Rapid creation of "all-Yugoslav" consciousness to replace group identities	Hierarchical federalism ("Bolshevik-type")
1953-1962	One-party/ moderate decentralization	Evolutionary merger: Gradual replacement of older cultural bonds by encouragement of "socialist Yugoslavism"	Quasi-federalism (enhanced local government authority)
1963-1971	Decentralization and regionalization of the single party	Pluralist socialism: Recognition that ethnic and regional interests are divergent and long term	"Cooperative federalism" among central, republican, and local authorities
1972-1973	Moderate one-party recentralization	"Revolutionary unity": Centrally directed purge of "ultranationalists" and "chauvinists" in republics	
1974-1980	(1974-76) Resurgent regionalization of the single party (1977-80) Confederalization of single party into eight regional machines	Pragmatism and group pluralism ("self-managing pluralism of interests"): All nonsubversive group interests including ethnicity are legitimate	Confederalization/ "polycentric federalism"

development, together with the transfer of funds from the more economically developed regions to the less advanced areas of the country, would quickly eliminate traditional loyalties and conflicts among ethnic and regional groups. Still imbued with "Partisan Yugoslavism," or their wartime faith that socialism would transcend interethnic conflict, the communist elite endorsed policies that would induce the country's cohesion and downplay its intrinsic diversity. Economic transformation, it was alleged, would be the key to the creation of an "all-Yugoslav consciousness" among producers throughout the society, a vision that some higher party officials later characterized as a kind of "homogeneous socialism."[53] This strategy of creating a new Yugoslav socialist man by means of high-tempo industrialization, which might be called *revolutionary fusion*, lasted until the early 1950s.[54] The largely "decorative" role of the federal system, and the relative powerlessness of Yugoslavia's republics and provinces during this early period reflected the regime's assertion that ethnic and regional identities were becoming less salient facets of Yugoslav society. Thus even though the state was formally organized as a federation, it essentially functioned as a spurious Soviet-type federal system, with power concentrated at the center of the unified party-state apparatus.[55] Basic manifestations of ethnic and cultural distinctiveness such as the use of one's own language or alphabet, were not prohibited—and in some cases such as Macedonian nationhood were actually fostered for symbolic political reasons—but traditional expressions of nationalist fervor, particularly religiously based ethnic affirmation, were harshly suppressed.

The general liberalization of the political system, and the commitment to establish a more humane form of socialism in the early 1950s, resulted in a noticeable change in the regime's policy on the "national question." Endeavoring to survive the break with the USSR and strengthen his regime's legitimacy, Tito could no longer afford methods that ignored deeply established group sensibilities. During the 1960s, the *evolutionary merger* of traditional groups and a more subtle encouragement of "socialist Yugoslavism" (through political socialization, education, and so on) rather than regime hopes for the rapid economically induced creation of a new ideological consciousness, became the official policy for managing presocialist ethnic and regional loyalties.[56] Economic change was still regarded as a means to create new bonds and attitudes, but the process was now viewed as a much longer-term enterprise, best achieved by the abandonment of insensitive "administrative methods."

The real power of the republics and provinces in the federal system did not change appreciably even after the adoption of the more liberal merger strategy, but the local government level of the federation became the beneficiary of enhanced attention and more formal authority as part of the new emphasis on Marxist strictures regarding communal self-government. As during the first phase of development after the war, however, those interethnic and interregional conflicts that did arise tended to be swept under the table or handled by the single-party elite behind closed doors. Thus although the communist party organization— renamed the League of Yugoslav Communists (LCY) in 1952—had abandoned its earlier invasive micromanagement of all socialist activities, it retained a monopoly position through its control of ideological "guidance" and the recruitment of key political and managerial personnel. Moreover, some party intellectuals worried that a combination of conservative communism and traditional Serbian nationalism in the state central bureaucracy in Belgrade still lurked behind the ostensible emphasis on official Yugoslavism. As the Serbian writer Dobrica Ćosić (who would later become an important anti-Titoist and post-Tito political actor) suggested in 1961:

> Today, the form of Serbian nationalism is often "Yugoslavism"....Serbia's "Yugoslavs" downplay the differences among the Yugoslav nations, they are for unification, unification is for them a creation of privileges for their language, and the assimilation of smaller nations, unification for them is never the overcoming of their "Serbianness," and in unification they seek to obtain their "historical rights" and "state-building aims." Serbian "Yugoslavs" carry a consciousness of their "historical mission," they are always for a strong unified state, they are always politically "concerned" about the fortunes and destiny of their people.[57]

It was only in the second half of the 1960s, following the removal of top Serbian communist leader and state vice-president Alexander Ranković and the restriction of secret police activities, that another strategic shift occurred in the management of ethnic diversity and conflicts. Adopting an outlook that can be conceptualized as *pluralist socialism*, the regime no longer treated intergroup conflicts as a taboo theme that needed to be suppressed or administratively resolved outside public view. In addition, state-encouraged "Yugoslavism," and the earlier vision of inculcating some kind of transcendent ideological consciousness, began to be regarded as a reactionary notion that encouraged centralism or anti-reformist "unitarian" policies. Increasingly, there was recognition that different and conflicting interests were normal and long-term phenomena during socialist evolution and that such plurality of interests would best be channeled and institutionalized through a politically more vital federal system that distributed power among all levels of governmental authority. As a result of the changed elite mindset regarding societal conflicts and ethnic relations, by the end of the 1960s the country's republics and provinces had begun to emerge as important centers of political authority and power.

As an internationally "nonaligned" country avowedly dedicated to eradicating Stalinist practices and also experimenting domestically with various methods of worker participation in management and government, Yugoslavia enjoyed enormous sympathy in the West, both from established opinionmaking elites and within radical intellectual circles. The momentum of regime reform was neither constant nor without strong conservative political opposition. But despite various obstacles to democratization (most significant was the retention of a single-party and an active secret police) and Tito's rather equivocal support for self-management's pluralistic facets, Yugoslavia stood out as a bastion of "liberal communism."[58] The reputation of Tito's regime as the cutting-edge of East European reformism was strengthened by the 1966 purge of the secret police, the reorganization of the party on a more decentralized basis in 1967, and constitutional amendments (1968-1971) devolving more authority to the republics and provinces.

In its initial stages, the Titoist reform model also proved quite successful in advancing Yugoslav economic development. During the 1950s and 1960s, for example, Belgrade's strategy of rapid industrialization benefited considerably from the abundance of low-priced factors of production such as capital, labor, energy, and raw materials and from the high export opportunities that existed in the international economy. Growth rates in terms of gross domestic product, labor productivity, and real personal incomes (Table 1.2) were the highest in the country's history and compared very favorably with other developing countries. In only two decades, Yugoslavia had been transformed from an underdeveloped agrarian society into a "moderately developed industrial country" with enhanced economic capacity, research infrastructure, technical competence, and participation in international trade.[59]

Yugoslavia's impressive economic progress during the 1950s and 1960s, its superficial ethnic tranquility, and the country's political consolidation as an independent state all seemed to confirm self-management's vitality as a reform alternative to "orthodox" state socialism. Thus at the end of the 1970s, foreign observers lavished praise on the participatory and pluralistic structural novelties of Yugoslav socialism as well as Belgrade's independent foreign policy. Observers devoted less attention, however, to various unsavory aspects of Tito's regime, such as

TABLE 1.2   Yugoslavia's Economic Growth, 1956-1984: Selected Indicators

	Average Annual Growth Rate (%)			
Indicators[a]	1956-1964	1965-1972	1973-1979	1980-1984
Gross domestic product (GDP)	8.8	6.0	6.1	0.4
GDP per capita	7.7	5.0	5.1	-0.3
GDP in industry	12.2	6.6	7.5	2.1
GDP in agriculture	3.6	2.0	2.2	2.9
Labor productivity in the public sector	4.8	4.3	2.7	-2.0
Real personal incomes	6.3	6.1	2.7	-2.0

[a]1972 Prices.

Source: Lojze Socan, Mark Kranec, *et al.*, *Trade: EC-Yugoslavia* (Ljubljana Institut za Ekonomska Raziskovanja, 1988), p. 76.

the brutal treatment of pro-Soviet communists and other political nonconformists during the 1940s and 1950s (many confined on the so-called Naked Island in the Adriatic), the monopolistic power and corruption of Titoist elite circles, and the regime's persistent containment and repression of intellectual dissent. Milovan Djilas and other Yugoslav dissidents had directed attention to many of these defects, but the novelties of Yugoslav socialism and Yugoslavia's unique position as a communist state outside the Soviet orbit during the Cold War generally distracted Western attention from its less attractive features.

It was not until after the regime's harsh use of central political and military power to stifle resurgent nationalism in the early 1970s that the authoritarian side of Titoism again (as prior to 1948) began to receive closer scrutiny outside the country. Thus Tito's purge and arrest of many nationalistically oriented Croatian communists in late 1971 and early 1972 and the subsequent purging of liberal political forces in several other republics revealed that even thought the regime had shed the classical features of its Stalinist past, and elaborated some highly original participatory mechanisms to animate political life, it remained an essentially single-party dictatorship when it came to fundamental issues of power and self-determination.[60] As a Yugoslav Marxist philosopher would later point out: "The entire heroic generation, with Tito leading it...could not break with statist and monopolist practices. The problem of democracy in all of its economic and political dimensions remained the insurmountable problem for that generation and its historical boundary."[61] Regime spokesmen, meanwhile, emphasized that Tito had simply acted to avert the disintegration of the country and that "flareups of nationalist and chauvinist" activity were essentially "ephemeral and transitory political phenomena."[62]

Official optimism during the early 1970s about Yugoslavia's unity was contradicted by public opinion surveys that revealed mounting popular apprehension concerning the state of interregional and interethnic relations in the country.[63] It is interesting that survey research also revealed that the majority of young people supported the notion of nurturing a more "unified Yugoslav nation." Exactly what such survey findings meant in terms of the country's long-term cohesion, however, was quite unclear. For example, some scholars saw support for Yugoslavism as a potential basis for the sustained unity of the country, whereas others interpreted the trend as an emotional reaction of the young against "national frictions" that might have no lasting significance and might even serve as a "shield" for political forces opposed to the individual and genuine self-determination of ethnic groups.[64] Vagueness about the meaning and consequences of public perceptions about Yugoslavism derived largely from the communist elite's own ambiguous perspective on the topic. Thus although the idea of fostering a single "Yugoslav nation" was officially frowned upon as exemplifying old state centralist thinking, Tito and other party conservatives still found the notion of Yugoslavism a useful antidote for combating ethnic particularism and what they saw as a trend away from "revolutionary unity." Moreover, the fact that the Yugoslavism of many young people derived from various sources (e.g., idealism, the fact that many children were the product of interethnic marriages) that differed markedly from the "statist" notion of Yugoslav identity prevalent in Tito's conservative circles created mixed signals and a conceptual confusion about the meaning of the Yugoslav idea and weakened its ability to serve as a unifying principle.

The Yugoslav communist elite, retaining its grip on power and stifling strident ethnoregional nationalism though strong-arm methods in the early 1970s, lost none of its earlier resourcefulness for innovative governmental and ideological improvisation. For example, the adoption of a new constitution in 1974, which formally advanced the role of "associated labor" and self-management through a novel system of "delegational representation" and the enhanced devolution of power to regional and local authorities, was heralded both domestically and abroad as evidence of Yugoslavia's ongoing commitment to socialist reform. The new constitution's elaborate provisions for equitable regional representation (on a parity rather than proportional basis) and for interregional negotiations and consensus formation seemed a hopeful basis for the maintenance of the country's stability. Stimulated by a new regime strategy encouraging the "self-management pluralism of interests" (outlined by Kardelj in 1977), all group interests, including ethnoregional interests, were deemed to be legitimate so long as they were not aggressively anti-socialist.

The constitution of 1974 invested each Yugoslav republic and province with theoretical "statehood," and along with the renewed strength of the single-party machines at the republican/provincial level of the LCY in the later part of the 1970s (Table 1.1), it effectively created a semiconfederative political structure in which powerful sectional leaderships from the single-party competed for influence and support at the top level of the system. Emphasis was now placed on achieving unanimity among all republics and provinces in the federal policymaking process, despite the often prolonged and futile character of such consultation and agreement-seeking procedures. Although frequently cumbersome and ineffectual in practice, the regionally balanced "collective" state and party leadership bodies elaborated by Tito at the federal level, as well as procedures for the frequent rotation of top officials, nevertheless appeared to extend the Yugoslav pursuit of interethnic concord and "debureaucratized" governance. Yugoslavia was beginning to show signs of internal strain and the renaissance of serious ethnic tensions, but the regime continued to exhibit a capacity to manage such problems within the confines of the one-party communist state.

Despite the institutional novelties of Yugoslav constitutional engineering in the mid-1970s, there were portents of future difficulty. Perhaps most important was the growing centrifugal pressures generated by the autarkic policies of Yugoslavia's regionally entrenched political elites. In place of the unified party elite that dominated the communist system in its initial postwar phase, the regime was now characterized by six republican and two provincial elites that skillfully utilized decentralized authority for their respective parochial interests. This situation resulted in an unusual proliferation of authoritarian leadership networks—sometimes referred to as "policentric statism" or a "pluralism of elites"—that effectively invalidated the regime's ambitious framework for democratic participation. Yugoslavia was undeniably more pluralistic as a result of Titoism's reforms, but the thousands of citizens serving short terms as part-time delegates in Yugoslavia's unique legislative system proved little match for the seasoned professional politicians controlling the single-party's eight regional organizations.

Moreover, Yugoslavia's decentralized political elite constellations, through their excessive interference in the economy, poor investment decisions, failure to consistently follow federal economic guidelines, and sometimes outright corruption, sowed the seeds of even more serious economic difficulties that would soon threaten the regime's cohesiveness and viability. Regime sponsored policies designed to create a "self-managed economy" often contributed to such negative trends. The introduction of procedures to create a so-called consensual economy, for example, sidelined the process of market price formation in favor of "self-management agreements" and "social compacts" among economic actors. Such methods prompted administrative intervention in the economy, reduced competition, and helped to fragment the Yugoslav economy into autarkic regional markets. The basis for regional autarky can also be traced to the regime's constitutional framework, which was highly decentralized with respect to such key areas as banking, taxation, monetary and fiscal policy, and the recording of balance of payments. Although the decentralized constitutional arrangements gave regional elites the incentive and capacity for adopting a regional rather than pan-Yugoslav perspective, the political imperatives of elite self-legitimization and ambition also worked in the same direction. Thus, many members of the various regionally entrenched elites often sought political advantages by skillfully manipulating the heightened economically based tensions between various regional and ethnic communities.

By the 1970s, all of Yugoslavia's regions were economically better off compared to the situation that existed when the communist regime assumed power after World War II (Figure 1.1), but the relative distance between the richer and poorer areas had increased markedly. Most significant in this regard was the steadily widening gap between the more economically advantaged regions (Slovenia, Croatia, Vojvodina, and Serbia proper) and the less-advantaged regions of the country (Bosnia-Hercegovina, Montenegro, Macedonia, and Kosovo). As citizens in the more affluent regions of the country came to resent their obligatory contributions to assist the country's more backward areas, republican elites discovered responsive constituencies for political manipulation. Meanwhile, leaders in the less advantaged areas of the country protested their constituent's perceived exploitation by the wealthier regions and the failure of the federal authorities to reduce interregional disparities.[65]

The growing horizontal fragmentation of the political and economic systems on an ethnic and regional basis during the 1970s was also accompanied by trends that seriously undercut the significance of self-management and the momentum of political and economic reform. For

FIGURE 1.1 Social Product Per Capita by Region, 1947 and 1974

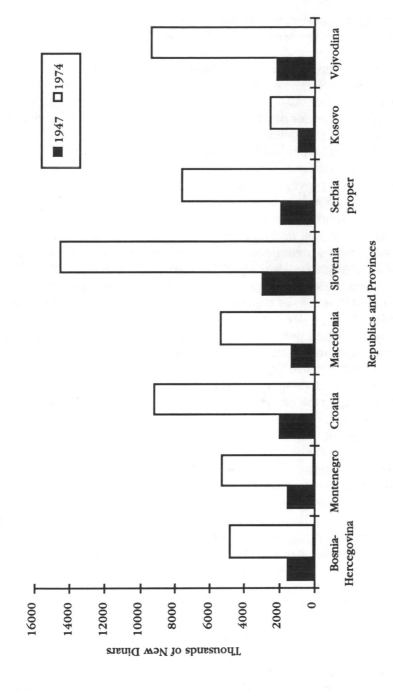

Source: Statistički Godišnjak.

example, political conservatives around Tito, fearing that unchecked centrifugal tendencies of marketization and political pluralism might restore capitalism and also eliminate the party's leading role successfully diverted reform initiatives into essentially formalistic schemes for the extension of self-management rights to the work force (e.g., the much-touted concept of "associated labor"), while informally maintaining various conventional modes of statist economic operation and hegemonic party control. As one prominent Yugoslav political scientist observed: "The conception of associated labor and the curtailment of market principles in the 1970s served more for the strengthening of the political bureaucracy's power, even more than before the economic reform [of 1965] when Yugoslavia was centrally organized."[66] "Self-management theory," as another critical Yugoslav sociologist has put it, "was one great utopia, which was really needed as an alibi for the absence of political democracy."[67] Foreign observers were fascinated by the potential and novelty of Yugoslavia's unique "labor-managed economy," but Tito did not permit various institutional mechanisms for mass participation to threaten the pattern of elite control. Thus recruitment to the republican, provincial, and federal assemblies remained carefully controlled by the LCY and its allied political organizations. The electoral process was less monolithic than in other communist states, but the so-called delegate system created dense filters in the political recruitment process, facilitating regime-managed cooptation and supervision of leadership candidates and eliminating the emergence of truly independent actors in the worker councils and assemblies.

Throughout the late 1970s, as economic and ethnic problems accumulated, the Yugoslav regime doggedly maintained its unique admixture of party monism, limited pluralism, and reformist rhetoric. Although the regime sponsored theoretical outline for a "pluralism of self-management interests" presented by Edward Kardelj promised more space for contending ideas, the LCY remained unwilling to abandon its single-party control over the political system. Kardelj admitted that elements of a one-party system still existed in Yugoslavia, but he claimed that the League of Communists had lost the characteristics of a classic political party fighting for monopoly control. Thus, he claimed, Yugoslavia was on its way toward a *nonparty* form of pluralism.[68]

Following Kardelj's death in 1978, Yugoslav scholars credited him with having facilitated "the 'opening' of socialism and marxism to pluralism" as well as having offered "an alternative to one-party monopoly and the fictitious pluralism of multiparty systems."[69] Although such claims were exaggerated and premature,[70] over the next decade Kardelj's pluralist notions provided ideological coherence for a relatively relaxed and unobtrusive form of single-party rule that continued to distinguish Yugoslavia from more authoritarian socialist states. Kardelj's brand of restricted pluralism did eschew free elections and party competition, and Tito did remain constitutionally ensconced as president of the republic "for an unlimited term of office," but considerable room existed for the expression of divergent opinions and critical views. Thus major defects of the regime, such as the party's continued interference in the economy, the expanding size and influence of the administrative apparatus, the impotence of the delegate legislative system, the oligarchic power distribution in Yugoslav enterprises, and growing interregional and ethnic tensions, were the subject of vigorous debate by opposing political factions and were candidly discussed by the country's lively media and scholarly community. Parameters on political dissent existed, but they were fuzzy and arbitrarily interpreted according to the changing whims of the central and regional party elites.

In many respects Yugoslavia at the end of the 1970s was living on borrowed time or, perhaps more accurately, the country was caught in a time warp, with its aging authoritarian leaders seemingly oblivious to the difficulties that were accumulating and lay ahead. Thus, although changes in the international economy such as higher costs of energy, technology, and capital, together with domestic mismanagement and bureaucratic impediments to reform, began to have a negative impact on Yugoslav economic development at the end of the 1970s, the regime still retained enough legitimacy, control, and economic buoyancy to avoid the full consequences of such problems. Despite a steadily mounting external debt in convertible currencies, Yugoslavia continued an economic growth strategy that emphasized heavy reliance on imports and foreign borrowing. During the 1970s (Table 1.2), the growth rates of labor productivity and real personal incomes declined substantially, but the overall economic growth of industry and agriculture remained at about the same levels as during the second half of the 1960s.

Unemployment levels were steadily increasing, but large numbers of Yugoslavs who were temporarily employed in Western Europe continued to send their earnings back to the country. Moreover, compared to the centrally managed communist regimes elsewhere in Eastern Europe at the time, Yugoslavia was a relatively open and dynamic society that seemed destined for a better future. The traditional refrain *biće bolje* ("it will be better") was still the optimistic presumption of most Yugoslav citizens and leaders. Political tensions among the society's diverse ethnic groups were more apparent than at any time since World War II, but most leaders and citizens felt that further reform of the federal system could accommodate such pressures and sustain the cohesion of the state. Indeed, the successful political leadership transition following Tito's death in 1980 initially seemed to confirm the value of the novel institutional legacy bequeathed by the regime's founder. Unfortunately, challenges that were even more difficult than elaborating a mechanism for leadership succession would soon threaten the stability and survival of socialist Yugoslavia.

Notes

1. Fred Taylor (ed.), *The Goebbels Diaries 1939-1941* (London: Hamish Hamilton, 1982), p. 285.

2. Malcolm Muggeridge, *Ciano's Diary 1939-1943* (London: William Heinmann, 1947), p. 93.

3. "Khrushchev's Secret Speech, February 25, 1956," in *The Anti-Stalin Campaign and International Communism* (New York: Columbia University Press), p. 62; and Roy A. Medvedev, *On Stalin and Stalinism* (Oxford: Oxford University Press, 1979), p. 145.

4. Stipe Dužević (ed.), *Program of the League of Communists of Yugoslavia* (Belgrade: Socialist Thought and Practice, 1977), pp. 192-193.

5. "Self-Management—A Law Governing the Development of Socialism," *Socialist Thought and Practice*, No. 51 (March-April 1973), p. 28.

6. Stipe Šuvar (while serving as president of the presidium of the Yugoslav League of Communists), *Foreign Broadcast Information Bulletin-Eastern Europe* (hereafter *FBIS-EEU*), February 2, 1989, p. 70.

7. "Statement by Ante Marković in the Assembly of the SFRY on the Occasion of His Election to the Office of President of the Federal Executive Council," *Yugoslav Survey*, Vol. 30, No. 1 (1989), p. 54. By 1987 it was estimated that Yugoslavia had dropped to a lower level of development than in 1950, with only Poland, Turkey, and Albania trailing behind it. Zoran Pjanić, "Trends in the Reform of the Economic System," *Socialist Thought and Practice*, Vol. 29, Nos. 1-2 (1989), pp. 5-20.

8. Susana S. Macesich, "The Illyrian Provinces: A Step Toward Yugoslavism," *Southeastern Europe*, Vol. 1, No. 2 (1974), pp. 119-125; Elinor Despalatovic, *Ljudevit Gaj and the Illyrian Movement* (Boulder: East European Monographs, 1975); Philip J. Adler, "Why Did Illyrianism Fail?" *Balkanistica*, Vol. 1 (1974), pp. 99-102; Jaroslav Šidak, *Studije iz hrvatske povijesti XIX stoljeća* (Zagreb: Sveučilište u Zagrebu, 1973), pp. 45-84; Gale Stokes, "Yugoslavism in the 1860s," *Southeastern Europe*, Vol. 1, No. 2 (1974), pp. 129-135; Dimitrije Djordjevic, "Yugoslavism: Some Aspects and Comments," *Southeastern Europe*, Vol. 1, No. 2 (1974), pp. 192-201; and Dimitrije Djordjevic, "The Idea of

Yugoslav Unity in the Nineteenth Century," in his *The Creation of Yugoslavia* (Santa Barbara, Calif.: Clio Books, 1980), pp. 1-17.

9. Duncan Wilson, *The Life and Times of Vuk Stefanovic Karadzic 1787-1864* (Oxford: Claredon Press, 1970), p. 301. See also Michael Petrovich, "Karadzic and Nationalism," *Serbian Studies*, Vol. 4, No. 3 (Spring 1988), pp. 41-57.

10. Mirjana Gross, "Croatian National-Integrational Ideologies from the End of Illyrianism to the Creation of Yugoslavia," *Austrian History Yearbook*, Vols. 15-16 (1979-1980), pp. 3-33; and also Charles Jelavich, "The Croatian Problem in the Hapsburg Empire in the Nineteenth Century," *Austrian History Yearbook*, Vol. 3, No. 2 (1967), pp. 83-115.

11. Gale Stokes, "Yugoslavism in the 1860's," *Southeastern Europe*, Vol. 1, No. 2 (1974), pp. 129-135.

12. Garašanin's detailed views on Serbian unification did not become public until 1906. David MacKenzie, *Ilya Garašanin, Balkan Bismarck* (Boulder, Colo.: East European Monographs, 1985), pp. 42-61, 296.

13. In the middle of the nineteenth century, only about one-third of all 3.2 million Serbs lived in the semiautonomous Principality of Serbia, while the other two-thirds were divided in roughly equal proportions between the Hapsburg and Turkish empires. Janko Pleterski, *Nacije Jugoslavija revolucija* (Belgrade: Komunist, 1988), pp. 41-42.

14. For the notion of federalism in Croatian perspectives on South Slav unity, see Petar Korunić, *Jugoslavizam i Federalizam u Hrvatskom Nacionalnom Preporodu 1835-1875* (Zagreb: Globus, 1989).

15. Charles Jelavich, "Serbian Nationalism and the Question of Union with Croatia in the Nineteenth Century," *Balkan Studies*, Vol. 3 (1962), pp. 29-42.

16. Leopold Ranke, *The History of Servia and the Servian Revolution* (London: Henry G. Bahn, 1853), p. 258.

17. Jovan Cvijić, "Studies in Jugoslav Psychology (II)," *Slavonic Review*, Vol. 9 (1930/31), p. 668.

18. R. W. Seton-Watson, *The Southern Slav Question and the Hapsburg Monarchy* (New York: Howard Firtig, 1911, 1969), pp. 174-208.

19. Fran Zwitter, "The Slovenes and the Habsburg Monarchy," *Austrian History Yearbook*, Vol. 3, Part 2 (1967), pp. 159-188.

20. Predrag Matvejević, *Jugoslavenstvo danas* (Belgrade: Mladinsko knjiga, 1984), pp. 57, 192.

21. Edward Woodhouse, *Italy and the Yugoslavs* (Boston: Richard Badger, 1920), p. 68.

22. Ivo J. Lederer, *Yugoslavia at the Paris Peace Conference* (New Haven: Yale University Press, 1963), p. 26. On their weak political position and other factors that prompted non-Serb representatives to downplay the idea of federalism at Corfu, see Dragoslav Janković, "Oko unitarnog ili federativnog uredjenja prve zajedničke jugoslovenske države," in Nikola Popović (ed.), *Stvaranje Jugoslovenske države 1918* (Belgrade: Institut za Savremenu Istoriju, 1983),

pp. 383-392; and Ivan Mužić, *Hrvatska politika i Jugoslavenska ideja* (Split: "Franjo Kluz," 1969), pp. 105-131.

23. The debate on Pašić is summarized in Nikolas P. Pašić, "Greater Serbia or Jugoslavia?" *Journal of Central European Affairs*, Vol. II, No. 2 (July 1951), pp. 133-152. For positive evaluations of Pašić, see Alex Dragnich, *Serbia, Nikola Pašić, and Yugoslavia* (New Brunswick, N. J.: Rutgers University Press, 1974); and Carlo Sforza, *Fifty Years of War and Diplomacy in the Balkans: Pasich and the Union of Yugoslavs* (New York: AMS Press, 1966).

24. Milada Paulova, *Jugoslavenski Odbor* (Zagreb, 1925), p. 569, cited in Charles Jelavich, "Serbian Nationalism and the Question of Union with Croatia in the Nineteenth Century," *Balkan Studies*, Vol. 3 (1962), p. 40.

25. A.J.P. Taylor, *The Habsburg Monarchy 1809-1918* (New York: Harper and Row, 1965), p. 249. For an excellent discussion of the negotiations leading to the creation of the state, see Wayne Vucinich, "The Formation of Yugoslavia," in Dimitrije Djordjevic, *The Creation of Yugoslavia* (Santa Barbara, Calif.: Clio Books, 1980), pp. 183-206.

26. Milorad Ekmečić, *Stvaranje Jugoslavije 1790-1918, Vol. 2* (Belgrade: Prosveta, 1989), pp. 829-832. See also, Marko Kostrenčić, "O Jugoslavanskoj ideji kao kohezionoj snazi ujedinjenja Jugoslavenskih naroda," in *Naučni Skup u povodu 50-Godišnjice raspada Austro-Ugarske Monarhije i Stvaranje Jugoslavenske Države* (Zagreb: Jugoslavenska Akademija Znanosti i Umjetnosti, 1969), pp. 8-16.

27. Nada Podgornik, *Narodnosti u demokratskoj statistici* (Belgrade, 1957), cited in Stane Stanić, "Nacije u popisu," *Nedeljne Informativne Novine* (hereafter *NIN*), No. 1116 (May 28, 1972), p. 33

28. Charles Jelavich, *South Slav Nationalisms: Textbooks and Yugoslav Union Before 1914* (Columbus: Ohio State University Press, 1990), pp. 272-273.

29. See Milorad Ekmečić, *Stvaranje Jugoslavije 1790-1918, Vol. 2* (Belgrade: Prosveta, 1989), p. 793; and Alex Dragnich, *Serbia, Nikola Pašić, and Yugoslavia* (New Brunswick, N. J.: Rutgers University Press, 1974), p. 133.

30. Charles Beard and George Radin, *The Balkan Pivot: Yugoslavia* (New York: Macmillan, 1929), p. 52.

31. For the argument that Serbian political predominance was unplanned and unprofitable, see Alex N. Dragnich, "The Anatomy of a Myth: Serbian Hegemony," *Slavic Review*, Vol. 50, No. 3 (Fall 1991), pp. 559-662.

32. *Temps*, February 18, 1908, quoted in Edward Woodhouse, *Italy and the Yugoslavs* (Boston: Richard Badger, 1920), p. 127.

33. Malbone W. Graham, Jr., "The 'Dictatorship' in Yugoslavia," *American Political Science Review* (May 23, 1939), p. 451.

34. Charles Jelavich has argued convincingly that the events of the 1920s and 1930s strengthened mass nationalist sentiments, "not Yugoslavism." "Comments," *Austrian History Yearbook*, Vols. 15-16 (1979-1980), p. 38-41.

35. *New York Times*, July 5, 1930, p. 2, cited in Bruce Bigelow, "Centralization Versus Decentralization in Interwar Yugoslavia," *Southeastern Europe*, Vol. 1, No. 2 (1974), p. 162 n. 10.

36. Serbs in Croatia complained of being subjected to various forms of discrimination and acts of terrorism. Bruce Bigelow, "Centralization Versus Decentralization in Interwar Yugoslavia," *Southeastern Europe*, Vol. 1, No. 2 (1974), p. 170.

37. Slobodan Jovanović, "The Yugoslav Idea," *Srpski glas*, No. 11 (1940), cited in *Politika: The International Weekly*, Vol. 1, No. 34 (November 10-16, 1990), p. 15.

38. Vladimir Dvorniković, *Karakterologija Jugoslavena* (Belgrade: Gregorić, 1939), pp. 20-22.

39. *Ibid.*, p. 42.

40. *Ibid.*, pp. 902-903.

41. *Ibid.*, pp. 903-904.

42. Drago Roksandić, "'Karakterologija Jugoslovena' Vladimir Dvornikovića i njena recepcija u srpskoj i hrvatskoj kulturi (1939-1941)," in *Srpska i Hrvatska Povijest i "Nova Historija"* (Zagreb: Stvarnost, 1991).

43. Vladimir Dedijer, *The Yugoslav Auschwitz and the Vatican* (Buffalo, N.Y.: Prometheus Books, 1992).

44. Edvard Kardelj, *Razvoj Slovenačkog Nacionalnog Pitanje* (Belgrade: Kultura, 1957), p. 441.

45. *Nacionalno pitanje u Jugoslaviji u svjetlosti narodno-oslobodilačke borbe* (Zagreb: Naprijed, 1945), p. 9.

46. David Martin, *Patriot or Traitor: The Case of General Mihailovich* (Stanford, Calif.: Hoover Institution Press, 1978), and also Martin's, *The Web of Disinformation: Churchill's Yugoslav Blunder* (New York: Harcourt Brace Jovanovich, 1990); Walter R. Roberts, *Tito, Mihailovic and the Allies, 1941-1945* (New Brunswick, N. J.: Rutgers University Press, 1973); Mark C. Wheeler, *Britain and the War for Yugoslavia, 1940-1943* (New York: Columbia University Press, 1980); and Michael Lees, *The Rape of Serbia: The British Role in Tito's Grab for Power* (New York: Harcourt Brace Jovanovich, 1990).

47. Milovan Djilas, *Wartime* (New York: Harcourt Brace Jovanovich, 1977), p. 356.

48. Milovan Djilas, "Novi tok istorije," *Socijalizam*, Vol. 33, Nos. 1-4 (1990), p. 37.

49. For purposes of convenience, this republic will be alternatively referred to in the book as Bosnia-Hercegovina, Bosnia, or Bosnia and Hercegovina.

50. For an interesting discussion of the Croatian perspective on Bosnia-Hercegovina and also an overview of other territorial controversies, see Franjo Tudjman, *Nationalism in Contemporary Europe* (Boulder, Colo.: East European Monographs, 1981), pp. 110-117.

51. Djilas, *Wartime*, p. 356.

52. For the Tito leadership's harsh treatment of Andrija Hebrang, the head of the Communist party organization in Croatia who during and after World War II advocated that the future regime adopt a genuinely "federalist state building strategy," albeit in a unified Yugoslav state, see Jill A. Irvine, *The Croat Question: Partisan Politics in the Formation of the Yugoslav Socialist State* (Boulder, Co.: Westview Press, 1993).

53. Josip Vrhovec, "Aktualni politički aspekti nacionalnog pitanja," in Gavro Lončar (ed.), *Socijalizam i nacionalno pitanje* (Zagreb: Centar za aktualni studij, 1970), p. 145.

54. The summary of communist strategies for the management of ethnic diversity draws on a framework first developed in Lenard Cohen and Paul Warwick, *Political Cohesion in a Fragile Mosaic: The Yugoslav Experience* (Boulder, Colo.: Westview Press, 1983).

55. For an interesting discussion of the regime's view regarding the relationship between federalism and Yugoslavism in this period, see Aleksa Djilas, *The Contested Country: Yugoslav Unity and Communist Revolution 1919-1953* (Cambridge, Mass.: Harvard University Press, 1991), pp. 163-180.

56. Surveys of elementary school students in multiethnic Vojvodina during the period from 1955 to 1961 claimed that the educational system was successfully engendering an identification with Yugoslavia on the part of young people from different ethnic backgrounds, although such "Yugoslav" consciousness did not, and was not intended to, erode an appreciation of cultural and linguistic differences among individual groups. Mihailo Palov, "Škola i formiranje shvatanja o otadžbini," *Društvo i Vaspitanje*, Vol. 13, No. 1 (1963), pp. 5-87.

57. *O savremenom nesavremenom nacionalizmu* (December 1961), cited in "Jugoslovenstvo kao Srpski nacionalizam," *Vreme*, Vol. 2, No. 41 (August 5, 1991), p. 21. At the time, Ćosić also attacked the dangers of non-Serbian ethnic and regional nationalism in polemics with Slovenian communist intellectuals. Slavoljub Djukić, *Čovek u svom vremenu* (Belgrade: Filip Višnjić, 1989), pp. 121-137.

58. Astute Yugoslav critics at the time noted that the regime's penchant for constant reform of the political structure was a classic example of putting old wine in new bottles: "There were endless reorganizations on all levels from the highest representative bodies down to the lowest agencies and authorities....It was all founded on the illusion that through interminable institutional changes social inertia can be prevented and social mobility maintained....The incessant changes of the institutions and the strong activity of their personnel created a fictitious dynamism, whose only utility probably consisted in precluding the demobilization and disbandment of their personnel." Veljko Rus, "Institutionalization of the Revolutionary Movement," *Praxis (International Edition)*, Vol. 3, No. 2 (1967), p. 206. A good summary of the strengths and weaknesses of Yugoslav reform in its initial stages is Mihailo Marković, "Self-Governing Political System and De-Alienation in Yugoslavia (1950-1965)," *Praxis*, Vol. 6, No. 2 (July 1986), pp. 159-174.

59. Lojze Socan, Marko Kranjec, *et al.*, *Trade: EC—Yugoslavia* (Ljubljana: Institut za Ekonomska Raziskovanja, 1988), pp. 76-77.

60. These issues are explored further in Lenard J. Cohen, *The Socialist Pyramid: Elites and Power in Yugoslavia* (Oakville: Mosaic Press, 1989).

61. Predrag Vranicki, "Titoizam i detitoizacija," *Danas*, December 5, 1989, pp. 28-29. The authoritarian facets of Titoism are elaborated in Kosta Čavoški, *Tito: tehnologija vlasti* (Belgrade: Dosije, 1990).

62. Kiro Hadživasilev, "National Equality and Social Self-Management," in Koca Jončić (ed.), *Nations and Nationalities of Yugoslavia* (Belgrade: Medjunarodna Politika, 1974), pp. 28-29.

63. For a discussion of public attitudes toward interethnic relations over several decades, see Ljiljana Baćević, "Medjunacionalni odnosi," in *Istraživački projekat CDI: Jugosloveni o društvenoj krizi* (Iztraživanje javnog mnjenja, 1985. godine) (Belgrade: Komunist, 1989), pp. 72-96.

64. Ivan Šiber, "Javno Mnjenje i nacionalno pitanje," in Gavro Lončar (ed.), *Socijalizam i nacionalno pitanje* (Zagreb: Centar za aktualni studij, 1970), pp. 190-191.

65. See, for example, Miloje Nikolić, "Economic Development of the First and Second Yugoslavia (1918-1990)," *Yugoslav Survey*, Vol. 33, No. 2 (1992), pp. 155-166; Nicholas R. Lang, "The Dialectics of Decentralization: Economic Reform and Regional Inequality in Yugoslavia," *World Politics*, Vol. 27, No. 3 (April 1975), pp. 309-336; and Diane Flaherty, "Plan, Market, and Unequal Regional Development in Yugoslavia," *Soviet Studies*, Vol. 40, No. 1 (January 1988), pp. 100-124.

66. Dušan Bilandžić, "Velika Reforma ili Propast," *Danas*, September 1, 1989, p. 16. The same author has surveyed the continuation of such problems during the first five years of the post-Tito era in *Jugoslavija posle Tita* (Zagreb: Globus, 1986).

67. Josip Županov cited in Milan Jajčinović, "Socijalizam je nešto drugo," *Danas*, July 18, 1989, p. 27. By 1989, although many Western enthusiasts continued to extoll the achievement of Yugoslav self-management, participant observers of the experiment candidly admitted that it "has in practice been shown to be uneconomical, socially unproductive and to a great extent unsuccessful." *FBIS-EEU*, October 16, 1989, p. 74. For the contribution of the self-management system to the Yugoslav crisis of the 1980s, see Svetozar Pejovich, "A Property-Rights Analysis of the Yugoslav Miracle," *Annals*, Vol. 507 (January 1990), pp. 123-132.

68. Edvard Kardelj, *Pravci razvoja političkog sistema socijalističkog samoupravljanja* (Belgrade: Komunist, 1978), pp. 110-116, 215-254.

69. Milan Matić, "Pluralizam samoupravnih interesa u delu Edvarda Kardelja," and Vućina Vasović, "Kardeljevo shvatanje pluralizma," both in *Arhiv za pravne i društvene nauke*, Vol. 65, Nos. 1-2 (January-June 1979), pp. 66 and 74. On Yugoslav self-management as a unique pluralist system see also Jovan Mirić, *Interesne grupe i politička moć* (Zagreb: Centar za kulturnu djelatnost SSO,

1980); and Vinka Tomić and Vukasin Pavlović, *Samoupravni pluralizam interesa* (Belgrade: Institut za političke studije FPN, 1981).

70. Zagorka Golubović maintains that Kardelj's conception of pluralism left the League of Communists in its monopolistic position and offered only "poor compensation" for those seeking genuine democratic competition of ideas and interests during the 1980s. Kardelj's idea "only established that different interests exist, while we can only speak about pluralism when organizations exist that defend different interests." *Kriza identiteta savremenog Jugoslovenskog društva* (Belgrade: Filip Višnjić, 1988), pp. 278-279.

2

Socialist Reform in Crisis:
The Post-Tito Debate

Already during Tito's life power devolved into the hands of republican and provincial oligarchies. But thanks to Tito the Yugoslav summit was preserved. At his death, that bond disintegrated. Everything was the same as earlier, the political summit, the military, the police, press censorship. But nothing was the same....Everything unravelled: only power was held as a kind of personal patrimony.

—Slavoljub Djukić

DURING THE 1980s Yugoslavia was beset by an economic and political crisis that seriously destabilized the country and eventually impaired its very existence. By the end of the decade the country's economy was afflicted by skyrocketing inflation, high unemployment, a huge foreign debt, and serious food shortages. According to official figures, salaries in the country dropped by 24 percent in 1988 (Figure 2.1) and living conditions plunged to the level of the mid-1960s. Accumulated inefficiencies in economic production that could be traced to the poor record of investment decisions by federal and regional leaders, as well as a failure to adjust to the changing world economy, led to plummeting economic growth rates, which undermined the country's ability to both finance technological revitalization and boost exports.[1] Despite the plethora of institutional channels for citizen self-management established by Tito-era reforms, strikes and mass public demonstrations became the preferred mode of participation for groups expressing strong dissatisfaction with the country's economic and political management. In 1988 alone, an estimated four million Yugoslavs took part in protest

FIGURE 2.1   Real Net Personal Income Per Capita: Yugoslavia, 1952-1988

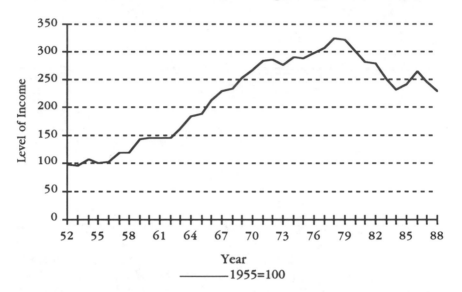

Source: Statistički Godišnjak 1989.

demonstrations. When unpopular government-sponsored controls proved unable to resolve the economic crisis, Yugoslavia's Prime Minister Branko Mikulić and his cabinet, the Federal Executive Council, were forced to resign from office in December 1988.

Throughout Yugoslavia, the economic discontent of the 1980s became closely intermingled with burgeoning ethnoregional nationalism. Only one year after Tito's death, nationalist protests by Albanians erupted in Serbia's economically underdeveloped province of Kosovo, setting in motion a pattern of ethnic conflict that intensified throughout the decade. Albanian nationalist leaders and much of the Albanian population (composing 77.4 percent of Kosovo's population in 1981) expressed resentment against what they viewed as the privileged position of Serbs and Montenegrins in the province and against Kosovo's subordination to Serbian republican officials in Belgrade. For their part, the Serbs in the province claimed that they were being subjected to "genocide" and "terror" by Albanian nationalists, who, they alleged, desired not only the complete elimination of all Serbs and Montenegrins from Kosovo, but also the eventual removal of the country's entire Albanian population from the control of Serbia and possibly even Yugoslavia.

The conflict between Albanians and Serbs in Kosovo spilled over and complicated other ethnoregional problems in the country. Nationality groups residing in Yugoslavia's more economically developed regions (such as Slovenia and Croatia), already resentful about having to foot the bill for economically questionable and frequently mismanaged development projects in Kosovo, were less than enthusiastic about further involvement and the rising costs (including police and military expenditures) to maintain Serbian hegemony over the Albanian population. The escalation of ethnic tensions in Kosovo—which followed on the heels of a major balance-of-payment crisis during 1980—and subsequent severe administrative restrictions on imports revealed serious problems with both domestic and external policy that had been festering during Tito's rule. Such problems also exposed the vulnerability of the post-Tito regime. Ethnic relations in Kosovo continued to deteriorate during the 1980s. Together with mounting economic problems and the antagonism between the more developed and less developed sections of the country, such worsening relations sharply intensified divisions within the ranks of Yugoslavia's communist elite. Already politically divided into regional party machines as a result of the increasing confederalization of the League of Yugoslav Communists (LCY) that had occurred near the end of the 1970s—and since Tito's death unable to halt the accelerating fragmentation of their ethnically and regionally divided organization— Tito's heirs were ill equipped to grapple with the country's rapidly growing economic difficulties or to take the steps necessary to preserve their regime.

As the economic crisis and interethnic bickering intensified in Yugoslavia during the mid-1980s, citizens throughout the country increasingly blamed Yugoslavia's ills on the post-Tito communist political establishment and the ruling party organization. The League of Communists consequently suffered a dual crisis of legitimation: a *vertical crisis*, as party members and citizens lost confidence in the party elite's capacity to resolve the country's difficulties and maintain Yugoslavia's territorial cohesion, and a *horizontal crisis*, as each of the eight republican and provincial party organizations and elites grew more autonomous and unwilling to implement the countrywide decisions that had been hammered out between their representatives in federal decisionmaking bodies.

The rapid loss of the League's previous legitimacy and vanguard role is illustrated by the organization's declining membership and reputation, especially among younger people (Tables 2.1a and 2.1b). Interviews

TABLE 2.1a   Surveyed Young People *Not* Wishing to Join the League of
Communists (in percent)

Region	1974	1986	1989
Slovenia	32	88	92
Croatia	13	70	75
Vojvodina	4	54	50
Serbia[a]	6	40	42
Macedonia	7	40	42
Bosnia-Hercegovina	5	36	40
Kosovo	4	35	33
Montenegro	8	18	34
Total Yugoslavia	9	50	51

[a]Not including the provinces of Kosovo and Vojvodina.
Source: Srečko Mihailović, "Od dobrih podanika ka pluralizmu," in Nadežda
Bogdanović (ed.), *Omladina Krajem Osamdesetih: Pregled Rezultat
Istraživanja* (Belgrade: Savez Socialističke Omladina Srbije, 1990), p. 21.

TABLE 2.1b   Participation of Young People in Membership of the League of
Communists (in percent)

Region	1976	1980	1984	1988	January-June 1989
Slovenia	27.7	26.0	16.6	8.3	7.3
Croatia	24.7	26.2	18.7	7.1	[a]
Vojvodina	31.2	28.9	20.7	14.0	13.2
Serbia[b]	32.5	33.3	24.8	16.3	15.8
Macedonia	20.9	25.3	20.2	12.1	10.3
Bosnia-Hercegovina	36.0	41.2	33.6	20.2	17.8
Kosovo	35.3	40.7	37.8	35.7	34.0
Montenegro	30.2	25.0	28.6	22.5	22.8
Total League of Communists	30.8	33.1	25.3	16.1	15.8

[a]Unavailable.
[b]Not including the provinces of Kosovo and Vojvodina.
Source: Dubravka Stankov, "Kretanja ka socialno-klasnoj i nacionalnoj strukturi
SKJ," *Komunist*, January 1, 1990, pp. 14-15.

conducted in the mid- and late 1980s revealed a sharp drop in the number of young people who expressed interest in joining the LCY compared with the situation approximately a decade earlier. The trend was particularly striking among younger people in the northwestern republics of Slovenia and Croatia, where the League's appeal, which was never very strong at the best of times, almost completely evaporated. Even in areas such as Serbia and Montenegro, where the LCY had traditionally been quite strong, the decline in the League's popularity among the younger generation was very striking.[2]

The younger generation's increasing aversion to the League of Communists in the mid-1980s is particularly interesting when contrasted with other information gathered only a few years earlier that revealed an increase in the number of young people who expressed a commitment to the notions of Yugoslavism and Yugoslav identity. In the 1981 census, for example, approximately 1.2 million inhabitants of Yugoslavia (5.4 percent) chose to identify themselves as Yugoslavs rather than by traditional ethnic labels. This figure represented a nearly fivefold increase from the 1971 census results, a trend that was heavily concentrated among younger and more educated citizens and those residing in urban localities and certain geographic regions.[3] Survey data gathered in 1985 revealed even higher levels of Yugoslav identification and also "latent" preferences for that identity among young people.[4] Researchers interpreted the surge of Yugoslav identity—which was particularly prevalent in multinational areas such as Bosnia-Hercegovina, Vojvodina, and Croatia—to various factors, including the preference for a pan-ethnic or state identity by children from interethnic marriages and an effort (especially among the large number of Serbs dispersed throughout the country who had reclassified themselves as Yugoslavs) to protest the political fragmentation of the state following Tito's death. Such Yugoslavism indicated the existence of a reservoir of support for the country's cohesion at approximately the same time that ethnic tensions and economic problems throughout Yugoslavia were becoming more serious, and many young people were turning away from the established one-party organization.

Exactly where these divergent, but not necessarily contradictory, dimensions of the Yugoslav political landscape would eventually lead depended in large part on the country's divided post-Tito ruling elite. Unfortunately, there was little consensus within the political leadership on what steps should be taken to resolve the country's difficulties. As one Yugoslav sociologist observed about the development of future attitudes toward the federal system and the process of redefining boundaries among ethnic groups: "In a socialist society, it depends primarily on the political elites, that is how they interpret the situations, what kind of political messages they emit to the population. In Yugoslavia, for example, it is mostly important how the political elites interpret events and transmit information."[5]

Contending Strategies of Socialist Reform:
1985-1989

Yugoslavia's economic and political deterioration during the 1980s spawned a cottage industry of domestic commentators who offered various explanations for the country's crisis and suggested a variety of strategies for putting things right—specialists in what some Yugoslavs facetiously termed the field of "crisisology." The economic and political crisis of the 1980s also resulted in a major replacement of top personnel within the country's discredited communist political elite. Faced with increasingly vocal citizen dissatisfaction and an exodus of young people from the League of Communists, many older communist leaders who had presided over the country in the 1970s and during the mounting crisis of the early 1980s, either retired from the scene or were pushed out of power by ambitious new leaders. The generally younger and technically specialized group of communist political leaders who emerged in the second part of the 1980s became increasingly preoccupied with developing new reform strategies to repair Yugoslavia's economy and renew the legitimacy of the socialist regime.

More often than not, however, the new generation of communist leaders—particularly in Serbia and Slovenia—sought to garner political support for themselves and their respective reform proposals by directly appealing to the parochial ethnic and regional concerns of their local communities. As prospects for the continued legitimacy and survival of the League of Communists rapidly diminished, members of each regional communist elite became increasingly focused upon their own survival and only secondarily concerned with cross-regional party unity, which had served as the avowed linchpin of the one-party regime during the Tito era. Thus, although elite turnover in the higher ranks of the League of Communists during the second half of the 1980s pluralized and enlivened the dialogue in the country about how to reform Yugoslav socialism, the growing divisions among the various ethnoregional segments of the elite, and the distance between those segments and members of the federal government, made it extremely difficult for the regime and the ruling party to formulate a comprehensive reform strategy acceptable to the entire country.

A wide spectrum of commentary regarding crisis management and reform could be found in Yugoslavia during the late 1980s. The post-Tito debate concerning the problems and future of the self-managed socialist model can be clustered around three major contending reform strategies: (1) *the Serbian strategy*, inspired by Slobodan Milošević, who emerged in 1987 as Serbia's most influential political leader; (2) *the Slovenian strategy*, representing the views expressed by the republican state and party (LCY) leadership in Slovenia; and (3) *the federal government's strategy*, associated with the program of Ante Marković, who in early 1987 became the head of the Federal Executive Council (FEC), Yugoslavia's federal state cabinet.

The Serbian Strategy:
Majority Control of a Renewed Federation

Nationalism as an Elite Resource

Throughout Yugoslav communist history, interethnic rivalry was viewed by some party leaders more as an opportunity than a danger. In the late 1960s and early 1970s, for example, several leaders of Croatia's League of Communists tapped the nationalism that was sweeping their republic to build a base of popular support.[6] A similar development occurred in the province of Kosovo between 1968 and 1981, when the regime's unprecedented tolerance for ethnoregional autonomy in that area allowed local Albanian communist leaders to politically mobilize the long suppressed aspirations of their ethnic group.

The most successful Yugoslav communist functionary to exploit ethnic nationalism as a political resource during the second part of the 1980s was Serbia's Slobodan Milošević. Born in 1941, Milošević joined the League of Communists in 1959 and finished Belgrade University's Law Faculty in 1964. He held a variety of political and economic jobs in Serbia before becoming a full-time LCY official in 1982.[7] As head of the party organization in Belgrade (1984-1986), he quickly gained notoriety as a strong advocate of Serbian economic grievances. It was not until Milošević assumed the post of party chief for the entire republic (1986-1989), however, that he turned his attention to the ethnic grievances of his Serbian constituency, particularly Serbian concern with rising Albanian nationalism in the province of Kosovo. Milošević's role as an ethnic spokesman became fully defined after a remarkable visit to Kosovo's Serbian community in April 1987, where he gave reassurance to anxious Serbs who had been pushed around by local police: "No one will be allowed to beat you! No one will be allowed to beat you!" Milošević declared, thereby instantly becoming a new Serbian folk hero, especially to Serbs living outside the Serbian republic. It was at this point that Milošević, rather stunned by the success of his own rhetoric, came to fully appreciate the potency of nationalism as a political tool.[8]

Deftly engineering the removal of regional Serbian political and media leaders considered "soft" on the issue of Albanian nationalism (at the Eighth Session of the Serbian League of Communists' Central Committee in September 1987), Milošević soon called for new constitutional provisions that would reassert the control of Serbian republican authorities over the autonomous provinces of Kosovo and Vojvodina (the latter province, though predominantly Serbian in ethnic composition, had traditionally protested the hegemony of officials in Belgrade). In effect, Milošević successfully exploited a backlash of Serbian nationalism in order to build a cross-regional alliance of ethnic Serbs unprecedented in Yugoslavia since the formation of Tito's World War II Partisan movement. When Serbs and Montenegrins began to regularly engage in mass protest demonstrations during 1987 and 1988, "Slobo" Milošević emerged as a hero to the crowds. By November 1988, when Milošević addressed a Belgrade rally attended by an estimated 800,000 to 1.3 million Serbs, it was apparent that he enjoyed more popular support (albeit regionally concentrated) than any other Yugoslav political leader since Tito and that the Serbian leader had completely transformed the character of Yugoslav political life.

Although fear of Albanian nationalism and economic grievances were certainly important catalysts for the sharp upsurge of Serbian ethnic consciousness during the late 1980s, Milošević's nationalist appeal also derived from the Serbs' more general and long-standing dissatisfaction with the course of Yugoslav political development. Many Serbs strongly believed that the regime's federal decentralizing policies and constitutional initiatives had seriously weakened the influence of both the Serbian republic and their ethnic group in the Yugoslav federation. A particular focus of such discontent was the 1974 constitutional arrangement, which reduced Serbia to one player in an eight-sided political game by establishing parity representation for each of the six republics in the Yugoslav federation and providing Serbia's two autonomous provinces a voice in federal decisionmaking. Most members of Milošević's ethnic constituency, as the core nationality in the 1918 creation of the original Yugoslav state, the nationality that predominated in the ranks of the wartime communist movement, and the country's largest ethnic group, felt that their interests were insufficiently recognized under the 1974 constitutional framework and that they had legitimate grounds for expressing their strong dissatisfaction.[9]

The pluralizing tendencies of Yugoslavia's "confederal" constitutional system, which formally diminished Serbia's influence in Yugoslav political life, were also blamed for the country's recent economic difficulties. From the Serbian vantage point, constitutional provisions requiring the representation and "harmonizing" of the country's many ethnic and regional interests—including the accommodation of smaller but ethnically aggressive nationalities such as the Albanians—prevented the central government from decisively responding to the economic crisis.[10] As Milošević explained to one interviewer concerning decisionmaking under Tito's 1974 constitution: "Even before his death the system didn't function, Tito functioned. After his death, nothing has functioned, and nobody has been able to reach agreement on anything."[11]

Many Serbs who flocked to Milošević also shared his view that the regime's Titoist precepts regarding frequent elite rotation and the use of "ethnic arithmetic" in elite selection had prevented the recruitment of a technically qualified and influential team of central officials. According to Milošević, the constitutional provisions limiting the tenure of high officials to one-year terms destroyed a feeling of responsibility on the part of decisionmakers, resulted in administrative errors, and prevented long-term policy implementation.[12] Milošević's advocacy of a so-called anti-bureaucratic revolution appealed to many Serbs who had concluded that federal politicians and senior administrators had been able to enrich themselves and evade accountability by means of short-term service—the constant rotation of officials mandated by law—in various public positions.

Although certainly benefiting from deeply-rooted facets of Serbian political culture that favor strong, heroic leadership in times of crisis (i.e., the notion of the tribal chieftain or ethnic savior required to employ the policy of the "hard hand"), Milošević's specific appeal within Serbian elite circles derived from a complex admixture of ethnic and nonethnic ingredients.[13] Many Serbian intellectuals, such as the writer and former communist Dobrica Ćosić (who had sharply criticized Serbian nationalism twenty-five years earlier), Belgrade philosopher Mihajlo Marković (who had been a prolific advocate of "humanistic socialism"), and supporters of the strongly nationalistic "Memorandum" prepared in 1986 by the Serbian Academy of Sciences, were attracted by Milošević's bold assertion of Serbian interests and his radical departure from Titoist strategies for managing the "national question."[14] Disillusioned with the failure and unpopularity of the Titoist system, and with socialism's inability to resolve multiethnic conflicts, many Serbian intellectuals tended to opportunistically view Milošević's advocacy of Serbian nationalism as a new avenue to influence political affairs.

Beyond the appeal of his nationalist views, Milošević's initial success in the mobilization of Serbian support may also be traced to the yearning of many Serbs for an honest and strong new leader who, after many years of economic decline, could "clean house" and establish an efficient and competent regime. During the late 1980s, for instance, some Serbian intellectuals and political dissidents (including Milovan Djilas)—who harbored serious reservations about Milošević's demagogic methods and his initial failure to enthusiastically embrace political pluralism—were, nevertheless, impressed by both his sincere commitment to "Serbian rights" and his vocal disdain for elite mismanagement and bureaucratic corruption. Many Serbs serving in top military posts—such as longtime Minister of Defense Nikola Ljubičić—also sympathized with Milošević's strong commitment to the country's unity, "nonparty pluralism," and enhanced Serbian influence in federal policymaking.[15] Finally, many conservative members of the LCY simply hoped that Milošević, as a strong advocate of public ownership and an opponent of multiparty pluralism, would be able to maintain the status quo and preserve the existing socialist-Titoist model. As critical Serbian journalists later put it, Milošević "succeeded in tricking both the communists and the nationalists: the communists believed he was only pretending to be a nationalist and the nationalists that he was only pretending to be a communist."[16]

Milošević's ability to simultaneously attract widespread support in Serbian elite circles and mobilize hundreds of thousands of frustrated citizens in Serbia was extremely unsettling to members of the Yugoslav communist establishment who had previously defined the proper mode of political participation in a "self-managed" socialist democracy. Some observers and politicians, particularly in Croatia and Slovenia, cautioned that Milošević's populist tactics—such as mass demonstrations at which crowds shouted slogans and demanded the resignation of unpopular officials—accentuated elitism rather than democracy. A Slovenian journalist observed in this regard that the crowds "want to have their say immediately and at any price and not in an organized way through political institutions, or in a soundly argued struggle of opinions. It is characteristic of this phenomenon that the political elite rules over the crowds of people and that the crowds accept this elite as their own and lcave everything in its hands: thus what is involved is a big step backwards in the development of democracy."[17]

Defending Milošević's break with traditional communist methods, some Serbian political analysts argued that mass political protests reflected positive facets of both socialist and Serbian political culture. Speaking in Milošević's defense, Belgrade political sociologist Mihailo Popović criticized politicians and journalists from the "so-called western republics" of Yugoslavia, who he suggested are generally "inclined to negatively evaluate mass demonstrations of solidarity with the Serbs and Montenegrins of Kosovo, and sometimes write about the masses like the conservative theoreticians Gustave Le Bon and Vilfredo Pareto." According to Popović, the mass Serbian demonstrations of 1988 were a positive reaction to the stagnation of the self-managing system: "Self-management is atomized and formalized, the delegate system is much more of an empty political forum, that masks the activity of the political elite, which, unfortunately is more often unsuccessful than successful."[18] Another Milošević adherent reconceptualized Yugoslav self-management to include "street democracy" (*ulična demokratija*):

> Street democracy when it is engaged in by the working class and when it is for socialism and self-management is constructive class struggle. It subverts bureaucracy, and makes possible the shattering of the 'fossilized' institutions of the system....Those in the leadership or outside it, who are against this form of class struggle in fact are on the other side of the barricades—they belong to the bureaucracy, the contra-class.[19]

Despite such promotion of mass protests and populist style of political leadership, Milošević was roundly criticized in many quarters (predominantly, but not entirely, outside Serbia) as a dangerous demagogic leader whose personal ambitions were served by plebiscitarian-style democracy and continued restraints on political pluralism.

The Reforms of the "Milošević Commission"

Troubled by criticism that his views were vague and essentially "anti-reformist," Milošević sought the assistance of prominent Serbian economic and political specialists in formulating a coherent reform program. One group of experts, headed by Milošević, was constituted as a "Commission of the Presidency of the Republic of Serbia: The Commission for Questions of Social Reform" (originally "Economic Reform"). An associated subgroup of experts was also formed under the aegis of the commission as the "Group of the Presidency of the Republic of Serbia for Reform of the

Political System." The "Milošević Commission," as it came to be known in Yugoslavia, first presented a broad outline for economic recovery in May 1988. Premised on the notion of "socialism as a wealthy society," the Milošević strategy envisioned market-oriented reforms in which the "world market and world competition represents the strongest generator of economic operation."[20] The way out of the economic crisis would be sought through the stimulation of investments and production in enterprises, introduction of new programs and technologies, stepped-up development of the small-scale economy, and increased foreign investments. Milošević urged Yugoslavs to overcome their "unfounded, irrational and...primitive fear of exploitation" by foreign capital. He added that such prejudices about foreign capital investment have been spread by the bureaucracy, "which itself is on the lowest level of education and cultured existence" and has frequently made wrong investment decisions regarding foreign loans "on the basis of personal criteria of the top leaders and not on the basis of economic criteria."[21]

The Milošević reform strategy criticized, in principle, the state's role as a regulator of economic development and particularly measures such as government direction of the banking system. Greater federal governmental authority was encouraged, however, for areas such as monetary, financial, and taxation policy as well as in foreign economic relations. According to Milošević's supporters, the major problem of the Yugoslav federation was the dearth of state power where it was required and an excess of state intervention where it was unnecessary. Stressing the importance of a "united" or "integrated" Yugoslav market, the Milošević reformers blamed the country's economic crisis on constitutional provisions and laws permitting the emergence of "autarkic republican economies." In this view, decisive action by the federal government should no longer be subordinated to the imperative of seeking unanimous agreement from all of the country's regions, the so-called "economy of accord-reaching" or the "consensus economy." In Milošević's opinion, the creation of a united market was an essential "condition for Yugoslavia's existence" and could not "be called statism or centralism."

> Yugoslavia is turning into a loose confederation, and with regard to its economic aspects, an increasingly poor hunting reservation in which the less developed are the objects of exploitation by the more highly developed....Yugoslavia must be a unified economic area where identical system-related solutions exist and where products and services, money and capital, people and knowledge move freely....And the state is doing this in all, even the most liberal market economies.[22]

The Milošević plan for economic reform advocated the stimulation and streamlining of the self-management system as it existed in the late 1980s, not its elimination. Applying the same exhortation/mobilization tactics to the economy that he had successfully employed in rallying ethnic indignation among the Serbs, Milošević aimed at motivating self-managers in Yugoslav enterprises to work harder, curtail bureaucracy, and recommit themselves to the regime. Enterprise "collectives," he said, "must function on economic principles...strive to create profits and constantly struggle for their share and place in the market."[23] The key problem targeted by Milošević, however, was the removal of bureaucratic "blockages" and waste in the enterprise that were allegedly responsible for previous failures. As a prominent member of the Milošević Commission put it: "One of Yugoslavia's paradoxes is that all reorganization in the name of debureaucratization, has had the result of strengthening the administrative apparatus, and with that increasing social costs and parasitism." The problem, he added, is not to eliminate all state functions, but to change "the mentality and style of administrative work."[24]

Although Milošević publicly claimed that he was working for a "mixed economy" and a "pluralism of property ownership," his reform program clearly emphasized the "social ownership" sector or "public means of production" rather than the private sector. According to Milošević, establishing real equality between the social and private ownership sectors would be a mistake:

> That would be the same as to demand that a society be socialist and capitalist in the same measure, or that one room be simultaneously hot and cold....That would threaten the interests of the working class and bring the question of socialism into question....Private property is not incompatible with socialism...but the chief, fundamental form of property in socialism remains social property....Private property is secondary and can develop up to specified limits.[25]

Thus at the end of the 1980s, Milošević was concentrating his reform efforts on the public sector, which was already generating approximately 85 percent of national income in Yugoslavia, rather than on the private sector which at the time, according to some observers, possessed more than 50 percent of the country's potential for economic growth.[26] Although social property was described as the "most developed and dominant form of ownership" in their reform proposals, members of the Milošević Commission nevertheless claimed that all forms of property should receive equal legal treatment and that the private sector should be equitably represented in the political system.[27]

In July 1989, the Milošević Commission announced a comprehensive proposal for the political reorganization of Yugoslavia. Reemphasizing Milošević's commitment to a "modern democratic and efficacious federation," the proposal recommended that decisionmaking in the Federal Assembly based on the principle of interregional unanimity and limited to only the "narrowest circle" of constitutional questions but that most voting follow the principle of "qualified majorities" (e.g., 51 percent, two-thirds, and so on). Decisionmaking along such lines would allegedly promote a federation capable of "actively influencing economic development" and regulating the economy in order to "express and defend general societal interests."[28]

The Milošević reform proposal also called for a political system that would guarantee civil liberties, freedom of political expression, democratic control over the work of state organs, the responsibility of all public officials, and an independent judiciary. Political pluralism was endorsed in terms of the "democratic expression of different social interests, ideas, and values," "freedom of association," and terminating the League of Communists' monopoly over personnel recruitment and the state. The organization of citizens in various leagues, alliances, and other associations was, however, expected to take place under the umbrella of the Socialist Alliance (the broad-based former national front organization that included both party members and nonmembers) and the legislative system—in other words, "organized in harmony with the social or interest structures of our society."

Recognizing that socialism was "in a transition period of its development," Milošević envisioned in his proposal the possibility that other forms of "pluralistic political organization" might need to emerge but suggested that such alternatives to the ruling party should be "created on a democratic and socialist basis and within Yugoslav frameworks." Multiparty pluralism was neither specifically ruled out nor encouraged in the political reform outline presented by the Milošević Commission in 1989. Thus the precise parameters of political pluralism appeared very indefinite, and the meaning of a phrase such as "within Yugoslav frameworks" was left unclear. When the head of the Milošević Commission's working committee for political reform was asked whether the draft proposals called for the legalization of opposition parties in Yugoslavia, he reiterated his opposition to unbridled political pluralism: "Logic doesn't exclude the possibility that tomorrow there would be eight communist parties and socialist parties, but not parties whose programs advocate the reprivatization of social wealth, a return to capitalism. Here is that barrier."[29]

The Slovenian Strategy:
"Asymmetric Federalism" and Competitive Pluralism

The reform option advanced by Slovenian political leaders at the end of the 1980s was developed partly in reaction to the Milošević phenomenon but also reflected developments within Slovenia that preceded the rise of the new Serbian leader. Tito's mechanisms for balancing regional representation in Yugoslavia's collective leadership structure had allowed Slovenian leaders to enjoy considerable influence in federal political life, but many Slovenes felt that their economically productive republic (in 1986 it provided 18 percent of total GNP and 23 percent of total exports) was contributing an unnecessarily high price for the operation of the federation. Particularly irksome to Slovenes was that each year their republic, with about 8 percent of Yugoslavia's population, contributed over 25 percent of the total federal budget and between 17 and 19 percent of the Federal Fund for Underdeveloped Regions. The Slovenian public and elite were particularly annoyed by revelations that the federal funds transferred to the less advantaged regions of the country had been wasted as a result of the federal state's economically unprofitable investments, corruption, and the financing of bloated bureaucratic structures.

Federal defense expenditures were also viewed as excessive by many Slovenes, particularly because Yugoslavia did not seem to be facing any imminent military threats and because citizens of their republic had traditionally played an extremely small role in the leadership of the armed forces. Such grievances became an important facet of the growing political ferment among students and Slovenian intellectuals during the first part of the 1980s.[30] The most outspoken voice of Slovenian dissent was the Socialist Youth Alliance journal *Mladina*, whose iconoclastic criticism of the Serbian-dominated Yugoslav armed forces, and also its support for the Albanian cause in Kosovo, engendered fierce criticism from party conservatives, especially in Serbia and southern Yugoslavia. By early 1989, however, Slovenia's burgeoning political diversity went well beyond the *Mladina* editorial board and was expressed in over 100 grass-roots organizations and ten independent political groups. Public opinion surveys (Table 2.2) revealed that a substantial majority of Slovenian citizens wanted their republic's political leaders to sharply curtail (though not necessarily completely sever) economic ties with the federal government in Belgrade as well as with the underdeveloped areas of the country. Most Slovenes viewed the emergence of "alternative" political organizations competing with the League of Communists as a positive

TABLE 2.2   Slovene Public Opinion on Factors Hindering Slovenian Sovereignty, 1988 (in percent)

Factor Hindering Sovereignty	Don't Agree At All	Don't Agree Generally	Undecided	Generally Agree	Completely Agree
Slovene political leadership is too yielding and wavering.	8.5	21.8	20.7	31.2	17.8
				(49.0)	
We have too great an economic association with the federation and the underdeveloped areas.	2.4	5.7	12.4	12.2	47.3
				(59.5)	
The federal organs authoritatively reject important Slovene proposals.	2.0	6.3	19.1	31.8	40.8
				(72.6)	
Slovene political pluralism and democracy are being attacked from outside Slovenia.	3.4	6.9	23.1	30.2	36.4
				(66.6)	
Alternative political movements and associations are destroying Slovenian solidarity.	20.1	22.0	29.9	17.3	10.7
				(28.0)	

[a]Numbers in parentheses are totals of those who generally agree and those who completely agree.

Source: Niko Toš (ed.), Slovenski utrip: rezultati raziskav javnega mnenia 1988-1989 (Ljubljana: Fakulteta za sociologijo, politične vede in novinarstvo, 1989), pp. 375-376.

development that enhanced their republic's autonomy. At the same time they also perceived attacks on such political pluralism from outside the republic as a major threat to Slovenia's sovereignty.

Reflecting the intensification of ethnoregional self-assertion and pluralism in their republic, Slovenia's communist state and party leaders gradually adopted a distinctive and radical perspective on reform. Although the Slovenian communists exhibited a unique reformist mindset, up to early 1990 they remained committed to Yugoslavia's basic territorial cohesion and to broad principles of economic change endorsed by most other Yugoslav political leaders, including members of the Milošević team in Serbia. For example, speaking at a 1988 press conference in Washington, D.C., Slovenia's state President Janez Stanovnik was highly critical of the Serbian political leadership's penchant for nationalist rhetoric, but he added: "There are no significant differences when it comes to the economy. The views of Mr. Milošević with whom I disagree on political issues do not differ from mine in economic matters. He is just as liberal as I am when it comes to economic matters."[31] The same point was made by the head of the Milošević Commission's working committee for political reform in mid-1989: "We all more or less agree that Yugoslavia needs to be a socialist, democratic, federal state, of equal nationalities, based upon the predominance of social property, on respect for the rights and freedoms of people, to be a legal state...but the essential difference, for example, with Slovenia, is in the domain of the state structure...and the way it functions."[32]

Institutionalizing Territorial Rights

In terms of Yugoslavia's political architecture, the reform-minded Slovenian communist leadership during the late 1980s remained generally supportive of the federal organization and principles elaborated in the 1974 constitution, that is, the model of parity regional representation and "consensus" decisionmaking that Milošević and his Serbian communist allies found so objectionable. Slovenian leaders shared the view of Milošević and the Serbian leadership that federal authorities must be adequately empowered to deal with major issues of economic policy. In their opinion, however, policy formulation must be the result of consensus rather than majority voting (*majorazacije*) or the inevitable "outvoting" that the Slovenes believed would result from the Serb's demographic predominance in the Yugoslav federation. In the Slovenian view, the requirement for unanimity of republican positions in federal decisionmaking under the 1974 constitution provided a safeguard against the potential subordination of the smaller republics and ethnic groups by the majority. Moreover, Slovenian writers pointed out, although Milošević might endorse the principle of "one man, one vote" for voting in federal level institutions, the Serbs would never permit such a principle to determine political decisionmaking in Kosovo, where their own ethnic community constituted a minority in the population.[33]

The Slovenian view of constitutional reform was advanced most forcefully in mid-1989 by Milan Kučan, who headed the League of Communists in Slovenia until the end of that year and was his republic's most prominent anti-Milošević spokesman:

> Can the imposition of majority decisionmaking in a multinational community by those who are the most numerous be anything else but the violation of the principle of the equality of nations, the negation of its sovereignty and therefore the right to autonomous decisionmaking....We will only live in such a Yugoslavia in which sovereignty is ensured, as the permanent and inalienable right to self-orientation of all the nations...where we will regulate common issues in a federal state according to the principle of agreement.[34]

Slovenian communists advocated the principle of "one unit, one vote" in federal decisionmaking with respect to the country's most important economic and political issues, a view that Serbian leaders denounced as a denial of democratic fair play. As the secretary of the Serbian party's ideological commission suggested in response to Kucan's attack on majority voting: "In the name of which democratic principles is the Slovenian leadership demanding that one Slovene is equal to five Serbs, or three Croats?"[35] The Slovenian rejoinder to this criticism was that although the concept of "one man, one vote" might historically reflect progressive, democratic principles, "Serbian political thought has stopped at this Jacobin maxim" and that any mode of representation and decisionmaking based on Serbian numerical strength in Yugoslavia denied the equality of nationalities.[36]

Throughout the late 1980s the Slovenian communist leadership not only stubbornly adhered to the idea of a federation operating on the basis of unanimity and equally weighted units but also further enraged the Serbian leadership by endorsing the idea of a so-called "asymmetric federation." As elaborated by Slovenian political and constitutional theorists, the notion of federal asymmetry referred to an arrangement whereby each republic would negotiate its own terms of power sharing and power distribution with the central government in a federation. A particular republic might, for example, enjoy wide-ranging autonomy in selected spheres of activity such as economic development, education, linguistic and cultural matters, yet other domains, such as defense and foreign policy would remain the responsibility of a federal government functioning on the basis of interregional agreement. As one Slovenian writer observed, the "asymmetric federation" is a relatively new "intermediate form" of organization that lies between a federation and a confederation.[37] For its part, the Milošević leadership regarded the Slovenian idea of federal asymmetry as a means of advancing the already "confederalist" or centrifugal aspects promoted by the 1974 constitution, and thus a prescription for a "feeble federation" that would presage the disintegration of socialist Yugoslavia.[38]

Undaunted by Milošević's criticism, Slovenian politicians claimed that an asymmetric federation would facilitate interregional agreements by obviating the need for "standard solutions where they are not necessarily needed."[39] Indeed, anxious to forestall the possibility that Belgrade decisionmakers might one day wish to impose "standard solutions" on their republic, the Slovenian Assembly adopted provisions in 1989 that required the assembly's agreement before federal authorities could intervene in Slovenian affairs as a result of any alleged "emergency" situation within the republic. The president of the Slovenian Assembly conceded that this step was taken in light of the federal presidency's declaration of emergency measures for Kosovo in late February 1989. No one had to ask the Kosovo Assembly for permission, the Slovenian official asserted, because the Kosovo Constitution did not address the issue of a provincial role in such a situation.[40]

Although Slovenia's adoption of the new constitutional provision on state emergencies, and an equally controversial amendment giving the republic the formal right to secede from Yugoslavia, were declared unconstitutional by the country's collective state presidency, the Slovenian Assembly formally promulgated the measures at the end of September 1989. The amendments immediately triggered negative commentaries by Serbian observers who claimed that the Slovenian elite had launched a "torpedo directed at the bow of Yugoslavia" and were interested in Slovenia becoming a "small Switzerland."[41] Urged on by the Belgrade leadership, mass protest demonstrations by Serbs and Montenegrins also took place, at which leaders and crowds demanded the removal of the Slovenian communist leadership.

Pluralism Without a Vanguard

Slovenian views advanced during the late 1980s concerning party pluralism were especially offensive to Milošević and his Serbian constituency. During 1989, for example, Slovenian communists amended their organizational statutes, dropping any reference to their party's "leading role." Acknowledging that one-party monopoly had impeded economic recovery and democratic development in their republic, top Slovenian officials insisted that the League of Communists must begin to compete "equally with other subjects" if it wished to assume a paramount ideological position in society.[42] Slovenian communists were also critical of the way their party organization operated on the countrywide level, particularly central party procedures that permitted decisionmaking by majority voting. The Slovenian communist leaders consequently opposed the convening of an "extraordinary" Fourteenth Party Congress scheduled for January 1990, fearing that such a convocation would prove detrimental to the relatively autonomous position they had incrementally been carving out for themselves. When, during preparations for the congress, it was announced that voting at the meeting would be conducted on the basis of one vote per delegate rather than by equally weighted regional delegations, Slovenian officials objected that such methods would give a decisive advantage to Serbia and its allies.

In an unprecedented statement on June 20, 1989, Slovenian party leaders warned that if their views were overridden by a system of majority decisionmaking at the extraordinary congress they would hold their own congress, and "decide either for a unilateral cancellation of democratic centralism or for the complete organizational independence of the League of Communists of Slovenia."[43] The Slovenian communist threat to assert regional party independence was made only after their unsuccessful efforts to engage Milošević and the Serbian leadership in negotiations regarding the League's interregional problems. Milošević refused such entreaties for bilateral party discussions and rebuked the Slovenian leadership for "the most vile stab in the back of Serbia" over the Kosovo issue.[44]

Serbian communist leaders were also angered by the tolerant attitude adopted by leading Slovenian politicians toward the spate of independent party-like political organizations that emerged within Slovenia at the end of the 1980s.[45] Slovenian communist leader Kučan, for example, described such pluralism as "not a danger, but a new chance for the country," although he indicated his personal preference for a *nonparty* form of pluralism.[46] Although the Slovenian communists did not initially endorse a multiparty political system, their interpretation of political pluralism went well beyond the Milošević Commission's much narrower notion of a "political pluralism on socialist foundations." Indeed, the 1989 Slovenian constitutional amendments offered wide scope for independent socialist *and* nonsocialist political organizations to compete with the communists in the nomination of candidates to run for election in legislative assemblies.

Throughout 1989, Serbia's leaders and other opponents of such full-blown pluralism warned that tolerance for a multiparty or multigroup system on the regional level, and subsequently in countrywide political life, would reintroduce the fractious pre-World War II squabbling among ethnically and religiously based parties. Moreover, other Serbian political analysts argued that the experience of many developing countries demonstrated that the existence of several different political parties provided no guarantee of economic development, democracy, or a solution to the type of crisis faced by Yugoslavia. Behind such concerns about the formation of new parties was, of course, the fear that pluralist developments in Slovenia and elsewhere in the country, including Serbia, would inevitably lead to the strengthening of "anti-socialist forces" that would eventually undermine the existing regime.[47] Macedonian party leader Vasil Tupurkovski, a Milošević ally at the time, pointed out that "the party must rid itself of the monopoly of power, but in such a way that it does not lose its vanguard position and find itself on the margins of social processes."[48] Members of independent noncommunist groups in Slovenia claimed that the notion of a "nonparty pluralism," frequently advanced by the Milošević camp as well as by other cautious communist leaders, constituted an absurd idea so long as the League of Communists maintained its controlling role in the political system.[49]

Relations between Serbia and Slovenia seriously deteriorated in November 1989 following a decision by the government in Ljubljana to prevent entry into their republic by Serbs who planned to stage a December 1 protest demonstration. The Serbian communist leadership responded by announcing the termination of all government and business links with Slovenia. The threat to interrupt trading ties between the two republics was supported by 130 enterprises in Serbia, creating the potential, if fully implemented, of seriously harming the country's economy. One Croatian sociologist suggested that the Serbian action meant the collapse of a unified market by breaking the country into two spheres of influence, Slovenia and Serbia, and that, as a result, "Yugoslavia has effectively been abolished as a state."[50] Whether the Slovenian-Serbian rift would presage the eventual disintegration of the Yugoslav state, or whether a compromise strategy could be found to maintain the country's cohesion was a very open question at the beginning of 1990.

The Federal Government's Strategy:
Marketization as a "New Type of Socialism"

The contrasting reform strategies of the Serbian and Slovenian communist leaderships advanced in the late 1980s were regionally based proposals that lacked countrywide endorsement or application. Slovenian and Serbian political leaders engaged in lively intraparty polemics about their respective reform theses, but the difficult task of actually elaborating and implementing a cross-regional or Yugoslav reform program remained the responsibility of the federal government, headed after March 1989 by Ante Marković. A Croat from Bosnia-Hercegovina, Marković was trained as an electrical engineer and had spent most of his career in the economic management of one of Yugoslavia's largest manufacturing enterprises. His two previous positions had been leadership posts in the Croatian government bureaucracy, where he had gained a reputation as a serious political technocrat committed to market reform.

In terms of broad economic goals, Marković's general program exhibited many similarities to the Serbian and Slovenian recommendations, such as enhanced implementation of a market-oriented economy. Calling for a "completely new type of socialism" to solve Yugoslavia's crisis, Marković expressed his belief that "the open market economy [is] the ultimate achievement of mankind for which no alternative has yet been found."[51] Untainted by earlier official failures to deal with the economic crisis, Marković began work on his "new socialism" by fleshing out a sweeping package of constitutional reforms adopted in the last days of the paralyzed former government.

In November 1988, the Yugoslav Federal Assembly promulgated thirty-nine amendments to the constitution as a basis for comprehensive economic and political reform. Most of the amendments involved deregulation of the economy to permit the implementation of free market principles and a pro-growth economic policy. The constitutional changes and the initial policy measures adopted by Marković included the elimination of most property limitations (with the exception of land-holdings, which were limited to thirty hectares); the reduction of state interference in the banking system; provision for unfettered competition among the social, private, and cooperative spheres of property ownership; liberalized rules for foreign ownership and joint ventures; preparations for the establishment of a money and securities market; and the encouragement of free initiative and profit motivation throughout the economy. Speaking to a German business group in June 1989, Yugoslavia's foreign trade minister claimed that the Marković government's new strategy constituted the "most revolutionary reforms since World War II" and that it was lack of courage by earlier governments to fundamentally change the system that had contributed to the current crisis. "Capital," observed the minister, "must be protected and profit possible."[52]

In order to expedite economic change, the FEC took a number of modest steps toward political reform during 1989. It was decided, for example, that federal regulations might be adopted without complete unanimity among the republics and provinces and that the "interrepublican committees," utilized since 1974 for the protracted and often impossible task of developing cross-regional unanimity on federal policies, would be dissolved. The balanced representation of republic and provincial personnel continued to be important in the selection of FEC members, but ethnic affiliation was dropped as a major criterion in personnel recruitment. In a move to eliminate the "excessive normativism" plaguing the economy, enterprises were allowed to regulate their internal and industrywide operations without the adoption of numerous "self-management" acts, agreements, and compacts.

As part of his pledge to streamline the administration and create a "modern state suited to a market economy," Marković also formed a smaller cabinet (from 29 down to 19 members) including several younger and highly qualified officials. The two FEC Vice-Presidents working directly with Marković—Aleksandar Mitrović, a 56-year-old Serb educated as an engineer, and Živko Pregl, a 42-year-old Slovenian trained in economics—had considerable experience in economic management and administration. Plans were also announced to cut the size of the federal bureaucracy from about 14,000 to 10,000 employees, although the government also announced that it would hire between 500 and 700 "new experts and professionals."

Beginning his work as prime minister, Marković cautioned that full implementation of his reform program would take at least five years. Moreover, while political reform constituted an important component of his "new socialism," primary attention during 1989 would focus on the country's pressing economic difficulties. In view of the serious regional divisions in the party elite regarding political reform, the federal government's economic priority seemed to make sense. In an unusually candid interview concerning the policies of the FEC, Vice-President Pregl stressed that although the current crisis would not be overcome without "profound changes in the political system," economic reform must take priority "because we agree much more on the country's economic matters than on how to harmonize political developments."[53] In contrast to Milošević and his supporters—who generally blamed the

Yugoslav crisis and reform failures on institutional flaws in the method of decisionmaking, or on deliberate sabotage by a conservative and corrupt bureaucracy—Pregl argued that the government's main problem was finding competent personnel who could understand market-type economic relations. Charges by Milošević that the federal government lacked sufficient power to override parochial republican and provincial interests were downplayed by Pregl: "We do not intend to haggle with anybody about anybody's interests. Our concept is clear—the market! The concept can break these state obstacles in Yugoslavia."[54]

A key political ally for the Marković government team, at least initially, was Yugoslavia's state President Janez Drnovšek, whose term ran from May 1989 to May 1990. At 39 years of age, Drnovšek was the youngest state president in Yugoslavia's history, holding a doctorate in economics and having a specialization in international finance (his Ph.D. thesis was on the International Monetary Fund and Yugoslavia). Unlike his predecessors, who were chosen by regional party machines, Drnovšek was elected to the collective state presidency in April 1989 by a large popular mandate in his native Slovenia (the first republic to use direct elections to fill such a post).

Drnovšek was a staunch supporter of a market-oriented economy and the policies endorsed by Marković. In his Slovenian election campaign, Drnovšek promoted the idea of making Yugoslavia's currency fully convertible within five years and suggested that a similar time frame be proposed to the European Free Trade Association and the European Council as an adjustment period for closer Yugoslav association with the European economy. Drnovšek also proposed that the state presidency ease interregional and interethnic differences so that "extremist politicians will lose ground for the further straining of conflicts."[55] He shared the view of the Marković government that the political crisis had been caused largely by economic difficulties and that if the size of the "social product" available for distribution would increase, "mutual political tensions will lessen."[56] Drnovšek's support for the government was particularly critical during 1989 and 1990 because of the presidency's authority to intervene in the operation of federal decisionmaking when difficulties (such as regional protests and stalemates in the Federal Assembly) arose.[57]

One of the most serious problems faced by the Marković government was how to control runaway inflation. Initially, Marković opted for a gradual approach to dampening inflation, concentrating on measures to revive production, alleviate tax burdens on the economy, reduce the federal budget, restrict the amount of money in circulation through borrowing limitations on federal authorities, encourage investment by greater participation of foreign and private capital, and liberalize imports and prices. Utilizing such measures, Marković initially envisioned a decline in the inflation rate beginning in fall 1990. Debt repayment was also viewed as an important anti-inflationary measure. Future investments were to be implemented through carefully conceived joint ventures because, as Marković argued: "The mistake in the past does not lie in the fact we have borrowed, but in the way we have used these funds."[58] Throughout most of 1989 the Marković government "categorically" rejected an anti-inflation policy based upon price or wage freezes—the method unsuccessfully employed by the former government of Branko Mikulić.[59] "Inflation," FEC Vice-President Pregl stressed, "can be partially stopped through a freeze but we are certain that this is not the right way to do it...we do not treat inflation as a special problem. This was done in the past and we have tonnes of paper with various anti-inflation titles. The effects of this are well-known."[60]

The difficulties inherent in Marković's long-term "systemic solution" to revive the Yugoslav economy, especially the postponement of immediate relief from the country's current hyperinflation, naturally provided grist for the mills of those forces unsympathetic to the central government. Pleading for quick adoption of his market reform package at the end of June 1989, Marković conceded that "time is our big enemy, if not the biggest enemy we need to confront in the next period."[61] Although Marković expressed satisfaction that "100% unity" existed in the FEC, and that none of its members had advanced views on regional or ethnic grounds, Marković's initial honeymoon with Milošević and the Serbian leadership ended after only a few months. In Serbia, a *Borba* journalist quipped in June 1989, Marković is "on the list of those whose replacement has not yet been sought, but for whom 'closed season' no longer applies."[62] Marković's claims about the potential of his reform strategy and its initial achievements in 1989 were ridiculed by Serbian leaders as excessively optimistic. One Serbian deputy in the Federal Assembly even suggested that the central government's failure to employ "shock therapy" against inflation—that is, a freeze on prices and income— derived from a desire by some of its members to turn the Serbian people against their leaders. More moderate voices in Serbia repudiated such extreme views, observing that "there have been all kinds of conspiracies in world history, but a conspiracy using inflation has never been recorded."[63]

By mid-1989 it was clear that the Milošević forces had decided to actively oppose the strategy of the federal government. Although Milošević and his Serbian Reform Commission were publicly on record as supporting the central government's nonfreeze policy (controlled prices undervalued Serbian exports of food and electricity to other parts of the country), they nevertheless attempted to channel popular dissatisfaction with high inflation away from themselves and toward the Marković government. Milošević adherents appealed to those citizens, particularly Serbs, who were dissatisfied with the continued fall in the standard of living. In Serbia there was little sympathy for Marković's argument that the population and regime needed to endure short-term difficulties, such as high unemployment and inflation that inevitably accompany market reforms. For Milošević and his supporters, marketization was deemed important, but paramount emphasis was placed on the political reorganization of the federal structure as a means of eliminating the so-called "absolute domination of partial interests" (Slovenia and Kosovo, for example), which allegedly obstructed both the influence of the central government and the interests of the country's Serbian majority.

Badly in need of support for his reforms, Marković had the unenviable task of charting a middle course between the strong centralizing pressure encouraged by populist mobilization in Serbia and the pluralistic pressure for regional autonomy promoted in Slovenia. At the end of July 1989, at a two-day session of the party Central Committee called to discuss worsening interethnic relations, Marković complained that most reform efforts initiated by the federal government had "either been stopped or slowed down" by regional officials, and he raised the issue of whether Yugoslav political leaders genuinely desired a "new system."[64] As one of the frustrated vice-presidents in the Marković cabinet explained, failure to implement the federal government's program was a major factor undermining comprehensive reform in Yugoslavia:

> Things that the Assembly adopted are not being done. Republics and provinces should have reduced their budgets and...established their deficits. This was not done. These deficits are one of the main causes of our inflation: they amount to more than our entire annual social product....We reach agreements and then spend however much we want....This works according to the system whereby I grab something today and someone else does the same tomorrow, and the inflationary spiral continues. There is no end to this...inflation demolishes everything, it destroys the economic system, creates bad blood, divides people, and even threatens the political system.[65]

By fall 1989, Marković, though visibly frustrated, remained committed to his reform strategy and denied reports that his government planned to resign. Visiting the United States in October to obtain financial assistance for Yugoslavia, Marković claimed that opponents of his program were concerned that state property was "threatened" by the planned economic liberalization of the country, and he expected "an intensification of the conflict between ideology and reforms."[66] In December, Marković accelerated his economic reform program with new measures to fight inflation, including a six-month wage freeze (a policy previously rejected by his cabinet), tight monetary and budget controls, the creation of a convertible dinar, and an end to state subsidies for unprofitable companies. The Serbian leadership completely rejected the Marković package, and large mass demonstrations were held throughout Serbia to protest the federal government's threatened austerity measures. Despite Serbian and Montenegrin opposition, however, the new Marković proposals had sufficient support from the other republics to permit their parliamentary adoption as "urgent measures" (requiring only a two-thirds vote rather than unanimity by all the republics). The initial success and popularity of Marković's early 1990 initiatives to check inflation took some of the steam out of Milošević's criticism concerning the federal government's economic program. But the Serbian leader continued to hammer away at the federal government over the question of Kosovo, Slovenian autonomy, and the political "disintegration" of the country.

Although the sweeping program of economic reforms promoted by Prime Minister Marković throughout 1989 enjoyed considerable cross-regional support, the strong political challenges to the central government in Slovenia, and by Milošević supporters in Serbia (and allied Montenegro), together with mounting popular protests against hyperinflation, made it very difficult to implement federal policy in a thorough and orderly manner. Of course, Marković and the federal government were not without resources and allies in the struggle of reform philosophies. Thus at the end of 1989 the prime minister still had the strong support of the military, the federal apparatus of the League of Communists, much of the federal legislature, important regional allies such as Croatian communist government and party officials, as well as those foreign countries and international organizations sympathetic to Yugoslavia's survival. Even such assets, however, could not ensure the implementation of the comprehensive reform program announced by the FEC, particularly in the context of a crisis that regularly engendered new episodes of ethnopolitical and economic conflict.

The main barrier to successful crisis management and reform by the Yugoslav communist regime at the outset of 1990 was the lack of political trust and cooperation among the members of the regionally divided political elite. Without such trust, and given the mobilization of ethnoregional constituencies around popular regional spokesmen in Serbia and Slovenia, the federal government's comprehensive plan of marketization and gradual democratization had little chance of success. Political dialogue and party factionalism in Yugoslavia had long been characterized by hyperbole, personalized attacks, and sharp polemics, but by late 1989 the rising pattern of intraelite mistrust had acquired more serious significance owing to the deep economic crisis, the sharply divergent strategies for political reform, and the absence of a powerful pan-ethnic authority figure such as Tito to end stalemates and push through difficult decisions.

Prime Minister Marković's pragmatic efforts at economic reform won him considerable popularity throughout Yugoslavia, but it was no longer possible—as during Tito's lifetime—for a federal leader to impose decisions in the face of strong opposition from regional political elites. Recognizing the depth of interregional elite dissension, the federal government postponed efforts at macropolitical reorganization (e.g., the adoption of a new constitution), concentrating instead on incremental economic renovation.[67] In doing so, however, the danger existed that economic reforms would be allowed to falter—as had happened several times before in Yugoslav communist history—because of resistance from entrenched regional political bureaucracies. The major problem was not the absence of political will by federal authorities to undertake major reforms, but the government's lack of the necessary cross-regional legitimacy to implement reforms on a sustained countrywide basis.

Although elite disunity significantly undermined the reform initiatives of the federal government, the basic sources of the systemic crisis afflicting the communist regime went much deeper and stood little chance of being resolved by those who had governed the country during the crisis of the 1980s. As the Serbian political scientist, Vladimir Goati aptly observed:

> The segmentation of the Yugoslav political elite answers the questions of why, despite its absolute control of society, it did not succeed in finding a way out of the crisis. The reason must be found in the fact that the ineffectiveness of the political (and other) elites is not only a function of their control, but also of their unity....The absence of the second element, unity, in the Yugoslav political elite is the key to explaining its total failure in the struggle with the social crisis over several years. From that, however, we must not draw the conclusion that a unified Yugoslav politocracy would successfully resolve the gigantic problems of economic development, and democracy; in the framework of the existing monocratic

political paradigm [such unity] would only have mitigated some of the irrationalism. A solution...requires a fundamental change in the paradigm, a change in which the politocracy looses its dominant position.[68]

During 1990 and 1991, the accumulated problems and tensions stemming from the communist regime's failed "paradigm," was compounded by the emergence of several new difficulties that would seriously challenge not only the maintenance of federal-guided reform and federal control, but also the very survival of the Yugoslav state.

Notes

1. From 1981 to 1985, Yugoslavia's rate of growth was roughly ten times slower than during the period from 1976 to 1980 as well as in relation to the entire period from 1948 to 1985. Božidar Franges, *Yugoslavia and the World Economy* (Belgrade: Medjunarodna Politika, 1987), pp. 22-23.

2. On the overall decline of public confidence in the League of Communists, see Vladimir Goati, *Politička anatomija Jugoslovenskog društva* (Zagreb: Naprijed, 1989), pp. 91-99. For the growing pattern of popular cynicism and disenchantment with the regime in Yugoslavia during the early 1980s, see Alvin Magid, *Private Lives/Public Surfaces: Grassroots Perspectives and Legitimacy Questions in Yugoslav Socialism* (Boulder, Co.: East European Monographs, 1991).

3. See Boris Vušković, "Tko su Jugoslaveni?" *Naše Teme*, Vol. 26, No. 10 (1982), pp. 1702-1712; and Aleksander Raić, "Jugosloveni u Vojvodini," *Naše Teme*, Vol. 26, No. 10 (1982), pp. 1713-1722.

4. Sergje Flere, "The Ethnic Attitudes of Youth in Yugoslavia," *Revija za narodnostna vprasanja, razprave in gradivo*, No. 21 (1988), pp. 133-142.

5. Vjeran Katunarić, "Interethnic Relations in Contemporary Yugoslavia: Some Theoretical Notes and Empirical Findings," *Revija za narodnostna vprašanja, razprave in gradivo*, No. 21 (1988), p. 108.

6. See Ante Cuvalo, *The Croatian National Movement, 1966-1972* (Boulder, Colo.: East European Monographs, 1989).

7. Slobodan Milošević is a son of a Serbian Orthodox clergyman of Montenegrin origin and is literally a "child of the revolution." He was born in August 1941, two months after the Yugoslav communist party began its wartime guerrilla struggle. Thus, Milošević was only seven at the time of the Tito-Stalin rift and just ten when "workers' self-management" became the regime's ideological platform. It is significant that the most formative stage of Milošević's education and career development from 1961 to 1986 coincides with the burgeoning of ethnic conflict in Yugoslav political life. After graduating from university, where he served in a number of posts connected with the League of Communists' ideological and political activities, Milošević worked as an economic adviser to

the mayor of Belgrade, in the Information Department of the Belgrade City Government (1966-1968), as deputy general director, and then general director of the enterprise "Tehnogas" (1970-1978), and then as president of a Belgrade bank (1978-1982). Both of Milošević's parents, who separated when he was quite young, would commit suicide. Milošević's wife, Mirjana Marković-Milošević, also became an active Serbian political figure in the mid-1980s and a close ally of her husband. In October 1989 she was elected to the presidium of the influential City Conference of the Belgrade League of Communists.

8. Slavoljub Djukić, *Kako se dogodio vodja: borbe za vlast u Srbiji posle Josipa Broza* (Belgrade: Filip Višnjić, 1992), pp. 124-130.

9. Milošević continuously emphasized that Serbs should not have a guilty conscience about Serbian nationalism during the precommunist era and that they should not be self-conscious about striving for their ethnic rights and a strong unified Yugoslav state today. Milošević's collected speeches are in *Godine Raspleta* (Belgrade: Beogradski Izdavačko-Grafički Zavod, 1989). See especially pp. 35-38, 220-221.

10. Survey data show that dissatisfaction with the constitution of 1974 was quite high among all regions and ethnic groups in the country but especially among the Serbs and in Serbia proper. Sergije Pegan, "Politički sistem," in Draško Grbić (ed.), *Jugosloveni o društvenoj krizi (istraživanje javnog mnjenja, 1985. godine)* (Belgrade: Komunist, 1989), pp. 61-63.

11. *Le Monde*, July 12, 1989, p. 6. Milošević claims that the 1974 constitution was one of Tito's late initiatives and that "he was unable to imagine the extent to which such a system would destroy the country." For Yugoslav analytical studies that are highly critical of the 1974 constitution's impact on economic life, see Marjan Korošić, *Jugoslovenska kriza* (Zagreb: Naprijed, 1989), and Stanko Radmilović, *Ekonomska kriza i društvena reforma* (Belgrade: Beogradski Izdavačko-Grafički Zavod, 1989).

12. *Le Monde*, July 12, 1989, p. 6.

13. Milošević's success is also closely related to his skill in political communication. As a Slovenian journalist observed: "He's not exactly a born speaker; his delivery is somewhat rapid and it is obvious that he is more accustomed to reading his speeches than to ad-lib. However, what he reads is something new in Yugoslav political practice. Milošević has simply 'stepped out' of the bounds of the iron political jargon of our politicians, a jargon that has continued to assert and petrify itself for decades. His speeches include no long and involved sentences whose meaning is grasped by the audience only after it has worked its way through five or six subordinate clauses. In his speeches there is none of that compulsive theorizing that appears in every speech—even on the most banal occasions....His speeches are delivered in short and simple sentences that are filled with metaphors, comparisons, and slogans that are easily understood by everyone and therefore can quickly turn into 'folk sayings.'" *FBIS-EEU*, October 28, 1988, p. 64.

14. The entire text of the Memorandum is in *Naše Teme*, Vol. 33, Nos. 1-2 (1989), pp. 128-163. Dobrica Ćosić has denied participation in the preparation of the Memorandum: "I was not a member of the commission of authors. The basic characteristics of the Memorandum are anti-Titoism and traditional Yugoslavism. I do not think that Milošević has taken anything from that." *FBIS-EEU*, August 11, 1992, p. 35.

15. It has been argued that the support of the military was an important ingredient in Milošević's consolidation of power in September 1987. Zoran Jeličić, "The Beginning and End of the Eighth Session," and Dusan Janjić, "The Role of Ljubičić," both in *Vreme News Digest Agency*, No. 52, September 21, 1992, pp. 7-8, 10-11.

16. Milos Vasić, Roksanda Ninčić, and Tanja Topić, "A Tired Serbia," *Vreme News Digest Agency*, No. 52, September 21, 1992, p. 6.

17. *FBIS-EEU*, November 25, 1988, p. 40.

18. *Nedeljne Informativne Novine* (hereafter *NIN*), November 20, 1988, p. 12.

19. Vladimir Stambuk, "Klasa i demokratija," *NIN*, No. 1987, January 29, 1989, pp. 17-18.

20. *FBIS-EEU*, November 22, 1988, p. 39.

21. *Ibid.*, p. 40.

22. *Ibid.*, p. 42.

23. *Ibid.*, p. 39.

24. Professor Kosta Mihailović, cited *NIN*, No. 1946, April 17, 1988, p. 16.

25. *NIN*, No. 1657, July 3, 1988, pp. 14-15.

26. Ivo Jakovljević, "Miloševićeva šansa," *Danas*, Vol. 8, No. 391 (1989), p. 21.

27. Oskar Kovač, "Sve svojine su ravnopravne," *NIN*, No. 2013, July 30, 1989, pp. 16-17.

28. Slobodan Vučetić, "Pravna država slobodnih ljudi," in *Ibid.*, pp. 10-15 (all quotations in this and the next two paragraphs are from this source).

29. *Ibid.*, pp. 10-11. Vučetić later reiterated his endorsement of a "pluralism of political organizations" under the condition that they be "generally viewed as being based upon socialist and Yugoslav options." He added that in his opinion a multiparty system is "less bad than a one-party system. In both systems the citizens and democracy are bounded." *NIN*, No. 2030, November 26, 1989, pp. 16-17.

30. For a good overview of this trend, see Miha Kovac, "The Slovene Spring," *New Left Review* (September-October, 1988), pp. 115-128.

31. *FBIS-EEU*, November 15, 1988, p. 65.

32. Vladimir Štambuk, "Klasa i demokratija," *NIN*, No. 1987, January 29, 1989, p. 14.

33. *FBIS-EEU*, June 21, 1989, pp. 67-68.

34. *FBIS-EEU*, June 20, 1989, p. 70.

35. *FBIS-EEU*, July 6, 1989, p. 71.

36. *FBIS-EEU*, July 11, 1989, pp. 65-66.

37. Mario Nobilo, "Asimetrična federacija," *Danas*, July 18, 1989, pp. 30-31.

38. Olivera Vučić, "Lažna asimetrija federalne konfederacije," *NIN*, June 11, 1989, pp. 24-25.

39. *Danas*, Vol. 8, No. 389 (1989), p. 12.

40. *Ibid*.

41. *FBIS-EEU*, September 29, 1989, pp. 58-59. Immediately prior to the decision by the Slovenian Assembly, members of the federal-level party Central Committee voted 97 to 40 (with 1 undecided) that Slovenia should delay its vote on the constitutional amendments. Only the 20 Slovenian representatives, 16 members from Croatia (4 were absent), and 1 or 2 members from other regions voted against the call for a postponement. The Serbian and Macedonian representatives voted unanimously for a postponement, as did almost the entire contingent from Bosnia, Montenegro, Vojvodina, and Kosovo. The amendments were later passed in the Slovenian Assembly by a vote of 256 to 1. The only vote opposed was by an army colonel who said that if he were an "ordinary delegate" he would have voted for the amendment. *Radio Free Europe Research, Situation Report, Yugoslavia*, October 23, 1989, p. 6.

42. *Ibid.*, p. 11.

43. *FBIS-EEU*, June 27, 1989, p. 69.

44. *FBIS-EEU*, June 2, 1989, p. 67. During 1989 Milošević also angered the Slovenian leadership by insinuating that its enthusiasm to become more closely associated with the European economy reflected an attitude of cultural superiority vis-à-vis the rest of Yugoslavia and also excessive deference to Western Europe. Slovenian leaders called the Milošević accusation "insulting" and expressed pride in having "blazed Yugoslavia's trail to Europe." *FBIS-EEU*, June 2, 1989, pp. 69-70.

45. The party-like organizations that began operating in Slovenia during 1989 included, the Slovene Social-Democratic Alliance, the Slovene Christian Social Movement, the Slovene Peasant Alliance, the "Greens" Union, the Slovene Democratic Alliance, and the Academic Anarchist Anti-Alliance Alliance.

46. *FBIS-EEU*, June 20, 1989, p. 69; and *FBIS-EEU*, June 22, 1989, p. 70.

47. Jovan Marjanović, "Reform SKJ i politički pluralizam," *Socijalizam*, Vol. 32, No. 1 (1989); Milijana Belančić, "Pluralizam zahteva jedinstvo," *Komunist*, May 26, 1989, p. 6; and Najdan Pašić, "Gvozdeni zagrljaj birokratije," *Komunist*, May 12, 1989, p. 11. Dr. Janko Pleterski, a member of the Slovenian League of Communists' presidium, told his colleagues that political pluralism cannot be rejected because parties or alliances might form on a regional and not a federal basis: "Such 'arguments'…resemble arguments for election laws in the prewar Yugoslav dictatorship, which permitted public activity only when it was state-wide." *FBIS-EEU*, July 11, 1989, p. 68. Slovenian communist activist Lev Kreft rejected the idea that ethnic parties destroyed interwar Yugoslavia. "Politički pluralizam," *Socijalizam*, Vol. 32, No. 1 (1989), pp. 84-87.

48. *FBIS-EEU,* June 5, 1989, p. 55. During late 1989, sources suggested that Tupurkovski and Milošević had a falling out over the latter leader's nationalist tactics.

49. *FBIS-EEU,* June 29, 1989, p. 65.

50. *Chicago Tribune,* December 4, 1989, p. 2.

51. *Associated Press Report,* January 28, 1989.

52. *FBIS-EEU,* June 6, 1989, pp. 44-45.

53. *FBIS-EEU,* June 8, 1989, p. 41.

54. *Ibid.,* p. 44.

55. *FBIS-EEU,* April 5, 1989, p. 49.

56. *FBIS-EEU,* April 18, 1989, p. 59.

57. Marković could serve up to five years as prime minister, but under the system of annual presidential rotation, Drnovšek was required to step down from his post in May 1990. At that time he was succeeded by the member of the collective presidency serving as vice-president, Serbia's Borisav Jović (a 61-year-old economist with a doctorate in economics, experience as a commercial and financial director, and a former member of the Milošević Commission).

58. *FBIS-EEU,* June 19, 1989, p. 65.

59. For a good overview of the unsuccessful reforms in the pre-Marković period, see Paul Shoup, "Crisis and Reform in Yugoslavia," *Telos,* No. 29 (Spring 1989), pp. 129-147.

60. *FBIS-EEU,* June 8, 1989, p. 44.

61. *FBIS-EEU,* June 21, 1989, p. 60.

62. *FBIS-EEU,* June 27, 1989, p. 59.

63. *Ibid.*

64. *FBIS-EEU,* July 31, 1989, p. 53.

65. *FBIS-EEU,* August 24, 1989, p. 60.

66. *Associated Press Report,* October 4, 1989.

67. During 1989, Marković generally avoided detailing a course of political reform, but when pressed on the issue during his U.S. visit he remarked that "the logic of pluralistic ownership, which demands a system of its own, will have to demand and open the society to a multiparty system." *Ibid.*

68. Vladimir Goati, "Ko poseduje političku moć?" in Mihailo Popović *et al.* (eds.), *Srbija krajem osamdestih* (Belgrade: Institut za sociološka istraživanja, 1991), p. 462.

Changing of the guard at the "Flower House," the Belgrade mausoleum of Josip Broz Tito (1896–1980), leader of Yugoslavia from the end of World War II to his death in 1980. *Credit:* Matija Koković.

Slobodan Milošević, president of Serbia (March 28, 1991). *Credit:* Josip Bistrović.

Franjo Tudjman, head of the Croatian Democratic Alliance (HDZ) voting in Croatia's first post–World War II multiparty election (April 22, 1990). *Credit:* Josip Bistrović.

Legislative deputies in the Croatian Sabor (legislature) celebrating a proclamation that affirmed Croatia's separate identity as a state (May 30, 1990). The Sabor also elected Franjo Tudjman, president of Croatia, the same day, but it would be over a year before Croatia would declare its independence. *Credit:* Josip Bistrović.

Croatia's President Franjo Tudjman (*left*) and Slovenia's President Milan Kučan meet at Celje (December 7, 1990) to discuss their joint proposal for a confederally organized state to replace the Yugoslav federation. *Credit:* Vreme News Digest Agency.

Serbia's first competitive election (December 1990); mass meeting of opposition party supporters in Belgrade. *Credit:* Ilija Bogdanović.

Opposition party supporters in Belgrade (December 1990). *Credit:* Ilija Bogdanović.

Police action against anti-Milošević demonstrators in Belgrade (March 1991). *Credit:* Vreme News Digest Agency.

Students protesting in Belgrade against the Milošević regime (March 1991). *Credit:* Vreme News Digest Agency.

Father and son observe federal army tanks assisting the Milošević regime in suppression of the March 1991 protests in Belgrade. *Credit:* Vreme News Digest Agency.

Croatian demonstrators attacking federal soldiers in an armored personnel carrier (APC) during violent clashes between the army and 50,000 demonstrators in Split, Croatia (May 26, 1991). The Macedonian soldier driving the APC was strangled to death by one of the demonstrators.

General Veljko Kadijević, the Yugoslav defense minister, September 1991. *Credit:* Canapress Photo Service.

Serbia's President Milošević and President Alija Izetbegović of Bosnia-Hercegovina on their way to a meeting of their two delegations (Belgrade, January 22, 1991). *Credit:* Vreme News Digest Agency.

Meeting in Belgrade of Croatia's President Tudjman and Serbia's President Milošević (March 25, 1991). *Credit:* Vreme News Digest Agency.

Meeting of the presidents of the Yugoslav republics at Brdo na Kranju to discuss Yugoslavia's future (April 11, 1991). *Left to right:* Slovenia's Milan Kučan, Bosnia-Hercegovina's Alija Izetbegović, Macedonia's Kiro Gligorov, Croatia's Franjo Tudjman, and Serbia's Slobodan Milošević. Milošević may be looking for his ally, President Bulatović of Montenegro, who is not present in the photo. *Credit:* Vreme News Digest Agency.

3

Toward Postsocialism:
The Emergence of Party Pluralism

I really see no reason why any society, if it is not thoroughly tyrannical, should prevent a diversity of political views and organizations....However if this so-called political pluralism is used as another term to supplant Yugoslavia and socialism, then we in Serbia are against it.

—Slobodan Milošević (December 1989)

Yugoslavia will continue to function, with or without the League of Communists.

—Ante Marković (January 1990)

The End of One-Party Rule

BY EARLY 1990 the dissolution of the communist regime was rapidly gaining momentum. The impetus to such centrifugal movement derived mainly from the widening political distance among communist elites in the individual republics and the heightened anti-communist nationalism boiling beneath the surface of the official and increasingly delegitimated political order. Indeed, with the economy in disarray and leaders of the League of Communists deeply divided about the prescription for reform, a glaring contradiction in all of the various strategies advanced by the Yugoslav communist regime for dealing with the national question from the early 1950s onward (Chapter 1) came into sharp relief. Thus, although the regime celebrated and thereby perpetuated the ethnoregional differentiation of Yugoslavia (e.g., through the federal system, the ethnic

79

key and leadership recruitment), the tenacious anti-pluralism of the communist system precluded the free political expression, interplay, and reconciliation of ethnoregional interests. Under such conditions of political monism, the country's burgeoning ethnoregional particularism, both within and outside the ranks of the League of Communists, had no political outlet and no alternative but to turn against the system of single-party socialism. Thus in a pattern very similar to other East European societies where communist rule had recently collapsed or had been seriously weakened, Yugoslavia's regime faced the danger of meltdown under the pressure of a burgeoning "civil society" that was outside the control of the state and the official regime.[1] Although superficially the most glaring example of intraregime fragmentation was the collision between the communist elites of Slovenia and Serbia, the country's unity was increasingly threatened by other nationalist forces and a broader deterioration of interethnic relations.

In the province of Kosovo, for example, Albanian nationalism continued to seriously challenge Serbia's Milošević regime and the more general cohesion of the country. Ethnic violence in Kosovo had intensified sharply during 1989 and early 1990 as Albanians protested the adoption of new constitutional measures giving Serbian authorities in Belgrade greater control over the province.[2] Although Albanian nationalism in its own right was unlikely to provoke Yugoslavia's disintegration, Serbia's heavy-handed response to Albanian demands for Kosovo's enhanced autonomy within the Yugoslav federation (for example, as a seventh republic) severely strained the already seriously troubled relationship between Serbian political leaders and their counterparts in northwestern Yugoslavia.[3] Whether out of conviction to advance their decentralized brand of socialist reform or a perverse desire to make trouble for Milošević, Slovenian communist reformers evinced support for Albanian protest against Serbian rule. Outraged by such meddling in their affairs, the Serbian leadership and population generally viewed their fellow citizens in Slovenia and Croatia as cruelly insensitive to the difficulties faced by the Serbian minority in Kosovo and deliberately blind to the dangers which unbridled Albanian nationalism posed for the unity of Yugoslavia. Already in a state of considerable anxiety over perceived threats to Serbian interests, and also to Yugoslavia's future existence, the Milošević controlled media in Belgrade launched a venomous propaganda campaign against the Slovenes and their Albanian "allies."[4]

At the onset of the 1990s, Croatian nationalism also reemerged as an important political force and a threat to Yugoslavia's stability and cohesion. Throughout the late 1980s, the leaders of the League of Communists in

Croatia, though generally appalled by Milošević's program and sympathizing with many of Slovenia's reform proposals, nevertheless steered clear of a major clash with the Serbian leadership. Most communist political leaders in Croatia, many of whom were first recruited for political service during the 1970s following Tito's suppression of Croatian nationalism (the so called MASPOK, or "mass movement"), were very cautious in their approach to both interregional and interethnic problems and to the question of their republic's relationship with the federal government. As a Croatian journalist pointed out, the "first criterion" of leadership recruitment in Croatia after 1971 was "not letting a single nationalist get through, even if people who were not nationalists were stopped because of it."[5] The Croatian elite's extreme prudence regarding the "national question" was heightened by the delicate relationship between the republic's Croatian ethnic majority and its Serbian minority community (roughly 12 percent of the population in 1981). Croatian-Serbian relations were particularly sensitive within the ranks of Croatia's League of Communists, where Serbs were significantly overrepresented compared to their relative size in the republic's population.

By the end of the 1980s, as the countrywide legitimacy crisis of the League of Communists enveloped Croatia and as noncommunist political organizations began to attract more support in the republic, regional and ethnic self-assertiveness dramatically increased within Croatian elite circles.[6] Throughout the 1970s and 1980s, a growth of nationalist feelings, together with a revival of Roman Catholic religiosity, had become increasingly apparent in the general Croatian population. Such views, however, had remained unmobilized and unarticulated by legitimate political actors and organizations.[7] It was only in 1989 that members of the Croatian intelligentsia and communist political leadership, after having stood on the sidelines for two years watching the increasingly acrimonious and nationalistic propaganda battle between the leaders of Serbia and Slovenia, became more aggressive in advancing their own ethnic and regional concerns.[8] Slowly, the so-called "silent republic" began to find its voice in Yugoslavia's building pluralist cacophony.[9]

The dramatic collapse of communist political hegemony and the rapid introduction of competitive party systems in one East European state after another during fall 1989, naturally caused enormous anxiety among all segments of Yugoslavia's political elite, including the Croatian communists. Years of communist foot-dragging on the question of party pluralism was now replaced by the communist leadership's transparent scramble to endorse a domestic model of political competition in the hope that the ruling party might somehow resuscitate its tarnished reputation as the vanguard of democratic reform, preserve some of its influence, and quell the deep discontent within its increasingly volatile membership. In the dismal context of their failed policies and the country's spiraling economic and political crisis, members of Yugoslavia's regionally and ethnically divided communist elite could no longer justify a restricted model of political pluralism, even in the name of building a unique self-managed form of industrial democracy. The quasi-democratic notions of a "self-managed pluralism of interests" or a "nonparty pluralism," previously touted by the regime as a substitute for multiparty competition, had completely lost credibility. After decades of vacillation and obstruction with regard to pluralist political development, most Yugoslav communist leaders now clearly saw that they would be forced to either adapt to the eventuality of competing in an open political market or—as had occurred elsewhere in Eastern Europe—face the prospect of extinction.[10] Moreover, deep and bitter conflicts among regional and ethnic branches of the ruling League of Communists had undermined the traditional argument of party conservatives that the perpetuation of the single-party system was essential to the unity of the country.

Yugoslavia's various regional elites had sharply divergent ideas concerning the best way to react to the developments in Eastern Europe and to confront the delegitimation of their own communist regime. In Serbia, the mobilization of mass protests by Slobodan Milošević's "anti-bureaucratic revolution" had demonstrated that one method by which communist leaders could enhance their support was through a populist appeal to their local ethnic constituencies. At the same time, the "Milošević phenomenon" had revealed the depth of anti-regime feelings situated directly below the thin crust of the one-party regime. Throughout the late 1980s, Milošević had managed to channel those alienated emotions to his advantage, perhaps because of Serbia's particular problems and political culture. Whether Milošević would be able to maintain his unusual plebiscitarian style of mass mobilization remained an open question, particularly as Yugoslavs watched the chaotic events unfolding in neighboring Romania and Bulgaria at the end of 1989.

As for Milošević personally, he had achieved his impressive success through a direct appeal to the Serbian population, but he was reluctant to grant the same opportunity to others—particularly nonsocialists—and appeared unwilling to take any lessons from the East European popular revolution of 1989: "There is no reason to equate the events in Yugoslavia with those in other socialist countries," Milošević explained. "They are now creating the kind of world we initiated in 1948."[11] As with so many issues of political reform, Milošević's fundamental antipathy to multiparty pluralism put him at odds with reform-minded forces in the northwestern region of Yugoslavia. Moreover, by explicitly attacking any expression of Slovenian and Croatian national sentiment, Milošević increasingly forced communist leaders in those republics to choose between continued support for pan-ethnic party unity—at the risk of further alienating their own ethnic constituents—or garnering popular backing through direct opposition to Serbian views.

In Slovenia and Croatia, where identification with Central European culture and multiparty democratic traditions was stronger than in Serbia, the advent of postcommunism in countries such as Czechoslovakia, Hungary, and Poland, intensified the already existing pressure for a fundamental transformation of the Yugoslav regime. Already politically threatened by the prevailing anti-communist mood and generally repelled by Milošević's brand of tutelary nationalist populism, Slovenian and Croatian communist reformers accelerated their efforts to institutionalize political pluralism both within and outside the League of Communists.[12]

In December 1989 the Croatian communist leadership— having received a petition signed by approximately 25,000 Croatian citizens urging the legalization of different political parties and the holding of free elections—admitted that it had been slow in recognizing "the historic exhaustion of the single-party system" and called for the establishment of a multiparty system in the country.[13] The Croatian initiative was followed shortly thereafter by the publication of a new draft platform by the federal party organization that advocated competitive elections and an end to the LCY's monopoly. "We are changing all of this now," the draft declaration stated, "in order that tomorrow it will not be too late for socialism in Yugoslavia."[14] At the end of December, the Slovenian League of Communists, which had pioneered the ruling party's advocacy of greater pluralism, announced that it would "strive for the creation of a multiparty system" and that all communist party organizations in state enterprises and government institutions would be dissolved.[15] In his speech to the Congress of the Slovenian League of Communists, reform leader Milan Kučan told the delegates that they were members of the first communist party in power that had introduced a multiparty system and free elections without direct pressure from the masses.[16] As the "virus of pluralism" spread to Serbia from Central Europe and northwestern Yugoslavia, even the Milošević-guided political leadership in Belgrade was eventually forced to formally support the idea of multiparty pluralism, although their endorsement was heavily laced with reservations warning against the formation of "anti-socialist" political organizations.[17]

Although the radical political changes sweeping Eastern Europe had finally persuaded most Yugoslav communist leaders that the adoption of multiparty pluralism within their country was urgent, the League of Communists' internal quest to combine political pluralism with organizational cohesion proved unsuccessful. The feud between Serbian and Slovenian communist officials regarding the correct model of socialist reform, especially the appropriate parameters of internal party pluralism, reached a climax at the Fourteenth Extraordinary Congress of the League of Communists held at the end of January 1990. What many party members had hoped would be a meeting to transform the LCY into a nonauthoritarian modern party instead turned into a bitter struggle between Slovenian and Serbian communist leaders. The Slovenes advocated the reorganization of the League into a union of "independent and free republican communist parties"—a "League of Leagues"—whereas Serbia's Milošević charged that those seeking further decentralization of the League were essentially calling for a "war among Yugoslav communists...and a war among Yugoslav nations."[18]

Already frustrated at losing every vote on its proposals, the entire Slovenian delegation finally made a dramatic exit from the meeting hall when Slovenia failed to obtain a congress majority in support of a previously negotiated reform platform calling for the enhanced autonomy of the country's republics, an end to laws allowing the prosecution of political opponents, and greater cooperation with Western Europe. Milošević implored the Congress to proceed with its work and elect a new leadership, but the Croatian delegation refused to continue without the participation of the Slovenes, which resulted in the abrupt suspension of the meeting one day ahead of its official schedule. "We left because this [League] is not an organization that can be responsible for social reform in this country," remarked Slovenian communist leader Milan Kučan. "When we left, the party ceased to exist."[19] An observer at the congress from Bosnia-Hercegovina echoed these sentiments and forecast the serious implication of intraparty fragmentation for communism's future in a pluralist environment:

> The League of Communists of Yugoslavia to all intents and purposes no longer exists....This outcome of the extraordinary Fourteenth Congress will definitely reduce the communists' standing in Yugoslavia. Simply, a party would find it difficult to obtain citizens' sympathies if its members trip each other up, and if one party of the organization sets traps for the other, and helps it lose authority in the community where it operates. This "fraternal" trip up, produced a schism, at the moment when it seemed that at least some agreement had been reached over helping each

other to gain citizens' votes in a situation where new political parties are being created.[20]

A Macedonian commentator at the congress noted that interethnic confrontation "between the Slovenian and Serbian party delegations had acquired the characteristics of a political and inter-state conflict between two entire republics" and predicted that as a result of the split "the entire political map of Yugoslavia will be completely different."[21] Meanwhile, spokesmen for Prime Minister Marković indicated that the conflict within the League of Communists would have no bearing on the federal government's existing plans to delete all references to the League's "leading role" from the constitution and to completely democratize the electoral system. Alluding to the fact that the League had approximately two million members in a population of some 23 million, the vice-president of the Federal Executive Council, Živko Pregl (a Slovene), bravely remarked that the government would not allow the fate of the country to be "decided in quarrels among people representing 10 percent of the population."[22]

The Military and Political Pluralism

While Prime Minister Marković and the federal government attempted to ignore the disunity in the League of Communists and to proceed with their ambitious economic reform program, the erosion of single-party control aroused considerable apprehension within Yugoslavia's military elite. Throughout the history of the Yugoslav communist regime, the military establishment of the Yugoslav People's Army (JNA) had viewed itself as a principal force ensuring the country's cohesion and territorial integrity.[23] That sentiment intensified with Tito's death in 1980 and was reinforced by the growing ethnic and regional divisions that emerged over the next decade within the political elite. Under the 1974 constitution, the military was mandated to utilize "armed struggle and other forms of self-defense" and to protect the country and its system of "socialist self-management." The constitution further provided that any military action would be a "unified" operation and that the high command "shall ensure the unity and indivisibility of armed struggle."[24] In the mindset of the military elite, this constitutional mandate implied a broad peacetime mission to defend the regime against both foreign and domestic "enemies of socialism" and included the military's vigorous opposition to the notion of competitive party pluralism. Such pluralism, as conceived by military and conservative communists, had destabilized and destroyed interwar Yugoslavia and remained a dangerous concept propagated by domestic dissidents, soft-headed communist reformers, and anti-socialist émigré politicians.

Developments within Slovenia during the late 1980s served to fuel the military elite's abhorrence of growing political pluralism. Not only did the proliferation of noncommunist groups in Slovenia undermine the prevailing elite strategy aimed at containing multiparty pluralism, but various Slovenian intellectuals had begun to directly attack the military's role in Yugoslav domestic and foreign policy. The military struck back when a small group of journalists working with the Slovenian youth journal *Mladina* publicly criticized the military in 1988 for its alleged connection with arm sales to the Third World and—based on information allegedly obtained from a secret speech of Slovenian party leader Kučan— for planning to assist in a police crackdown against dissidents. Several of these young journalists were arrested by the police and military and charged with possession of secret military documents. Although the arrests generated widespread outrage in Slovenian intellectual and political circles and provoked mass protests, the accused were prosecuted in closed trials in Ljubljana and sentenced to prison terms ranging from five to eighteen months. An army sergeant major implicated in the matter received a four-year jail sentence from a military court for allegedly leaking a classified document to the accused journalists.[25] The legal proceedings temporarily silenced the young critics involved in the affair, but Slovenian public opinion at both the mass and elite levels, was deeply offended by the JNA's heavy-handed action. A retired high-ranking Slovenian judge expressed the views of most observers in his republic when he characterized the trials in Ljubljana as an attempt by the military establishment to "hinder and eliminate the process of democratization in Slovenia, because the Army is very concerned about the spreading of this process to other parts of Yugoslavia."[26]

Despite the Ljubljana trial, *Mladina* continued its vitriolic attacks on the military throughout 1989, which included commentaries about the "brutal reprisals in Kosovo" carried out by "Yugoslav Army Shogun authorities" and the "dirty business of the Yugoslav military industry."[27] In June 1989, the most well known of the convicted journalists, Janez Janša, was able (during a brief leave from prison) to participate in the founding congress of the Slovene Democratic Alliance, one of the many noncommunist protoparty-type organizations established in the republic during this period. At the meeting Janša advocated the formation of so-called "parallel armies" within each republic (to be constituted from existing "territorial defence units"), which would function alongside the regular JNA forces. At the time of Janša's statement in 1989, few observers would have believed that such an idea might one day actually lead to full-scale armed conflict between the JNA and local armed forces in Slovenia.

The ongoing dispute with *Mladina* and Slovenian intellectuals, the creation of new party-like organizations within Slovenia, as well as the drive by Slovenian communist officials for increased constitutional autonomy only intensified the military elite's strong opposition to the spread of political pluralism. Although accused of improper intervention in Yugoslav domestic politics and obstruction of democratic reform, members of the JNA elite adamantly protested that they were simply supporting the enhanced unity of the country so that the serious economic and political crisis could be resolved, and maintained that such advocacy did not constitute taking sides in the conflicts among regional communist leaders.[28] Attending a television roundtable at the end of October 1989, top-ranking military officers reiterated their reasons for opposing multiparty pluralism. Ironically, it was a conservative Slovenian officer, Deputy Federal Secretary for National Defence Vice-Admiral Stane Brovet, who most stridently attacked the notion of party pluralism and objected to the idea that the Yugoslav military might become an "apolitical army in the service of whatever party was in power."[29]

> We are against multiparty pluralism for a number of reasons. First of all, the programmatic reorientation of the majority of groups and movements who pretend to come into being as parties in our country, contain elements of nationalism, anti-socialism, confederalism, and also separatism. Secondly, it is a question of a struggle for power, but a struggle for power, in our opinion in these conditions cannot extricate us from the crisis, but in contrast can dangerously cause the crisis to deepen or even sharply threaten the integrity of our country.[30]

Brovet's view was characteristic of the widespread sentiment in the top military command structure.[31] Only when federal and most regional political authorities belatedly accepted the concept of party pluralism near the end of 1989, in the wake of the East European democratic revolution, was the military grudgingly forced to soften its position. Thus as one military officer explained to foreign reporters, the army "would not stand in the way of the country's democratic development," and it would "adjust itself to the changes in society."[32]

Despite their tactical retreat, the military elite's demonstrated record of anti-pluralist views made its future role in the country's democratic transformation highly problematic. When the Fourteenth Congress of the LCY ended in failure at the end of January 1990, for example, the General heading the League's organization in the military revealed the superficial support of the JNA for party pluralism when he placed responsibility for developments at the congress on the "the narrow national interests" advanced by the League's "bureaucratized leading elites" and singled out the Slovenian communists for special blame. Although conceding that the League was losing its "membership, action capability, national reputation, and integrative power," the General defiantly maintained that the communists in the military "do not accept the League's fragmentation into several parties, or the League's transformation into a social democratic party with a name change."[33]

As the ruling League of Communists fractured and atrophied in a context of ethnic quarreling and continued economic crisis, speculation increased about potential military intervention in domestic politics. Although the possibility of a military coup could not be entirely ruled out, there were also good reasons to discount the probability of such a scenario. For one thing, even strongly conservative and anti-pluralist military officers were aware that expanded military involvement in the political realm would be a very high-risk enterprise, potentially provoking a violent and unmanageable backlash in several sections of the country. Thus the predominantly Serbian military elite, already deeply involved in the costly and difficult suppression of Albanian ethnopolitical dissidence in Kosovo, undoubtedly recognized the intense reaction and political opposition that direct military intervention would engender in areas such as Slovenia and Croatia. Moreover, even if they were initially successful in taking power and suppressing any resistance to such intervention, members of the military establishment could expect to face the same daunting economic and political challenges that had plagued the squabbling political elites throughout the 1980s.[34]

Political Pluralism Stage One:
The Elections in Slovenia and Croatia

Despite diehard opposition from conservative military and political leaders, in the first months of 1990 support for party pluralism had become commonplace and indeed fashionable in elite circles throughout Yugoslavia. Although various "alternative" groups, movements, and parties had been emerging throughout the country for some time,[35] by mid-March only two republics, Slovenia and Croatia, had formally legalized the establishment of political organizations outside the communist fold and had scheduled competitive elections. The announcement of legitimate electoral contests in the two republics quickly intensified pluralist development. Political groups that had been operating in the constricted pluralist environment tolerated during 1989 accelerated their activities, and many new groups were founded and legally registered to compete in the upcoming elections.[36] An equally important development during this period was the effort by the League of Communists, both in Slovenia and Croatia, to reconfigure their organizations as a means of better exploiting the new competitive situation.

Recognizing that their past failures had made them politically vulnerable, communist leaders hoped that measures such as self-criticism, the symbolic renaming of their organizations—as the League of Communists of Slovenia-Party of Democratic Reform (ZKS-SDR) and the League of Communists of Croatia-Party of Democratic Change (SKH-SDP)—and a repackaging of their message might enable them to survive politically. Notwithstanding these measures, the Slovenian and Croatian communists lacked any comprehensive and deep-rooted support within their respective republics, and after more than four decades of their monopoly control and dithering reform efforts, they had engendered considerable opposition to their continued rule. Thus the communist elite's overnight conversion to pluralism, their hyphenated organizational reidentification, and their disassociation from the countrywide communist party organization at the Fourteenth Congress in January 1990 seemed unlikely to provide a sufficient basis for widespread communist appeal in the upcoming elections.

Slovenia: A New Equilibrium

As the first genuinely democratic party competition in Yugoslavia since 1938, the April 1990 election in Slovenia was a showcase for the entire country. One of the first campaign developments was the consolidation of the wide variety of different political groups founded in Slovenia during the emergent pluralist phase of 1988 and 1989. For example, several of the major opposition political groups established a center-right coalition organization labeled the Democratic United Opposition of Slovenia (DEMOS). By election time, this broad coalition consisted of the Slovene Democratic Alliance, the Slovene Christian Democrats, the Slovene Farmers' Alliance, the Greens' Alliance of Slovenia, the Slovene Craftsmen's Party, and the Social Democratic Alliance of Slovenia. DEMOS was headed by Jože Pučnik, the leader of the Social Democratic Alliance. Pučnik, a philosophy professor and former communist, had served several years in prison during the 1950s for his dissident views, and for the past twenty years had been living in exile in West Germany. DEMOS was a hodgepodge of social democratic, Christian democratic, agrarian, and ecological ideas along with a commitment to parliamentary democracy and a free market economy. The common denominator uniting DEMOS's diverse membership was the goal of defeating the ruling communist party.

Outside the DEMOS coalition, at the center of the political spectrum, was the League of Socialist Youth of Slovenia-Liberal Party (ZKM-LS), whose program stressed democratic principles and Slovenian control of its military affairs. The reconstituted communist organization, the ZKS-SDP, led by reform communist Milan Kučan, advanced an essentially social-democratic program and advocated the strengthening of Slovenian political autonomy within a reorganized and "confederal" Yugoslav state. A smaller group of center-left Slovenian reform communists also competed in the election as the Socialist Alliance of Slovenia. Pučnik and Kučan, in addition to being leaders of the two strongest party formations, were candidates in a parallel contest for president of Slovenia, a race also contested by several less well known candidates from smaller political parties.

For Slovenian voters, the election contest essentially boiled down to a choice between reform socialism or postsocialism. On several other important matters, however, the positions of the competing parties were not that far apart. For example, all the major parties favored Slovenia's closer association with the European Economic Community as well as a loose confederation of Yugoslavia's republics that would allow Slovenia full sovereignty over its internal affairs and require only a limited commitment to other areas of the existing federation. Preelection surveys revealed that most Slovenes (58 percent) favored autonomy *within Yugoslavia*, many citizens were undecided, and only 20 percent supported outright secession. Parties operating under the umbrella of the DEMOS coalition made it clear that notwithstanding their support for a confederal Yugoslavia, their priorities lay outside the existing Yugoslav framework. As a top DEMOS official claimed: "Yugoslavia as a concept is exhausted. Slovenia simply wants to join Europe and is not willing to wait for the rest of Yugoslavia to catch up with it."[37] Even the Slovenian communists, who stressed their desire to work out some continued association with the other regions of the country, presented a campaign platform pointedly entitled "Europe Today."

Differences among the parties on the crucial issue of Slovenian political autonomy were a matter of degree, with the communists tending to be somewhat more cautious than DEMOS and the smaller parties. Members of DEMOS generally advocated an "independent" or "sovereign" Slovenia, though the exact relationship of the republic to Yugoslavia differed among the diverse members of the coalition—from a minority advocating outright separation to a majority supporting confederation—and was often left very vague. DEMOS President Pučnik, for example, advocated independent statehood for Slovenia, although not "secession at any cost."[38] If political leaders in other sections of the country failed to demonstrate an understanding of Slovenian demands, there would be no other course, in Pučnik's view, but to separate from Yugoslavia. For his part, the communist leader Kučan emphasized that his reform leadership team had worked for Slovenia's autonomy within Yugoslavia and claimed that such initiatives were slowly "bearing fruit." Consequently, in Kučan's opinion, secession should be viewed only as "an extreme and ultimate possibility."[39] Whereas the reform communists saw the possibility of Yugoslavia's long-term success as a confederation, members of DEMOS viewed confederation primarily as a transitional arrangement on the way to Slovenia's full independence. DEMOS's support for the abolition of special laws protecting the republic's ethnic minorities (primarily Italians, Hungarians, and Austrians) also revealed its more nationalistic orientation when compared to the communists. On two major issues relating to Slovenia's status within Yugoslavia, almost all of the major parties were united: it was believed that Slovenia should substantially trim back its existing obligations to the federal military establishment, and should cease making federally mandated contributions to assistance programs for the underdeveloped regions of the country.

Two relatively minor issues during the election campaign revealed the high level of anxiety among Belgrade's military elite with respect to Slovenia's pluralist development. The first was the attempt by military judicial authorities to have DEMOS leader Pučnik prosecuted for a campaign poster that allegedly insulted the JNA. A civilian public prosecutor declined to press charges, remarking that the poster was simply an "election gesture" made during a "heated" campaign. The incident not only demonstrated the futility of military pressure on Slovenia, but also that in the new legalized multiparty environment the boundaries of "political crime" had been considerably narrowed. The second, and somewhat more serious, episode was the election-eve visit to the republic by the federal Secretary of National Defense Veljko Kadijević. The visit was viewed by both the opposition parties and the communists as a blatant attempt, albeit an unsuccessful one, to exercise undue influence in the election by publicly signaling the military's serious concern with the situation in Slovenia.[40] Following the election, top Slovenian communist leader Ciril Ribičić detailed a number of official meetings that had taken place during the first months of 1990 between republican authorities and high-ranking military leaders. Ribičić claimed that the talks became increasingly cool and then were stopped altogether owing to the military's accusations that the Slovenian communists were abandoning socialism, intending to form a republican army, and causing ethnic divisions within the League of Communists.[41]

After decades of one-party rule, the "founding election" for Slovenia's (and Yugoslavia's) new pluralist phase of development was an impressive success. In the contest for the Socio-Political Chamber, for example, approximately 920 candidates ran in sixteen multimember districts, and over 80 percent of the electorate turned out to vote. Although seventeen parties took part in the election, it was the DEMOS coalition, the reconfigured communists, and the Liberal Party that constituted the major political options. In voting for the tricameral legislature's important Socio-Political Chamber, DEMOS took 55 percent of the vote, the communists 17 percent, the Socialist Alliance (closely allied with the communists) 5 percent, and 15 percent went to the Liberals. If parties are ranked individually, the communists and the Liberals actually placed first and second in the legislative election, followed by the various individual parties that together constituted the winning DEMOS coalition: the Slovenian Christian Democrats (12.9 percent), the Slovenian Farmers' Alliance (12.5 percent), and the Slovenian Democratic Alliance (9.9 percent). A smaller, but notable, success in DEMOS was the showing by the Greens, who took a larger share of votes (8.9 percent) than environmental groups in any other European country. The Social Democratic Alliance (7.3 percent) and the Slovene Craftsmen's Party (3.5 percent) were the least successful partners in the DEMOS coalition. On the basis of a proportional representation list system, the 80 seats in the Socio-Political Chamber were distributed as follows: DEMOS 47, the Communists 14, the Liberals 12, the Socialist Alliance 5, and 1 seat each reserved for the Italian and Hungarian minority parties (Figure 3.1). No seats were awarded to the seven parties that each received less than 2.5 percent of the vote.

The outcome of the race for president of Slovenia proved to be particularly interesting. When no candidate emerged with an absolute majority on the first ballot, the two front-runners—reform communist Kučan (44.4 percent) and DEMOS's Pučnik (26.6 percent)—took part in a run-off election. The final result was Kučan 58.3 percent and Pučnik 41.7 percent. Kučan's success clearly derived from his personal popularity,

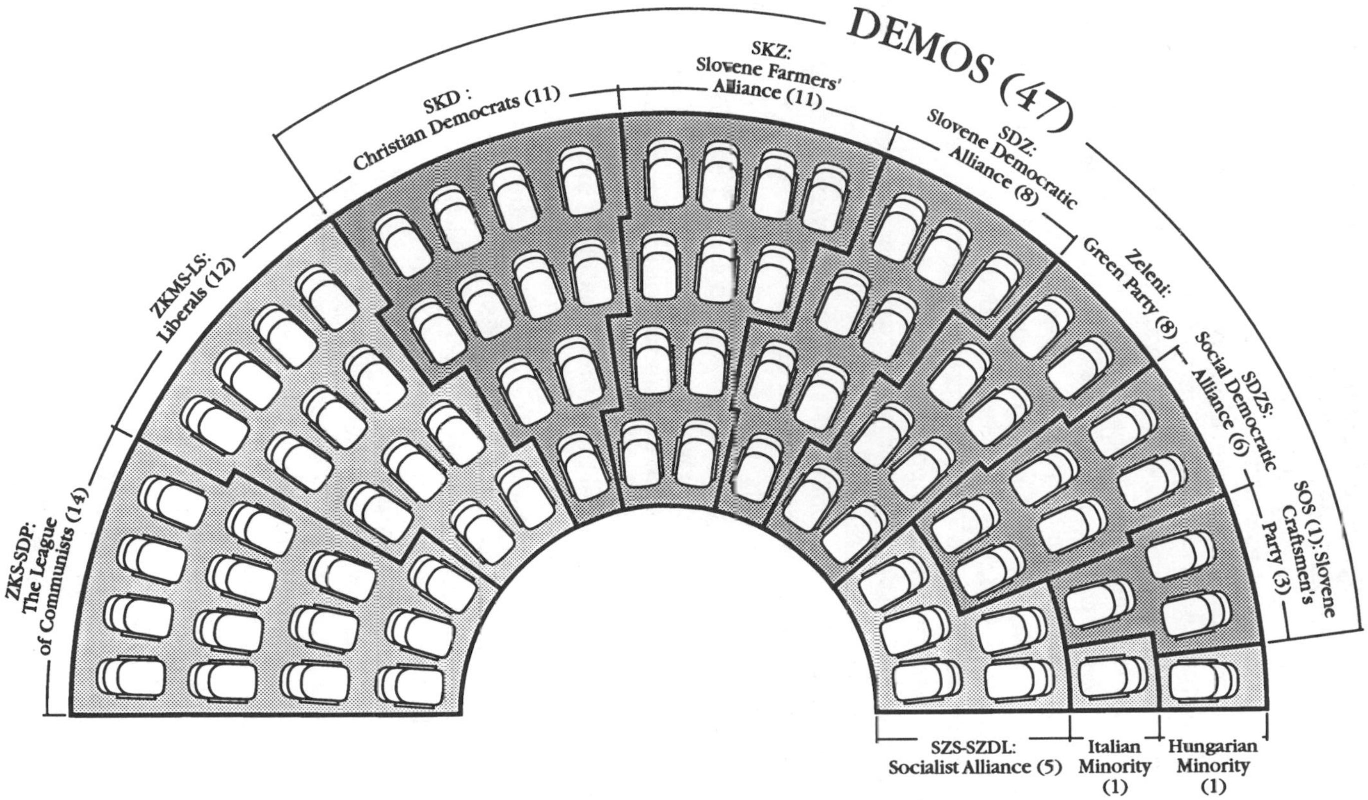

FIGURE 3.1 Distribution of Seats in the Sociopolitical Chamber of the Slovene Legislature, 1990

which was closely related to his strong advocacy of Slovenian interests in the ongoing dialogue with the federal government and military establishment and his skillful defiance of Serbia's Slobodan Milošević and communist conservatives during the late 1980s.

The communists had lost the legislative elections to the broad DEMOS coalition, but Kučan's stunning victory in the presidential race provided them with some consolation. Well aware that he had won a personal victory for his leadership style and regionally oriented policies, Kučan delivered on his campaign promise to give up active membership in the League of Communists and devote himself to representing his entire republic. Shortly after the election Kučan attributed his victory to the popular perception that he was best qualified to defend "Slovenia's right to self-determination in a non-disruptive manner" and also the difference of his own policies when compared with those of Milošević. "Undoubtedly," Kučan pointed out, "the constant contrast between these two ideas over the past four years did persuade Slovenes of the wisdom of the Slovene communists' policy…in a way the election results are a demonstration of the criticism of Serbia."[42]

Slovenia had peacefully undergone a major regime change, yet maintained an internal equilibrium between political forces. The legislature was controlled by the noncommunist opposition, and the president of the republic was a born-again communist with a strong ethnoregional, if not outright nationalistic, orientation.[43] The nonviolent and balanced nature of Slovenia's political transformation did not mean, however, that business would proceed as usual. The new prime minister of the republic, Lojže Peterle, was from the Christian Democratic Party (which had attracted the most votes within the DEMOS coalition). When asked about his political vision for Slovenia, Prime Minister Peterle responded: "All of my dreams are based on a Christian foundation. In my dreams, the ecology and economy are linked with social responsibility. Neighborhoods play an important role. Yugoslavia failed twice in this century because it failed to solve its nationalities' problems. In both cases it acted as a dictatorship. A third attempt, if successful, could only be made on the basis of democratic structures."[44]

Croatia: The Tudjman Phenomenon and Ethnic Polarization

Croatia's first multiparty election since World War II occurred only one week after the conclusion of the election in neighboring Slovenia. Whereas the Slovenes had experienced several years of quasi-party development prior to the legalization of parties, the Croatians had much shorter lead time to prepare for real democracy. Thus between January and late April 1990, Croatia underwent a "political shock" that had two important consequences for the outcome of the election. First, the Croatian communists, who were distinguished in the public's mind for failing to advance the republic's interests, did not have sufficient time to reorient themselves and establish a new image with the electorate beyond the change in their organization's name. Second, under these circumstances the opposition party best positioned to offer a sharp break with the dismal communist record and to present itself as an effective representative for Croatian ethnoregional interests would have a particularly good opportunity for electoral success.

At the beginning of the electoral campaign, the Croatian communists were assisted to some extent by the relative organizational inexperience of the approximately one dozen major alternative groups. Most of these opposition groups had been formed during 1989 and had little opportunity to solicit public support. The legalization of opposition party organizations and the termination of regime-sponsored harassment against them, however, quickly transformed the situation. The largest and best financed alternative political party was the Croatian Democratic Alliance (HDZ), led by 66-year-old Franjo Tudjman. A historian and former communist official who had fought with Tito's Partisans during the war and attained the rank of army major general, Tudjman had broken with the regime and his old comrades owing to his devotion to Croatian nationalist perspectives. His impressive credentials as an opposition leader included having spent several years in jail for nationalist activities during the 1960s and 1970s. Moreover, Tudjman had incurred the ire of the communist regime for his historical analyses, which maintained that the communists had deliberately exaggerated the wartime atrocities (against Serbs, Jews, and others) committed by the pro-Axis Independent State of Croatia.[45]

By early 1990, Tudjman's HDZ, which had already been functioning illegally for about one year, was operating offices throughout all of Croatia's 116 townships and had established branches among Croatian communities in neighboring Vojvodina and Bosnia-Hercegovina. The HDZ also received considerable support from Croatians living outside Yugoslavia, which gave the new party a major advantage over the financially strapped communist party and the smaller opposition groups.[46] More than thirty-five parties and movements were officially registered in the campaign, but as the election approached, an essentially three-way race had emerged among the following parties: (1) Tudjman's HDZ (leading a bloc that included five smaller parties);[47] (2) the communists (with their smaller left-wing ally, the Alliance of Socialists) led by reformer Ivica Račan; and (3) the Coalition for National Accord (KNS), a fragile centrist alliance eventually consisting of eight parties, several movements, and some prominent "nonparty" individuals.[48] Interestingly, the three most prominent members of the opposition—the HDZ's Tudjman and the KNS's Mika Tripalo and Savka Dapčević-Kučar—all had been former high-ranking communists and leaders of the Croatian nationalist upsurge some twenty years before and had been ousted from their positions by the Titoist leadership as a result of their nationalist activities.

Beyond their acceptance of free elections and parliamentary democracy, all of Croatia's major parties, including the reform communists, advocated the introduction of a market economy and various schemes for the privatization of public property. It was the question of Croatia's future relationship to the Yugoslav state that revealed the clearest differences among the various parties. With Tudjman's campaign posters promising to assert the priority of Croatian interests ("Let us decide ourselves the destiny of our own Croatia"), the HDZ appealed directly to voters' patriotic and nationalist sentiments and to their dissatisfaction with the existing regime and situation in the country. The core of Tudjman's program was the affirmation of Croatian "identity and sovereignty" and the reorganization of Yugoslavia into a confederation or "alliance of states." According to Tudjman, such a confederation would grant only very limited powers to a central or interstate coordinating authority. Each member of the confederation would operate as a more or less independent unit, much like the existing pattern of the European Economic Community. Functioning along confederative principles, Croatia would no longer participate in a centrally directed military establishment and it would not assume obligations for financing economically underdeveloped areas outside the republic. Thus without explicitly calling for Croatian secession or the immediate dismantling of the existing state—as did some of his more extreme allies—Tudjman left no doubt that should he win the election, Croatia would strive to operate on an independent basis within a radically reorganized Yugoslavia.

Tudjman regarded his argument for the establishment of a confederative state as a continuation of views that had been unsuccessfully advanced by Croatian national spokesmen, such as Stjepan Radić, in the first decade after World War I.[49] His preference for a loose confederation also derived from his belief in the fundamental irreconcilability of different South Slav political and cultural outlooks and temperaments. As he explained to one German interviewer:

The Serbs either want a Greater Serbia or a unitary Yugoslavia. Contrary to this we are demanding either a Yugoslav confederation or separation....Croatians and Serbs do not only have different historic characteristics: they also belong to different cultures. Therefore any attempt to create a unitary Yugoslavia is doomed to fail. The future new federation of states must guarantee a high degree of independence both for the Serbs and the Croatians....According to our tradition we are closely linked with central Europe and with Germany....Croatia will have closer ties with Germany than with any other country.[50]

The most controversial aspects of Tudjman's sovereigntist platform were his statements regarding Bosnia-Hercegovina and the Serbian minority in Croatia. Echoing a widely held Croatian perspective, Tudjman suggested that the Croatians and Moslems (who in his view were mainly Islamicized Croats) living in Bosnia-Hercegovina be included in the new affirmation of Croatian sovereignty. Moreover, he implied that this perspective might eventually involve certain adjustments in the territorial boundaries between the existing units of the presently constituted Yugoslav state. "Croatia and Bosnia," Tudjman would remark in an interview shortly after the election, "constitute a geographical and political unity, and have always formed a joint state in history."[51] Tudjman did not mince words about his belief that under communist rule the Croatian people had suffered ethnic discrimination owing to the disproportionately large number of Serbs occupying posts within Croatia.

Croatian sovereignty means above all that we restore Croatian legitimacy. In the last 45 years Croatism has not only been exposed to pressure but also to persecution....Streets and squares named after Croatian kings were changed. Croatian children were not allowed to sing innocent Croatian songs. Look at who the editors of radio, television, and newspapers are...we cannot agree with there being 40 percent Serbs in the government of Croatia, and 61 percent in the trade unions administration, when 11 percent of the total population is Serb. Nor can we agree with there being 6 1/2 Serbs among the seven chief editors on television (because one of them is half Croatian and half Serb).[52]

For most Croatians, Tudjman's views concerning ethnic symbolism and ethnic representation in Croatia and the issue of Bosnia-Hercegovina's association to Croatia raised important and legitimate questions that had previously been politically taboo. Moreover, Tudjman's supporters noted that he was always careful to mention that the Serbs in Croatia would be granted democratic rights should his party attain power, and that any changes to Bosnia-Hercegovina's status could only follow a democratic referendum in that republic. Tudjman's reassurances notwithstanding, among Serbs within Croatia and Bosnia-Hercegovina any schemes advanced by Croatian nationalists were highly inflammatory, considering that during World War II thousands of their brethren under Croatian rule had perished as a result of ethnic genocide.[53] Watching Tudjman's nationalist electoral campaign and his ability to excite popular emotions, it was hardly surprising that some of his more prescient Yugoslav critics unflatteringly referred to Tudjman as the "Croatian Milošević" whose "Croatism" would be a "bomb planted under the republic."[54]

In contrast to Tudjman's high-profile nationalist campaign, the communists and their smaller allies on the left advocated the democratic reform of the existing Yugoslav federation in order to permit Croatia more control over its internal affairs. In the Croatian communists' view, the federal government headed by Ante Marković (a Croat) was on the right track, and its economic reforms and proposed constitutional amendments should be provided with an opportunity to work. The centrist Coalition for National Accord took a position not much different from the communists, advocating enhanced autonomy for the republic but stopping short of endorsing full independence. "We are neither for, nor against Yugoslavia at any cost," remarked coalition leader Mika Tripalo, clearly keeping his options open for anticipated postelection negotiations with the other sections of the country.[55] Eager to differentiate themselves from Tudjman's notions about Bosnia-Hercegovina, however, Tripalo's coalition opposed any changes in the borders between Yugoslavia's six republics. "Changing republican borders in Yugoslavia," remarked the head of one party in the coalition, "means civil war, and by no means do we want that."[56]

The elections held in late April and early May were a rout for the communists and an impressive victory for Tudjman's HDZ. The HDZ won a total of 205 out of 356 seats in Croatia's legislature, including a majority in each of that body's three chambers. The communists ranked second with 75 seats, and their smaller "left bloc" allies picked up 26 more seats. In the most important branch of the legislature, the 80-seat Socio-Political Chamber, the HDZ won an over two-thirds majority (54 seats), compared with 19 seats for the communists and left bloc, and only 7 seats for the other parties. The performance of the centrist Coalition for National Accord was much weaker than anticipated, despite the personal popularity of some of its top leaders. In essence, the vote was a clear shift to the right or what might be viewed as a combination of assertive Croatian nationalism, and a kind of "anti-communist plebiscite." As could be expected, most Serbs in Croatia voted heavily against the

HDZ, choosing to support either the communists or the increasingly vocal and more nationalistic Serbian Democratic Party (SDS).[57] Jovan Rašković, the outspoken psychiatrist heading the SDS, claimed that the Serbs of Croatia recognized the contributions of Slobodan Milošević, although not necessarily his "remnants of Bolshevik type behavior."[58] Interestingly, survey research conducted during the election campaign revealed that a large majority of Serbian citizens in Croatia were strongly opposed to plans by Croatian nationalists such as Tudjman to work for the restructuring of the Yugoslav federation on a confederal basis or perhaps even Croatia's outright secession from Yugoslavia. Even more disturbing for future political development, the same data also demonstrated that a large segment of the Serbian minority population believed, even prior to the election, that they were discriminated against by the republic's majority Croats, a viewpoint particularly prevalent in the heavily Serbian-populated regions of Croatia.[59]

The nature of the electoral system—an absolute majority single-member district, with a double-ballot model similar to the one employed in France—was certainly a contributing factor to the Croatian communists' electoral debacle. The electoral system required candidates to obtain an absolute majority to win on the first ballot. In those districts lacking a majority winner in the first round, a second run-off ballot was held two weeks later (limited to those candidates receiving at least seven percent of the votes in the first round). In this second round, only a plurality was necessary for victory. Because the system favors strong popular parties on the first ballot and coalitions among like-minded parties on the second ballot, the organizational strength and popularity of the HDZ, and the desire of most opposition parties to defeat the old regime at any cost, helped to ensure a major communist defeat.

Thus when the percentage of the vote for each of the three major political constellations—the HDZ, the left wing, and all others—is considered in the election for the Socio-Political Chamber (Table 3.1), it appears that quite a large number of voters opposed Tudjman's HDZ in each round. But as the leading party, it was still able to accumulate the required majorities necessary to win the largest proportion of contested seats (a large number of voters also chose to abstain from the election entirely, particularly on the second ballot). The majority/winner-take-all electoral system substantially enhanced the HDZ's relative position in the distribution of legislative seats.[60] It is not surprising that some communists and members of the smaller center-right parties emphasized that the HDZ's victory was not as impressive as it seemed[61] and complained that it would have been more democratic for Croatia to have adopted a

TABLE 3.1 The Croatian Elections of 1990: Voting and Distribution of Seats for the Sociopolitical Chamber of the Sabor

	First Round		Second Round		Legislative Seats	
	Total Vote	Percent of Vote	Total Vote	Percent of Vote	Total Seats	Percent of Seats
Croatian Democratic Alliance (HDZ)	1,200,691	41.8	708,007	42.2	54	67.5
The League of Communists (SKH-SDP) and smaller parties of the left	994,060	34.5	627,345	37.3	19	23.7
Serbian Democratic Party	46,418	1.6	34,682	2.0	1	1.2
Centrist Coalition and all others	633,892	22.0	308,378	18.3	6	7.5
Total/votes cast for parties/seats	2,875,061	100.0	1,678,412	100.0	80	100.0
Voter turnout (as a percent of registered voters)	84.5		74.8			

Source: Dopunski izvještaj o provedenim izborima za zastupnike u Sabor Socijalističke Republike Hrvatske (Zagreb: Republička izborna komisija, 1990).

proportional representation electoral system (such as the one used in Slovenia a few weeks earlier). The HDZ dismissed such complaints as sour grapes and pointed out that the Croatian electoral system had been specifically designed to avoid the extreme party fragmentation and political instability that historically had bedeviled new democracies, such as Weimar Germany. In view of the total number of individual parties competing in the election, the HDZ had a rather strong case.

The vicissitudes of the electoral system aside, the HDZ had won a clear victory in the election. Tudjman's successful mobilization of Croatian national sentiments, and popular opposition to the communists' long monopoly rule and failed policies were undoubtedly the most important components in the electoral outcome. A related, and only slightly less conspicuous factor was Croatian resentment against the countrywide surge of Serbian nationalism inspired by Slobodan Milošević. Thus it was a classic case of Croatian and Serbian nationalism feeding upon one another, a pattern that had tragically emerged several times before in Balkan and Yugoslav history. Indeed, in a postmortem interview about the campaign, communist leader Račan identified popular dissatisfaction with his party's earlier "policy of silence" with regard to Croatian national interests as a major reason for its defeat as well as the Croatian communist regime's earlier "lukewarm attitude" toward the question of "greater Serbian and hegemonistic pretensions."[62] Ironically, the belated effort by some Croatian communists to raise the issue of "Serbian neoexpansionism" during the campaign may actually have aided their opponent Tudjman's mobilization of nationalist anxiety among Croatian voters. In any case, on May 30, 1990, deputies in the Croatian legislature elected Tudjman as the republic's president, by a margin of 281 out of 331 votes cast. The HDZ's Stipe Mesić, a lawyer who like Tudjman had served time in prison during the communist regime for his support of Croatian nationalism, became the first prime minister of Croatia.

The Slovenian and Croatian elections of spring 1990 radically altered the character of political life in Yugoslavia. As a result of the elections in the two republics, parties and political activists who just six months before had operated in a gray zone of semi-legality and quasi-pluralism were now vested with decisionmaking authority for the most economically developed regions of the country. Individuals who had only recently been incarcerated as "political criminals" by the communist regime now presided over the process of postcommunist transition, which included responsibility for sensitive areas such as military affairs, and the administration of justice. Perhaps more important, these newly elected leaders were committed to programs which disavowed Yugoslavia's 45-

year old federal structure and aimed at the transformation of the country into a loose confederation of sovereign states. The election of noncommunist governments in Slovenia and Croatia also added a new paradox to the country's many other underlying contradictions, namely, a situation in which the northwestern part of the country was under the political control of noncommunist governments and elites democratically chosen in multiparty elections, while the country's federal elite and political leaders in the southeastern part of Yugoslavia had been selected through one-party authoritarian methods. Yugoslavia was still in transition, but it had crossed the Rubicon into the unpredictable and chaotic world of democratic pluralism.

The Pluralist Virus Spreads:
"Ante's Party" and "Wild Pluralism"

Faced with the new pluralist climate and the defeat of communist power in the northwestern regions of the country, remaining members of the communist regime elsewhere in Yugoslavia responded in a variety of ways. On the federal level, Prime Minister Marković—who had been cast adrift in terms of party backing as a result of the collapse and delegitimation of the League of Communists as a countrywide organization at the Fourteenth LCY Congress in January—decided to establish an entirely new political party. Although still technically a member of the League of Communists, Marković believed that already by March 1990 the LCY's dissolution as a countrywide organization had effectively resulted in a "transfer of power" at the center of the political system.[63] Marković's aim, already apparent in April 1990, was to develop a new base of support for his government's reform program. He did so by forging a coalition of forces throughout the country that supported his nonideological brand of regime restructuring along market economic principles and wished for an alternative to the nationalistically oriented forces holding sway in Slovenia, Croatia, Serbia, and Montenegro. Marković also hoped to capitalize on the popularity of his federal economic policies which had at least temporarily reduced inflation and halted the drop in the standard of living. Because regionally centered nationalist elites were opposed to holding federal elections, Marković was unable to launch his new organization in a countrywide political contest. The remaining republican and provincial level elections scheduled for fall 1990, however, offered the innovative prime minister an alternate arena for his program. Indeed, public opinion surveys commissioned by the federal government in the late spring and early summer of 1990 revealed that most citizens in Yugoslavia, though disenchanted with the League of Communists, had still not committed themselves to the emerging spectrum of new party organizations. Thus in areas such as Serbia proper, Vojvodina, Montenegro, Macedonia, and Bosnia-Hercegovina, which still had not held competitive elections, considerable room existed for an appeal to a politically alienated and uncertain electorate.[64] Marković maintained that his broad goal was to create a truly democratic political system that would "function regardless of which party is in power," adding that it made no difference what ideological labels were attached to him or his new party.[65]

Endeavoring to maximize the pan-ethnic or cross-regional aura of his new enterprise, Marković announced on July 29, 1990 the formation of his new "Alliance of Reform Forces" at a meeting held in Bosnia-Hercegovina (the country's most heterogeneous region and the area having the largest number of inhabitants self-identified as "Yugoslavs"). Speaking to a cheering, multiethnic crowd of over 100,000 people, Marković made clear his intention to offer an alternative to the narrow nationalist platforms advocated by most of the country's new political groups:

> You do not want any bloodshed any more and least of all fratricide…there are many forces which want us to quarrel among ourselves again, which want to divide us, which want to build their own power on our differences….Let every party that struggles for the confidence of the voter, and for obtaining power prove that it is capable of further developing and advancing this system in the interests of every citizen in every part of the country….If a party is not able or not capable of doing so, do not give it your confidence.[66]

Although strongly criticized, especially in Serbia, for using his prime ministerial position to intervene in the country's emergent pluralist development and for having improperly created a "government party," Marković was soon able to establish branches of his alliance throughout Yugoslavia. Nationalist parties claimed that Marković was seeking an artificial consensus or a "new Yugoslavism," not unlike earlier royalist and communist strategies.[67] In his defense, the prime minister maintained that he was simply filling a gap in Yugoslavia's fragmented pluralist spectrum. Thus just days before formally announcing his new alliance, Marković pushed legislation through the Federal Assembly that legalized the formation of new parties on a countrywide basis. As the possibility of holding a federal election waned, however, Marković and other political actors focused their attention on the republics and provinces as the main arena for political competition. Indeed, the disintegration of the LCY and the emergence of party pluralism and free elections in the republics rapidly refocused citizen allegiances away from the federal level—a perspective quite advanced in some areas such as Slovenia and Croatia even before the emergence of legalized party pluralism—and significantly contributed to the growing delegitimation of Yugoslavia as a federation and cohesive state. Because of the so-called "republicanization" of multiparty competition, Yugoslavia had entered a completely new stage of political development.[68]

As Yugoslavia's pluralist development accelerated during the second half of 1990, Prime Minister Marković's Yugoslav-oriented reformist alliance, though a bold and original initiative, was quickly swamped by a plethora of new parties catering to a variety of different interests and perspectives. By the end of July, with political pluralism legalized in all of the republics as well as on the federal level, new parties rapidly proliferated. Only about 60 parties were in existence at the outset of the year, and approximately 90 parties existed just after the elections in Slovenia and Croatia. But by September, roughly 150 party organizations had been officially registered. At the end of 1990, over 235 parties were in existence, and the upward trend continued during the first six months of 1991, at which time 290 parties had been registered.[69] The new competitive environment that followed years of one-party monopoly fostered a trend aptly described as "wild" or "neurotic" pluralism, which included the formation of several very small organizations (less than 1,000 members) that focused on some narrow special interest or issue.[70] Almost all of the newly formed parties were registered in only one republic.

An examination of the new parties registered in the republics during late 1990 (Table 3.2) in terms of their avowed principles and programs reveals some noteworthy trends and interregional contrasts. Most interesting was the proliferation of parties explicitly committed to some nationalist, ethnic, religious, or regional interest. Nearly 30 percent of all registered parties fell into this category, and the percentage was even higher when Serbia (33.3 percent), Macedonia (36 percent), and Croatia (40.4 percent) are considered separately. In an environment previously characterized by feuding among regional communist party leaders devoted to their own parochial nationalist strategies, but in which the political expression of alternative viewpoints was constrained, it was natural that new ethnopolitical groups would find fertile soil among citizens disappointed with the communist regime.

TABLE 3.2   Political Parties in Yugoslavia, December 1990, by Predominant Goal Orientation (in percent)

Predominant Goal Orientation of Party Program[a]	Slovenia	Croatia	Bosnia-Hercegovina	Serbia	Montenegro	Macedonia	All Republics
Communist and socialist	12.7	11.9	18.6	10.5	40.0	16.0	16.3
Liberal-democratic	21.2	16.6	23.2	21.0	20.0	8.0	19.2
Labor/farmer/business	8.5	7.1	13.9	10.5	4.1	16.0	10.0
Ethnopolitical/religious/ regional	14.8	40.4	23.2	33.3	24.0	36.0	28.4
Special interest[b]	31.9	14.2	6.9	10.5	4.0	8.9	15.0
Yugoslav state unity	2.1	2.3	13.9	1.7	4.0	4.0	4.6
Other	8.5	7.1	-	12.2	4.0	-	6.2
Total	100.0	100.0	100.0	100.0	100.0	100.0	100.0
Number of parties	(47)	(42)	(43)	(57)	(25)	(25)	(239)

[a]The breakdown is intended to illustrate general tendencies of Yugoslavia's emergent pluralist party system, based upon the predominant beliefs or organizing principles of parties and disregarding significant overlap in orientations and differences among the parties with respect to size and influence.

[b]Parties organized to advance specific interests (e.g., the environment, peace, women, pensioners, unemployed, consumers, human rights, culture).

Source: Based on information supplied by the Federal Executive Council, Belgrade, 1991.

Disillusioned by the artificial cross-ethnic and cross-regional solidarity under the old regime, many former members of the LCY and new participants in the political process sought a novel basis for solidarity closer to home and to their traditional cultural identities. The hurried quest for personal security and stable relationships during a period of socioeconomic turbulence and rapid political disorientation was undoubtedly an important factor contributing to the proliferation of small ethnopolitical parties on the republican and local levels.[71] The heightened interethnic and interregional tensions surrounding the elections in Slovenia and Croatia, followed by the victory of nationalist parties in those republics, also contributed to a growing belief that each region or subcultural group should and could organize to become master of its own fate. Moreover, the proportion of new parties committed to ethnopolitical goals was actually much higher than may be superficially apparent from the rough classification of parties in Table 3.2 (which is based upon each party's general programmatic orientation).

Whatever the formal designation or official platform of their new party, a large number of activists and members in all categories of the parties operating on the republican level could accurately be described as either "anti-communist nationalists" or "communist nationalists." Thus a large number of new parties, though not explicitly nationalistic in terms of their platforms or ideological labels, nevertheless were emphatically anti-federalist or linked to the achievement of their particular goals within a single ethnic constituency. For example, although the data on registered parties in Slovenia revealed the lowest percentage of explicitly ethnopolitical parties and the highest proportion of special interest parties, it is important to consider that a large number of the latter organizations hoped to pursue their goals within the context of the Slovenian regional or ethnic milieu and had very little commitment to the retention of the existing Yugoslav state.[72] Similarly, although Montenegro had the highest proportion of left-wing parties utilizing the communist or socialist label, most of these organizations were strongly devoted to the attainment of Serbo-Montenegrin ethnic interests.

The confusion between party labels, party programs, and actual party orientation is especially pertinent in the case of Serbia, where about one-tenth of the parties are explicitly communist or socialist, and only about one-third are explicitly oriented to ethnopolitical goals. The data in Table 3.2 illustrate interesting general trends, but mask the fact that the dominant political force in Serbia throughout the second half of 1990 and beyond was the Socialist Party of Serbia (SPS), a passionately pro-Serbian party organization presided over by Slobodan Milošević. Organized in mid-July

1990 by leading members of the Serbian League of Communists, together with a sprinkling of previously independent intellectuals and other Serbian notables, the SPS was designed to put a fresh face on the unique mixture of socialism and nationalism (first developed by Milošević's communist regime during the late 1980s), as part of preparations for the Serbian elections to be held at the end of 1990 (Chapter 7).

What is most clearly evident from the data in Table 3.2 on the regional breakdown of political parties according to their predominant goal orientations is the relative dearth of parties explicitly devoted to preserving the unity of the country and also those parties primarily devoted to the attainment of liberal-democratic goals. Bosnia-Hercegovina stood out in 1990 and 1991 with the largest proportion of explicitly Yugoslav-oriented and liberal-democratic parties perhaps because its citizens were acutely aware of the need to preserve interethnic harmony in their diverse and potentially explosive republic. Unfortunately, as will be explored in later chapters, narrow and uncompromising ethnopolitical commitments, rather than support for Yugoslavia's preservation or democratic consolidation, would soon emerge as the strongest facets of pluralist development in Bosnia-Hercegovina, and most other areas of the country.

Notes

1. For the growth of "alternative" associations and forces in Yugoslav society in the late 1980s, see Momir Krizan, "Of 'Civil Society' and Socialism in Yugoslavia," *Studies in Soviet Thought*, Vol. 37, No. 4 (May 1989), pp. 287-306.

2. From January 24 to February 6, 1990, ethnic protests in Kosovo resulted in the deaths of 28 Albanians (pushing the death toll for that group to approximately 60 over the previous year) and the wounding of another 94 demonstrators. Some Serbian leaders continued to pour oil on the fire by advocating Slavic migration into Kosovo and even an armed Serbian uprising against the Albanians. Regime efforts to restore order included the imposition of a nighttime curfew, restrictions on public gatherings, and action by the security forces assisted by tanks, armored vehicles, jets, and helicopters of the Yugoslav military. On February 6, 1990, there were demonstrations of 20,000 Albanians in Priština calling for the release of jailed Albanian activists and free elections. The Democratic Alliance of Kosovo, a new independent group of Albanians, claimed to have more than 200,000 members, but the organization was denied official recognition.

3. A public opinion survey conducted in Slovenia during early 1990 revealed that in a projected referendum 55.4 percent of the respondents would vote for separation from Yugoslavia, whereas 52.8 percent felt it would be impossible to

reconcile the political conceptions of Serbia and Slovenia. *Danas*, No. 418, February 20, 1990, p. 18.

4. On the role of the press in Yugoslavia's emergent pluralism, see Stevan Niksić, "Pluralizam nije demokratija"; and Ljiljana Baćević, "Demokratizacija medijskog sistem Jugoslavije," *Novinarstvo*, Vol. 26, Nos. 3-4 (1990), pp. 10-13, 23-25.

5. Jelena Lovrić, "Usamljeni uvodničar," *Danas*, No. 390, August 8, 1989, p. 10.

6. Data from Croatia indicated that the League of Communists in the republic was rapidly losing membership while newly forming opposition parties were rapidly gaining in strength. In the Croatian city of Osijek, for example, research revealed that approximately 15 percent of the League membership intended to vote for the nationalist and noncommunist Croatian Democratic Union in the elections scheduled for April 1990. The hemorrhage of members from the League of Communists in Croatia was particularly heavy among ethnic Croats, who have traditionally constituted a significantly smaller proportion of communist membership in Croatia than their percentage in the republic's total population. *Danas*, February 20, 1990, p. 12.

7. Dragomir Pantić, *Klasična i svetovna religioznost* (Belgrade: Institut društvenih nauka, 1988), pp. 23-45; and Ivan Perić, *Suvremeni hrvatski nacionalizam* (Zagreb: August Cesarec, 1984).

8. The rising tide of Serbian nationalism inspired by Slobodan Milošević made it extremely difficult for Croatian communist leaders to remain aloof or neutral on interethnic and interregional questions during the late 1980s. Thus even an anti-nationalistic and anti-pluralist Croatian politician such as Stipe Šuvar—serving as president of the League of Communists—became a minor hero in his native republic when he crossed swords with Milošević.

9. Jasna Babić, "Novi pluralizam šutljive republike," *Danas*, February 28, 1989, pp. 14-15.

10. During 1989, official tolerance of party pluralism varied from one republic to another depending on the attitudes of communist officialdom. In February 1989, a group of prominent intellectuals from Zagreb, with support from others in Belgrade and Ljubljana, established the first nonofficial organization—the Association for a Yugoslav Democratic Initiative (UJDI)—seeking to establish branches throughout the country and committed to the preservation of the Yugoslav state. The organization was first legally registered in Montenegro in December 1989. By March 1990, it had 1,000 members and sixteen branches throughout Yugoslavia. *FBIS-EEU*, March 8, 1990, p. 73.

11. *Borba*, January 2, 1990, p. 2.

12. Survey research indicated that between October 1988 and October 1989, open support for the idea of multiparty pluralism and the ideas of the Slovenian reformists, as well as opposition to Milošević's strategy for reorganization, had intensified within Croatian opinionmaking circles. Slaven Letica, "Znanstvenici o krizi," *Naše Teme*, Vol. 33, Nos. 1-2 (1989), pp. 109-118, and "Politika i

politolizi: Bit će kako jest," *Danas*, October 10, 1989, pp. 16-17. For a brief overview of changing perspectives in the Croatian League of Communists during fall 1989, see Milan Andrejevich, "Croatia: Reform Intention," *Report on Eastern Europe*, January 19, 1990, pp. 33 and 36.

13. *Associated Press Report*, December 11, 1989.

14. *Canadian Press Newstex*, December 15, 1989.

15. *Associated Press Report*, December 24, 1989.

16. Cited in Marinko Ceulić, "Kongres SK Slovenije: Pobjeda srednjeg puta," *Danas*, December 26, 1990, p. 25.

17. *Danas*, No. 409, December 19, 1989, pp. 20-21. By 1990, Milošević's halfhearted commitment to pluralism began to engender increased criticism from emergent noncommunist democratic forces within Serbia. See Milan Andrejevich, "Growing Opposition to Milošević in Serbia," *Report on Eastern Europe*, January 19, 1990, pp. 26-29.

18. *Associated Press Report*, January 21, 1990.

19. *Washington Post*, February 4, 1990, p. AO1.

20. *FBIS-EEU*, February 1, 1990, p. 83.

21. *Ibid.*, pp. 83-84.

22. *Associated Press Report*, January 21, 1990.

23. A. Ross Johnson, *The Role of the Military in Communist Yugoslavia: An Historical Sketch* (Santa Monica, Calif.: Rand Corporation, 1978).

24. *The Constitution of the Socialist Federal Republic of Yugoslavia* (Belgrade: Secretariat of the Federal Assembly Information Service, 1974), pp. 70-71.

25. Marko Hren, "The Role of the Army in Yugoslavia: Background on the Case of Ivan Borstner, Janez Jansa, et al. (Mimeo)," and "Secret Military Trial in the Middle of Europe at the End of the Twentieth Century," *Independent Voices from Slovenia, Yugoslavia*, July 13, 1988.

26. *FBIS-EEU*, August 18, 1988, p. 25.

27. *FBIS-EEU*, May 15, 1989, p. 75.

28. While publicly affirming their "ideological and action oriented unity," some members of the Yugoslav military establishment were undoubtedly troubled, cross-pressured, and divided by the overall breakdown of unity in the political elite. For example, the pro-Milošević Belgrade weekly *NIN* reported "whispered" commentaries that recent retirements from the military elite ordered by the collective state Presidency stemmed from the "nearness" of certain high-ranking officers to "Serbian viewpoints" on the diagnosis and the way of curing the crisis. Aleksander Tijanić, "Promene u armiji," *NIN*, No. 2022, October 1, 1989, p. 11. Milovan Djilas has suggested that with the "arrival of Milošević, the unity between the Army and the Serbian leadership was destroyed. The Army does not support leaderships of individual republics. This also applies to Serbia." *FBIS-EEU*, February 9, 1989, p. 61.

29. *FBIS-EEU*, November 1, 1989, p. 74.

30. *NIN*, No. 2026, October 29, 1989, p. 11.

31. For example, at a meeting of the LCY Central Committee in October, several high-ranking military officers attacked the idea of political pluralism put forth by Ivica Račan, who was then a member of the presidium of the Croatian LCY. Račan's views are presented more fully in Jelena Lovrić, "Raspada li se partija," *Danas*, No. 407, November 28, 1989, pp. 12-15.

32. *Globe and Mail*, December 16, 1989, p. A2.

33. *FBIS-EEU*, February 16, 1990, p. 73.

34. See Marko Milivojevic, "The Political Role of the Yugoslav People's Army in Contemporary Yugoslavia," in Marko Milivojevic, John Allock, and Pierre Maurer (eds.), *Yugoslavia's Security Dilemmas: Armed Forces, National Defense and Foreign Policy* (Oxford: Berg Publishers, 1988), pp. 15-59. Milan Andrejevich suggested that a military solution to the Yugoslav crisis was unlikely given "the armed forces' penchant for barking and not biting." *Radio Free Europe Research, Situation Report, Yugoslavia*, October 23, 1989, p. 19.

35. Vukašin Pavlović, "New Social Movements in Yugoslavia," *Socialist Thought and Practice*, Vol. 29, Nos. 3-5 (1989), pp. 70-79.

36. At the end of 1989 Slovenia had over one hundred alternative political organizations, whereas Croatia, with a shorter experience in quasi-party development, had approximately a dozen protoparties (usually utilizing the title, "alliance," "community," "union," "movement," "league," "association," and others). By the end of March 1990, however, one analyst in Croatia could identify at least fifty such organizations and the number increased each week. Slaven Letica, "Crven, Zelen, Plav," *Danas*, March 3, 1991, pp. 18-19. By the time of the actual elections in May 1990, however, the number of political groups emerging as viable options had been considerably reduced.

37. *Reuters-AP*, April 10, 199.

38. *Reuters-AP*, April 13, 1990.

39. *FBIS-EEU*, April 9, 1990, p. 64.

40. *Ibid.*, p. 65

41. *FBIS-EEU*, April 26, 1990, p. 84.

42. *FBIS-EEU*, May 3, 1990, p. 69.

43. Two weeks after the election, the head of Slovenia's League of Communists explained his party's new thinking: "We are breaking with communism....We prefer to be described as "reformers" or "social democrats" and not as communists. We support democratic socialism and our program lies somewhere between the social democratic and socialist programs of left-wing European parties." *FBIS-EEU*, May 14, 1990, p. 75.

44. *FBIS-EEU*, June 1, 1990, p. 74.

45. Tudjman, born in 1922 and educated as a historian, served in Tito's Partisans during World War II. After the war, he attended the Higher Military Academy in Belgrade and left the army in 1961 with the rank of major general. Appointed a professor of history at Zagreb's political science faculty, he became active in nationalist activities in the late 1960s, was expelled from the LCY, and was twice tried and imprisoned for his nationalist views (during the early 1970s and the early 1980s). In June 1990, he told an interviewer: "I was on the wrong

side when I was very young. I joined the communist movement to fight for a free Croatia with revolutionary means. Today I know that there are better ways. My hopes are linked with the national democratic consciousness of Croatia." *FBIS-EEU*, June 22, 1990, p. 72. For other biographical details on Tudjman, see also *Croatia on Trial: The Case of Croatian Historian Dr. F. Tudjman* (Amersham, Bucks: United Publishers, 1981). Tudjman's controversial ideas on the genocide during World War II and other aspects of his mindset can be found in his *Bespuća povijesne zbiljnosti: Rasprava o povijesti i filozofiji zlosila*, 2nd ed. (Zagreb: Matice Hrvatske, 1989).

46. Tudjman claimed to have HDZ branches in thirty-five American cities, each with fifty to several hundred members and some branches with up to 2,000 members.

47. The Croatian Democratic Bloc consisted of the Croatian Democratic Alliance (HDZ), one wing of the Croatian Peasant Party, the Croatian Party, the Croatian Party of Justice, the Democratic Christian Party, and the Democratic Action of Croatia.

48. The core of the KNS consisted of the Social Democratic Party of Croatia, the Croatian Christian Democrats; the Croatian Peasants' Party, the Croatian-Liberal Alliance, the Croatian Democratic Party, the Moslem Party, the Democratic Alliance of Albania, and the "Peace Lovers."

49. "Franjo Tudjman, Stjepan Radić i Hrvatska suverenost," *Hrvatska revija*, Vol. 40, No. 1 (March 1990), pp. 28-38.

50. *FBIS-EEU*, April 26, 1990, p. 81. Tudjman has frequently directed attention to the cultural differences between the Serbs and Croats, but it is interesting to note that in his early historical writings of the 1960s he condemned the Ustasha movement that ran Croatia during World War II for similar cultural distinctions. "The ustashi ideologists...explain their separatist nationalist program by the theory that the people of Croatia had developed under the influence of West-Roman Catholic culture whereas the Serbs had belonged to the eastern Byzantine and Turkish, and Orthodox cultural spheres. Therefore the mentality of the two peoples was quite different in spite of language similarities; so that the border on the Drina River was not only a political, spiritual and cultural border between two different peoples but the dividing line between two (eastern and western, or even European and Asian) civilizations. By such geographic and political theorizing, the constitution of NDH [the Independent State of Croatia] was presented as a national Croat but also an international necessity which served to defend Western Civilization from the threatening East....The ustashi movement spoke of its historic mission to defend Europe from the new eastern, bolsheviks." Franjo Tudjman, "The Independent State of Croatia as an Instrument of the Policy of the Occupation Powers of Yugoslavia, and the People's Liberation Movement in Croatia from 1941-1945," in Petar Brajović, Jovan Marjanović, and Franjo Tudjman (eds.), *Les Systèmes d'Occupation En Yougoslavie* 1941-1945 (Belgrade: Institute for the Study of the Workers' Movement, 1963), pp. 188-189.

51. *FBIS-EEU*, May 8, 1990, p. 57; and *Kurier*, May 10, 1990, p. 5.

52. *FBIS-EEU*, April 24, 1990, p. 66. Tudjman also argued that the Serbs and Croats had lived together peacefully in Southeastern Europe for centuries but that hatred and struggle had arisen between the two groups after the Yugoslav state was created. "At no point after the founding of the state were the different groups asked whether they wanted to live together in a common Yugoslav state. In Scandinavia, too, there were struggles as long as efforts persisted to create a common Scandinavian state. Now they are living peacefully side by side, as independent states. I am in favor of the Scandinavianization of the Balkans." *FBIS-EEU*, April 24, 1990.

53. Vladimir Dedijer, *The Yugoslav Auschwitz and the Vatican: The Croatian Massacre of the Serbs During World War II* (Buffalo, N.Y.: Prometheus Books, 1992).

54. *FBIS-EEU*, April 23, 1990, p. 63; and *FBIS-EEU*, May 3, 1990, p. 65.

55. *FBIS-EEU*, April 18, 1990, p. 54.

56. *FBIS-EEU*, March 27, 1990, p. 69.

57. Tudjman was later questioned by a journalist for *Le Figaro* about whether his comments made during the campaign and his earlier writings had given the Serbs in Croatia and other minorities reason for concern: [*Tudjman*]: "I was and still am anti-fascist. I am a fervent advocate of democracy. My whole life proves it....I fought the Nazi occupier for four years. My brother was killed by the fascists. My father and my [step-mother] were killed by the communists..." [*Interviewer*]: "What about the remark you made during the spring 1990 election campaign: 'Fortunately my wife is neither Serbian nor Jewish.' [*Tudjman*]: "That remark was taken out of context. This is stupid. I still have the Jewish friends I had." *FBIS-EEU*, June 26, 1992, p. 18.

58. *FBIS-EEU*, April 2, 1990, p. 80.

59. See Ivan Grdešić, *et al., Hrvatska u izborima '90* (Zagreb: Naprijed, 1991), pp. 151-155. The author would like to express his appreciation to Dr. Grdešić for providing data from this survey for closer analysis, and also to Larry Boland and Mark Baskin for their generous assistance.

60. For this aspect, see Ivan Grdešić, "1990 Elections in Croatia (Yugoslavia): Political Consequences of the Electoral Law," *Paper for the 1990 Annual Meeting of the American Political Science Association*, San Francisco, August 30-September 2, 1990.

61. For example, Mladen Zvonarević, "Tko je zapravo pobijedio," *Danas*, July 17, 1990, pp. 30-31.

62. *FBIS-EEU*, May 7, 1990, p. 70.

63. *FBIS-EEU*, May 31, 1990, p. 67; and *FBIS-EEU*, July 6, 1990, p. 72.

64. Niko Toš, "Stavovi gradjana o promenama političkog sistema," in Ljiljana Baćević (ed.), *Rezultati ispitivanja Jugoslovenskog javnog mnenja* (Belgrade: Savezno izvršno veće, 1990), pp. 36-37.

65. *FBIS-EEU*, May 31, 1990, p. 67.

66. *FBIS-EEU*, July 30, 1990, pp. 65-67.

67. *FBIS-EEU*, August 8, 1990, p. 39.

68. *FBIS-EEU*, June 20, 1990, pp. 66-67.

69. *Documentation*, Federal Executive Council (Belgrade, Yugoslavia).

70. Vladimir Goati, "Politički pluralizam u nas—stanje i prespektive," in Vladimir Goati (ed.), *Smisao Jugoslovenskog pluralističkog šoka* (Belgrade: Književne novine, 1989), pp. 10-13.

71. Branko Horvat, "Više sutra nego danas," *Vreme*, January, 21, 1991, p. 34.

72. An analysis of the programs of Croatian parties competing in the 1990 election indicated that most left-wing and liberal-democratic parties supported some variant of a reorganized federal system. Most of those parties, however, expected that such arrangements would be far more decentralized than under the communist regime. Vjekoslav Afrić and Tvrtko Ujević, "Analiza sadržaja političkih programa političkih stranaka u Hrvatskoj (Izbori 90.)," *Revija za sociologiju*, Vol. 21, No. 1 (1990), pp. 11-34.

4

Sovereignty Asunder:
The Fragmentation of State Authority

There is a danger of everyone starting to do what they want, and when they want it, in their own territory. Such a situation cannot be allowed.

—Borisav Jović, President of the [Collective] Yugoslav Presidency
(May 13, 1990)

The federation is de facto dead, but it is de jure still operating. What is recently taking place in Yugoslavia implies the gradual disintegration of the federal state.

—Lojze Peterle, Prime Minister of Slovenia (August 26, 1990)

EVEN BEFORE THE SPRING 1990 victory of noncommunist parties in Slovenia and Croatia challenged Yugoslavia's political unity, the country's major federal political institutions had been undergoing a process of enfeeblement. An attempt at the end of March 1990 to reintegrate the fragmented League of Communists as a countrywide organization proved unsuccessful, and the LCY's membership and remaining influence plummeted in the context of the country's economic crisis and growing competition from other political parties. State authorities on the federal level fared little better. When, for example, the Constitutional Court of Yugoslavia ruled in March that certain constitutional amendments adopted by different republics were illegal and should be revoked—including the September 1989 amendments to Slovenia's constitution, which gave the republic greater autonomy (e.g., the right of secession, the right to declare emergency measures)—republican political decisionmakers simply ignored the federal judicial decision and proceeded with their respective agendas. Indeed, Slovenia had not even bothered to send representatives to the Constitutional Court's public debates concerning the controversial constitutional provisions. The president of the Constitutional Court admitted that the refusal of the republics to comply with the court order illustrated "the domination of the political over the legal sectors."[1]

The federal government under Prime Minister Marković continued to press ahead with its ambitious reform program and achieved considerable initial success with its package of anti-inflationary measures, but the increasingly autarkic policies in most of Yugoslavia's republics and provinces tended to vitiate the countrywide impact of the reforms. Political leaders in Serbia, for example, not only continued their efforts to restrict trade between their own republic and Slovenia but also refused to eliminate certain local price controls or close down various unprofitable enterprises. Obstacles to coordinated federal decisionmaking increased in April and May, when Slovenian and Croatian representatives in federal bodies—such as the Federal Assembly's Chamber of Republics and Provinces and the collective state presidency—submitted to instructions and pressures from the newly elected postcommunist center-right politicians in the two republics.

In June, Prime Minister Marković explained to members of the Federal Assembly that the main obstacle to the achievement of Yugoslavia's reform goals, and its smooth entry into the European economy, was the upsurge of extreme nationalism and the festering of unhealed wartime scars. He pleaded for each republic and province to show more "tolerance and mutual respect."[2] In its quest for unity, the government had the strong support of the military establishment, but even this bastion of "Yugoslav" cohesion faced enormous internal strains as a result of the centrifugal forces that were intensifying in the country. Moreover, the decision of Slovenia's new government to appoint Janez Janša as the republican minister of defense—a man who had only recently been jailed for his criticism of the military and was the *bête noire* of the military elite—set the stage for further conflict between that republic and the JNA leadership.

Deepening interregional conflicts and the federation's growing delegitimation came into sharp focus in May 1990, following the election of Serbia's representative, Borisav Jović, as annual president of the collective federal state presidency. Jović, who like his Serbian political ally Slobodan Milošević supported the maintenance of a federal system with a strong central government, immediately generated a firestorm of criticism after implying that the multiparty elections held only weeks before in Slovenia and Croatia were illegitimate and that "urgent measures" would have to be adopted if separate units of the federation pursued policies and practices that could change the character of the country. "What is happening now in Yugoslavia in the domain of political pluralization," Jović asserted, "is threatening to lead the country in new difficulties and uncertainty." "To move now," he added, "for a greater weakening of the federal state would mean the further disintegration of Yugoslavia which would be illogical and out of step with European and world developments."[3] Although he acknowledged the need for discussion about the future structure of the federation, and even the right of secession in principle, Jović left no doubt that he viewed the "aspirations for confederation" in Slovenia and Croatia to be a destabilizing force that he intended to vigorously oppose from his new state position. In contrast to Prime Minister Marković, who had pleaded for unity within a more pluralistic framework, Jović was promising to *impose* unity in order to halt pluralistic "chaos."

The immediate reaction of Croatia's President Tudjman was to claim that Jović's comments had "threatening overtones" and to assert that "sovereignty belongs to the people and not to the federation."[4] Tudjman (whose party had already won the Croatian elections but was not yet officially installed in power) hurriedly consulted with the new political leaders of Slovenia in order to coordinate a response to Jović. According to one member of the Slovenian delegation, the meeting "was a warning to all of Yugoslavia, and especially to the group around Jović, that the times have passed when, as before the [Second World] war, Slovenia was more of a toy in [central-regional] relations, and Croatia so to speak had to be neutralized by an alliance [of Serbia] with Slovenia."[5] The joint Croatian-Slovenian statement issued at the end of the meeting reasserted the sovereignty of the two republics and rejected Jović's alleged "centralist-unitarist model," which assumed that Yugoslavia's stability depended on the "primacy" of the federal constitution and federal legal system or on the country's "socialist organization."[6] Elite reaction to Jović's remarks also revealed the division between the federal government and the federal presidency concerning the best way to resolve the country's difficulties. Thus the vice-premier of the Marković government, Živko Pregl (a Slovene), suggested that President Jović's comments reflected "a nervous reaction, which is one of the last echoes of the old manner of thinking." Pregl admitted that political developments in Slovenia and Croatia might be at odds with certain aspects of the existing federal constitution, but, exhibiting the Marković government's characteristic pragmatism, he suggested that Yugoslavia would have to live, at least temporarily, with the obvious "conflict between life and the federal constitution."[7]

The controversy surrounding Jović's remarks represented only a brief episode in Yugoslavia's heated political infighting, but it revealed the widening distance and friction among key political actors and institutions as well as deep differences regarding the way sovereignty should be shared or distributed among Yugoslavia's various governmental units and "peoples."[8] As conflicting views about Yugoslavia's future constitutional organization assumed more importance—centered around the rival notions of federalism and confederalism—the course of political development was seriously complicated by a dramatic upsurge of ethnoregional nationalism and the assertion of republican sovereignty in various parts of the country.

Slovenia:
Between Autonomy and Independence

During the second half of 1990, developments in Slovenia provided the most pronounced example of the growing disparity between "life and the federal constitution." Technically, Slovenia remained a constituent part of the Yugoslav federation, but the new leaders of its noncommunist government (and lapsed communist President Kučan) wasted little time in asserting the region's political sovereignty and laying the groundwork for possible future independence. Not surprisingly, the first significant confrontation between the newly elected government and federal authorities centered on the issue of military affairs. Slovenian officials were particularly incensed by an order from the Federal Secretariat for National Defense that required the republic's Territorial Defense (TD) forces to hand over their weapons and ammunition to units of the JNA. Indeed, the joint Croatian-Slovenian statement in May responding to President Jović's more general "threat" singled out the order for the surrender of arms as unconstitutional and demanded that it be rescinded. The Slovenian presidency's noncompliance with the federal order opened a new round of friction between the republic and the federal military that would continue and intensify throughout 1991.

As expected, difficulties concerning the military question were exacerbated by the appointment of Janez Janša as Slovenian defense minister. Only two weeks after taking his new post, Janša—a seasoned and bitter critic of the Yugoslav military elite—remarked that it would be necessary to quickly end the situation whereby Slovenian troops were commanded by Serb officers in the Serbo-Croatian language, and he added: "There is no known case in history where the less developed part of a state would have commanded the more developed part."[9] He also observed that the republic was paying more than four times as much as it should for the support of the military and that it would be possible to "very quickly" organize "a Slovene Army for the defense of Slovenia's independence."[10] In early June, the Slovenian legislature requested that the Federal Assembly adopt a new amendment to the existing law on military service that would depoliticize the military, and would also permit army recruits, "as a rule," to perform their military service in their native republics.

As conflict over military issues escalated, Slovenian politicians announced several other measures to assert their republic's sovereignty in both internal and external affairs. Delivering on a promise made by the DEMOS leadership during the spring election campaign, for example, Slovenia halted the bulk of its payments to the Federal Fund for Underdeveloped Regions. In effect, this move was an extension of the policy of partial cutbacks previously made by the reform communist leadership. Commenting on the further cuts, Slovenia's Prime Minister Peterle announced that the republic would continue payments only to that portion of the fund earmarked for Slovenian enterprises operating in less-developed regions of Yugoslavia. Denying that the cancellation of Slovenian contributions would encourage the further dissolution of the country's federal system, Peterle claimed that the "germs of disintegration" actually resulted from complaints regarding the Fund's existence and inefficiencies.[11] Despite Slovenia's relatively prosperous position in Yugoslavia, he dismissed any moral imperative for his republic to provide aid to the less well-off parts of the country: "We face an economic collapse, and considering we ourselves have nothing, we cannot help others."[12]

The newly elected Slovenian leadership also introduced initiatives intended to give the republic a more independent profile in foreign economic and political relations. The new government quickly announced, for example, that in order to enhance closer relations with Europe, Slovenia would accelerate its activities in the Alpine-Adriatic Working Community (a regional organization founded in 1978 consisting of Germany, Hungary, Austria, Italy, and Yugoslavia). Plans were also introduced to expand Slovenia's banking, trade, and information facilities in Western Europe and the United States. "We have to put Slovenia on world maps," observed the head of the Slovenian Assembly's International

Affairs Committee. "Our products should be stamped 'Made in Slovenia,' not 'Made in Yugoslavia.'"[13] Complaints were also lodged with federal authorities concerning Slovenia's inadequate representation in the Yugoslav diplomatic corps, and demands were made for the location of more foreign diplomatic missions in Ljubljana. Slovenia's Foreign Affairs Minister Dimitrije Rupel, one of the most ardent advocates of enhanced Slovenian political autonomy in the new coalition government, put the matter of diplomatic representation bluntly: "We do not want the Serbs to represent Slovenia in Europe. We simply do not want to enter Europe via Belgrade."[14]

Anxious to flesh out a firmer basis for its new sovereignty initiatives, the Slovenian regime also proceeded with the preparation of a new constitution for the republic. Slovenian state President Kučan made it clear that it would be the constitution of a "sovereign state" within a planned confederation, not the constitution of a "Yugoslav federal unit."[15] On July 2, 1990, in an initial step in constitutional engineering, the Slovenian legislature adopted by a vote of 178 to 3 (with 2 abstentions) the "Declaration on the Sovereignty of the State of the Republic of Slovenia." Beyond proclaiming the sovereignty of the republic on the "basis of the Slovenian nation's right to self-determination," the six-article declaration's most important features included assertions concerning the primacy of the Slovenian legal system, constitutional provisions, laws, and regulations over similar federal provisions; a call for the preparation of a new republican constitution within one year's time specifying which federal laws were still valid in the republic; and a mandate for the republic's government to assume full control over the units of the Yugoslav Army stationed on Slovenian territory.[16]

The Slovenian sovereignty declaration naturally provoked instant protests from those political forces seeking to obstruct any further devolution of authority in the Yugoslav federation, most notably the Serbian political leadership and the military high command. Federal president Jović demanded the repeal of the declaration, claiming that it "denigrated and infringed upon the shared interests of Yugoslav nations and nationalities."[17] The presidency also initiated proceedings before the Constitutional Court of Yugoslavia to determine the constitutionality of the declaration, although Slovenian sovereigntists seemed to have little to fear from this quarter. "Everything is now in the hands of the politicians," observed the president of the Constitutional Court. The "Court might officially confirm that the proclamation of Slovenian sovereignty is not in accord with the Constitution of Yugoslavia, but this would not be binding on anyone."[18] Only the Slovenian member of the federal presidency, Janez Drnovšek, downplayed the impact of the declaration, characterizing it as something that was "expected" and really only a "tactical move" prior to a new round of interregional negotiations on Yugoslavia's future.[19]

Slovenia's Prime Minister Peterle rejected the idea that the declaration marked the beginning of Yugoslavia's dissolution. "Sovereignty," he said, "does not mean secession straight away. In the fields where federal laws are acceptable to us we want to keep those laws....Our watchword is not independence, but sovereignty....To us Yugoslavia is acceptable as a confederation if Slovenia enjoys full sovereignty there. If not, the alternative is Slovenian independence."[20] The declaration was clearly a transitional political act, designed to improve Slovenia's position in future discussions with the other republics and the federal government concerning Yugoslavia's reorganization or dissolution. For the moment, independence was only an extreme option for Slovenian leaders, although Peterle and his colleagues frequently pointed out that their commitment to Yugoslavia was not unconditional and that there were sixty states in the world smaller than Slovenia.

At the end of July, the new Slovene regime, signaling its temporary flexibility and prudence on countrywide reorganization, rescinded an earlier decision to end the participation of Slovenia's representatives in the Federal Assembly at Belgrade. However, the Slovenian government's decision to temporarily cooperate in the work of amending the federal constitution was made not to enhance Yugoslavia's federal structure but to further "reduce the competence of the federal state."[21] At least for the time being, Slovenia still had more to gain politically and economically from involvement in Yugoslavia than from separation and independence. Conceding the incremental strategy of the leadership in Ljubljana, Prime Minister Peterle observed that "Slovenia is more and more sovereign every day."[22]

Kosovo Versus Serbia:
Sovereignties in Collision

The same day that the Slovenian Assembly issued its declaration of sovereignty, 114 ethnic Albanian delegates to the provincial Kosovo Assembly met in the street outside their legislature and adopted a declaration proclaiming Kosovo an independent unit within Yugoslavia, having equal status with Serbia and the other republics. The July 2 declaration described the Albanian population of Kosovo and Yugoslavia as having the status of a "nation"—not just the politically inferior status (in Yugoslav constitutional parlance) of a "nationality" or a "national minority"—and thereby entitled to its own republic and right of self-determination. The Albanian delegates also annulled a March 1989 decision of the Provincial Assembly to approve amendments to the Serbian constitution that diminished Kosovo's provincial autonomy within the Serbian republic. The unusual venue of the meeting resulted from a decision made by the Serbian government some ten days earlier to stifle Albanian political and constitutional demands by arranging (through its Serbian president) for the adjournment of the Kosovo Assembly, thereby effectively locking out the elected legislators.

The declaration of Kosovo's sovereignty expressed the growing political self-assertion of the province's Albanian population—a phenomenon that had accelerated markedly during the previous sixteen months owing to a number of factors. Perhaps most important were the extremely harsh measures that had been taken by Serbian and central government authorities to suppress Albanian protests following the curtailment of Kosovo's autonomy in March 1989. Those measures, which resulted in the deaths of over sixty Albanians by mid-1990 and the imprisonment of hundreds of Albanian activists, completely polarized the already very strained pattern of ethnic relations in the province. The contrived indictment of popular Albanian leader Azem Vlasi on charges of "counterrevolutionary activity," which was followed by a drawn-out and farcical trial, also proved to be a political blunder on the part of the Serbian authorities. Vlasi's ordeal and his subsequent acquittal in April 1990 also stimulated Albanian political self-confidence and won the Albanians support outside Serbia.

While the Serbian authorities strengthened their grip over Kosovo in June 1990 by taking direct control over local security organs and militia, the political mobilization of the Albanian population continued unabated. Encouraged by the growth of pluralism and the scheduling of elections elsewhere in Yugoslavia, Albanian leaders began to organize political parties in the province. By mid-1990, the largest such party—the Kosovo Democratic Alliance (originally formed in December 1989)—was estimated to have several hundred thousand members and had already begun agitating for new elections and the adoption of a liberal provincial electoral law. It was the promotion of these demands by Albanian legislative delegates in Kosovo, and their request that the central authorities allow work to proceed on a new Kosovo constitution, that finally prompted Serbian officials to manipulate the adjournment of the Provincial Assembly in June 1990. Although the assembly was scheduled to reconvene on July 5, Albanian delegates decided to proceed with their extraparliamentary declaration of sovereignty for two reasons. First, the declaration was scheduled to coincide with a similar move toward sovereignty by Slovenian legislators. Second, and even more important, Kosovo's Albanian sovereigntists hoped to preempt a referendum called for July 2 and 3 in the province by the Serbian government to obtain popular approval for the preparation of a new republican constitution *prior* to holding free elections. Albanian leaders correctly suspected that such a constitution would reconfirm Kosovo's inferior political status as a province within Serbia, thereby legally precluding Albanian hopes of forming a seventh republic within Yugoslavia. In effect, the Serbian referendum concerning further constitutional development was an exercise designed by Slobodan Milošević to drum up support and legitimacy for his political platform.

Milošević had been embarrassed by the impressive electoral mandate received by nationalist forces in Slovenia and Croatia a few months earlier. Facing the prospect of an electoral challenge from noncommunist opposition political parties that had been slowly organizing over the past year within Serbia, he urgently needed to obtain some affirmation of popular approval. For the Albanian leadership in Kosovo, however, it was equally imperative that Albanians both boycott the Milošević referendum and clearly assert Kosovo's autonomy from Serbian control. Thus the July 2 declaration of Kosovo's sovereignty represented not only a serious struggle between Serbian and Albanian political leaders for power in Kosovo but also a race to shore up their respective constitutional and political positions for probable future negotiations on Yugoslavia's political structure. Although in the referendum on a new constitution Milošević was able to obtain a 96.8 percent "yes" vote, almost all Kosovo's 90 percent Albanian majority boycotted the process. Voting turnout was approximately 78 percent in the republic as a whole, but the figures were 86 percent in "Serbia proper" compared to roughly 25 percent in Kosovo.

Heartened—despite such contrived plebiscitarian-style legitimacy—and anxious to obstruct momentum toward Albanian sovereignty, Serbian authorities moved on July 5 to suspend the operation of the still "adjourned" Kosovo Assembly as well as the Kosovo government. A widespread purge of Albanian employees from the government and state administration began, along with the gagging of the independent Albanian media, or what Serbian officials like to refer to as the "mouthpieces of separatism."[23] Serbian leaders explained that it was necessary to eliminate "the political domination of the majority" in Kosovo, that the province must remain an "integral" part of Serbia, and that Kosovo must "get used to the fact that it is not a state."[24] The Belgrade media attributed the timing of the Kosovo declaration of sovereignty to a coordinated Slovenian-Albanian plan—the "Ljubljana-Priština axis"—endeavoring to disrupt and destroy Yugoslavia.

Serbia's heavy-handed measures to thwart Albanian sovereignty in Kosovo were officially condemned as illegal by the new regimes in Slovenia and Croatia. The federal presidency and the federal government, however, sidestepped the issue, having previously condemned Kosovo's declaration of sovereignty as an illegal act. Prime Minister Marković's desire to obtain concessions from Milošević on larger constitutional and political issues was undoubtedly an important factor in the decision by federal government authorities to soft-pedal the matter of Kosovo. Within the collective federal presidency, only the new Slovenian and Croatian members favored requesting Serbia to rescind its suspension of Kosovo's governing bodies. Thus, Albanian sovereigntists faced hostile opposition from President Jović and his pro-Serbian perspectives, and other republican representatives, such as the Macedonians and Montenegrins, were anxious to discourage the ethnopolitical demands of the sizable Albanian populations in their own republics. Meanwhile, Bosnian leaders who had to look after their own delicately balanced interethnic situation (Moslems, Serbs and Croats) prudently chose to steer clear of the sensitive Albanian question.

Moderate Albanian leaders who advocated Kosovo's sovereignty, but still supported the province's continued affiliation in either a federal or confederal Yugoslav state, were particularly bitter about federal acquiescence in the suspension of Kosovo's elected governing bodies and about the continued violation of Albanian civil liberties. The president of the Kosovo Democratic Alliance (KDA), Ibrahim Rugova, suspected, for example, "some kind of a game having been played by the Federal and Serbian government."[25] KDA leaders explained that Kosovo's majority Albanians only wanted free elections in the region, which would permit the elected majority party to enjoy the privilege of governing:

> We are an ethnic group and not a minority. Serbia is treating us like a colony. It acts like the European colonial lords in Africa. The latest Serbian special laws are nothing else but apartheid policy....We are for Yugoslavia, if it is possible to find a democratic solution in the European spirit. However, if the oppression of the Kosovo Alliance continues, one has to think about the other possibilities.[26]

By fall 1990, enhanced Serbian control over Kosovo temporarily thwarted efforts by the province's Albanian leadership to achieve sovereignty as a seventh republic in the Yugoslav federation or even to achieve their modest goal of passing a provincial electoral law that would allow newly formed Albanian political parties to campaign for seats in a reconvened Kosovo legislature. Albanian leaders, having watched the progress of sovereignty assertion and political pluralism in other regions of the country during the summer and early fall, and especially the support offered by Serbia (and pro-Serbian) federal authorities to the sovereignty claims of the Serbian minority in Croatia, naturally maintained that there was some kind of double standard in the country. In particular, Albanian leaders were amazed that Serbian politicians could advocate special political recognition and protection of Serbian minorities throughout the country when it came to negotiations on Yugoslavia's macropolitical structure yet simultaneously obstruct all Albanian attempts to express their majority position in Kosovo. KDA leader Rugova claimed that the country was "moving backward" to the situation in the interwar period when Albanians were denied meaningful political representation and were thought of as a "foreign body" in Yugoslavia. The concept of Yugoslavia, he observed, could no longer be simply "a state of the South Slavs in which other Balkan peoples like the Albanians are simply incidental residents.... The independence of Kosovo within the Yugoslav federation is the only acceptable solution."[27]

On September 7, 1990, ethnic Albanian delegates of the dissolved Kosovo Assembly met secretly and proclaimed a 140-article constitution of the "sovereign Republic of Kosovo" and also adopted a law permitting citizens to organize themselves into political parties. The Belgrade newspaper, *Borba*, reported that "on September 7 Yugoslavia got its 'seventh republic' without knowing it."[28] Meanwhile, the Serbian government characterized the proclamation of the "so-called" Kosovo constitution as an illegitimate action on the part of "a movement directly and exclusively targeted at breaking up the territorial integrity of Serbia and Yugoslavia."[29] Serbian authorities also took steps to criminally prosecute those Albanian constitution-makers they could apprehend. Many of the Albanian legislative deputies involved fled to the relatively more liberal environment of northwestern Yugoslavia, or abroad, whereas some urged their ethnic brethren to begin "Gandhian"-type resistance to the Serbian authorities.[30]

Near the end of September, after four months of discussion, the Serbian Assembly adopted a new constitution, which in many respects amounted to a sovereignty declaration for Serbia. Despite protests by the extraparliamentary opposition that a new constitution should not be adopted until after the republic's first competitive election in December, Milošević regarded such constitutional engineering as an important further step in legitimating his position, both within and outside Serbia. Under the new constitution, Serbia became "a sovereign, integral, and unified" state with the authority of its republican governmental bodies extending to the entire territory of Serbia, including its two "autonomous provinces." The two provinces (Vojvodina and Kosovo) were permitted to exercise what was referred to as "territorial autonomy" but "cannot have the jurisdiction of a state." Moreover, the constitution provided that if provincial or local authorities failed to implement regulations and laws adopted in Belgrade, republican organs of authority were empowered to ensure their implementation. As for Serbia itself, one of the republic's leading legal specialists—using language almost identical to that of Slovenian leaders regarding their July sovereignty declaration—observed that the republic's new constitution "isn't conceptualized as the constitution of a federal unit, but as the constitution of an independent state."[31]

For the moment at least, the new constitution essentially allowed Milošević and his political team to implement a strong-handed approach to Kosovo and an independent course with respect to Yugoslavia's broader interregional issues. Thus, Article 135 of the new Serbian constitution constrained Kosovo in some vague and bounded "autonomy" and also accorded republican authorities in Belgrade wide latitude to "adopt acts seeking to defend the interests of the Republic" should Serbia face threats to its "rights and duties" from either the federation or "other republics." In a separate constitutional provision (Article 72), pregnant with political implications for the entire country, the Serbian republican government was also empowered to "maintain connections with the Serbs who live outside the republic of Serbia, working to guard their national and cultural-historical identity."[32]

The "Serbian Question" and the "Knin Republic"

Serbian political influence in communist Yugoslavia had never been an issue relating solely to developments within the Serbian republic or only to the question of Serbian sway in federal decisionmaking. In 1981, for example, Serbs constituted the largest ethnic group in Yugoslavia (36 percent of the total population), but approximately 3 million of the over

8.1 million Serbs living in the country resided outside the Serbian republic and its two provinces. Moreover, in two republics, Croatia and Bosnia-Hercegovina, where Serbs in 1981 made up roughly 12 percent and 32 percent of the republican populations respectively, the relationship between the Serbian ethnic communities and other major nationality groups (Croats in Croatia, and Moslems and Croats in Bosnia-Hercegovina) had been an important determinant in regional political development both before and after the creation of the Yugoslav state in 1918.

In addition to the usual problems posed by ethnic diversity, three major background factors had a significant impact on the relationship between the Serbs and their neighbors in Croatia and Bosnia-Hercegovina. Perhaps most important has been the historical yearning of the diasporic Serbian communities for closer cultural and political ties with their ethnic brethren in "Serbia proper." Indeed, such sentiments contributed to Serbian support for the Yugoslav idea before World War I, to the violent catalyst that precipitated that war in June 1914, and also to the subsequent formation and maintenance of the Yugoslav state. As discussed in Chapter 1, for most Serbs—especially those dispersed outside of the Serbian heartland—support for various "Pan-Yugoslav" notions was closely linked to the idea of "Pan-Serbianism" or interregional Serbian solidarity. As a result, although the Yugoslav idea historically attracted considerable multiethnic support, the particularly strong advocacy of that idea by the Serbs of Croatia and Bosnia-Hercegovina often collided with the nationalist sentiments espoused by other major ethnic groups in those two regions.

Second, the genocide waged against the Serbian communities in Croatia and Bosnia-Hercegovina by ultranationalistic Croats and Moslems during World War II severely poisoned interethnic relations in those two republics. Although throughout the postwar period the communist regime more or less successfully suppressed most overt manifestations of ethnic unrest in the two republics, underlying antagonisms and tensions constituted an important latent force waiting to erupt on the political landscape. Tito's one-party state restrained interethnic animosities, but it did not, as it was so often claimed by regime supporters, fundamentally resolve the "national problem."[33] Finally, the relatively privileged political position of the Serbs in Croatia and Bosnia-Hercegovina during the communist regime—owing to the disproportionately high participation of Serbs from those regions in the ranks of Tito's Partisan Army—exacerbated the other latent interethnic tensions in the two republics and provided grist for the mill of anti-Serbian nationalism. Indeed, for the most part Serbian communists in Croatia and Bosnia identified more with the centralizing facets of the Tito regime's strategies for maintaining the cross-ethnic and the cross-regional cohesion of the country, rather than other strands of the Partisan legacy that emphasized the federal character of the Yugoslav state.[34] By 1990, as nationality conflicts intensified and communist control waned throughout Yugoslavia, all three of these factors would seriously complicate interethnic relations and political developments in both Croatia and Bosnia-Hercegovina.

In Croatia, the advent of party pluralism in early 1990, and the surge of support for Franjo Tudjman's nationalistically oriented Croatian Democratic Union, naturally aroused the concern of the Serbian minority in the republic. Rather comfortably overrepresented for over four decades in the membership of the League of Communists' republican organization, and also in Croatia's political elite and state administration, the Serbs of Croatia were well aware that the demise of communist control would have a negative impact on their influence and status. Tudjman's stunning defeat of the League of Communists in the April-May elections, his commitment to the assertion of "Croatian sovereignty," and particularly his plans to rectify the underrepresentation of Croatians in the political, administrative, and media sectors were all factors intensifying Serbian anxiety in Croatia and once again positioning Serbian-Croatian relations at the center of the Yugoslav political stage.

Although in the immediate aftermath of the 1990 Croatian elections Serbian officials retained their posts in the republican administrative organs, the situation at the summit of the political hierarchy shifted dramatically. Serbian political elite representation was reduced largely to those Serbs belonging to the "opposition" communist caucus in the republic's legislature. It was not the rump Serbian communist legislators, however, but another five Serbian deputies belonging to the recently formed Serbian Democratic Party (SDS), led by Jovan Rašković, who quickly emerged as the principal spokesmen of Croatia's Serbian minority. The SDS derived its main support from a chain of thirteen communes in the Croatian regions of northern Dalmatia, eastern Lika, the Kordun, Banija, and western Slavonia—parts of the so-called "Krajina" or borderland—an area (Map 4.1) where in 1991 Serbs constituted an absolute majority of the population in eleven communes and a relative majority in two communes. These Serbian-majority communes roughly coincided with the boundary region that constituted the famous Austrian Military Frontier and had long served (1578-1881) as a defensive buffer against Ottoman expansion in the Balkans. A good portion of the original Serbian inhabitants of the area had migrated to the region to escape persecution by the Ottomans and had been recruited specifically to serve as border guards for the frontier garrisons. During the eighteenth and

MAP 4.1   Serbs in the Population of Croatia, by Commune (1991)

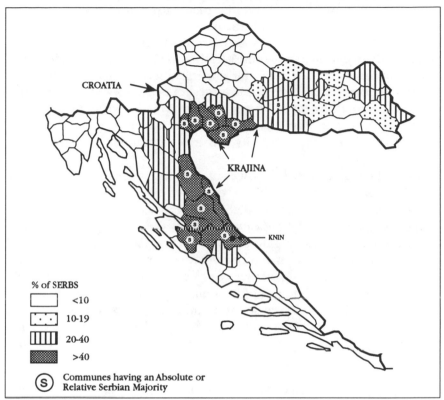

nineteenth centuries, Austrian and Hungarian political authorities frequently exploited Serbian ethnic marginality and concerns in Croatia in order to counterbalance the pressures of Croatian ethnic nationalism. In 1981, ethnic Croats made up 22 percent of the combined population of the approximately 207,000 persons living in the eleven communes of Croatia with an absolute Serbian majority, whereas Serbs constituted 69 percent (and were a significant portion of another 8 percent of the total population classified as "Yugoslavs"). Although the Serbs in the eleven communes constituted only 26 percent of all Serbs residing in Croatia, their regional concentration, intense ethnic consciousness, and proximity to an even larger Serbian ethnic enclave in Bosnia-Hercegovina made them a very significant factor in the political life of Croatia and Yugoslavia.

Exploiting the pluralist political environment in Croatia at the beginning of 1990, Rašković's SDS was able to mobilize significant support from the republic's Serbian community. The political headquarters of the SDS was located in the commune of Knin, the most populous and southernmost unit in the Dalmatian cluster of Serbian majority communes often referred to as the "Knin region" (*Kninska krajina*). Even before Tudjman's electoral victory, Knin had become a hotbed of resurgent tension between Serbs and Croats. In July 1989, for example, Serbian demonstrations in Knin in support of the Serbs of Kosovo echoed the type of nationalist rhetoric advanced by the Milošević leadership in Serbia and provoked a major confrontation between local Serbian leaders (several of whom were arrested) and the ethnically sensitive communist government in Zagreb.

With Tudjman's election, however, and his official support for the transformation of Yugoslavia into a "confederation of sovereign states"— which held out the possibility that links between Serbia and the Serbs living in Croatia might be radically severed—the attitudes and behavior of the Serbs in the Knin region escalated beyond a localized or regional ethnopolitical issue. In an interview at the end of June, SDS leader Rašković attempted to explain why Yugoslavia's breakup or even confederation along the lines of Tudjman's notion of a "constitutional union of sovereign states" was so frightening to all Serbs, especially those living as minorities outside the Serbian republic. He also touched on one of the basic problems undermining the continued cohesion of the entire country:

> There is something about Yugoslavism that has not been thoroughly cleared up. For the Serb, Yugoslavism is something identical with Serbianism. There is an alloy of Yugoslavism and Serbianism. For other peoples, this alloy does not exist and therefore this is one of the greatest divisions in the political and psychological life of Yugoslavia. One people identify with Yugoslavia, but other people accept it conditionally.... Federalism is something that is tied to the ideas of the Serbian people....As regards a confederation, nobody in the world knows what a confederation is.[35]

Rašković and his compatriots claimed they were willing to acknowledge Croatia as their "homeland," but perpetuation of the Yugoslav state with its relative Serbian majority was crucial to their "Serbianism" and their perceived security.

Serbian-Croatian tensions escalated during June 1990 when Tudjman's new government proposed draft amendments to the Croatian constitution that made specific reference to the republic as the sovereign state of the Croatians and other nations and national minorities living in Croatia, but no longer explicitly mentioned the Serbs. The amendments provided for the adoption of traditional Croatian ethnic symbols (a coat of arms, flag, and national anthem) as the official insignia of the republic. The Latin script was also explicitly identified as the republic's official alphabet (use of Cyrillic and other alphabets would be regulated by law). The new ethnic symbolism was offensive to many of Croatia's Serbs, but their deeper fear was that Tudjman planned to sever Croatia from the Yugoslav state—either through creation of a loose confederation or outright secession—thereby leaving the Serbian minority at the political mercy of a Croatian majority and the nationalist government in Zagreb.

Persistent efforts by Tudjman and his more moderate colleagues to reassure the republic's Serbs that their rights would be protected were deeply distrusted in the Serbian community and were at odds with the nationalist and anti-Serb rhetoric frequently adopted by Tudjman and certain quarters of his party's leadership. Serbian anxiety was also fueled by the steady and sensational campaign of anti-Croatian propaganda emanating from Serb nationalists linked to media and government circles in Belgrade. Thus, the most aggressive leaders of the Serbian minority in Croatia from the Knin area not only enjoyed the strong support of an ethnically self-conscious and relatively territorially compact population but were also encouraged by their ethnic brethren and the Milošević leadership in the Serbian republic. Pressure from Belgrade and also from hawks in his own party may have been the main reason that Rašković turned down an invitation to join the new Croatian government as a deputy prime minister, and later informed the Croatian Assembly that all five of his party's deputies would cease participation in legislative activities. A meeting between Rašković and Tudjman failed to resolve matters, and became bogged down in disagreement over the issue of the Serbian leader's vague demand that the republic's Serbian community be granted some kind of "ethnic sovereignty." Moreover, the meeting would actually exacerbate difficulties, after Tudjman's office publicly released a transcript of the supposedly private meeting at which Rašković had attempted to assert his political independence by making deprecatory comments about Milošević.[36]

In July, Rašković's Serbian Democratic Party rejected the draft amendments to the Croatian constitution, characterizing them as an attack on the Serbian people and making an exception only for the amendment that removed the word *socialist* from the republic's official title. Although Croatian political leaders appeared willing to guarantee the rights of the Serbian community (e.g., use of Cyrillic in predominantly Serbian localities, provision for Serbian cultural associations and media), they were opposed to any arrangement for "autonomy" that would compromise the republic's authority over the Serbian majority communes. According to Tudjman and his colleagues, not only were the Serbian majority localities part of "historical" and "natural" Croatia, but they also contained a substantial ethnic Croatian population as well as other non-Serbian peoples who had rights and ethnic interests. When Rašković, ignoring Croatian authorities, announced plans to hold a referendum among the republic's Serbs on the matter of their autonomy in Croatia, Croatian leaders claimed, with some justification, that they were witnessing the creation of a "state within a state." For the Croats, Rašković's tactics were viewed as a carefully orchestrated and dangerous challenge to the sovereignty of Croatia's first democratically elected government since before World War II.

Developments in Croatia assumed crisis proportions in the period from the end of July to the end of August, following a mass meeting of between 100,000 and 150,000 Serbs in the Knin region, when the Serbian community leadership—newly organized into a Serbian National Council—formally adopted the "Declaration on the Sovereignty and Autonomy of the Serbian People." According to the declaration, the Serbs in Croatia "on the basis of their geographical, historical, social, and cultural specificities, are a sovereign people with all the rights that constitute the sovereignty of peoples."[37] In view of Yugoslavia's unsettled future, the declaration left open the precise nature of Serbian autonomy. According to Serbian leaders, if the country would remain a federation, then the areas in Croatia having a Serbian majority would need to have only the rights necessary for *cultural autonomy*. Should Croatia secede from the Yugoslav federation, however, Serbian leaders in the republic held out the possibility that their community would seek *political autonomy*.[38]

Croatian leaders, meanwhile, claimed that the declaration, and also Rašković's plans to hold a referendum on Serbian autonomy in Croatia, were part of a conspiracy hatched in Belgrade to divert Yugoslav and world attention away from Serbia's harsh suppression of Albanian autonomy in Kosovo. In a speech to the Croatian legislature on July 25, 1990, Tudjman explicitly warned of a "scenario of Kosovization and destabilization" in Croatia, whereby the Serbian minority would try to provoke military intervention on their behalf from outside the region by falsely claiming to suffer persecution at the hands of the republic's Croatian majority.[39] As Croatian-Serbian relations deteriorated sharply in Croatia, Rašković claimed that the Serbian community was engaged in an "unarmed" or "psychological uprising" to gain respect and that a referendum on Serbian autonomy was necessary because of the "Ustashe core" (the World War II Croatian ultranationalists) in Tudjman's HDZ. Tudjman himself was not an adherent of the Ustashe, conceded Rašković, but only a "Croato-centralist."[40]

Meanwhile, Tudjman's government announced that it would prohibit the Serbian referendum on autonomy scheduled for August, and it banned the operation of the "intercommunal" association formed by the Serbian-majority communes in Croatia. "Territorial autonomy for the Serbs is out of the question," declared Tudjman, "we will not allow it."[41] The Croatian political leadership also announced that it would proceed with the formation of special new police detachments that would not be dominated by Serbs, as the police had been under the communist regime. Plans for the reorganization of the police and administrative justice system were particularly offensive to Serbian officials in the Knin region, who not only feared for their jobs but also would be required to display the new regime's insignia which were based upon traditional Croatian ethnic symbols. As the date of the referendum approached, armed Serbian vigilante groups began to form in the Knin area, setting up barricades on the approach roads to the predominantly Serbian communes. Anticipating that the Croatian government would take some action to prevent such activity and obstruct the referendum, Serbian leaders from Croatia succeeded in arranging a meeting with Yugoslav President Jović in order to request federal protection. Tudjman complained that the meeting represented federal intervention in Croatia's affairs, and cited the episode as evidence of a "well-organized conspiracy" to undermine the republic's legal authority.[42]

The crisis reached a climax on August 17, when helicopters sent to the Knin region by Croatia's secretariat of internal affairs were intercepted and forced to turn back by JNA air force MIG fighters. Although the Yugoslav federal defence secretariat strenuously denied Croatian government allegations that the incident represented military interference in the republic—later claiming that the MIGS responded only to a radar alert after the Croatian helicopters strayed off their flight path—the dangerous implications of the confrontation for Croatia's political autonomy caused Tudjman to back away from his vow to administratively obstruct the planned referendum on Serbian autonomy. Meeting in emergency session, the Croatian government condemned the vigilantism in the Knin region as well as Milošević's alleged role in inciting Croatia's Serbs and the illegality of the Serbian referendum, but decided to refrain from direct action against the Serbian leadership and the communes organizing the vote. Thus moderate voices in Tudjman's inner circles, and his own desire not to provide justification for further military intervention, had resulted in a temporary retreat by the Zagreb government.

The rules of the August 18, 1990 referendum gave the right to vote to every Serb over the age of eighteen who was either a resident of Croatia, a Serb born on the territory of the republic of Croatia, or a Serb holding Croatian citizenship but living outside the territory of the republic.[43] The over 45,000 Croats living in the eleven Serbian majority communes of Croatia were, however, disenfranchised. According to Serbian leaders, the referendum attracted a "100 percent turnout" of those eligible to vote and resulted in a near unanimous outpouring of support for the Declaration on the Sovereignty and Autonomy of the Serbian People. Tudjman, however, described the referendum as an event that "had no legal basis whatsoever" and "will mean nothing for the Croatian republic."[44] "We kept our cool, we did not let ourselves be involved in bloodshed, in a civil war," Tudjman told the Croatian legislature on August 24, blaming the entire crisis on the failure of Serbian leaders to cooperate in the elaboration of sensible provisions to protect the rights of their minority community, on pressure from Serbian nationalists in Belgrade (including the leadership of the Serbian Orthodox church), and on the "indecisiveness" of the Yugoslav federal government.[45] In the weeks following the referendum, overt interethnic tensions subsided somewhat in Croatia, although efforts by Croatian authorities to disarm Serbian vigilante groups met with little success. Tudjman's government wisely eschewed any direct confrontation with the Serbian minority, hoping instead to let the republic's court system invalidate "the usurpation of power" by the so-called "Knin republic" (i.e., the intercommunal council that had been established by the Serbian-majority communes).

In postmortems on the July-August crisis, Croatian leaders explained that their desire to avoid any pretext for federal military intervention was uppermost in their minds when they decided to refrain from direct action against the architects of the Serbian vote on autonomy. Tudjman claimed that apart from the brief JNA air force incident, and some military officers who personally aided the vigilantes in Knin, the Yugoslav "army has not supported the uprising of the Serbs as a whole."[46] There was also praise from Tudjman and his colleagues for the two dozen Serb deputies in the Croatian legislature who belonged to the communist opposition and had not joined with Rašković and the four SDS Serb deputies in support for the referendum.[47] Tudjman, however, leveled sharp criticism against Serbian political and intellectual circles in Belgrade that, he claimed, had prodded Rašković and the nationalist wing of the

SDS to take an intransigent position. "The Serbs," observed Tudjman, "are obviously returning to their traditional political attitude. A Greater-Serb policy is pursued against the non-Serb nations."[48] Croatia's second most powerful politician, Stipe Mesić (prime minister of Croatia from May to August 1990 and thereafter the republic's representative in the federal presidency), was equally critical of the Serbs' desire to establish some type of special status in Croatia.

What kind of referendum in Croatia is this when the Croats are not taking part in it, only Serbs and nobody else....They are not a God-given nation, they are equal to everybody else, not more equal. If there are problems we should discuss them within the system's institutions....Who gave them the right to go to [Federal President] Jović, to speak on behalf of the Serbs of Croatia? Who authorized Jović to have talks with them without the presence of representatives of the republic of Croatia? I am not aware that he held talks with Albanians, and Kosovo is a greater problem than Knin. These people think that everything in this country should be measured with criteria that suits the Serbs.[49]

Although Tudjman's government chose to ignore the results of the Knin referendum and to characterize the vigilantism of the Serbs as a modern form of *hajducija* (Serbian brigandage against Ottoman rule), the stalemate between Zagreb and the Serbian minority in the republic remained a troublesome obstacle in the path of projected Croatian sovereignty. Meanwhile, Serbian leaders such as Rašković, increasingly isolated in their "autonomous" Knin stronghold, under attack from even more nationalistic Serbs in their own party, and now shunned as rebels by the Zagreb authorities, continued looking for ways to promote the interests and "ethnic sovereignty" of Croatia's Serbs. Not surprisingly, their focus turned southeast toward Bosnia-Hercegovina—the largest center of Yugoslavia's Serbian diaspora—and also to the important political developments taking place in the Serbian republic.

Notes

1. D. Štrbac, "The Court Assesses and Rules," *Politika: The International Weekly*, April 14-21, 1990, p. 3.

2. "Speech Presented by Ante Marković on Results Achieved and Further Measures to Implement Economic Reform Programme," *Yugoslav Survey*, Vol. 31, No. 2 (1990), pp. 46-48.

3. *FBIS-EEU*, May 15, 1990, pp. 78-82.

4. *FBIS-EEU*, May 17, 1990, pp. 72-74.

5. *FBIS-EEU*, May 18, 1990, p. 73.

6. *FBIS-EEU*, May 21, 1990, pp. 72-73.

7. *FBIS-EEU*, June 6, 1990, p. 55.

8. In a speech at the end of May, Jović clarified his position asserting that the presidency was not considering a state of emergency because of rising internationality and interregional tensions or planning to annul the elections in Slovenia and Croatia. He also proposed new talks between the presidency and leaders from all the regions on the matter of the adoption of a new constitution. *FBIS-EEU*, May 30, 1990, pp. 61-68.

9. *FBIS-EEU*, June 5, 1990, p. 83.

10. *FBIS-EEU*, June 12, 1990, p. 55.

11. *FBIS-EEU*, June 6, 1990, p. 58.

12. *FBIS-EEU*, June 22, 1990, p. 70.

13. Carol Williams, "Nationalism Tugging Apart Yugoslav Unity," *Los Angeles Times*, July 21, 1990, p. 1.

14. *FBIS-EEU*, June 22, 1990, p. 68.

15. *FBIS-EEU*, July 2, 1990, p. 69.

16. *FBIS-EEU*, June 20, 1990, p. 66.

17. *FBIS-EEU*, July 9, 1990, p. 71.

18. Dragan Bujošević, "Declaration Against Law," *Politika: The International Weekly*, No. 16 (July 7-13, 1990), p. 1.

19. *FBIS-EEU*, July 9, 1990, p. 73.

20. *FBIS-EEU*, August 1, 1990, p. 58.

21. *Ibid.*, p. 60.

22. *FBIS-EEU*, July 11, 1990, p. 62.

23. Jim Fish, "Yugoslavia Seeks Repeal of Slovenian Sovereignty Declaration," *Washington Post*, July 7, 1990, p. A17.

24. *FBIS-EEU*, June 19, 1990, p. 82.

25. *Tanjug*, July 20, 1990.

26. *Neue Kronen Zeitung*, July 14, 1990, p. 4.

27. *FBIS-EEU*, September 6, 1991, p. 58.

28. *FBIS-EEU*, September 18, 1991, p. 51.

29. *FBIS-EEU*, September 14, 1990, p. 54.

30. *FBIS-EEU*, July 13, 1990, p. 56.

31. Miodrag Jovičić, "Konfederacija vodi u haos," *Stav*, November 2, 1990, pp. 20-23.

32. *The Constitution of the Republic of Serbia* (Belgrade: Kultura, 1990), p. 35.

33. Lenard Cohen and Paul Warwick, *Political Cohesion in a Fragile Mosaic: The Yugoslav Experience* (Boulder, Colo.: Westview Press, 1983).

34. On the importance of such attitudes among the Serbian communists in Croatia, see Jill Irvine, *The Croat Question: Partisan Politics in the Formation of the Yugoslav Socialist State* (Boulder, Colo.: Westview Press, 1993), pp. 225-231, 285-287.

35. *FBIS-EEU*, June 26, 1990, p. 57.

36. For Rašković's objections to such publicity, see *FBIS-EEU*, August 10, 1990, p. 41.

37. *FBIS-EEU*, July 31, 1990, p. 72.

38. *FBIS-EEU*, August 2, 1990, p. 42.

39. *FBIS-EEU*, August 7, 1990, p. 72.

40. *FBIS-EEU*, July 27, 1990, p. 36.

41. *FBIS-EEU*, August 6, 1990, p. 53.

42. *FBIS-EEU*, August 15, 1990, p. 36.

43. *FBIS-EEU*, August 17, 1990, p. 26.

44. *FBIS-EEU*, August 22, 1990, p. 28.

45. *FBIS-EEU*, August 27, 1990, p. 51.

46. *Ibid.*, p. 28.

47. *FBIS-EEU*, August 12, 1990, pp. 54-55; *FBIS-EEU*, September 5, 1990, p. 54. The election of a Serb from the communist caucus as speaker of the Croatian legislature was used by Tudjman to indicate that the Serbian community in Croatia was not politically homogeneous in opposition to the new government. *FBIS-EEU*, August 27, 1990, p. 55. Radical Serbs from Knin described the election of the new speaker as a "provocation." *FBIS-EEU*, September 5, 1990, p. 56.

48. *FBIS-EEU*, September 4, 1990, p 37

49. *FBIS-EEU*, September 7, 1990, p. 73.

5

Pluralism in the Southeast: Nationalism Triumphant

Nowhere has Marxism become rooted among Moslem peoples. Moslem identity is so imbued with Islam, that atheistic thought of any kind can't have any success with the Moslems.

— Alija Izetbegović (July 1990)

We do not demand an absolution of sins or a pardon. We shall simply disassociate ourselves from the classic Bolshevik tradition, but the idea of socialism cannot be superseded.

— Momir Bulatović (June 1990)

Bosnia-Hercegovina: Electoral Politics and Ethnic Balance in Jeopardy

THE COMPLICATED INTERMINGLING of different ethnoreligious communities in Bosnia-Hercegovina—in 1991, 43.7 percent Moslems, 31.4 percent Serbs, and 17.3 percent Croats (along with 5.5 percent "Yugoslavs," a good portion of whom were Serbs)—had long made the region one of the Balkan's most volatile environments for intergroup relations.[1] A desire to transcend the strong historical animosities among the republic's three major ethnic groups, and also to forestall the persistent contending claims to the region by nationalists in adjacent areas (e.g., advocates of "Greater Serbia" and "Greater Croatia"), were major considerations underlying the communist elite's post-World War II decision to recognize and develop Bosnia-Hercegovina as a separate unit within the Yugoslav federation. Such an arrangement, it was hoped, would gradually neutralize the strong tensions generated by the interethnic bloodletting in the region during the war and would also frustrate any future conflict in the area that might be generated by ultranationalists. Although Serbian communists enjoyed a privileged political position in Bosnia-Hercegovina during the postwar years, the republic's status as a separate republic in the Yugoslav federal system and official recognition of the republic's tripartite ethnic makeup were viewed by most observers as crucial ingredients in both the region's and the country's political stability. Thus, the ethnic and political self-assertion of Bosnia-Hercegovina's Moslem nationality during the 1970s and 1980s, a development encouraged by the policies of Yugoslav federal authorities, somewhat reduced Serbian political influence and brought the ethnopolitical balance of power in the republic closer into harmony with its ethnic composition. Moreover, the underlying prerequisites for regional stability were preserved and strengthened by various legal provisions for proportional ethnic representation within Bosnia-Hercegovina's political structure as well as equal representation for the republic in federal decisionmaking.[2]

Unfortunately, the failed policies and enfeeblement of the Yugoslav federation, compounded by ascending nationalistic political forces in both Serbia and Croatia during the late 1980s and early 1990s, gradually led to the reopening of the "Bosnian question" in Yugoslav political life. Although the mobilization of Serbian ethnic consciousness by Slobodan Milošević had initially been focused on the position of Serbian communities in Kosovo, his concerns gradually escalated into a more general appeal to Serbian nationalism throughout Yugoslavia. Thus even before the May 1990 victory of Tudjman's HDZ party in Croatia, political and media circles within Serbia had begun to focus on the difficulties faced by the Serbian community in Croatia and Bosnia-Hercegovina. Controversy over Bosnia became more pronounced during the Croatian electoral campaign when Tudjman emphasized the special ties between Croatia and Bosnia-Hercegovina and suggested that it might become necessary to raise the question of the republic's territorial reorganization in future negotiations about the restructuring of Yugoslavia along confederal lines. Such controversial statements raised considerable anxiety among Bosnia-Hercegovina's over 1.3 million Serbs, who were already troubled by the recent upsurge of Croatian and Moslem nationalism in their midst. For Serbian nationalists both within and outside Bosnia-Hercegovina, Tudjman's insinuations represented a direct challenge to Serbian interests that also served their own agenda of building cross-regional Serbian solidarity. Thus while Tudjman took every opportunity to suggest that Milošević's nationalist rhetoric and policies had generated reactive Croatian nationalism, the Croatian leader's own mobilization of ethnic identity tended to spawn a similar nationalist backlash on the part of Serbs in both Croatia and Bosnia.

During summer 1990, the shock waves from the Knin crisis in Croatia, and from preparations for free multiparty elections in Bosnia-Hercegovina scheduled for the fall, intensified the political mobilization of Bosnia-Hercegovina's Serbs and their links with Serbs in other republics. As in Croatia, the concentration of a substantial portion of the Serbian population in various sections of Bosnia, enabled local Serbian leaders to quickly mobilize their ethnic constituency. By July 1990, a branch of Rašković's Croatian-based Serbian Democratic Party (SDS) had been organized in Bosnia-Hercegovina and was particularly active in the eighteen heavily Serbian populated communes in the northwestern and central parts of the republic directly adjacent or close to Croatia's Krajina region (Map 5.1). Of the approximately 670,000 people living in those eighteen communes in 1981, 63.1 percent were Serbs, 15.1 percent Moslems, and 9.5 percent Croats, with another roughly 10 percent classified as "Yugoslavs."

MAP 5.1   Serbs in the Population of Croatia and Bosnia-Hercegovina, by Commune (1981)

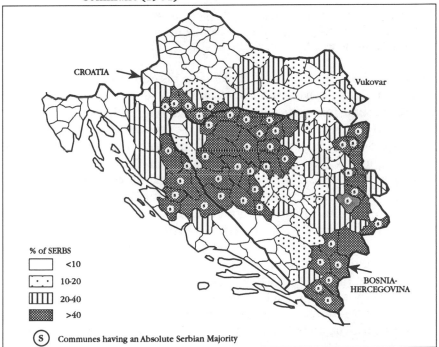

The combined population of nearly 564,000 Serbs—when the Serb population in the communes of Croatia having a Serbian absolute majority are added together with the Serbs in the eighteen Bosnian communes—fueled Serbian leaders' self-confidence that their collective political activities could make a difference in both regional and countrywide political life.[3] Indeed in 1981 the total number of Serbs in Croatia and Bosnia-Hercegovina together was over 1.8 million. The possibility of such joint action by the Serbs of Croatia and Bosnia was clearly on Rašković's mind in June 1990 during his unsuccessful negotiations with Tudjman to obtain some sort of future autonomy for the Serbian minority communities.

> *Rašković:* Tell me, in the case of the disintegration of Yugoslavia—and probably it will disintegrate, because within it beats two powerful potentials, freedom is beating and hate, and that will destroy anybody, not the least a feeble Yugoslavia—how do you envision a way for the Serbs...to be independent, but [still] part of the Croatian state?
>
> *Tudjman:* I haven't thought about that, but if one would create Croatia in its historical borders, then they would come into the framework of such a structure.
>
> *Rašković:* Good, but it isn't so simple because if Yugoslavia disintegrates, Bosnia will fall to pieces. You can't easily introduce the Serbian part of Bosnia into Croatia.[4]

By fall 1990, the ideas of Rašković and his Serbian Democratic Party colleagues had evolved from advocacy of cultural autonomy within Croatia, to some form of territorial-political autonomy within that republic, to support for an autonomous state unit incorporating at a minimum the adjacent Serbian-majority communes of both Croatia and Bosnia-Hercegovina. As Rašković saw it, such a "Krajina" or "border" state had specific historical characteristics: "It was originally formed on the territory of the present Croatia, but it is significant that the Krajina was outside the jurisdiction of the Croatian Sabor [legislature] for three hundred and three years."[5] Rašković's SDS counterpart in Bosnia-Hercegovina, Radovan Karadžić,[6] suggested that it would be difficult to sustain an independent Serbian political unit composed of sections of Croatia and Bosnia-Hercegovina. But should Yugoslavia disintegrate, Karadžić believed that it might be possible for such Serbian enclaves to form a new federation with other sections of the country (e.g., Serbia, Macedonia, and Montenegro). The one notion, however, that enjoyed widespread support among Serbs in both Croatia and Bosnia-Hercegovina was a determination not to be cast adrift or effectively cut off from the Serbian republic as a result of some future confederal arrangements (e.g., a Slovenian-Croatian-Bosnian confederation, a configuration that at the time of Bosnia-Hercegovina's first multiparty election in November 1990 seemed more likely than the formation of independent Bosnian and Croatian states).

As Bosnia-Hercegovina prepared for competitive elections, the republic's political landscape became more complex and representative of the region's innate diversity. Although electoral laws had prohibited the formation of parties explicitly organized along ethnic principles, this provision was soon invalidated by Bosnia-Hercegovina's Constitutional Court. Only two political parties participating in the electoral campaign— the long-ruling League of Communists (which had modernized by adding the label "Party of Democratic Change" to its traditional name, becoming the SK-SDP) and the republic's branch of Prime Minister Marković's relatively new Alliance of Reform Forces—could be characterized as pan-ethnic in terms of both their programs and bases of support. The communists and reformists were quickly overshadowed, however, by three nationalist parties, which respectively sought to represent Bosnia-Hercegovina's three major ethnic groups: the previously mentioned Serbian Democratic Party (SDS), the Moslems' Party of Democratic Action (SDA), and the Bosnian branch of Tudjman's Zagreb-based party, the Croatian Democratic Alliance (HDZ). Despite their parochial constituencies, all three ethnically oriented parties expressed general support for the continuation of Bosnia-Hercegovina's unique multiethnic and multiconfessional makeup as well as a commitment to the termination of communist rule.

The most notable differences of opinion among the three major nationalist parties concerned the future shape of the Yugoslav state and Bosnia-Hercegovina's position in any such new arrangements. For the Serbs in the SDS, Bosnia-Hercegovina's separation from the Yugoslav federal system was a threatening prospect, whereas most nationalist Moslems in the SDA and Croats in the HDZ found the idea of a confederation, with or without Serbia, as an option worthy of consideration. Enthusiasm for the confederal idea was most prominent among the Croats, the smallest of the three principal ethnic players in Bosnia-Hercegovina, who viewed their group's expanded participation with Croatia and Slovenia as a means to offset their minority situation.

Political alignments and tensions within Bosnia-Hercegovina were further complicated by the existence of ultranationalist wings within each of the three ethnically oriented parties. Such extremist elements benefited considerably from the uncertainty about Yugoslavia's future and increasingly raised the specter of imminent civil war among the country's different ethnic groups and regions. Thus, militant Serbian nationalists spread the fear of an Islamic-Catholic ("Khomeini-Ustashe") conspiracy by Moslems and Croats, whereas militant Croats viewed support for "ethnic sovereignty" on the part of Bosnian Serbs as a local version of the "Kosovo-Knin" methods allegedly orchestrated by the Belgrade authorities and Serbian Orthodox church.

At his organization's founding assembly, for example, Davor Perinović, the first president of the Croatian HDZ in Bosnia-Hercegovina, cautioned that "the enemies of Croats and Moslems never lay still."[7] Perinović also endorsed the traditional Croatian perspective that the Moslems of Bosnia-Hercegovina were Islamicized Croats and therefore were the natural ally of other Croats within and outside the republic. Even Perinović, however, soon came under attack from more nationalistic Croats in Bosnia-Hercegovina, who believed that their party organization should maintain closer ties with Tudjman's HDZ headquarters in Zagreb. Some HDZ hawks went so far as to advocate Zagreb's annexation of predominantly Croatian areas in western Hercegovina or at least considerable political autonomy for that region. The Moslem SDA was also divided between the more militant and religiously nationalistic majority in the party led by Alija Izetbegović (who had spent eight years in jail under the communists for his Islamic fundamentalist beliefs)[8] and a more moderate, secular faction led by Adil Zulfikarpašić, who prior to 1990 had lived for twenty years in Switzerland.[9] Less than two months before the Bosnian elections, Zulfikarpašić's minority moderates broke off from the SDA under pressure and formed the Moslem Bosjnak Organization (MBO).

The SDA's more nationalistic core stressed the need for suitable recognition of its ethnic group's relative majority status in Bosnia-Hercegovina and of Moslem religious values. It also opened the issue of Bosnia's territorial interest in the Sandjak, a predominantly Moslem area that had been divided between Serbia and Montenegro in 1945. Launching a Sandjak branch of his party in June 1990, SDA leader Izetbegović argued that should Serbia and Montenegro decide to unify in some future new federation or confederation, the Moslems of the Sandjak would demand both cultural and political autonomy. As for Bosnia-Hercegovina, however, even center-right Moslem leaders such as Izetbegović conceded that in view of the republic's tripartite ethnic composition and traditions, and also the fact that no single party was likely to obtain a majority in the upcoming election, some kind of a coalition government should be formed in Sarajevo, preferably from among the three major noncommunist nationalist parties. Moreover, endeavoring to find a middle way between the sovereignty schemes of the most nationalistic Serbs and Croats (who threatened to divide Bosnia-Hercegovina between themselves), Izetbegović emphasized the distinctiveness and complexity of Bosnia-Hercegovina's ethnic composition and also the need for the preservation of its existing borders. "Bosnia has lasted 1,000 years. I do not see any reason to break it up now. Bosnia is impossible to divide, because it is such a mixture of nationalities, just like the apartment bloc where I live."[10]

During the election campaign, Izetbegović remained noncommittal about Bosnia-Hercegovina's future ties with the HDZ government in Zagreb, despite Serbian anxiety about a future confederative alliance between Croatia's Tudjman and Bosnia-Hercegovina's Moslem nationalists and the even greater threat that the republic might become totally detached from the Yugoslav state. "I know Mr. Tudjman, and respect him," observed Izetbegović. "When I say he is a Croatian nationalist, one must not forget that one can be a nationalist in the positive sense. Perhaps his course is a bit too Croatian-oriented for our taste, but he has his right to be that way, to fight for his people."[11] Explicitly adopting the tactics of the interwar Bosnian Moslem centrists (the Yugoslav Moslem Party, or JMO) who sought advantages for their own group by straddling the Serbian-Croatian confrontation, both in Bosnia-Hercegovina and Yugoslavia in general, Izetbegović explained:

> The Croats and the Serbs determined the character of Yugoslavia, and will to a large extent determine it in the future. We must adopt a balancing posture in that situation, and thereby maintain our national interests....Intelligent and conscious people in Bosnia desire to maintain their independent position toward both Croatia and Serbia. Moslem national consciousness is the only answer to the great-state pretensions from both sides. We are neither Serbs nor Croats, and that must be clear.[12]

As the election campaign progressed, Izetbegović endeavored to project evenhandedness toward his ethnic neighbors in Bosnia-Hercegovina, undoubtedly hoping to emerge as the primary political actor in the republic and also to maximize his leverage in any future interrepublican negotiations on Yugoslavia's future. The Moslem leader, however, found it difficult to mask his bitterness about Serbian attacks on Moslem nationalism and his more positive estimation of Croatian behavior.

> The Serbian minister of Foreign Affairs...and the vice-president of the Serbian Executive Council go to Israel and the people living there convince

them, and adopt them as allies in the struggle against some kind of Islamic conspiracy against Yugoslavia and Europe. To me that shows unbelievable political blindness. We see that as a search 2,000 miles away for allies against your fellow citizens. We are not aware of anything similar in Zagreb...the writing of the Belgrade press also is excessively anti-Moslem, while in Zagreb there is no such effort....For us in Bosnia the behavior of our Bosnian Serbs is what is really important, but regarding this we will make no comments.[13]

In the two-round elections held during late November and December 1990, the three major nationalist parties in Bosnia-Hercegovina made a clear sweep in their respective ethnic constituencies, confounding trends identified by many observers and public opinion polls which indicated that voters would support parties espousing nonethnic or cross-ethnic programs. Utilizing electoral arrangements that combined features of both the majority system and the proportional representation system, 202, or 84 percent, of the 240 seats in the republic's two chamber legislature were awarded to the three leading ethnic party organizations: 87 seats (33.8 percent) to the [Moslem] Party of Democratic Action, 71 seats (29.6 percent) to the Serbian Democratic Party, and 44 seats (18.3 percent) to the Croatian Democratic Alliance. The reformed communists and their left-wing allies won only 18 seats in the new legislature, or less than 8 percent of the seats, and the Bosnian branch of Prime Minister Marković's Alliance of Reform Forces elected only 13 legislators (5.4 percent).

The leader of the Serbian Democratic Party attributed the defeat of the Yugoslav-oriented reform Alliance to the Serbs' ethnically based preference for freedom to live together in their own state (i.e., the Yugoslav federation or, in lieu of that, in an enlarged Serbia) rather than the "bread, democracy, and dollars" platform of Prime Minister Marković.[14] Although the communists and Marković reformers together offered a small nonnationalist opposition voice to the three dominant ethnic parties, the weakened position of the "Yugoslav option" in Bosnia-Hercegovina was reflected in the ethnic composition of the newly elected representatives. Thus, whereas 9 percent of all delegates in the previous legislature had been self-defined as "Yugoslavs," members of that group constituted only 2.9 percent of the new multiparty legislature, and all belonged to the opposition ranks. Croats made up one-fifth of both the former and the new legislative assembly, but the proportion of Moslems rose from 37 percent to 41 percent, and Serbs from 31 percent to 35 percent.[15] In the new multiparty Bosnia-Hercegovina, ethnic representation was certainly more genuine and spontaneous than under the communist regime—when the composition of legislative bodies was balanced according to a mandated "ethnic key"—but there was now little room for legislators committed to any pan-ethnic form of political identification.

Bosnia-Hercegovina's strategically important geographic location at the center of Yugoslavia, the interspersion of ethnoreligious groups throughout the republic, and the area's traditional role as a meeting ground and contested territory for Serbs and Croats were all factors contributing to the polarization of the electorate along distinct ethnic lines in 1990—a very serious and threatening matter for those forces hoping to preserve the cohesion of the Yugoslav state. Attempting to at least temporarily maintain interethnic harmony in the republic in the wake of an electoral contest that had bitterly divided voters, the leaders of the three nationalist parties negotiated a shaky coalition government in which ministerial positions and administrative posts were distributed along ethnic lines. The SDA leader, Alija Izetbegović, was elected president of a seven-member multiethnic presidency; a Croat from the HDZ was selected as prime minister; and a Serb from the SDS was chosen to be president of the republic's legislature. However, in view of their varied ethnopolitical commitments and contrasting perspectives on the best way to reorganize the Yugoslav federation, the effort by the three coalition partners to jointly govern proved to be a nearly impossible task.[16] Any glimmer of hope that a tripartite model of rule might succeed gradually dimmed under the strain of other developments that would soon threaten the unity of the country and seriously exacerbate interethnic conflict.

Macedonia:
A Fragile Identity in Search of Sovereignty

The polarization of nationalist forces in Bosnia-Hercegovina was a potentially disturbing factor in Yugoslavia's political development, but the character of emergent pluralism in other republics also had important consequences for the cohesion of the country. Only one week before the elections in Bosnia-Hercegovina, voters in Macedonia went to the polls in the first round of a competitive electoral process that would stretch into late December. As in other Yugoslav republics, a spate of new parties had emerged in Macedonia over the previous six months, the majority of which were committed to various ethnopolitical goals. By the time the election was held, over twenty parties were operating in Macedonia, although only a half dozen would emerge as major electoral contenders. The two most important parties espousing a nationalist platform on behalf of ethnic Macedonian voters were the Movement for Pan-Macedonian Action (MAAK) and the Internal Macedonian Revolutionary Organization-Democratic Party for Macedonian National Unity (VMRO-DPMNE). A third important nationalist party, the Party of Democratic Prosperity (PDPM), represented most of Macedonia's Albanian population (which constituted 19.8 percent of the republic's population in the 1981 census). The PDPM not only endeavored to represent the republic's large Albanian community concentrated in western Macedonia but was also closely linked and sympathetic to the goals of Albanians living in adjacent Kosovo and in Montenegro.

The rather moderate anti-communist nationalists in MAAK advocated a "spiritual union of all Macedonians" in a sovereign Macedonian state that would be affiliated with a confederally organized Yugoslav state but no longer subject to Serbian "hegemonism." VMRO-DPMNE, meanwhile, comprised more radical nationalist elements that had split off from MAAK and had claimed the mantle of the infamous and violent Internal Macedonian Revolutionary Organization (IMRO) which had been active in both Macedonia and Bulgaria between the two world wars. VMRO-DPMNE was strongly committed to Macedonian sovereignty, possibly in some kind of future Yugoslav confederation but preferably, in the opinion of most party militants, through some form of union with Macedonians from Yugoslavia, Bulgaria, and Greece. United in their desire for Macedonian political autonomy, and also in their strong opposition to the growing political influence of the republic's Albanian community, MAAK and VMRO-DPMNE (together with three smaller parties) formed an electoral coalition known as the All-Macedonian National Front.

Other prominent parties that not only explicitly focused on a nationalist platform, but also sought enhanced recognition for Macedonian sovereignty in some type of "Yugoslav framework," included the League of Communists of Macedonia-Party of Democratic Transformation (SK-PDP), the federally-based Alliance of Reform Forces (SRSJ), and the Socialist Party (SPM). Although the reform communists had initially supported the existing federal structure, by the early fall of 1990 their leader, Petar Gošev, was advocating a position similar to the confederal sentiments emanating from the new postcommunist governments in Slovenia and Croatia.

Anxious to distance themselves from the popular perception that they were under the influence of Serbian nationalists in Belgrade, Gošev and the Macedonian communists endorsed the idea of "Macedonian identity and dignity" within a reorganized political system.

> We will organize Macedonia as a sovereign state which accepts union
> with other peoples of Yugoslavia only on a voluntary and equal basis, and
> of course with the right of secession....Yugoslavia is possible at this
> moment only as a union of sovereign states with those delegated and
> agreed powers at the union level that each of the several members of the
> union is willing to delegate without pressure. It seems to me that the time
> has come when we can reach togetherness only "from the bottom
> up"...."Yugoslavization" of Macedonia would be pernicious for all its
> citizens.[17]

Despite their various programmatic differences, all of the major
Macedonian parties shared a general commitment to the republic's
sovereignty and at least temporary association with the other parts of the
disintegrating Yugoslav federation. There was also general agreement on
the need for further market-oriented economic reforms along the lines of
Prime Minister Marković's federal policies as well as closer ties to the
European Community. Such consensus was hardly surprising in view of
Macedonia's poor economic situation, its landlocked geographical
position, and also the strong opposition to the territorial and nation-
building aspirations of ethnic Macedonians traditionally exhibited by
neighboring countries and non-Macedonian ethnic groups. For most
Greeks, for example, the name "Macedonia" merely constitutes a
"geographical expression" that is appropriately applied to the existing
northern Greek province of Macedonia, but should not be used as a state
designation by some agglomeration of South Slav inhabitants who happen
to be living within Yugoslavia and wish to establish an independent
country to the north of Greece. For most Bulgarians, the territory of
Macedonia represents an extension of their own state's historic patrimony,
and its Slavic inhabitants represent a branch of the Bulgarian ethnic tree.
Among Albanians, within or outside Albania, Macedonians are just one of
several hostile Balkan Slavic groups who historically have endeavored to
dominate the area's quite sizable Albanian population.

Most Serbs, in contrast, have traditionally viewed Macedonia as the
southern part of their historic state territory and see its inhabitants as
South Slavic junior cousins who should cheerfully accept Serbian political
tutelage. Recaptured from Ottoman Turkey at the end of the Balkan
Wars, Macedonia was designated as "South Serbia" by the Belgrade
government throughout the interwar period, and it was only in 1945 that
Tito's one-party regime recognized Macedonia as one of six constituent
units in the new Yugoslav communist federation. Such short-lived and
restricted experience in modern national and state development, together

with the serious challenges to Macedonian territorial and ethnic identity from neighboring states and peoples, contributed to a certain ambivalence on the part of Macedonia's fledgling parties to clarify the details of their republic's future position in relation to other parts of Yugoslavia or with respect to other well-established Balkan states. Clearly the idea of "sovereignty" enjoyed widespread appeal as a means of fostering and preserving the very fragile Macedonian identity. However, the steps necessary to invest this notion with form and substance were left vague by all political parties at the time of the 1990 election.

The outcome of the long election process did little to evoke coherence or certainty regarding Macedonia's future course of action. Despite the use of a majority-type electoral system, none of the major parties competing for seats to the 120-member unicameral legislature were able to secure the 61 seats necessary for an absolute parliamentary majority. The nationalist VRMO-DPMNE was the most successful party, obtaining a plurality of 38 seats (31.7 percent) in the legislature. Unfortunately for VMRO-DPMNE, however, its leader, the 25-year-old poet, Ljubčo Georgievski, failed in his own bid to win a legislative mandate. The reform communists ranked next with 31 seats (25.8 percent), followed by the Albanian PDPM with 17 seats (14.2 percent) and the Macedonian branch of Prime Minister Marković's Alliance of Reform Forces with 11 seats (9.2 percent). The remaining 23 seats were distributed among several smaller parties, 5 of which belonged to Albanian organizations jointly sponsored by the PDPM and the smaller National Democratic Party.

The strong appeal of the nationalist VMRO-DPMNE, and the relatively poor showing for Marković's Yugoslav oriented reform forces were surprising developments to many observers who had expected the republic's population to endorse a moderate course of development.[18] Meanwhile, the communists remained in a kind of limbo, with more parliamentary representatives than their defeated comrades in Bosnia-Hercegovina, Croatia, and Slovenia but no longer in a position to control events, even with the help of the left-oriented reformers from Marković's Alliance of Reform Forces. Such a highly fragmented outcome—with federally oriented reformers, national communists, and two ethnically opposed anti-communist nationalist parties all pitted against one another—was a recipe for interparty bickering, short-lived coalitions, and constant parliamentary crises, all well-known features of highly polarized multiparty legislatures. After considerable wrangling, the Macedonian Assembly adopted a Declaration of Sovereignty in January 1991. Shortly thereafter the government managed to elect Kiro Gligorov, an experienced communist, as president of the republic, but it was not until late March that a new government of mainly nonparty experts was finally selected. The Declaration of Sovereignty asserted that the independence and territorial integrity of the Macedonian peoples, based upon their right to self-determination and secession, should be guaranteed in a forthcoming constitution and validated through a popular referendum. Although the declaration also envisioned an equal role for Macedonia in forthcoming interrepublican negotiations on Yugoslavia's future, the deep political divisions in the republic, and also its chronic identity crisis, suggested that the practical projection of sovereignty and influence would not be an easy task.

Pluralism Without Change:
The Elections in Serbia and Montenegro

In early December, following elections in Bosnia-Hercegovina and the first phase of voting in Macedonia, Serbia and Montenegro were the only two republics where ruling communists had not been subjected to the baptism of free elections. Although in July the Milošević regime had grudgingly supported legislation legalizing multiparty pluralism and scheduling future elections in the republic (and had also reconfigured the Serbian League of Communists as the Socialist Party of Serbia), the fundamental spirit of competitive party politics remained antithetical to the mindset of the ruling authorities in Belgrade. Thus although a pluralist electoral process had begun, the Serbian regime's authoritarian cast would soon complicate political opportunities for the republic's proliferating opposition parties.

Having already promulgated a custom-made constitution in September 1990 proclaiming Serbia's sovereignty (a maneuver that had previously been legitimated in a popular referendum on the draft constitution), Milošević entered the electoral campaign in a very strong position. Moreover, although he faced growing criticism from the republic's new opposition forces, the Serbian leader still enjoyed immense popularity as a spokesman for Serbian interests and Serbia's enhanced role in a remodeled Yugoslav federation. Free elections, however, would expose Milošević to the first major challenge to his established political power. Whereas he had successfully utilized conventional methods of factional infighting to attain his position as the top communist leader in Serbia, and had subsequently employed plebiscitarian-type techniques ("street democracy") to rally the Serbian people around his eclectic platform of nationalist and warmed-over socialist principles, Milošević now faced a plethora of noncommunist and anti-communist parties each promising voters attractive platforms espousing a mixture of nationalism, economic progress, and democracy.

As the electoral process in Serbia acquired momentum in fall 1990, over three dozen competing parties had entered the fray and the number of new organizations was steadily growing. Generally speaking, most of these parties were small and poorly organized anti-regime groups that were both internally factionalized and extremely reluctant to cooperate in any joint opposition to Milošević's SPS. The two most powerful opposition parties were the Serbia Movement for Renewal (SPO) headed by Vuk Drašković, a bearded and mystic-looking writer and former junior communist official who had been trained as a lawyer and the Democratic Party (DS), jointly headed by Professor Dragoljub Mićunović and a small group of other leading Belgrade intellectuals. Both the SPO and DS were anti-communist, but like most other opposition parties they shared the Belgrade regime's strong commitment to Serbian national interests and a remodeled Yugoslav federation. As with Milošević's SPS, the SPO and DS also supported continued Serbian political control over Kosovo (with its 90 percent Albanian population) and opposed the establishment of a confederated South Slav state unless border changes were made to preserve the unity of the Serbian people currently living in the different Yugoslav republics.

Indeed, survey interviews probing the major parties at the time of the election revealed that the intensity of nationalist feeling was actually stronger among members of the SPO and DS than among supporters of Milošević's SPS (Figure 5.1). Thus although the SPO and DS leadership were highly critical of the regime's quasi-authoritarian features as well as its penchant for socialist formulas, they were strongly committed to the affirmation and protection of Serbian nationalist interests—a concern that they believed to be compatible with the pragmatic maintenance of a unified Yugoslavia. Vuk Drašković, for example, who eventually emerged as Milošević's most formidable rival within the fragmented opposition camp, was outspoken regarding his primary loyalty:

> I am not a Yugoslav, and there are no conditions that would make me a Yugoslav. Because that would mean I'm 18 percent Croat, 15 percent Shiptar [Albanian], 8 percent Slovene....And I really, as much as I would wish otherwise, can't feel anything other than a Serb and—a man. I think that Yugoslavia is the greatest error and misfortune of the Serbian people....At the same time that misfortune shouldn't be compounded by a new misfortune of destroying Yugoslavia.[19]

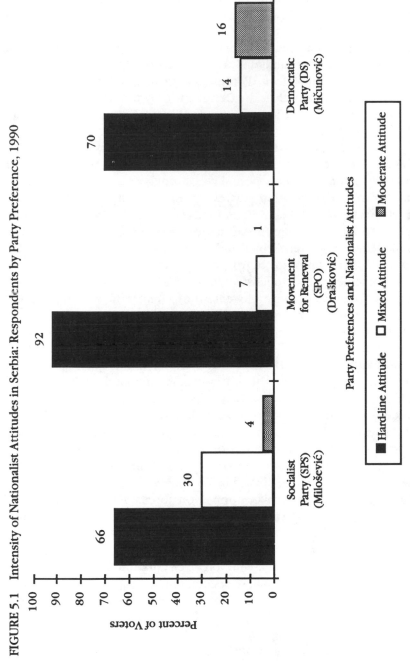

FIGURE 5.1 Intensity of Nationalist Attitudes in Serbia: Respondents by Party Preference, 1990

Source: Srečko Mihailović, "Izbori 90: mnjenje gradjana Srbije," in Srečko Mihailović, Vladimir Goati, et al., Od Izbornih rituala do slobodnih izbora (Belgrade: Institut Društvenih Nauka), 1991, p. 121.

Against a background of rising ethnopolitical fervor, some of the smaller Serbian opposition parties and quasi-party groups did make an effort to stake out a "third option," between the center-right anti-communist nationalism of the SPO and DS on the one side and Milošević's ruling communist nationalism on the other. In this regard, the most notable centrist and fundamentally nonnationalistic parties were the pro-Marković Alliance of Reform Forces and small intellectual dominated quasi-party groupings such as the Democratic Forum, the Association for a Yugoslav Democratic Initiative, and the Liberal Forum. Unfortunately, the nonnationalistic moderate groups and others sharing their views, such as the National Peasants' Party, made little headway in the struggle to challenge the dominant mood of Serbian nationalism, which had been successfully tapped by Milošević and was strongly reflected in the outlook of the two major opposition parties. Meanwhile, at the fringes of the political spectrum in Serbia, waiting for the entire exercise in competitive pluralism to falter, were extreme nationalists such as Vojislav Šešelj's Chetnik Movement (Šešelj had earlier been expelled from the SPO), which was officially prohibited from participating in the election because of its endorsement of nationalist violence, and even conservative leftists such as the New Communist Movement of Yugoslavia, which sought to restore the Titoist system.[20]

Parties organized along ethnopolitical lines tended to have the most appeal among the republic's non-Serb population. In Kosovo, for example, the pro-Albanian Kosovo Democratic Alliance was the largest party. Like other Albanian groups in the province, it encouraged the Albanian population to boycott the Serbian election as a protest against the Belgrade government's suppression of Kosovo's autonomy. In Serbia's other province, Vojvodina, the large Hungarian community strongly supported the Democratic Union of Vojvodina Hungarians. Ethnically oriented parties were also formed to represent the Gypsy minority, the Moslems of Serbia, and the Croats in Vojvodina.

Although the major Serbian opposition forces waged an aggressive electoral campaign, they suffered from a number of major disadvantages including limited financial resources, organizational inexperience, and, perhaps most important, Milošević's near-monopoly control over the republic's television, radio, and large-circulation newspapers and magazines. Early in the campaign, several of the cooperating opposition parties threatened to boycott the election unless the regime adopted a more democratic electoral law granting broader media access to the new parties and accommodating other concerns, such as the right to monitor the voting process. Such opposition tactics, however, were largely unsuccessful in modifying the regime's determination to fully utilize the traditional privileges of one-party control, especially Milošević's well-oiled propaganda machine.

Regime spokesmen characterized the threat of a boycott as "disloyalty," calculating that the yearning of the opposition for legitimate representation would ultimately ensure their participation in the election. Indeed, many opposition leaders were painfully aware that a sustained boycott and a decision to turn to extra-institutional protest would be of only limited value to Serbia's democratic development and would probably also be counterproductive in their efforts to displace the Milošević regime. As one of the leaders of the Democratic Party aptly observed: "Perhaps power is in the streets, but democracy isn't."[21] Concerned about potential international protests that the electoral results were not democratic or legitimate, Milošević eventually decided to permit limited media access for the new parties in October. Following yet another boycott threat in November, the regime also finally met opposition demands for participation in the vote count.

In the December 9, 1990 election, more than 50 parties competed for the 250 seats in Serbia's unicameral legislature. Thirty-two candidates (12 were sponsored by parties and 20 were independent citizens) also competed in a separate race for president of the republic. The results were a stunning victory for Milošević and his SPS, with Milošević obtaining two-thirds of the votes cast for president under the majority (double-round) electoral system and the SPS capturing 194 seats (77.6 percent) in the legislature. The remaining 56 legislative seats were divided among 14 parties, 7 of which were awarded 1 seat each. The SPO was the largest opposition winner with 19 (7.6 percent) of the legislative seats and its leader, Drašković, receiving 16.4 percent of the vote in the presidential contest. Prime Minister Marković's Alliance of Reform Forces won only 2 seats, both in the multiethnic province of Vojvodina. The Democratic Party took only 7 seats (2.8 percent), a particularly poor showing in view of the party's aggressive campaign. Almost all opposition gains—including the defeat of some Milošević cronies in Belgrade and in the largest cities of Vojvodina—were made after 20 of the new parties formed a coalition (the United Opposition of Serbia) to contest the runoff round of the legislative elections.

Beyond Milošević's grip on the media, his exceptional resources, and demonstrated popular nationalist appeal, opposition parties attributed their defeat to several additional reasons. Perhaps the most important factors discussed in this regard were the population's lack of experience with democratic competition after a long period of authoritarian rule and the strong tendency toward political conformism in Serbian political culture. Indeed, it was pointed out that throughout Serbian political history the successful political party was invariably the party that had organized the elections and that the ascendancy of new parties followed only some major destabilizing event or exceptional political episode. Fear of change on the part of the Serbian electorate was also considered an important factor in the Milošević victory. The electoral slogan employed by the SPS—"With Us There Is No Uncertainty"—not only appealed to voters worried about the political turbulence and economic deterioration in Yugoslavia during 1989 and 1990 but was also especially convincing to the thousands of state employees and their families in Serbia, who feared that additional disruption might flow from the defeat of the ruling socialist authorities. Many Serbian citizens directing the state apparatus and economy were particularly worried about the danger of postsocialist revanchism, which might seek scapegoats for earlier mismanagement. A portion of the working class also feared that opposition support for privatization of the economy would result in rampant unemployment. The insecurity of that "parastate stratum"—including thousands of "socialist pensioners" and members of the military forces—translated, it was observed, into considerable support for Milošević at the ballot box.[22]

Fear of change also affected other conservative strata, such as the highly nationalistic agrarian population of southeastern Serbia that, though never especially enthusiastic about socialist ideals, preferred to support a seasoned politician such as Milošević, who had an established record of standing up for Serbian interests. Unlike the reform communists of Slovenia and Croatia, who had endorsed nationalist views only after they were challenged by anti-communist nationalist parties, the reconfigured communists directed by Milošević had established their nationalist credentials several years prior to the appearance of competing parties. Some SPS supporters voted for the party based on their unshakable belief in socialist policies, a view that continued to be shared by many voters in the underdeveloped areas of Serbia throughout the postwar period.

Survey interviews with voters both before and after the election revealed that support for the leading opposition parties was considerably higher in the larger cities, among voters under 35 years of age, and in the intelligentsia (Table 5.1). Voters who felt that Milošević's nationalism was either too strident or, just as frequently, too moderate, also supported the opposition. Nearly two-thirds of the seats taken by opposition parties were in the multiethnic province of Vojvodina—with its large Hungarian minority and its traditional Serbian reservations about Belgrade-based political control—and in the metropolitan Belgrade area, with its high percentage of university students, better educated citizens, and more prevalent traditions of political nonconformism. In contrast, the dwindling and very anxious Serbian population of Kosovo voted overwhelmingly for Milošević, who had begun his meteoric career by arousing Serbian sentiments in that province. The majority Albanians in the region boycotted the election, as they had threatened.

The majority electoral system employed in the 1990 Serbian election also favored the better-organized Socialist Party, which had inherited a republic-wide political organization from its communist predecessors.

TABLE 5.1   Social Background of Party Supporters in the 1990 Serbian Election (in percent)

	Socialist Party of Serbia (SPS)	Serbian Movement for for Renewal (SPO)	Democratic Party (DS)
Location of Residence			
Village	32	28	12
Small town	13	13	5
City	34	36	45
Large city	21	23	38
Age			
29 and younger	13	35	30
30-39	20	27	27
40-49	22	18	26
50-59	23	12	12
60 and older	22	8	5
Education			
No or incomplete elementary	18	6	2
Elementary school	25	17	8
Secondary workers' school	26	32	18
Other secondary (technical and employee)	20 ⎱ 51	31 ⎱ 45	33 ⎱ 72
Postsecondary	31 ⎰	14 ⎰	39 ⎰

Source: Srečko Mihailović, "Izbori 90: mnjenje gradjana Srbije," in Srečko Mihailović, Vladimir Goati, *et al.*, *Od Izbornih rituala do slobodnih izbora* (Belgrade: Institut Društvenih Nauka), 1991, pp. 89-90, 96-97, 100-101.

Thus with the local power structure still in the hands of lower-ranking socialist functionaries, the SPS found it relatively easy to obtain pluralities throughout Serbia.[23] But the strength of the opposition parties tended to be concentrated in only a few distinct locales and, owing to the short span of party pluralism in Serbia, was far less entrenched. As a result, although the SPS received less than half the total popular votes in the election, the comprehensive distribution of its votes in constituencies throughout the republic entitled them to take 77.6 percent of the seats in the legislature. When the relatively low turnout in the election—71.5 percent of the eligible voters in the first round and 48.3 percent in the second round—is considered together with the advantages accruing to large and established parties under the majority electoral system, the relative narrow margin of the Milošević victory becomes apparent. For example, in the first round of the election only 32 percent of all registered voters in Serbia actually voted for Milošević's SPS, or 46 percent of those turning out in the election, but his party was nevertheless awarded 91 percent of the 96 seats decided in the first electoral contest. Ironically, despite the low rate of participation, the various localized instances of voter intimidation and procedural improprieties, and the considerable advantages enjoyed by the SPS as the entrenched regime party, the 1990 election in Serbia was still much more democratic than the one-party (albeit plural-candidate) electoral "rituals" held by the former communist regime.[24]

On December 9, Milošević's allies in neighboring Montenegro also won an impressive electoral victory. Under a proportional electoral system with more than 20 parties competing, the ruling League of Communists of Montenegro (SKM) won 83 seats (66.4 percent) in the 125-person legislature. SKM chief, Momir Bulatović, also won a three-way run-off race for president of Montenegro with 42.2 percent of the votes. Bulatović and other younger communists had first come to power in January 1989, when they had used techniques borrowed from Milošević's populist anti-bureaucratic revolution to oust established communist officials. Marković's federally oriented Alliance of Reform Forces won 17 seats (13.6 percent), and the People's Party, favoring a union of Serbia and Montenegro in a new federal Yugoslav state, took 12 seats (9.6 percent). Several small Moslem and Albanian parties operating together in the Democratic Alliance won 13 seats (10.4 percent).

Communism's popular roots in Montenegro (going back to before World War II) undoubtedly played an important role in the SKM victory, but, as in Serbia, conformism, support for the established order, and fear of change were more significant factors than mass enthusiasm for communist ideological precepts. Montenegrin enthusiasm for Milošević's communist nationalism, and his tough stance against the nationalist activities of Yugoslavia's Moslems and Albanians (who together composed one-fifth of Montenegro's population in 1991), also accounted for the success of the SKM. A great many Montenegrins still shared, as Milovan Djilas explained in an historical assessment of his native land, "an age old dream—the alliance of the two Serbian states....If they were for Montenegro out of necessity and feeling, their thoughts were of Serbia."[25] There were also, as Branko Horvat suggested, pragmatic reasons for the Montenegrins to support the communists:

> Montenegrins are undoubtedly the best Yugoslavs....For them Yugoslavia is simply an extraordinarily broadened possibility to achieve positions which carry great respect in their milieu. They become generals, state and party functionaries in numbers disproportionate to the size of their ethnic group. They accomplished this up until now through the communist party. Montenegrins became members of the communist party more than any other group. Consequently why would a people, where one still knows who originates from which tribe, change a party which has been shown to be such a good instrument of satisfying traditional aspirations.[26]

The Fruits of Pluralism

The elections of 1990, and particularly the status quo pluralist outcome in Serbia and Montenegro, would prove to be extremely important for the future of the Yugoslav state. First, the elections legitimated the strong political divisions already present between the newly elected anti-communist nationalists (many of whom were former communist officials) in Slovenia and Croatia and the victorious communist nationalists of Serbia and Montenegro. In this regard, support for Milošević and his Montenegrin communist allies was especially significant, emboldening them to maintain their opposition to ideas being advanced in Slovenia and Croatia (and which by fall 1990 seemed to be gaining more support in Bosnia-Hercegovina and Macedonia), for the transformation of Yugoslavia into a loose confederation of sovereign states. Thus, two out of the country's six republics, Serbia and Montenegro were now firmly committed to the creation of a reorganized federation with a strong central government that would enable all ethnic Serbs to remain in a single state. Divergent conceptions of future state development—the federalism versus confederalism debate—were now on a collision course unless a major compromise could be negotiated.

Second, the electorally validated division between communist and anti-communist (or noncommunist) nationalists also reinforced the important conflict between Serbian nationalism and non-Serbian nationalism within and among the different regions of the country. Newly elected center-right nationalist leaders outside Serbia and Montenegro could now argue domestically, and also to members of the international community, that they were struggling not just against the hegemonic pretensions of Serbian nationalism but also against the last bastion of "Bolshevism" in Europe. That viewpoint seemed to gain some credence in November 1990 when a group of communist politicians from Montenegro, Serbia, and Bosnia-Hercegovina, including Milošević's wife, joined with several high-ranking Serbian and non-Serbian conservative military officers in Belgrade to establish a new federally oriented communist organization, the League of Communists-Movement for Yugoslavia (SK-PJ). Claiming they would support any political party endorsing socialism and federalism in the remaining republican elections, or a proposed federal election (that never took place), the framers of the SK-PJ pointedly did not invite reform communists from other republics or Prime Minister Marković's Alliance of Reform Forces, to participate in the new movement. Anti-communists and reform communists outside Serbia, and liberal forces within the republic, looked upon the SK-PJ leadership as a "military-political clique" closely tied to Milošević's SPS and determined to maintain the Yugoslav federation at any cost.

Finally, the elections of 1990 also clarified the weakness of those political forces that were focused on transcending interregional and interethnic divisions in Yugoslavia. Thus, the Marković-led Alliance of Reform Forces had been able to win only 50 out of 735 seats in the four republican elections it contested. Moreover, with no prospect of a federal election in sight, citizen allegiances were now firmly centered on the increasingly "sovereign" republican political systems and their contending elites, a development that further weakened the already shallow support enjoyed by the federal government in most regions. "Yugoslavism," or "Yugoslav" consciousness, was becoming an increasingly rare phenomenon, and a perspective lacking any important political-organizational underpinning.

Notes

1. In 1991 Bosnia-Hercegovina had approximately 4,364,574 inhabitants, distributed as follows: Moslems 1,905,829; Serbs, 1,369,258; Croats, 755,895; "Yugoslavs," 239,845; others, 93,747.

2. For the development of Moslem political consciousness see Atif Purivatra, *Nacionalni i politički razvitak Muslimana* (Sarajevo: Svjetlost, 1972).

3. Seven of the Bosnian communes with large Serbian communities border directly on Croatia and are known as the "Bosanska krajina" region. Together with the "Kninska krajina" region the entire area is sometimes simply referred to as "the Krajina" and is understood to be the epicenter of Serbian ethnopolitical activity in Croatia and Bosnia-Hercegovina.

4. Cited in Slaven Letica, *Obećana zemlja: Politički antimemoari* (Zagreb: Globus International, 1992), pp. 155-156.

5. *Borba*, November 10-11, 1990, p. 13.

6. Karadžić, like Rašković, is a psychiatrist, which may say something about the skills necessary for political leadership in the region during the early 1990s.

7. *FBIS-EEU*, August 20, 1990, p. 75.

8. Izetbegović, who was born in 1925 and received a higher education in law, was the principal defendant in the Sarajevo trial of thirteen Moslem intellectuals on charges of "hostile and counter-revolutionary activities" during July and August 1983. The chief evidence used by the prosecution in the trial was the treatise "The Islamic Declaration," written by Izetbegović. See *Sarajevski process: Sudjenje Muslimanskim intelekualcima 1983 g.* (Zurich: Bosanski Institut, 1987), pp. 236-269.

9. For an interesting account of Zulfikarpašić's views, see "The Moslems of Bosnia—A Peace Factor Between Croatians and Serbs," *South Slav Journal*, Vol. 6, No. 2 (Summer 1983), pp. 2-18.

10. *FBIS-EEU*, June 12, 1990, p. 60.

11. *Ibid.*, p. 60.

12. Alija Izetbegović, "Mi nismo turci," *Start*, No. 560 (July 7, 1990), pp. 35, 37.

13. *Ibid.*, p. 37.

14. Radovan Karadžić, "Zašto nije bilo stihije," *NIN*, No. 203, November 23, 1990, pp. 16-17.

15. *Službeni list SRB i H*, December 19, 1990, p. 1245.

16. In mid-June 1991, Bosnia-Hercegovina's Minister of the Interior Alija Delimustafić publicly admitted that the operation of his ministry was completely stalemated by the "Lebanonization" of the police and that the leaders of the three ethnic parties enjoyed influence which placed them above the law. He pointed out, for example, that if someone "interesting" happened to be arrested, the top party leaders "Izetbegović (SDA), or Karadžić (SDS), or Kljuić (HDZ) depending on the case, say: 'don't keep him, he is a good Moslem, or Serb, or Croat, (depending on the case), he gave 10,000 Marks to our party.'" Delimustafić also claimed that the intervention of ethnic parties in the allocation of jobs in Bosnia-Hercegovina exposed the administration of justice to "classic corruption," weakened the professional standards of the police, and reduced the authority of his ministry over police recruits who had essentially become segmented "party police." Dragica Pusonjić, "Ministar optužio lidere," *Vreme*, June 17, 1991, pp. 28-29.

17. *FBIS-EEU*, August 28, 1990, pp. 72-74.

18. M. Ilić and N. Djurić, "MAAK na konac," *Intervju*, November 9, 1990, pp. 74-76; and Ljuba Stojić, "Parlamentarna kriza," *NIN*, December 6, 1990, pp. 30-33.

19. Vanja Bulić, "Izmedju ideja i pameti," *Yu novosti*, No. 517 (April 23-May 15, 1990), p. 50.

20. Other small groupings were committed to various single-issue causes ranging from royalist restoration to environmentalism.

21. Zoran Djindjić, "Magla kabinetskog uma," *Borba*, October 13-14, 1990, p. 2.

22. Slobodan Antonović, "Odlučili neodlučni," *Stav*, January 11, 1991, pp. 12-13.

23. Desimir Tosić, "Kad svi podanici glasaju," *Borba*, February 9-10, 1991, p. 2.

24. Srečko Mihailović, Vladimir Goati, *et al.*, *Od izbornih rituala do slobodnih izbora* (Belgrade: Institut društvenih nauka, 1991).

25. *Land Without Justice* (New York: Harcourt Brace, 1958), p. 224.

26. "Više sutra nego danas," *Vreme*, January 21, 1991, p. 37.

6

Drifting Apart: "New" Elites and a Delegitimated Federation

In the nineteenth century, people thought that the Yugoslav idea would save the Slavs from the Germans, on the one side, and the Italians, on the other. But that was a romantic notion....Despite similarities in language, we cannot be together. Now nothing remains of the Yugoslav idea.

—Franjo Tudjman, President of Croatia (July 1990)

The Yugoslav idea has been in existence for almost two centuries. Yugoslavia as a state has existed for over seventy years....We cannot today allow political mediocrities and chameleons, self-professed leaders and demagogues, and incidental witnesses of tumultuous historical trends to bring it to its knees.

—General Veljko Kadijević, National Defense Secretary (December 1990)

THE COMPETITIVE ELECTIONS held in Yugoslavia's republics from April through December 1990 constituted a major watershed in the country's political development. In the space of nine months, the already fragmented League of Yugoslav Communists had either been swept from power or forced to enter into a dialogue with opposition forces in every region of the country. Although the "founding" elections were an impressive exercise in regime transition from one-party rule to competitive politics, the experience left the country even more politically fragmented than it had been in the last days of the one-party state. Indeed, as 1990 drew to a close, Yugoslavia's major republics had become relatively self-contained political units that were constitutionally equipped—in stark contravention of rulings by the country's highest judicial and legislative bodies—to challenge, or if regional elites deemed it necessary, to completely discard the already enfeebled federal system. Yugoslavia's most important republics were governed, moreover, by popularly legitimated political leaders devoted to sharply conflicting visions of the country's future constitutional organization.

In Serbia, for example, Slobodan Milošević, who had successfully consolidated his power in a competitive (albeit not fully democratic) election, was strongly committed to establishing what he termed a "modern federation," that is, an arrangement in which the country's dispersed Serbian population would remain united in a single state and acquire political influence commensurate with its position as Yugoslavia's largest ethnic group. In contrast, political leaders in Slovenia and Croatia supported the radical transformation of the existing federation into a "confederation of sovereign states," although they threatened to proceed with unilateral secession from the existing state should planned 1991 interrepublican negotiations on the country's future prove unsuccessful.

Before discussing the course and outcome of the negotiations on Yugoslavia's political reorganization during late 1990 and the first part of 1991 (see Chapter 7), this chapter first examines the characteristics of the political elites and leaders who had come to power, or who had consolidated their power, during the 1990 multiparty elections and the new political climate in which they were operating. In short, what kind of decisionmakers governed Yugoslavia's contending republics at the onset of 1991, and what was the political mood of the voters who elected them to power?

"New" Elites, Old Leaders, and Divided Followers

The Political Class in Flux

The collapse of single-party dominance, the proliferation of new political parties competing in hotly contested multiparty elections, and the emergence of nationalist regimes in each of the republics (directed by either reconfigured communists or noncommunists), profoundly altered the composition and outlook of the political leadership in Yugoslavia. An examination of the political and social characteristics of the legislators elected in the various republics during 1990, however, reveals some interesting aspects of both change and continuity.

Undoubtedly, the most striking break with the past was the appearance of elected deputies representing a variety of different parties and expressing sharply divergent points of view. Such party and opinion differentiation represented a clear contrast with the factionalized, but essentially oppositionless, legislatures that had functioned under the previous regime.[1] The deputies elected in 1990 also varied widely in their professional political experience. The majority had no prior experience as elected officeholders. But many others had been political officials in the communist regime and had recently changed their party affiliation. Still others had been dissidents and activists in various extraparliamentary opposition movements and associations. Although the novel exercise in party pluralism resulted in a transformed political class that was largely unfamiliar with the dynamics of a democratic polity, most legislators nevertheless viewed themselves as the architects of completely "new" regimes, legitimated by popular consent.

If the republican legislators elected in 1990 qualified as "new" in terms of their mode of election, party labels, and their previous legislative service, there were other facets of their political and social composition that could hardly be characterized as fresh or forward looking. Data on the age composition of the newly elected legislators in selected republics (Table 6.1), for example, reveal that on the whole these deputies are a considerably older group than their predecessors who served in the legislative assemblies during the last days of the communist regime. As might be expected, there are important differences among the republics with respect to the social background and characteristics of the new deputies, and among different party caucuses within each republic. For example, although on average the newly elected legislatures of Serbia, Croatia, and Slovenia all have an older age profile than the previous communist assemblies, the seasoned age makeup of the Serbian legislature at the end of 1990, dominated by a large majority from Milošević's ruling Socialist Party, stands out in comparison to the legislatures of Slovenia and Croatia. A very sharp drop in the number of women elected to the legislatures in those republics is also evident, with Serbia having the most male-dominated legislature and experiencing the most precipitous decline in female representation (from 23.5 percent in 1986 to 1.6 percent in 1991).

Although the legislative recruitment process under the communist regime was deliberately aimed at recruiting young people and women for symbolic purposes, most of the new parties participating in the competitive elections of 1990 were not as concerned with the age and

TABLE 6.1   Composition of Republican Legislatures, January-June 1991 (in percent)

	Bosnia-Hercegovina	Croatia	Macedonia	Slovenia	Montenegro	Serbia
Women deputies, 1991	2.9	1.5	4.1	11.2	3.2	1.6
Women deputies, 1986	27.6	15.0	17.2	24.0	11.5	7.9
Age of Deputies						
29 and younger	5.4	5.4	6.6	9.1	1.6	0.8
30-39	37.9	29.6	29.1	25.4	24.8	21.2
40-49	32.0	38.7	41.6	32.5	39.2	38.8
50-59	16.6	20.6	19.1	25.8	28.8	34.0
60 and older	7.9	5.4	3.3	7.0	5.6	5.2
Total	100.0	100.0	100.0	100.0	100.0	100.0
N	(240)	(351)	(120)	(240)	(125)	(250)
Nationality of Deputies						
Moslems	39.5	-	0.8	-	14.4	2.0
Croats	21.6	86.5	-	-	0.8	0.4
Macedonians	-	-	77.5	0.8	-	-
Slovenes	-	0.5	-	92.5	-	-
Montenegrins	-	-	-	-	67.2	5.2
Serbs	35.4	8.1	-	0.4	8.0	83.6
Yugoslavs	3.3	2.8	0.8	1.6	4.0	1.2
Albanians	-	-	19.1	-	5.6	-
Hungarians	-	-	-	0.8	-	0.8
Others	-	0.5	1.6	1.6	-	-
Unknown	-	1.4	-	-	-	-
Total	100.0	100.0	100.0	100.0	100.0	100.0
N	(240)	(356)	(120)	(240)	(125)	(250)

Source: Based on data supplied by the Federal Institute for Statistics (Belgrade 1991) and the Republican Electoral Commission of Croatia (Zagreb 1991).

gender of their candidates running for legislative office. Particularly in the case of the nationalistically oriented parties that achieved electoral success in 1990, it was the ethnicity of candidates and, even more important, their loyalty to ethnopolitical programs that constituted the primary criterion in legislative recruitment. The attraction of older males to the conservatism and traditional views of the nationalist parties, and possibly the aversion of younger people and many politically active women within each ethnic group to such political organizations, may also have played a role in the altered composition of the legislatures after 1990.[2] For example, other partial data reveal that there were relatively more women candidates seeking office on the lists of smaller opposition parties than on the lists of the successful nationalist parties. Whatever the reasons for the generational and generic changes, however, older and predominantly male deputies devoted to various nationalist platforms dominated the legislatures in the key republics of Serbia, Croatia, and Slovenia.

The most salient cleavages in the new legislatures of the more ethnically homogeneous republics (e.g., Slovenia, Serbia, and Montenegro) were among different parties and subgroups of deputies exhibiting "harder" or "softer" attitudes on nationalist issues and on the future role of the republics in the federation. In the legislatures of the more ethnically heterogeneous republics, however, the nationalist divisions and different perspectives regarding Yugoslavia's reorganization appeared to be linked to the sharp differentiation among parties representing different ethnic groups. For example, in Bosnia-Hercegovina, each one of the three rival nationalist party contingents in the legislature was ethnically homogeneous. Thus, legislators from the Serbian Democratic Party were all Serbs, those from the Croatian Democratic Alliance were all Croats, and those from the Moslem Party of Democratic Action were all Moslems. Only the small legislative caucuses from Prime Minister Marković's Alliance of Reform Forces, and the reformed communists were multiethnic in composition.

The occupational composition of the newly elected legislatures also revealed interesting facets of change and continuity. In Slovenia, for example, where the meltdown of the authoritarian communist system and the rise of a vigorous "civil society" had been under way for several years—exemplified by the proliferation of alternative social movements and party-like associations during the 1980s—a new generation of political activists eagerly sought and won legislative office. Very few members of the newly elected legislature in Slovenia were seasoned "sociopolitical workers" from the old regime, and those who were in that category—

mainly members of the reformed League of Communists—now preferred to identify themselves by occupational labels other than "politician." Not all of the relatively young Slovenian legislators from the victorious noncommunist opposition parties in 1990, however, were youth activists and political novices. Most of the Slovenian legislators were "intellectuals of the mid-generation" who had either deserted from the former ruling elite, or were mature individuals who had calculated that it was an opportune time for them to become politically involved. Another, but much smaller, group of the new Slovenian legislators elected in 1990 had worked as activists in the "alternative" media and various youth organizations during the 1980s, and were politically seasoned from their infighting with the former political establishment, and federal military officials.[3]

Why the former youth activists from the 1980s did not assume legislative and political decisionmaking positions in postcommunist Slovenia can be explained by several factors. Many of the earlier "regime critics" were unable to adapt to the new climate of legal multiparty competition, whereas others were marginalized by the leaders of the new center-right parties in the DEMOS coalition who generally distrusted the left-oriented youth activists of the 1980s. Moreover, most of the leaders in DEMOS were strongly oriented to an anti-communist and nationalist strategy— described by a Slovenian analyst as: "[one] who is against us, is against the nation"[4]—that left little room for "free-floating" or undisciplined styles of intellectual dissent that were so typical in earlier years. The new cabinet organized by DEMOS after their electoral victory in 1990 was quite young, including the 43-year-old Christian Democratic Prime Minister Peterle, and 18 out of 26 other ministers who were under 50 years of age. But for the most part, the new elite were drawn from the former practitioners of "anti-politics" who had been active in challenging the communist regime during the early 1980s. There were, however, important exceptions in the DEMOS coalition government. Thus, the youngest cabinet members in 1990—Janez Janša (32), who was the new Defense Minister, and Igor Bravčar (35), who was the new Minister of Internal Affairs—had been prominent activists in the opposition struggles with the communist military and political elite during the mid-1980s and had decided to become involved in party politics, even if this meant joining the establishment and managing the "repressive apparatuses of the state."[5]

At first glance, the occupational background data supplied by newly elected legislative deputies in Serbia would also seem to indicate a massive entry into the political class by members of the intelligentsia, in a pattern similar to that found in Slovenia.[6] Closer examination of such information, however, reveals that a large number of seasoned professional politicians from the Serbian communist regime, having migrated directly into Slobodan Milošević's ruling socialist party in mid-1990, simply chose to reclassify themselves (based on their educational backgrounds) as members of the humanistic and technical intelligentsia when seeking election. The Milošević regime did, however, co-opt for legislative candidacy a substantial number of genuine intellectuals, specialists, and other community notables who were generally former members of the League of Communists, sympathized with Milošević's nationalist goals, and had become SPS loyalists. Medical doctors and lawyers were especially favored in the SPS legislative recruitment strategy. For example, doctors constituted 18 percent of the SPS candidates for office and 20 percent of its elected deputies. Serbia's major opposition parties, the Serbian Movement for Renewal and the Democratic Party, also recruited a large number of doctors and lawyers to run as candidates for legislative posts, although the opposition lawyers were mainly self-employed professionals rather than state employees. Interestingly, neither the victorious Socialist Party nor the opposition saw the need for the recruitment of "direct producers" into a legislative role, that is, an occupational group that had been prominently featured under the old regime. Thus, the number of industrial and agricultural workers in the Serbian legislature declined from 30 percent in 1986 to 3 percent in 1990.

In Serbia, Milošević's winning SPS successfully utilized the familiar communist pattern of maintaining legislative control through the recruitment of professional politicians and the carefully selected co-optation of politically trustworthy members of the intelligentsia, a strategy that was also emulated by the electorally victorious Montenegrin League of Communists in 1990. Even in republics where the reconfigured communists suffered electoral defeat (Slovenia, Croatia, Bosnia-Hercegovina, and Macedonia), however, many of the members from the large contingent of the intelligentsia who had been recruited into the new parties and political leadership groups, and who now were either overtly anti-communist or noncommunist, had formerly been active members and sometimes officials in the League of Communists. As a Zagreb political scientist suggested in an analysis of political change in Croatia and Bosnia-Hercegovina during 1990:

> A large number of the members of the old elite succeeded in infiltrating the "new" elites, taking also into account those supporters of the old regime who at a particular moment in the past had been burned in the

[communist] struggles for power, and now returned as "avengers." In general the "new" methods of rule are the same as the old ways: managers and intellectuals, or specialists, and others are under [political] tutelage....Chances for modernization are thrown on the rubbish heap by the incessant intensification of political conflicts in the name of the national question, thereby ensuring for the populist elite a dominant position in society.[7]

The same writer also points to the diminished representation in the new political elites of groups such as the technical intelligentsia and managerial stratum—whose members tend to exhibit a commitment to "transethnic" professional values—a development that served to enhance the nationalistic orientation of new political decisionmakers.

Prior affiliation with the defunct League of Communists and a strong commitment to nationalist views were also characteristics shared by most of the top-ranking republican and federal leaders in Yugoslavia. For example, Alija Izetbegović, the president of Bosnia-Hercegovina, was the only republican president not formerly a prominent functionary of the communist regime (Table 6.2). Service on behalf of the old regime—not atypical for most politically active citizens over 30 years of age in Yugoslavia—did not, however, provide a bond that could compensate for significant differences of opinion dividing the country's principal leaders. Thus, with the exception of federal Prime Minister Marković, whose Croatian origin was submerged by his commitment to pragmatic pan-Yugoslav reform, all of the major leaders appeared to place parochial ethnic or regional interests above the fate of the country as a whole. Even Izetbegović, whose predisposition to the unity of Yugoslavia and his own republic had been shaped in his ethnically divided Bosnian environment, was strongly devoted to the concerns of his Moslem coreligionists, including the maintenance of their traditionally close relationship with ethnic Croatians.

Most of the new political leaders fell into three categories: (1) communist/socialist nationalists, such as Serbia's Milošević and Jović, and Montenegro's Bulatović; (2) regional nationalists, such as Slovenia's Kučan, and Macedonia's Gligorov (who had both tactfully shed their recent close association with the League of Communists); and (3) anti-communist nationalists, such as Croatia's Tudjman and Mesić (who had broken completely with the communist regime over two decades earlier). The fact that Izetbegović, Tudjman, and Mesić had all been jailed and harassed by the former regime naturally put them at odds with the Serbian and Montenegrin leaders who still professed support for the

TABLE 6.2   Principal Political Leaders in Yugoslavia (January-May 1991)

Republic Presidents		Age	Ethnopolitical Orientation/Background
Bosnia-Hercegovina	Alija Izetbegović	76	Moslem fundamentalist/anti-communist
Croatia	Franjo Tudjman	69	Croatian nationalist/communist
Slovenia	Milan Kučan	50	Slovene regional nationalist/reform communist
Macedonia	Kiro Gligorov	77	Macedonian regional nationalist/reform communist
Serbia	Slobodan Milošević	49	Serbian nationalist/communist
Montenegro	Momir Bulatović	35	Serbo-Montenegrin nationalist/communist
Federal prime minister	Ante Marković	66	"Yugoslav"/reform communist
Federal president	Borisav Jović[a]	63	Serbian nationalist/communist
Federal vice-president	Stipe Mesić[b]	57	Croatian nationalist/communist

[a]Resigns post on March 15, 1991, over presidency's failure to adopt emergency measures against Croatia and Slovenia. Resumes post on March 20.

[b]Scheduled to become president of collective state presidency on May 15, 1991, but blocked by Serbia and its allies. Assumes post of president on June 30, after compromise negotiated by European Community.

ideology of Yugoslav socialism. Thus, to some extent ideology and ethnicity reinforced each other in dividing the principal leaders of Yugoslavia's republics and the federation at the outset of 1991, although contending perspectives derived from divergent ethnoregional interests appeared to be the major basis for contention. These divisive factors, together with other problems that would influence leadership interaction (mutual distrust borne of recent experiences, personality conflicts, pressure from their respective constituencies) made it difficult to imagine that these leaders would be able to successfully negotiate the peaceful restructuring or dismantling of the Yugoslav state.

Trends in Public Opinion

The emergence of nationalist regimes in Yugoslavia's republics—each of which was governed by leaders having strong differences with their counterparts in the other republics and who were unwilling to accept direction from federal authorities—constituted both a cause and a consequence of intensifying interethnic divisions in the country's general population. A countrywide public opinion survey of over 4,000 citizens in Yugoslavia conducted in mid-1990 revealed (Table 6.3), for example, that Slovenes, Croats, and Albanians tended to attribute far less importance to their affiliation with Yugoslavia, than did groups such as the Moslems of Bosnia-Hercegovina, the Montenegrins, and the Serbs. Orientation to one's republic, rather than to Yugoslavia as a whole, had already become the primary focus of political allegiance for citizens of Slovenian background and, to a somewhat lesser extent, for Croatians as well.

The same survey research data (Figure 6.1) indicate very low levels of public support in Slovenia (17 percent) and Croatia (38 percent) for the notion that federal constitutional provisions should have precedence over republican constitutions. The percentage of those individuals surveyed from Croatia who supported the supremacy of the federal constitution dropped even lower—from 38 to 28 percent—when ethnic Croats in that republic were considered separately. In contrast, citizens of Bosnia-Hercegovina (70 percent), Montenegro (84 percent), Serbia (83 percent), and especially in the very Yugoslav-oriented province of Vojvodina (87 percent) were more supportive of the principle of federal constitutional paramountcy. It interesting that although citizens in Serbia were in the top rank of those supporting federal control, in actual practice Milošević and the Serbian regime behaved similarly to the leaders of Slovenia and Croatia when it came to adopting constitutional provisions and policies at variance with the federal constitution.[8]

TABLE 6.3   The Personal Attachment of Citizens in Yugoslavia to Different
Levels of Territorial Organization, May-June 1990 (in percent)*

| | Level of Territorial Affiliation | | |
Ethnic Group	Local	Republican/ Provincial	Yugoslavia
Slovenes	51	66	26
Croats	45	51	48
Macedonians	31	52	68
Moslems	43	50	84
Yugoslavs	25	32	71
Montenegrins	37	47	80
Serbs	36	51	71
Albanians	48	47	49
Hungarians	60	62	79
Others	37	43	58
Total Sample	39	52	62

*Percent of respondents in each ethnic group who felt a particular level of
affiliation was "quite important" or "very important" for them personally. Based
on interviews with 4,230 randomly sampled adults throughout the country.
     Source: Dragomir Pantić, "Širina grupnih identifikacija gradjana Jugoslavije:
Vrednovanje pripadnosti od lokalne do mondijalne," in Ljiljana Baćević *et al.*,
Jugoslavija na kriznoj prekretnici (Belgrade: Institut Društvenih Nauka, 1991),
p. 266.

Data from Yugoslavia's 1991 population census (Table 6.4) tend to
give some support to the general pattern of regional divisions and
variation exposed by the 1990 survey research project. Thus, the census
reveals a substantial fall in the number of citizens who identified
themselves as "Yugoslavs," from approximately 1.2 million individuals,
or 5.4 percent of the population, in 1981 to roughly 710,000, or 3
percent, in 1991. The rate of decline was highest in Croatia and Slovenia,
although Serbia's assertion of greater republican sovereignty by 1990
undoubtedly also contributed to the substantial decrease in Yugoslavs in
that republic as well. Self-identification as Yugoslavs was highest in the
two most ethnically diverse sections of the country, the Serbian province
of Vojvodina and the republic of Bosnia-Hercegovina, both areas where
large numbers of citizens were offspring of interethnic marriages and
whose environment suggested the wisdom of pan-ethnic allegiance
(whether as a means to escape more parochial classification or to exhibit
support for interethnic harmony).

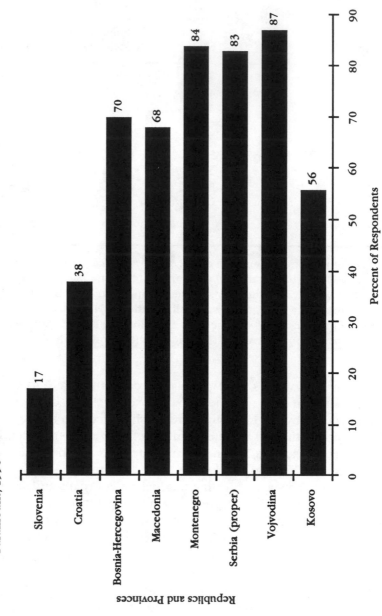

FIGURE 6.1   Federal Versus Republican Constitutions: Percent of Sample Agreeing that the Federal Constitution Must Be Paramount, 1990

Source: Šta Misli Jugoslavija (Belgrade: Savezno Izvršno Veće, 1990), p. 31.

TABLE 6.4   Citizens of Yugoslavia Self-Identified as "Yugoslavs" in the 1981 and 1991 Censuses

	1981		1991		Percent of Decline or Growth, 1981-1991
	N	Percent	N	Percent	
Bosnia-Hercegovinia	326,280	7.9	239,845	5.5	-26.5
Slovenia	26,263	1.4	12,237	0.6	-53.4
Croatia	379,058	8.2	104,728	2.2	-72.3
Macedonia	15,673	0.7	—[a]	-	-
Montenegro	31,243	5.3	25,845	4.0	-17.3
Serbia proper[b]	272,195	4.8	145,810	2.5	-46.4
Vojvodina[c]	164,880	8.2	168,859	8.4	+2.4
Kosovo	2,676	0.2	3,070	0.2	±14.7[d]
Total	1,218,268	5.4	700,394	3.0	-41.7

[a]The first results of the census in Macedonia did not report data on "Yugoslavs."

[b]Without the provinces of Vojvodina and Kosovo.

[c]Fifty-three percent of all the "Yugoslavs" in the republic of Serbia are in the province of Vojvodina, and persons declaring that identity made up ten percent or more of the population in eight of Vojvodina's municipalities.

[d]Information for Kosovo is incomplete because almost all Albanians (about 90 percent of the province) boycotted the census. The growth rate of Yugoslavs in the province reflects a small increase in their absolute number, most likely among inhabitants of Serbian and Montenegrin background.

Sources: Stanko Žuljić, Narodnosna struktura Jugoslavije i tokovi promena (Zagreb: Ekonomski Institut, 1989), p. 141; and Nacionalni Sastav stanovništva po opštinama (Belgrade: Savezni Zavod za Statistiku, 1992).

Overall, however, and in stark contrast to the surge of Yugoslav identity in 1981, the 1991 census reveals a marked return by many citizens of the Yugoslav state to their specific ethnic group origins or—when such origins were mixed—to chose an ethnic commitment other than Yugoslav.[9] To what degree this trend is a result of the changed views of citizens, or of elite-led nationalism, is difficult to gauge, but the two dimensions tended to reinforce one another in a manner that encouraged stronger political identification with one's ethnic group and region. The diminished level of popular commitment to the Yugoslav state, as either a focus of territorial affiliation or a focus of personal identity, certainly encouraged, or at least provided a rationale, for the efforts of those regional leaders who sought to dismantle the existing federation.

The Collapse of Constitutional Authority: From Pluralism to Postfederalism

By fall of 1990 Yugoslavia's constitutional structure was rapidly crumbling. Despite fierce criticism from the Serbian political leadership and other enthusiasts of a strong federal system—particularly in the top ranks of the military establishment—the postcommunist governments in Slovenia and Croatia continued to press ahead with their plans for political sovereignty during the second half of 1990.[10] In early October the Slovenian legislature adopted a draft constitution asserting that "Slovenia will become an independent state which will take on and exercise all the sovereign rights including those which it had transferred—either upon the foundation of federal Yugoslavia or later—to the Socialist Federal Republic of Yugoslavia."[11]

This move was followed by a plebiscite in the republic on December 23 in which approximately 88.5 percent of the citizens turning out to vote expressed support for Slovenia's secession from Yugoslavia should that step be deemed necessary. On December 26, based on the results of the plebiscite, Slovenia's legislature adopted a declaration of its republic's sovereignty. Two days prior to Slovenia's plebiscite, Croatia's somewhat more cautious leaders adopted a new constitution that enabled their republic to secede from the Yugoslav federation should Croatia's legislature support such a decision by a two-thirds vote.[12] In view of their ongoing problems with the republic's militant Serbian minority, and also their hope that interrepublican negotiations might result in the peaceful restructuring of the country on a confederal basis, Croatian authorities temporarily preferred to avoid a potentially divisive popular referendum on the republic's future status.

As challenges to Yugoslavia's state unity entered a critical stage in late 1990, the country's "constitutional judiciary," which had been a pillar of socialist legality under the Titoist system, proved helpless to prevent the collapse of the federal system. Indeed, the Yugoslav case is a vivid illustration of just how contingent judicial authority is upon regime legitimation.[13] Courts can assist political leaders in preserving a federal union, but the authority of judges and judicial sanctions ultimately depends on political will and political support. Near the end of 1990—months after the deadline had expired for republican and provincial compliance with federal judicial decisions regarding the repeal of unconstitutional amendments—the new president of the Constitutional Court could only lament the depleted authority of his institution and what he called the "constitutional-legal confusion" in his country:

> The decisions of the Constitutional Court are obligatory, their implementation is secured by the Federal Executive Council, and we can demand that measures are taken against the responsible people if they do not implement them. That opinion goes so far, reality is something else....The problem is the different conceptions of the legal nature of [Court] opinions. In one view it has the force of a decision, but according to others it is only an evaluation, that is "information," but the elimination of contradictions is a question of political mediation. In place of the elimination of contradictions, we see the adoption of new amendments to the republican and provincial constitutions...and these amendments and the constitution of Serbia contain provisions which are in contradiction to the constitution of Yugoslavia.[14]

Although the inherent murkiness of constitutional provisions relating to the actual paramountcy of the highest constitutional court over interregional matters undoubtedly assisted political forces in the country seeking to ignore the court's decisions, it was the political segmentation of the country along regional and ethnic lines that fatally undermined the rule-of-law and the authority of federal institutions. In November 1990, Prime Minister Marković once again requested that the federal Constitutional Court assess the constitutionality of the various sovereignty-seeking legal provisions adopted by Serbia, Croatia, and Slovenia during 1990. Given the steady decline of support for federal judicial and political authority, however, there was little expectation that the three republics would pay any heed to the court's rulings. Indeed in January 1991, the court concluded that the key elements of Slovenia's July 1990 declaration of sovereignty were unconstitutional, and also annulled several pieces of legislation that had been adopted by the Croatian and Serbian legislatures. Such rulings, however, had no effect on the political assertiveness of the offending republics. Thus in February 1991 Slovenian and Croatian lawmakers voted overwhelmingly to formally annul the validity of all federal laws pertaining to their republics. The inability of the federal judiciary to secure compliance with its decisions was a crucial factor in the overall delegitimation of the federal structure because without recourse to legal sanctions, other sectors of the regime, such as the federal presidency, the federal government, and the federal assembly, were also unable to implement its decisions. Increasingly such federal bodies were ignored by the political elites in the republics, who in some cases (Slovenia and Croatia) chose to alternatively boycott or immobilize the operations of Yugoslavia's federal institutions.

Disregard for republican-level legal authority and constitutional courts was also apparent during this period. For example, when the Tudjman government in Croatia proceeded with a proclamation of the republic's sovereignty and the adoption of a new republican constitution in December 1990, political leaders in the Serbian majority areas of Croatia responded by proclaiming a statute that purported to establish a new intercommunal governmental unit called the "Serbian Autonomous Region." The move by the Serbs was motivated by their real fear that in view of current support for confederation by the Zagreb regime their community would soon be at the mercy of a politically independent Croatian state. The Constitutional Court of Croatia moved quickly to invalidate the Serbian entity, just as the court had done with respect to the earlier Serbian Declaration of Sovereignty adopted during the summer. In the spirit of Yugoslavia's disintegrating and regionalized legal system, however, the Serbian communes of Croatia exhibited the same disdain for the republican Constitutional Court's ruling as the Croatian government persistently had demonstrated toward the decisions of the federal Constitutional Court.

Anxiety in Croatia's Serbian community intensified in early October 1990 when the presidencies of Croatia and Slovenia published a draft proposal of a confederal agreement that would replace the current federation with a loose alliance of sovereign states. The future constitutional shape of the country, and the confederal option in particular, had been lively topics of discussion since the spring electoral campaigns in the two republics. But in response to a request from the federal presidency that all republics specify their views on constitutional reorganization, Croatia and Slovenia now provided a more coherent presentation about the way in which they planned to restructure their political and economic relationship with other parts of the existing Yugoslav state. The proposal, which combined separate drafts prepared by experts in Croatia and Slovenia, included various alternative suggestions for establishing mutual cooperation among "sovereign states" and was explicitly said to be based on "theoretical generalizations of confederative examples from history and the experience of the European community."[15] Entry into the confederal alliance was characterized as a "voluntary" act, based upon "the inalienable and unexpendable right of every nation to self-determination, including the right to unite with and separate from other nations and states."[16] Member states would also be free to leave the confederation by their own decision.

According to the proposal, such a confederation would operate as a custom's union, common market, and monetary union (with or without a single currency), and matters such as environmental protection and economic and technological development would be coordinated or handled jointly. Various common governing institutions would also be established by the members of the alliance—a consultative parliament, council of ministers, executive committee, and confederal court, and so on—although several alternative versions of the organization and functioning of such institutions were offered for purposes of future discussion. Under the Slovenian-Croatian proposal, unanimity among the member states would be the basis for decisionmaking in the council of ministers, and the languages of all the member states would officially be used in the confederation's various institutions. Each member state would be a "separate subject of international law" and have independent diplomatic representation, but the question of whether to also establish a common foreign policy and diplomatic corps was left open. In the period before possible demilitarization the proposal suggested that defense planning should be coordinated, and a supreme command comprising the presidents of all member states was envisioned to coordinate military affairs in case of aggression against the confederation. Each member state would finance its own portion of any common military units placed under the joint command of the alliance, and the commander of any optional joint military force would have to be agreed upon by all member states.

The introduction to the draft proposal asserted that the document was intended as a starting point for debate, not a final negotiating position. It was also anticipated that countrywide discussion of constitutional restructuring and the proposal would ensue after free elections could be held in all Yugoslavia's republics. It is interesting, however, that only weeks after the publication of the Slovenian-Croatian proposal one of its key architects, Tudjman adviser Slaven Letica, suggested that the outline for a confederation was actually the "last straw" for maintaining a Yugoslav state framework and that it might already be too late for such arrangements to attract genuine support in other regions of the country: "One could even say that in Yugoslavia the assumptions don't even exist for creating a confederation. Namely, a confederation is an alliance of friendly states, but the present Yugoslav states are no longer friendly they are continuously on the brink of war. Not only civil war, but inter-state war. Consequently, one could say that confederalism has become a rather obsolete form."[17]

Just days before public dissemination of the Croatian-Slovenian proposal, the federal presidency had outlined its own proposal for constitutional change.[18] The presidency—still composed of a majority of representatives from republics that had not yet held free elections—recommended that the country support the idea of a remodeled federation rather than a confederative arrangement. Explanatory information accompanying the federal presidency proposal suggested that "efforts" had been made to stress the independent position of the republics and "their full right to manage their affairs."[19] Notwithstanding this language, the spirit and letter of the presidency's proposal were clearly intended to reassert strong federal political authority and to prevent the country's drift into a loose confederation. According to the proposal, for example, the functions of the future state presidency which would include control over the armed forces and foreign affairs, would remain "essentially similar" to the situation under the 1974 constitution.[20] Violations of decisions of the Constitutional Court would purportedly become "impossible" under the remodeled federal scheme, although the manner in which this new judicial authority would actually be implemented remained unspecified.

Explaining the views of the presidency to the Federal Assembly on October 17, 1990, federal state President Jović emphasized that a "growth of nationalism and separatism" was threatening to undermine the cohesion of the country. "Everything," he claimed, "which symbolizes Yugoslavia or carries the Yugoslav name is despoiled in the most crude and primitive manner." Jović placed special blame on Slovenia and also Albanian political forces in Kosovo for current violations of the constitution. Slovenia was also singled out for assisting "unscrupulous actions intended to breakup the unity of the armed forces."[21] Thus at the end of October 1990, as Yugoslavia's southeastern republics prepared for their first free elections, deep divisions still remained among the republics and between most of the republics and the federal authorities regarding the country's future constitutional shape. Ruling elites in Serbia and Montenegro strongly supported Jović's position and the federal presidency's concept of a remodeled federation, whereas Slovenia and Croatia pressed forward with plans for sovereignty and their proposal for a loose confederation. The political leaders in Bosnia-Hercegovina and Macedonia, who at this point were still members of the ruling League of Communists, tended to support the federal presidency's view. But as the republican elections approached, the confederal option gained popularity among governing circles in both republics—who sought to put forward a new image—as well as among many of the opposition parties.

Popular attitudes with respect to the federation-confederation debate during 1990 tended to closely resemble the evolving patterns of elite-level polarization. For example, mid-1990 public opinion surveys regarding support for the contending confederal and federal options paralleled the lack general lack of elite consensus, with citizens of Kosovo, Slovenia, and Croatia most enthusiastic about confederation and the majority of respondents in Serbia proper, Macedonia, and Montenegro favoring a federation. Ethnic alignments on the same issue were closely related to the regional breakdown, with Slovenes, Croats, and Albanians very supportive of confederation and Serbs, "Yugoslavs," and Montenegrins generally inclined to the federal option. Serbs living outside Serbia proper—especially in Croatia, Bosnia-Hercegovina, and Vojvodina—who feared that the disintegration of the country would leave them in the position of a repressed minority—were the least enthusiastic about confederation. More than one-fifth of the citizens surveyed, however, simply did not have a clear position on matters of constitutional restructuring, a situation that undoubtedly gave wider latitude to the country's divided political elites in determining Yugoslavia's future.[22]

Military Legitimacy and State Cohesion:
The JNA's Political Mission

The erosion of constitutional authority in Yugoslavia in late 1990 was particularly disconcerting to the members of the country's military elite. Conservative military leaders had already exerted considerable pressure on civilian authorities in an unsuccessful attempt to forestall competitive party pluralism prior to the spring 1990 elections, and they subsequently watched with outrage and disbelief as brash anti-federalists and nationalist noncommunist leaders were elected to power in several republics. Faced with the prospects of increasing challenges to communist rule and federal power, and also the glaring inability of the courts to maintain a unified constitutional system and legal order, most top-ranking military officers in the Yugoslav People's Army (JNA) viewed themselves as the last bastion of Yugoslavism and state unity. Indeed, whereas the number of citizens self-identified as Yugoslavs was decreasing in the country as a whole (Table 6.4), that identity was actually on the rise within the JNA officer corps.

Most of such Yugoslavs in the top military ranks were officers of Serbian and Montenegrin ethnic backgrounds, although many were also Slovenes and Croats from the JNA's older generation of officers. Such "military Yugoslavism" was also accentuated in the military elite's overall ethnic structure (Table 6.5). Thus, it is reasonable to assume that the majority Serbian contingent (including Montenegrins) in the officer corps—approximately 60 percent in 1990—was also imbued with a strong preference for the Yugoslav idea and preservation of the country's unity. Moreover, although the formal one-party control structure in the military was gradually dismantled during 1990, and activities of all political parties in the armed forces prohibited, most Serbian military officers remained strongly opposed to the notion that portions of a depoliticized military might come under the control of the noncommunist civilian authorities elected in Croatia and Slovenia.

TABLE 6.5   Ethnic Composition of Officers in the Yugoslav People's Army (JNA)

	1971	1981	1990
Croats	8.4	12.6	12.5
Slovenes	3.7	2.8	2.3
Serbs	60.4	60.0	54.3
Montenegrins	7.0	6.2	5.2
Yugoslavs	6.1	6.7	9.6
Moslems	1.3	2.4	5.3
Albanians	0.3	0.6	1.5
Macedonians	5.8	6.3	7.3
Hungarians	0.5	0.7	1.0
Others	1.5	1.6	1.4
Total	100.0	100.0	100.0

Sources: Teodor Geršak, "Kdo drži v rokah Jugoslavansko armado," *Revija Obramba*, Vol. 23, Nos. 6-7 (1991), pp. 48-50; and Vlatko Cvrtila, "Tko je što u armiji," *Danas*, Vol. 10, No. 468 (February 5, 1991), pp. 16-17.

Although only a minority of Serbs in the military elite may have been deeply and philosophically committed to the socialist ideals elaborated during the Titoist period, most Serbian officers realized that the military's organizational unity was an essential prerequisite for the retention of their positions and substantial privileges. Thus for most Serbs in the Yugoslav military establishment, the breakup of the country's armed forces into separate republican armies constituted both a personal career threat and an ethnic calamity. Moreover, the potential disintegration of the existing federation, and the establishment of a loose alliance of sovereign states advocated by Croatia and Slovenia, not only placed their future job prospects and perks in jeopardy but would also result in the unacceptable division of Yugoslavia's Serbian ethnic community among several small successor states. Consequently, in the mindset of the Serbs who dominated the military elite, career aspirations, life-style, organizational unity, and ethnic solidarity were all inextricably linked to the preservation of Yugoslavia.

The anxiety felt by Yugoslavia's military elite led to a fundamental shift in the JNA's strategic thinking and self-justification.[23] Prior to early 1990, and the end of the League of Communists' monopoly over the political system, the legitimacy of the Yugoslav military establishment derived primarily from its constitutionally stipulated role to defend the country and, by implication, the one-party regime. With the collapse of the one-party communist state, the ascendancy of anti-federalist and nationalist forces in several republics, and the diminished external threat to the country as the Cold War drew to a close, the JNA urgently needed to elaborate a new legitimating formula that could justify its activities and also its large share of the country's budget. One obvious course of legitimation was to focus the military's attention upon perceived *internal* threats to state unity and away from the country's defense against external foes.

Having lost its traditional rationale for existence, and the political backing of the communist hierarchy, the military establishment thus embraced a new mission of preserving internal peace and order. As a result of this strategic reorientation, by early 1990 the military elite viewed the nationalist parties that were emerging as electoral front-runners in Slovenia and Croatia not only as subversive elements threatening Yugoslavia's cohesion, but also as the country's primary security problem. Indeed, the nationalist forces that appeared likely to take power in Zagreb and Ljubljana were now characterized by the JNA leadership as Yugoslavia's number one enemies, demanding the full engagement of the military's energies and resources. If a general fear of pluralism was a prominent element in the military's outlook during 1989 and early 1990, anti-pluralism *and* anti-separatism became its major concern during the pluralist "revolution" of 1990.

As the electoral victory of nationalist forces appeared increasingly imminent in both Slovenia and Croatia during the early spring of 1990, the military elite focused its attention on maintaining control of military forces located in those republics. The JNA's main concern was the facilities associated with the Territorial Defense (TD) units, the branch of the Yugoslav military structure designed in the 1960s to provide localized regional forces and resources for a guerrilla-type struggle against an external foe. The TD units were essentially an auxiliary military force, composed of reservists residing in a particular locality. According to military specialists in Slovenia, between mid-April and mid-May 1990, JNA leaders secretly arranged to bring the TD units located in Slovenia and Croatia under their control through the transfer of weapons from TD armories to JNA armories. The prevention of the possible theft of arms served as the pretext for such transfers. This operation was only partially completed when it came to the attention of the newly elected Slovenian authorities and was quickly terminated.[24] For the leaders of the JNA elite, however, the issue of who would control the TD forces in Slovenia, and also in other areas of Yugoslavia, was still an open question.

By mid-1990, popular antipathy to the federal military in Slovenia and Croatia—a sentiment that had been on the rise in those republics for several years—became extremely intense. Survey research interviews conducted throughout Yugoslavia in May and June 1990, for example, revealed major regional differences in the population's willingness to provide financial support to the JNA (Table 6.6). Citizens in Slovenia (78 percent), Kosovo (65 percent), and Croatia (54 percent) felt most strongly that there should be a reduction of republican funding for the federal military. In Montenegro, Serbia, and Bosnia-Hercegovina, however, respondents expressed high levels of support for either maintaining such assistance at existing levels, or even increasing available funds. Yugoslav researchers interpreting such data concluded that the "high percentage of citizens from Slovenia and Kosovo supporting a decrease in assistance reveals how, within such areas, the JNA is considered primarily a means for internal repression, and not as a force for defending Yugoslavia."[25]

As multiparty elections continued in the fall of 1990, and chances increased that anti-federalists and noncommunists might assume power in Yugoslavia's southeastern republics, the military elite attempted to consolidate its control over the armed forces by escalating pressure on the new governments already established in Slovenia and Croatia. The

TABLE 6.6   Public Attitudes Toward Financing the Yugoslav People's Army (JNA), mid-1990

Desirable Amount of Financial Support for JNA	Total Yugoslavia	Bosnia-Hercegovina	Montenegro	Croatia	Macedonia	Slovenia	Serbia	Kosovo	Vojvodina
Less than now	36.0	24.0	10.0	54.0	28.0	78.0	18.0	65.0	21.0
About the same as now	39.0	41.0	56.0	33.0	47.0	10.0	51.0	18.0	52.0
More than now	16.0	24.0	24.0	6.0	16.0	3.0	23.0	9.0	20.0
Don't know	9.0	11.0	10.0	8.0	9.0	9.0	9.0	9.0	7.0
Total	100.0	100.0	100.0	100.0	100.0	100.0	100.0	100.0	100.0

Source: Štefica Bahtijarević and Goran Milas, "Reakcija javnost na mere i politiku SIV-a," in Ljiljana Baćević (ed.), *Jugoslavija na kriznoj prekretnici* (Belgrade: Institut Društvenih Nauka, 1991), pp. 97-98.

JNA's decision to take such action was reinforced in December when a Slovenian constitutional amendment was adopted that transferred formal direction over the republic's TD units from the federal presidency to the Slovenian presidency. As one of a series of measures adopted in Slovenia to extricate the republic from the ambit of federal jurisdiction, the JNA considered this amendment as a political precursor of Slovenian political autonomy and possible independence. On September 28, 1990, the Yugoslav secretary for national defense announced that republican military units would no longer be able to operate outside the control of the federal military structure. When Slovenia reacted by dismissing the commander of the Slovenian TD forces and replacing him with a person loyal to the republic, the Yugoslav presidency, under pressure from the JNA elite in Belgrade, acted to regain control over Slovenia's TD units. On October 4, federal military police took control of the headquarters of Slovenia's TD forces in Ljubljana, and senior JNA officers indicated that if necessary further military action would be taken to reestablish federal control over the republic's military structure.

Having won a minor skirmish in the matter of the Slovenian Territorial Defense forces (although TD weapons were still in depots controlled by the republic's officials), the JNA elite opened a major propaganda campaign against both Slovenian and Croatian efforts to assert republican political and military sovereignty. The views expressed by top JNA officers revealed the military's relatively new political mindset regarding its internal "mission" to preserve the Yugoslav polity and also provided insights into later military developments in the country. For example, speaking in London on November 22, former Yugoslav Minister of Defense Admiral Branko Mamula observed that the two previously separate components of the armed forces—the regular JNA and TD forces—were being integrated into "one system" with "the aim of preventing any possible abuse of territorial defense." Mamula claimed that the JNA had thus far exercised restraint in dealing with the country's crisis and had no intention of further interference unless circumstances demanded it. He also asserted, however, that the JNA "must not allow itself to be pushed to the margins."

The "circumstances" most likely to trigger military involvement were clear from Mamula's sharp criticisms of Slovenian and Croatian proposals for a confederal state to replace the Yugoslav federation. It was not the matter of potential secession by the existing republics *per se* that made a confederation "unacceptable," claimed Mamula, but rather that efforts to establish "national" states by either the Croats or the Serbs would undoubtedly lead to conflict over Bosnia-Hercegovina, a development that could not be resolved without resort to violence. Many of the political parties established in the republics, Mamula also pointed out, had brought back the "ghosts of the past" and had created a constitutional crisis. He rejected charges that the JNA leadership was reactionary, but he also emphasized that any kind of political pluralization which threatened Yugoslav cohesion must not be tolerated: "The army leadership is not conservative as it is often described, nor does it defend anything from the past that is not of lasting value. Not all of our former values should be summarily discarded, nor should we have to base our reformation on the discretion of others. The army supports the profound transformation of society...but within realistic boundaries imposed by Yugoslav conditions."[26]

Just ten days after Admiral Mamula's comments, and on the eve of Serbia's first multiparty elections since World War II, Yugoslavia's national Defense Secretary, Veljko Kadijević, gave a long interview in which he went even further in criticizing developments in Slovenia and Croatia. The rise of subversive "anti-socialism" and "anti-Yugoslav" forces within the country, claimed Kadijević, would invite foreign meddling in internal politics. In other words, by fighting against putative internal subversion, the JNA was also fulfilling its long-standing constitutional role to preserve Yugoslavia's integrity. Kadijević claimed that the military opposed the continuation of a one-party monopoly but was also against any type of political pluralism "directed from the outside and unsuited to Yugoslavia's conditions." For Kadijević, the entire system of Territorial Defense forces created under Tito's direction during the 1960s amounted to "a great deceit" that was originally designed and currently being exploited to develop republican armies separate from the federal military structure. "Nationalist and separatist forces"—a code phrase of the newly elected leaders in Ljubljana and Zagreb—would not, Kadijević pointed out, be allowed to breakup the JNA. "No state in the world has several armies, Yugoslavia should not and will not be like Lebanon....All armed formations outside a uniformed forces as defined by [Yugoslavia's] constitution will be disarmed."

Kadijević also signaled the voters of Serbia that he personally, and the "communists in the army," supported "an all-Yugoslav and socialist orientation" consistent with the views of the recently launched League of Communists-Movement for Yugoslavia (SK-PJ). The SK-PJ was not directly competing in the Serbian election, but the fact that a large number of Milošević activists, including Milošević's wife, were cofounders of the new party along with Kadijević could not fail to be noticed by Serbian voters. In the words of the defense minister: "The socialist idea cannot be rejected because of the crude failures of the real socialist model...the idea of socialism, viewed historically, belongs to the future."[27]

Serbia's anti-socialist opposition, who were engaged in an electoral contest with Milošević, viewed the Kadijević comments as a highly improper example of military intervention in internal politics. In Slovenia and Croatia, however, the defense minister's remarks were viewed as a serious portent of federal military action designed to reverse the results of the spring 1990 elections. President Tudjman stated that federal military intervention in his republic would be resisted with force, and he observed that the JNA's interference in Croatia's affairs had actually begun in August 1990 when JNA air force helicopters had been used against the Croatian police in their attempts to suppress Serbian militancy in the Knin region.[28] Meanwhile, Janez Janša, the Slovenian defense minister and an old foe of the JNA leadership (referred to in army publications as "Janša, the former convict"),[29] claimed that General Kadijević's interview was part of a "planned scenario" to intensify pressure on Slovenia. According to Janša, Kadijević and the army leadership had "decided to go to extremes" to avoid the possibility that Slovenia and Croatia would soon transfer republican based defense forces from the "federal armed forces to confederal ones" and that the JNA was equally worried that nationalist forces in Serbia were opposed to support for a "socialist army." Janša also strongly implied that the imminent Slovenian plebiscite on independence would permit the republic to organize its own army, which would "not be political, but strictly professional."[30]

Such statements, and Janša's frequent assertions that Slovenian military recruits should serve only in Slovenia, that Slovenian funds supporting the military should no longer be sent to the federation, and that federal military property should be divided up among the republics, enraged the same JNA military leadership that had prosecuted the young Slovenian minister for treason only three years earlier. Faced with Janša's self-confident management of Slovenia's security affairs, and the growing possibility of Slovenia's independent state development, the Yugoslav presidency warned the Slovenian government that its planned December plebiscite was illegal. Admiral Stane Brovet, a Yugoslav-oriented Slovene, went even further, referring to the coming plebiscite as an act of "treason."[31]

The overwhelming opposition to the existing federation expressed in Slovenia's December plebiscite, together with the growing cooperation on defense related matters by the new elites in Slovenia and Croatia, only intensified the JNA leadership's determination to take strong action against the allegedly "separatist" republics. Slovenian and Croatian leaders urged that the federal military undergo a genuine depoliticization and a reduction in size, but the JNA top brass vehemently demanded that all military forces in the country become integrated under a single command structure. On January 9, 1991, under pressure from the military, a majority in the collective presidency outvoted representatives from Slovenia and Croatia and set a ten-day deadline for dissolution of all armed units that were not a part of the Yugoslav armed forces and police, and the surrendering of all illegal weapons to the JNA. This time, the main thrust of the presidency's decision was focused on Croatia, which had been outfitting its own special reserve police with clandestine arms imports and had been making plans for a republican based armed force. As federal military forces moved to a state of alert in preparation for carrying out the presidency's order, the Croatian government announced that it intended to resist such measures and placed its own forces on alert. The long-simmering differences between the federal military and the nationalist elites in the northwestern republics had finally led to a dangerous military face-off.

Responsibility for representing Croatia's interests in the federal presidency fell upon Stipe Mesić, a key member of the new political elite in Zagreb and a close associate of President Tudjman. Mesić had been the first prime minister of postcommunist Croatia following the election of Tudjman's HDZ in May 1990, but was soon selected to become the republic's representative in the federation's collective presidency, replacing the Croatian communist Stipe Šuvar. Because a representative from Croatia was scheduled to become Yugoslavia's next president of the collective presidency in May 1991 (according to the rotational system established by Tito), Mesić automatically assumed the post of vice-president of that body for the 1990-1991 period. As the deadline for disarming illegal forces approached, and threat of armed conflict between the JNA and Croatian forces grew more likely, Mesić and Tudjman worked hard to diffuse the situation and allow all sides to save face. Mesić's task in Belgrade was not an easy one. In a meeting of the presidency on January 9, 1991 to discuss the issue of disarming the republic's forces, Mesić engaged in "fierce polemics" with JNA General Blagoje Adžić over the right of Croatia to pursue its own course of internal development.[32] Viewed from the perspective of the military elite, and most of the country's Serbian community, Mesić represented a dangerous threat to Yugoslavia that had been sent to the presidency by a "separatist" republic that had been arming its ethnic Croatian citizens in preparation for armed rebellion against the federation. On January 26, after the deadline for compliance with the disarmament order had been twice ignored by the Croatian leadership, a compromise was finally reached at a meeting of the presidency. According to the agreement, Croatia would disarm its reserve police forces, and the JNA would terminate its state of combat alert. President Tudjman, obviously relieved, declared that the country had been on the verge of civil war.

Looking back at the January 1991 crisis over a year later, Mesić advanced three reasons for the compromise.[33] First, according to Mesić, Prime Minister Marković intervened with Ambassador William Zimmerman of the United States to organize U.S. and German pressure on the JNA elite and forestall direct military intervention. Second, the federal military had not received formal backing from the collective presidency, at a time when the armed forces were still, to a considerable extent, accountable to civilian political control. Finally, Mesić believed that the predominantly Serbian military elite decided to postpone their action against Croatia until it could muster additional evidence that the government in Zagreb was undemocratic and anti-Serb.

Although Mesić's analysis may be correct, the question naturally arises as to what might have transpired had the JNA launched military action to enforce the federal decision dissolving illegal paramilitary forces. In retrospect, it seems likely that such action would have led to a full-scale military conflict between the JNA and Croatian forces and very probably would have spread to Slovenia and other regions of the country. If the JNA had successfully carried out such military action in January, the army might have severely crippled the capacity of new political elites in the northwestern republics to move ahead with their plans for "disassociation" from the existing federation and thereby significantly altered the course of events during the coming months. Indeed, the danger of such an eventuality is probably what motivated Tudjman's government to tactically back down during the crisis and formally agree to dissolve Croatia's paramilitary units. In doing so, the Croatian leader bought himself valuable time to pursue his strategy of peacefully confederalizing Yugoslavia and, should that option not prove possible, unilaterally move ahead to proclaim Croatia's independence. Moreover, despite the formal agreement, Croatia did not actually dissolve the republic's paramilitary units. That the JNA stood by and watched this course of events while pursuing a less costly propaganda campaign against the alleged "separatists" in Zagreb suggests that the federal military leadership probably lacked confidence in January 1991 regarding the capacity of the armed forces to successfully carry out a punitive operation against either Croatia or Slovenia. As subsequent events would demonstrate, such reservations on the part of the military establishment were certainly well warranted.

Whatever the reasons for the January compromise on the dissolution of paramilitary forces, there was no cessation in the fierce war of words between federal military leaders and the northwestern republics. On January 25, the same evening that the compromise was reached, the JNA publicized a film in the possession of the military intelligence services purporting to reveal high-ranking Croatian officials—including Croatia's Minister of Defense, Martin Špegelj—plotting to use violent methods in order to sever their republic from the federation.[34] The alleged conversations included plans to kill JNA officers and their families who were living in Croatia. When the film was shown on TV Belgrade, it caused a firestorm of mass indignation that intensified the already high level of Serbian anxiety concerning developments in Croatia and further raised tensions in areas of mixed Serb and Croat population. Top Croatian officials challenged the authenticity of the film, and it was quickly submitted to examination by a panel of independent experts who concluded that the film was "half genuine, half fake."[35] Despite this finding, the Zagreb government refused to cooperate with federal military authorities who had issued a warrant for Špegelj's arrest. Not long after the incident, Špegelj told an interviewer that the army's film and the recording of his comments constituted "a monstrous frame-up of the Stalinist type" and that he could not be "arrested for doing his job, which includes his duties to defend Croatia."[36] Whatever the truth, after several years of worsening relations between Serbs and Croats, the film significantly heightened the distrust and political distance between the two groups.

The constant sparring between the JNA leadership and the new political elites in Slovenia and Croatia throughout 1990 and early 1991 not only had come close to precipitating a major military clash but had also poisoned the general atmosphere for calm discussions about Yugoslavia's future state development. In the highly charged climate of political rhetoric, threats and counterthreats, and interethnic tension, the reform-minded Prime Minister, Ante Marković, seemed to be the only major political actor still intent on using economic arguments and persuasive methods to resolve the Yugoslav crisis. Despite accelerating centrifugal nationalism, the impotence of the federal judicial system, and the increasing intervention of the military in political affairs, Marković endeavored to maintain a semblance of state cohesion and to proceed with economic reforms. At a time when the international community was beginning to become seriously concerned about Yugoslavia's potential disintegration, Marković used his excellent relationship with international leaders and financial institutions to encourage external support for the country's unity.

Unfortunately, the Marković government was unable to obtain support from the major republican leaders for either federal multiparty elections (Slovenia was most strongly opposed) or the adoption of long-proposed amendments to the federal constitution that might have relegitimated federal governmental institutions and restructured the country in a cohesive and rational manner. Anxious to increase their own influence, both of the principal actors crucial to Yugoslavia's existence—the advocate of Croatian sovereignty and confederalism, Franjo Tudjman, and the supporter of a Serbian-led centralized federation, Slobodan Milošević—had a common interest in weakening and marginalizing Marković's role in political matters.

In late December 1990, the undaunted Marković called a meeting of government leaders from all the republics "to reach an agreement on minimum assumptions for the functioning of a federal state until the final agreement on the future state structure." He added that "Yugoslavia must decide whether it will stop the current erosion of the functioning of the legal and economic systems and create normal conditions for reaching an agreement on new options for the future, or continue with practices which inevitably lead to anarchy and chaos."[37] Marković preferred not to take a firm stand concerning the confederation-federation debate, choosing instead to focus on the issues of economic development and the need for a stable countrywide legal framework. At the outset of 1991, Marković warned the country's immobilized Federal Assembly that as a result of the refusal of the republics to either economically or politically support the federation, the country's economic system and reform program faced total collapse. Quoting from his own government's report on the crisis, Marković asserted that "the coming year would be crucial not only for the success or failure of the reform, but also for the survival of Yugoslavia as a state."[38] It was against this backdrop of economic crisis and an ongoing propaganda battle between the federal military and the sovereignty-seeking northwestern republics that Yugoslavia's republican and provincial leaders embarked upon the most difficult negotiations in the country's 72-year long history.

Notes

1. Of the 1,248 delegates elected to four sessions of the Federal Assembly from 1974 to 1986, for example, only 9, or less that 1 percent, were *not* members of the League of Communists. *NIN*, February 21, 1988, p. 18.

2. Milorad Antonić, "Demokratija je muškog roda," *Nedjelja*, February 17, 1991, p. 14, and; Nadežda Cetković, "Muška skupština—Ženski parlament,"

Vreme, Vol. 2, No. 12 (January 14, 1991), pp. 63-64. Milica Antić argues that during the democratization of the Yugoslav federation that began in 1990, "the interests of the so-called 'social minorities' have been less important than the interests of the newly-arising nation-state. Women's issues are considered to be, yet again, less important than questions about the survival of the nation, national protection and security, the need for armies, and other such issues." She adds that: "politics in this transitional period...has been a very dirty business....Women involved in women's groups are seldom prepared to get involved in 'dirty' party politics, quite apart from the fact that they are given little incentive to do so." "Yugoslavia: The Transitional Spirit of the Age," in Chris Corrin (ed.), *Superwomen and the Double Burden* (London: Scarlet Press, 1992), pp. 173, 177-178.

3. Tomaz Mastnak, "Civil Society in Slovenia: From Opposition to Power," *Studies in Comparative Communism*, Vol. 23, No. 3 (August-Winter 1990), pp. 314-315.

4. *Ibid.*, p. 315.

5. *Ibid.*

6. Sergije Pegan, "Pluralizacija parlamenta—socijalni sastav Narodne skupštine Srbije," in Srećko Mihailović, Vladimir Goati, *et al.* (eds.), *Od izbornih rituala do slobodnih izbora* (Belgrade: Institut društvenih nauka, 1991), pp. 231-249.

7. Vjeran Katunarić, "Uoči novih etnopolitičkih raskola Hrvatska i Bosna i Hercegovina," *Sociologija*, Vol. 33, No. 3 (July-September 1991), p. 376.

8. Bojana Oprijan-Ilić, "Jugoslavija do dve kapi," *Borba*, January 25-26, 1992, p. 10.

9. Ruža Petrović, "The National Composition of Yugoslavia's Population, 1991," *Yugoslav Survey*, Vol. 33, No. 1 (1991), p. 12.

10. The autumn of 1991 also saw the emergence of a more open trade war between Serbia and the northwestern republics. For example, Serbian government regulations imposed an import duty on Slovenian and Croatian goods entering Serbia, and a special property tax on Slovenian and Croatian enterprises in Serbia. The governments in Zagreb and Ljubljana introduced counter-measures against Serbia, and also stopped paying their contributions to the federal budget. Meanwhile, the federal government proved powerless to enforce the removal of protectionist measures among the republics, or compel the republics to pay their share of taxes to the federation.

11. T. Gerdina, *Information on Slovenia* (1990).

12. Article 140 of the new Croatian constitution was a "transitional provision" specifying that the "Republic of Croatia shall remain part of the Socialist Federal Republic of Yugoslavia, until a new agreement is reached by the Yugoslav republics, or until the Croatian Sabor decides otherwise." *The Constitution of the Republic of Croatia* (Zagreb: 1991), p. 70.

13. For details on this aspect, see Lenard J. Cohen, "Regime Transition in a Disintegrating Yugoslavia: The Law-of-Rule vs. the Rule-of-Law," *Carl Beck Papers in Russian and East European Studies*, No. 908 (April 1992).

14. M. Buzadžić, "Tarzen u džungli paragrafa," *Borba*, December 1-2, 1990, p. 7.

15. "A Confederate Model Among the South Slavic States," *Review of International Affairs*, Vol. 41, No. 973 (October 20, 1990), p. 11.

16. *Ibid.*, p. 12. The full text is found on pp. 11-16.

17. *Borba*, November 10-11, 1990, p. 6.

18. "A Concept for the Constitutional System of Yugoslavia on a Federal Basis," *Yugoslav Survey*, Vol. 31, No. 4 (1990), pp. 13-25.

19. *Ibid.*, p. 23.

20. *Ibid.*, p. 24.

21. "Address by President of the SFRY Presidency Dr. Borisav Jović," *Yugoslav Survey*, Vol. 31, No. 4 (1990), pp. 50, 52.

22. Vladimir Goati, "Stavovi gradjana o promenama političkog sistema: o državnom uredjenju i višepartizmu," in Ljiljana Baćević, *et al.*, *Jugoslavija na kriznoj prekretnici* (Belgrade: Institut društvenih nauka, 1991), pp. 118-120.

23. Ljubica Jelušić, "Legitimacy and Integration of the Military in Yugoslav and Slovene Society: Public Opinion Approach," in Philippe Manigart (ed.), *The Future of Security in Europe: A Comparative Analysis of European Public Opinion* (Brussels: Defence Study Center, 1992), pp. 387-406.

24. Military experts later estimated that Slovenian officials were able to retain control over about half of the TD arms in their republic whereas the federal military was able to reassert its control over almost all of the TD weapons in Croatia. Miloš Vasić cited in *Reuters*, July 13, 1992.

25. Štefica Bahtijarević and Goran Milaš, "Reakcija javnost na mjere i politiku SIV-a," in Ljiljana Baćević (ed.), *Jugoslavija na kriznoj prekretnici* (Belgrade: Institut društvenih nauka, 1991), p. 98.

26. Branko Mamula, "Yugoslavia at a Time of Change—Her Future, Cohesion and Security," *RUSI Journal*, Vol. 136, No. 4 (Winter 1991), p. 45.

27. *FBIS-EEU*, December 3, 1990, pp. 63, 65.

28. *FBIS-EEU*, December 17, 1990, p. 71.

29. *FBIS-EEU*, August 14, 1990, p. 56.

30. *FBIS-EEU*, December 19, 1990, p. 73.

31. *Politika: The International Weekly*, December 22-December 28, 1990, p. 1.

32. *FBIS-EEU*, January 16, 1991, p. 52.

33. Stipe Mesić, "Kako sam srušio Jugoslaviju," *Vreme*, Vol. 3, No. 83 (May 25, 1992), p. 23.

34. "Istina o naoružavanju terorističkih formacija u Hrvatskoj," *Narodna Armija*, Vol. 46 (January 26, 1991), (Specijalno izdanje).

35. *Guardian*, February 1, 1991, p. 1.

36. *Associated Press*, February 5, 1991.

37. *FBIS-EEU*, January 14, 1991, pp. 54-56; and *FBIS-EEU*, January 15, 1991, pp. 51-53.

38. *Statement by the President of the Federal Executive Council, Mr. Ante Marković* (Belgrade: Federal Executive Council, January 3, 1991), p. 15.

7

The Politics of Intransigence: Prelude to Civil War

Tito's Yugoslavia does not really exist any more. Whereas we in Croatia and Slovenia want Tito's concept of a federalism, which also included some elements of confederalism, to be developed further, Belgrade wants to return to centralism....Yugoslavia is currently in a phase that cannot last long.

—Franjo Tudjman (November 1, 1990)

The approach that Yugoslavia does not exist, that only republics exist...is not acceptable to us...in our opinion, any division into several states that would separate parts of the Serbian people and put them within separate sovereign states cannot be acceptable...in our opinion, a confederation is not a state.

—Slobodan Milošević (January 15, 1991)

Zero-Sum Negotiations: The Slide Toward Disintegration

NEAR THE END OF December 1990, in an effort to resolve outstanding differences among the republics concerning Yugoslavia's future structure, the federal presidency organized a special round of discussions that were to include all of the country's principal regional and federal decisionmakers. Eight sessions of the so-called "expanded" collective presidency were subsequently held between January 10 and April 3, 1991. Convened during and directly after the January face-off between the JNA top command and the leaders of Croatia, the first meetings got off to an extremely rocky start. The deep political differences among the republics, and also the various interrepublican alliances that had been evolving for some time, quickly became apparent.

Four closely related issues proved to be especially divisive from the outset of the talks: (1) the status and value of maintaining the Yugoslav federation, (2) the right of republics to secede from the existing federation, (3) the character of republican borders, and (4) the most desirable type of future political arrangements among the republics. For the ruling circles in Ljubljana and Zagreb, the Yugoslav federation had all but ceased to exist, and they had no intention of renovating the federal structure. Thus at the initial meetings of the expanded presidency, and in a round of parallel bilateral meetings arranged among the republican leaders, representatives from Slovenia and Croatia reiterated their proposal (first publicized in October 1990) for a confederation of sovereign republics. The entire confederation notion was premised on the belief that each republic had the right to self-determination and secession and that the future organization of the country must preserve the "inviolability and permanence" of the existing republican borders. It is significant that Slovenia and Croatia entered negotiations with a two-track strategy. One track involved efforts to persuade the other republican leaders that immediate work should begin on restructuring the existing federation into a confederal alliance. The second and parallel track, permitted authorities in Zagreb and Ljubljana to proceed with their own incremental steps toward complete political and military independence from the existing federal structure. Indeed, at the very first negotiating session held on January 10, 1991, the president of Slovenia asserted that whether or not the discussions would actually lead to the formation of a "new community" among the republics, "only independent and sovereign republics could be parties to the agreement" and that "the process by which republics become independent…did not mean secession, but was rather a form of disassociation and settling the relationship among them."[1]

For the representatives from Serbia and Montenegro in the negotiations, the Yugoslav federation not only remained a political and international reality but needed to be revivified and strengthened, albeit in a modified form. The strategy of the ethnically related and politically allied Serbs and Montenegrins was to stand pat on their preference for a "modern democratic federation" that would permit all Serbs to reside in a single state and would also grant the country's Serbian majority a stronger voice in a remodeled version of the existing federation. Serbia and Montenegro completely rejected the notion that a republic could unilaterally decide to leave the federation simply by proclaiming its "administrative borders" to be "state borders." In the view of Slobodan Milošević and his allies, such unilateral secession by republics was both politically unacceptable and constitutionally illegal because such action would result in the partitioning of major ethnic groups, such as the Serbs, into separate states against their will. For the political leadership in Belgrade in 1991, just as for so many earlier Serbian leaders and their followers since 1918, the continuity of Yugoslavia's statehood and Serbia's interests were inextricably linked.

As the negotiations among the republican and federal leaders began, the representatives of Bosnia-Hercegovina and Macedonia advanced the most flexible positions. In contrast to the former leaders of those republics who had governed prior to the fall 1990 competitive elections and who generally supported the federal option proposed by the Yugoslav federal state presidency, the newly elected leaders in Sarajevo and Skopje favored the idea of combining aspects of both confederalism and federalism in a new Yugoslav state. In the case of Bosnia-Hercegovina, the new and fragile tripartite coalition of Moslems, Serbs, and Croats generally believed it was imperative to seek consensus and avoid taking any extreme positions. The republic's Moslem President, Alija Izetbegović, together with the Croatian leaders of Bosnia-Hercegovina, endorsed each republic's right to sovereignty and secession as well as the inviolability of republican borders. The Serbian leaders in Bosnia's ruling coalition, however, adopted perspectives similar to the representatives from Serbia and Montenegro.

For the moment, notwithstanding their endorsement of different models, all of the coalition partners in Bosnia-Hercegovina agreed that some sort of united Yugoslav state should be established to bring together the different constitutional ideas currently under discussion. For their part, the Macedonian representatives believed that formal state sovereignty, permanent borders, and equal standing in a confederation would be useful mechanisms for asserting their own autonomy from traditional Serbian political hegemony yet still maintaining the economic resources and security against external pressures that the republic had enjoyed from its membership in the Yugoslav federation. Thus, very early in the 1991 negotiations Macedonian and Bosnian representatives found themselves cooperating to advance some middle ground, or a "third variant" in the federation-confederation debate.

The serious differences among the republics regarding Yugoslavia's future suggested that reaching a negotiated compromise would be exceedingly difficult, but the escalating atmosphere of interrepublican and interethnic distrust and tension outside the negotiations made the chance of a peaceful political settlement even more remote. In addition to the ongoing conflict between the military and Croatia, other problems and episodes cast a shadow over the initial negotiations. On the eve of the first summit meeting, for example, a major scandal erupted over the Serbian republic's unauthorized appropriation of approximately $1.4 billion from the federal bank.[2] The Slovenian government maintained that the financial maneuver—which was denounced by Yugoslavia's Prime Minister Marković as an "unwarranted encroachment on monetary policy"—illustrated the attitude of Serbian authorities toward the resolution of the country's crisis and was evidence of "who is breaking up Yugoslavia."[3] Slovenia's Prime Minister Peterle observed that Serbia's "incursion" into the monetary system did not change Slovenia's fundamental strategy of becoming "independent as soon as possible," but "it would only substantially accelerate, that is, change the pace of the entire independence process."[4]

Although Yugoslavia's divided republican leaders had begun to negotiate about the country's future—a communications breakthrough that was an accomplishment in its own right—they seemed incapable of transcending fixed positions and mundane political conflicts to find common ground. Slovenian and Croatian protests concerning the military's growing role in political affairs overshadowed other issues during the second negotiating session held on January 31, although Bosnia's Izetbegović claimed that any meeting "when people simply show up" should be considered a success.[5] The negotiating atmosphere deteriorated further in early February when Slovenia and Croatia adopted measures to invalidate the authority of federal laws in their republics. Croatia's President Tudjman and his republic's representative in the federal presidency refused to attend a third summit session scheduled on February 8 in Belgrade because of noisy anti-Croatian demonstrations organized by pro-Milošević Serbian women outside the building where the negotiations were to take place. Slovenia's President Kučan traveled to Belgrade to attend the session but soon walked out of the meeting to express his sympathy with the Croatian representatives. Kučan subsequently stated that the course of developments had already destroyed the possibility of making any progress on a confederal agreement. At the next meeting on February 13, Tudjman emphasized that if Slovenia would leave the Yugoslav federation, Croatia would not remain part of the existing state.

During the February 22 meeting in Sarajevo, the key actors continued to talk past each other, with Serbia and Montenegro detailing their views concerning a federal state structure, and representatives of Slovenia and Croatia announcing that their republics had taken further legislative steps to advance the "negotiated disassociation" of the country. Slovenia's

Prime Minister Peterle characterized the developments in his republic as constituting "the formal part of the process of becoming independent. This decision means that Slovenia has legally separated from Yugoslavia as a federation."[6] From the outset, this fourth summit session was characterized by each republic reviewing and justifying its maximum goals rather than by the parties negotiating a mutually acceptable compromise.

Endeavoring to find a way out of the stalemate between the federal and confederal positions at the February 22 meeting, Bosnia's Izetbegović suggested the idea of an "asymmetric" or "graded federation" in which Serbia and Montenegro, either jointly or separately, would be closely linked to Bosnia-Hercegovina and Macedonia in a federal arrangement that would collectively maintain relations with a looser and more independently functioning confederation composed of Croatia and Slovenia. Izetbegović claimed that he was looking for an alternative so that each republic could live in the "kind of Yugoslavia that they want." He explained that he had arrived at his proposal—which became known as the "2+2+2 formula"—after hearing the usual republican positions being advanced for the "umpteenth time."[7] In adopting a position for his republic that, Izetbegović conceded, was closer to the Serbian position, the Bosnian delegation temporarily got at cross-purposes with Macedonia, whose President Gligorov, under pressure from nationalist parties in Skopje, quickly let it be known that his republic had no intention of joining a "reduced federation" in which the balance of interests would heavily favor Serbia. For the moment, Macedonia preferred to maintain its own views, altering the symmetry of the "2+2+2" formula into a "3+2+1" equation.[8]

Although Croatia's representatives in the negotiations acknowledged that Izetbegović's ideas offered some hope, it was also apparent that the intransigence of the top leaders in Serbia and Croatia was preventing any real progress toward a final agreement. In one of his frequent press interviews, Izetbegović offered a rather direct appraisal of how specific political personalities were impeding the negotiations:

> Of all of the participants I personally find Milan Kučan and Kiro Gligorov most appealing. For my taste they are two people who are democrats. On the other side stand two men who will probably play a decisive role— Tudjman and Milošević. In a certain sense they are completely opposite men, but from another side they are temperamentally too similar, and that makes things difficult. Both in my opinion are people who are insufficiently flexible, which of course is not always a defect, but in the business of negotiating, is usually a defect...some people are simply incapable of

compromise. I think Milošević and Tudjman are such people, and as much as one would want, one can't change some of their views...it seems to me that if Serbia and Croatia were headed by people such as Gligorov and Kučan, Yugoslavia would find it much easier to extricate itself from pat positions.[9]

Izetbegović's positive comments about Gligorov were reciprocated by the Macedonian leader who, despite his opposition to the idea of an "asymmetric" federation, identified the reasons for the close cooperation between the Macedonian and Bosnian representatives:

> From our first meeting with Izetbegović I encountered an exceptionally intelligent, moderate, and cooperative man who wished to intelligently listen and understand others, but who defended himself when he considered it necessary. Such people are at this moment very useful. In conversations we concluded that the similarity of our views does not arrive so much from identical positions in Yugoslavia, as much as from the interests of both republics to preserve Yugoslavia.[10]

In the fifth summit session held on March 1, Slovenia's president once again attacked initiatives for a remodeled federation, claiming that such proposals ignored the results of the December Slovenian plebiscite and his republic's desire to be a fully independent and sovereign state. For their part, Bosnia-Hercegovina and Macedonia claimed that there was no contradiction between the sovereignty that might be asserted by each republic and the establishment of joint mechanisms for cooperation in a single state. In support of this theory, President Izetbegović pointed out that a breakthrough in the process would be made only when the supporters of a federal option genuinely recognized the sovereignty of the republics and when supporters of the confederal option recognized the necessity for a single state (albeit with reduced powers). For the intractable Slovenes and Croats, however, sovereignty for the republics meant full statehood, and they would entertain the possibility of maintaining the former Yugoslav framework only as an alliance or community of states, and not as a single overarching state. When no breakthroughs had occurred at the conclusion of the March 1 summit, Slovenia's Kučan observed that the talks were continuing only because "nobody is prepared to take the responsibility for breaking them up."[11]

Political tension, interethnic conflicts, and the delegitimation of the federation intensified during spring 1991 as hope waned that the republics and existing political leaders could reach a mutually acceptable agreement on the future of the country. At the beginning of March, ethnic violence escalated throughout Yugoslavia after the Zagreb government's Ministry of Internal Affairs (MUP) sent special Croatian police units to the town of Pakrac in the Krajina area, where local Serbian authorities had disarmed the town's Croatian police officers. Zagreb's move was a response to a declaration of autonomy by the Krajina Serbs on February 28, not long after the Croatian legislature had called for that republic's "disassociation" from the Yugoslav federation. After clashes between the MUP forces and Serbian police reservists, Yugoslav President Jović ordered a unit of the federal armed forces to Pakrac in an attempt to maintain order. The use of JNA forces, and their subsequent exchange of fire with Croatian police, angered Zagreb authorities as well as the government in Slovenia, which had both been embroiled in an ongoing conflict with the federal military over the question of illegal paramilitary forces. President Tudjman charged that the army was "creating conditions" for its planned intervention to topple the democratically elected governments in Croatia and Slovenia, adding that "the predominance among the top brass of forces that want to install a centralist unitarist Yugoslavia, and return to communism, is a threat that Croatia must take into account."[12]

The increased political role and autonomy of the JNA was underscored when armored units of the JNA were utilized from March 9 to March 13—without authorization from the federal prime minister but with the tacit support of federal President Jović from Serbia—to assist Serbian authorities in restoring order following large street demonstrations in Belgrade organized by the anti-Milošević Serbian opposition. The demonstrations, which were held as a protest against the republican regime's monopoly over the media, led to clashes with police that resulted in 2 people being killed and approximately 90 wounded and ended only after the Serbian minister of internal affairs offered to resign and after about 100 arrested demonstrators had been released. Whereas the Belgrade demonstration was primarily a matter of internal Serbian politics, the presence of federal army tanks on the streets of Belgrade was viewed as an ominous development in the northwestern republics. Slovenian President Kučan observed that "the army, a federal institution, has for the first time intervened in an internal quarrel in a republic between the government and the opposition."[13]

Milošević and conservative forces in the federal military, faced with the determination of the Zagreb authorities to end local Serbian control in the Krajina, and with the increasingly independent stance of Slovenia, and also badly shaken by the Serbian opposition's challenge to the socialist regime in Belgrade, concluded that the situation in the country called for more decisive action. On March 12, state President Jović—a close ally of Milošević and top army officers—presented the collective Yugoslav presidency with a plan drafted by the military that provided that a 48-hour ultimatum be issued demanding that Croatia and Slovenia fully comply with the January 9 decree ordering that all illegal paramilitary units be disbanded. The ultimatum also demanded that Slovenia permit the resumption of federal control over the republic's Territorial Defense forces and that the Ljubljana government abrogate legislation interfering with the recruitment of young Slovenes to the JNA. Should Croatia and Slovenia refuse to comply, the military's plan called for a state of emergency to be declared, presumably followed by some sort of military action against the two offending republics.

When a majority of the representatives in the eight-member federal presidency (Slovenia, Croatia, Macedonia, Bosnia-Hercegovina, and Kosovo) twice refused to adopt the military initiative (on March 12 and March 14), Jović abruptly resigned from his post. Representatives from Montenegro and the province of Vojvodina also followed suit. Jović explained that he was unable to accept the "vote of nonconfidence" in the military, blamed the state presidency's majority for "supporting anti-constitutional and illegal moves conducive to the disintegration of Yugoslavia," and accused Slovenia and Croatia of "openly forming their own republican armies."[14]

In a dramatic television address on March 16, 1991, Slobodan Milošević stated that Serbia would no longer recognize the authority of the federal presidency. According to the Serbian leader, the failure of the presidency to take action against Slovenia and Croatia illustrated that "the plan for the destruction of Yugoslavia had entered its final agonizing stage." Claiming that Serbia's vital interests were threatened, Milošević also ordered the mobilization of Serbia's police reserve units and called upon all the republic's political parties to ignore their "mutual disputes and differences in the interests of Serbia."[15] At Milošević's request, Kosovo's representative to the presidency, who had failed to support Jović, was dismissed by the Serbian legislature, and a loyal Albanian from the province was found to take his place. As a result the presidency was now left with only four of its participating members, which effectively immobilized its authority by the absence of a voting quorum and left the country and the JNA without direction from any central political authority.

At a meeting with Serbian municipal officials on the same day as his television address, Milošević hinted at what he thought should be done to resolve the country's crisis. After two months of fruitless summit meetings with the leaders of the other republics, and having been blocked by the majority in the presidency, Milošević apparently had become convinced that more forceful measures were warranted:

> The army has the constitutional authority and constitutional obligation to defend the constitutional order....Consequently, it isn't a question of some kind of coup. What kind of coup is it, if tomorrow the army exercised its constitutional authority and proceeds to disarm those units of the Croatian Democratic Alliance [*hadezeovske formacije*]? This isn't some kind of coup. The army must disarm paramilitary formations in the interest of defending the constitutional order...to defend peace in the country and its territorial integrity....I believe that the army will exercise its obligation, but if it would not, to consider a theoretical situation as an example, in that case Serbia must act as an independent state on the basis of its own constitution, and that is understood by our own armed forces, and everyone else understands that.[16]

Milošević's hope that the Jović resignation and the vacuum at the top of the federal political system (as well as demonstrations orchestrated by his party in Belgrade on behalf of the military) would be a sufficient impetus to launch military intervention against the northwestern republics proved to be in vain. Following a three day public silence and internal discussions—during which Minister of Defense Kadijević had refused to attend sessions of the rump presidency—the JNA top command announced that the army would refrain from interference in political matters, although it warned that the army would not stand by and allow any changes to Yugoslavia's borders or permit interethnic clashes that could provoke civil war. Reports suggested that the military's decision to exercise restraint resulted from a split in the high command with, on the one side, General Kadijević (of mixed Serbian and Croatian background) and his deputy, Admiral Brovet (a Slovene) who were opposed to further involvement by the armed forces without clear orders from top military authorities, and on the other side, Chief of the General Staff Adžić (a Serb whose family had been killed by Croatian fascists during World War II), arguing that the military should take a "firm course."[17] It was also reported that federal Prime Minister Marković had strongly lobbied for military noninterference and threatened Kadijević that should the JNA interfere in internal politics, the government would use its control over federal funds and its existing ties to international financial institutions to withhold assistance from the armed forces.

In retrospect, the entire episode leading to the Jović resignation "crisis" has the appearance of a carefully staged maneuver by Milošević to simultaneously push the federal military into direct action against Croatia and Slovenia and also—through a countrywide state of emergency and distraction—undercut his political opposition inside Serbia. Failing to obtain a majority vote in the presidency, Milošević apparently engineered Jović's resignation to heighten the country's putative crisis and to thereby provoke the support of the army. When the ploy failed, and federal Vice-President Mesić from Croatia announced that he would become acting state president in view of Jović's resignation (he normally would not have been scheduled to assume the post until May 15), Milošević was forced to back down and hastily arranged for the Serbian legislature to send Jović back to the presidency on March 20. The JNA high command remained true to its Yugoslav convictions and its self-proclaimed internal mission to safeguard the country's fragile interethnic unity, but at least for the moment it was unwilling to become Milošević's pawn and unilaterally engage in the costly and potentially risky business of full-scale military action against the northwest republics.

The events in the first part of March dashed any remaining hopes that the Yugoslav federation could still function as a normal state or could be reconstituted as a state from its existing regional units. Any pretense of a viable federal authority dealing with the country as a whole as its paramount concern was ended by the polarization and immobility in the federal presidency and particularly by Serbia's blatant manipulation of its representatives and allies. Although Jović resumed his post as state president, most of the country now viewed him as a Milošević puppet. Prime Minister Marković—perhaps the last major politician with a genuinely "Yugoslav" outlook—had probably helped to restrain the military, but even he had been politically marginalized by the country's powerful republican elites and had been forced to the sidelines during the futile summit meetings among the republican leaders. As a result, the federal government under Marković found it increasingly impossible to implement its policies or to conduct a coherent program of countrywide reform.

As for the JNA, which purported to remain an institution devoted to Yugoslav unity, its heavily Serbian command structure and strong opposition to the confederal policies of Croatia and Slovenia was now viewed by the two independence-minded republics as a major motivating factor for their planned disassociation from the federation. Indeed, the JNA's role as a literal loose cannon, working closely if still not exclusively with conservative political forces in Serbia, had clearly increased during the opposition protests in Belgrade, during the temporary vacuum in the state presidency, and with the growing ethnic violence in Croatia. The top leaders of the JNA were not at Milošević's beck and call, as the March events in the presidency had demonstrated, but the military elite and the Serbian leadership shared a common interest in preserving Yugoslavia as a centralized state. Reluctant to act—whether because of internal divisions or out of trepidation about how it would perform in any wider struggle that might ensue—the JNA remained cautious. In late March the question of when, or if, the military would choose to actually use armed force on a major scale still remained a very open question. For over three months the JNA had threatened Croatia and Slovenia that failure to disband illegal military units would lead to federal military intervention and that unilateral secession from the federation was an illegal act that would attract similar consequences. The two northwestern republics, however, continued to play clever mice to the JNA cat, proclaiming their intention to become independent states either within or outside a confederal alliance and continuing to buy arms from foreign suppliers for their local quasi-military forces.

In the second part of March, the atmosphere of imminent military crisis in Yugoslavia temporarily abated, and although the cold war of words among contending parties persisted, the focus of attention shifted away from the federal institutions. After the seventh and next-to-last negotiating session in Belgrade ended in failure on March 21, Croatia and Slovenia, frustrated by the stalemated federally sponsored negotiations and having long maintained that federal authorities did not have a legitimate role in arbitrating between the republics, suggested that a new series of purely interrepublican talks be convened *without* the participation of federal officials. Moreover, since Jović's mid-March call for military intervention, the leaders in Ljubljana and Zagreb clearly no longer trusted the federal presidency and were determined to abandon the federal structure as soon as possible. Just prior to the beginning of the new nonfederal round of talks on March 25, an unusual bilateral summit meeting took place between Croatia's Tudjman and Serbia's Milošević at a secretly arranged location on the border between the two republics.

The Tudjman-Milošević talks attracted a great deal of interest throughout Yugoslavia. Not only were Serbian-Croatian relations traditionally the most crucial dimension influencing unity in Yugoslavia, but bad relations between the two ethnic groups and their leaders—a latent source of tension in the country at the best of times—had been steadily deteriorating during the past year.[18] If any progress was to be made in finding a negotiated settlement among the republics, it would have to include the agreement of the political leaderships in Zagreb and Belgrade.

Unfortunately, although the meeting generated many contrasting rumors, compromise once again eluded the two strong-willed leaders on the major issues dividing the country. The official communiqué of the meeting diplomatically stated that in view of the country's "deepening economic crisis," discussions had taken place about "changes in the work and composition" of the federal government. Unofficial reports claimed that Tudjman had endorsed Milošević's plans to oust Prime Minister Marković and to recognize Serbian control over Kosovo and Vojvodina in return for Milošević's commitment not to interfere in Tudjman's handling of Croatia's Serbian minority providing that group adhered to federal and Croatian laws.[19]

The Tudjman-Milošević talks caused mixed reaction in the other republics. For example, Slovenia's prime minister suggested that he welcomed the bilateral summit, considering that it dealt with issues strictly between Croatia and Serbia and that in his view any such communication should hasten the "normal dissolution of Yugoslavia."[20] Members of the Serbian opposition, however, felt that Tudjman had betrayed the cause of democratic change by allegedly agreeing to give Milošević a free hand on internal matters in Serbia. Tudjman would later claim that the Serbian opposition had indeed asked for his help during the March demonstrations in Belgrade but that he had refused to get involved and had made no special deals with Milošević.[21]

Despite the media hype and rumors concerning the Tudjman-Milošević summit, the meeting did nothing to improve the steadily worsening climate of Serbian-Croatian relations in Yugoslavia. On the last day in March, Croatian police took action to prevent the Plitvice National Park area from falling under the control of local Serbian officials who sought to join with other municipalities belonging to the Serbian Autonomous District of Krajina. After military clashes and bloodshed, the Yugoslav federal army intervened to prevent further conflict, just as it had in Pakrac earlier that month. For Zagreb authorities, the emerging pattern of federal military intervention to control ethnic conflict in Croatia was considered unacceptable interference in the republic's domestic affairs that was aimed at undermining Croatia's political control over its Serbian-majority region.

The mounting tension and military presence in the Krajina during early 1991 illustrated how the "Serbian question," that is, the position of the roughly 25 percent of Yugoslavia's Serbs living outside Serbia proper, had become a major impediment to progress in the interrepublican negotiations and thus to any political compromise on the reorganization

Slovenian border guards hoist the new flag of an independent Slovenia at the Yugoslav-Austrian border (June 26, 1991). *Credit:* Canapress Photo Service (Gapa).

Yugoslav federal army soldiers take down the Slovenian flag at a border crossing between Austria and Slovenia (June 27, 1991). *Credit:* Canapress Photo Service (Genberger).

Barricade of buses and other vehicles to block federal military forces at Ljubljana, Slovenia (June 27, 1991). *Credit:* Marjan Garbajs, *Revija Obramba.*

Blocked JNA tanks firing during the federal military's invasion of Slovenia in the fiercest battle of the war at Medvedjek, Slovenia (June 30, 1991). *Credit:* Marjan Garbajs, *Revija Obramba.*

JNA forces retreating under the surveillance of Slovenian Territorial Defense forces at Brnik, Ljubljana Airport (July 4, 1991). *Credit:* Marjan Garbajs, *Revija Obramba.*

Conversation between Croatia's Stipe Mesić (*left*), the last president of the Socialist Federal Republic of Yugoslavia (SFRY), and Ante Marković, the last SFRY prime minister, during a meeting with European Community ministers on the Island of Brioni (July 8, 1991) just prior to the signing of the "Brioni Declaration." *Credit:* Canapress Photo Service, (Alik Keplicz).

European Community monitors—the "ice-cream men"—observing hostilities in eastern Croatia at the end of 1991. *Credit:* Colonel Don S. Ethell.

Serbian soldiers marching Croatians out of their village near Vukovar (November 19, 1991).
Credit: Vreme News Digest Agency.

Refugees from Sarajevo (April 20, 1992). *Credit:* Vreme News Digest Agency.

Residents of Sarajevo digging fresh graves at a Moslem cemetery during a lull in the fighting (May 5, 1992). *Credit:* Vreme News Digest Agency.

President Izetbegović of Bosnia-Hercegovina shaking the hand of President Tudjman of Croatia after signing an agreement of "Friendship and Cooperation" between the two republics (July 21, 1992). *Credit:* Vreme News Digest Agency.

Radovan Karadžić, leader of the Bosnian Serbs, at the United Nations after talks with Cyrus Vance and Lord David Owen about their peace plan for Bosnia and Hercegovina (February 4, 1993). *Credit:* Canapress Photo Service (Ed Bailey).

Croatian and Moslem prisoners of war at the Serbian detention camp of Manjača, near Banja Luka (August 1992). *Credit:* Vreme News Digest Agency.

Croats and Moslems forced to leave an area occupied by Serbian forces in Bosnia (November 1992). *Credit:* Vreme News Digest Agency.

A refugee near Bijeljina in eastern Bosnia (1992). *Credit:* Vreme News Digest Agency.

A distraught Moslem woman and her child at a refugee holding center in eastern Bosnia (July 1992). *Credit:* Vreme News Digest Agency.

Scenes like this one in Bosnia (1992) have grown common. *Credit:* Vreme News Digest Agency.

(*Above*): Hans-Dietrich Genscher, the German foreign minister, with President Franjo Tudjman of Croatia (February 23, 1992). *Credit:* Josip Bistrović. (*Above, right*): Canadian peacekeeping troops from the United Nations protection force prepared to deploy at Daruvar, Croatia (March 26, 1992). *Credit:* T. Hnojčik. (*Right*): An elderly Serbian woman in Kruševac, Serbia, holds an election poster of Milan Panić during his campaign for the presidency of Serbia (December 16, 1992). *Credit:* Vreme News Digest Agency.

Members of a local election board in Belgrade count votes in the race for president of Serbia, the Serbian legislature, and the legislature of the "Third Yugoslavia," Serbia-Montenegro (December 20, 1992). *Credit:* Pierre Guimond.

Vojislav Šešelj, the ultranationalistic leader of the Serbian Radical Party (SRS) (May 2, 1991). *Credit:* Robert Šipek.

Dobroslav Paraga (*center*), the ultranationalistic leader of the Croatian Party of Right (HSP), at his headquarters (November 15, 1991). He is seated before a picture of Ante Starčević, one of the nineteenth-century fathers of radical Croatian nationalism. *Credit:* Siniša Hančić.

Croatian President Tudjman with other Croatian officials in front of the presidential jet (January 9, 1993). Tudjman's expenditures in connection with his official office were the source of considerable media comment within Croatia. *Credit:* B. Kelemenić.

Serbian-Croatian summit at Geneva (October 1992). *Left to right:* Croatian President Tudjman; cochairmen of the International Conference on the Former Yugoslavia, Cyrus Vance and Lord David Owen (speaking at the microphone); and President Ćosić of the Federal Republic of Yugoslavia.

of the Yugoslav state. For the Milošević leadership in Belgrade, obsessed with the idea of preserving the federal state and enhancing Serbian influence, support for the "unity" of the Serbs and particularly protection of the large Serbian communities in Croatia and Bosnia-Hercegovina were crucial bargaining chips in discussions about Yugoslavia's future. Thus, Milošević claimed that in principle he had no opposition to the self-determination of Yugoslavia's nations, or even legal secession by the republics, as long as those rights did not infringe on the equal right of Serbs in a particular republic to exercise their own self-determination. Accordingly he maintained that if the majority of citizens in Croatia or Bosnia-Hercegovina, for example, wanted to become independent, it would be necessary to change the borders of those republics. Grounding his argument on the "Serbian question," Milošević argued that self-determining or seceding non-Serb majorities in a republic could not have it both ways, that is, the dissolution of the Yugoslav state and also the expectation of inviolable borders.

Although in Milošević's opinion the unilateral secession of any republic from Yugoslavia would be illegal, by spring 1991 he had begun to acknowledge that the secession of a nearly ethnically homogeneous republic, such as Slovenia, with no substantial Serbian community, might become politically inevitable and even acceptable.[22] In the cases of Croatia and Bosnia-Hercegovina, however, with their large Serbian communities, such a secession scenario was completely out of the question for Milošević, unless of course major border adjustments would be negotiated.

Focused on his larger goal of Yugoslav unity under Serbian influence, Milošević cleverly supported and encouraged the incoherent and fragmented strivings of Yugoslavia's major diasporic Serbian communities for self-determination yet still carefully withheld full recognition of their political autonomy or acceptance of their plans to become part of the Serbian republic. By keeping the "Serbian question" on the front burner, and opening the issue of border changes, Milošević and his allies among the Serbs in the JNA hoped they could prevent Croatia's Tudjman, and also the Croat and Moslem leaders of Bosnia-Hercegovina, from making any precipitous decisions about leaving the Yugoslav federation. Moreover, Milošević believed that should negotiations collapse, the same issue could be used as a pretext for armed intervention against secession by either Croatia or Bosnia. The tactic of directing special attention to the diasporic Serbs in Yugoslavia also served Milošević's domestic agenda. Thus by concentrating attention on the countrywide plight of the Serbs,

Milošević could try to excuse, or deflect attention away from, the authoritarian cast of his ruling socialist regime and also appeal for political unity and support against the Serbs' putative internal and external enemies.

Croatian political leaders saw the "Serbian question" quite differently, although their frequently insensitive approach to Serbian-Croatian interethnic relations often played into Milošević's hands. For President Tudjman, the Serbs of Croatia were simply a minority living in a new democratic state and therefore would have to cohabit peacefully with the Croatian majority, whether or not Croatia happened to be inside or outside the Yugoslav federation. The fact that there were substantial numbers of Serbs living in Croatia or elsewhere outside Yugoslavia did not entitle the Belgrade leadership or the military to deny Croatia the right to exist as a sovereign state. But the Croatian president went out of his way to reassure the republic's Serbs, and also international observers, that minority rights would be respected in postcommunist Croatia. He also emphasized that the traditional use of Croatian nationalist rhetoric and symbols in the republic should not be a source of apprehension on the part of the Serbian minority community. The frequent references by Tudjman and his colleagues to the wide differences in the cultures and mentalities of the Serbs and Croats, however, deeply offended and angered the republic's Serbs. As Tudjman told one interviewer:

> Croats belong to a different culture—a different civilization from the Serbs. Croats are part of Western Europe, part of the Mediterranean tradition. Long before Shakespeare and Molière, our writers were translated into European languages. The Serbs belong to the East. They are Eastern peoples, like the Turks and Albanians. They belong to the Byzantine culture....Despite similarities in language we cannot be together.[23]

Tudjman's persistent complaints about earlier Serbian privileges in Croatia under the communist regime, and his intention to reduce the disproportionately high number of Serbs in political life, the state administration, the police, and the media, though understandable also served to fuel Serbian anxiety and their refusal to extend allegiance to the new regime in Zagreb.

For Tudjman and his supporters, if there was any real "Serbian question" at all worth considering it was essentially the issue of whether the Serbs in Croatia, and particularly the roughly 25 percent of that group living in the Krajina, would acknowledge the sovereignty of the new regime, or whether Zagreb authorities would have to take stronger measures to maintain order. An exasperated Tudjman, claiming that from August 1990 to March 1991 his officials had prudently refrained from using police force against the illegal action of armed Krajina Serbs—blocking roads, seizing control of local facilities, establishing autonomous enclaves—stated on April 4 that the March events in Pakrac and Plitvice were the last straw: "We have played democracy for long enough and it is high time to say that Croatia is a republic and that it has a right to establish order."[24] Unfortunately, although the unwillingness of Croatian leaders to accept interference with their republic's administration and legal system was justifiable, their constant reference to the political activities of the Krajina Serbs as the work of "outlaws," "terrorists," and the "mob" only intensified Serbian intransigence and lessened chances of resolving conflicts at the negotiating table.

Although Tudjman and his colleagues publicly maintained that the "Serbian question" was simply an issue of the republic's sovereignty and a matter of internal law and order, the problem in fact had much broader significance and created enormous pressure in the political struggle regarding Yugoslavia's future. Indeed, Croatian leaders fully realized that unless they would be able to reach a negotiated accommodation with the Krajina Serbs and, even more important, with Milošević and the large Serbian segment of the military leadership concerning the acceptability of Croatian-Slovenian proposals for an alliance of sovereign states, Croatia would probably have to fight its way out of the Yugoslav federation in a protracted armed struggle. Tudjman's pointed remarks during the early part of 1991—that if Slovenia would disassociate from Yugoslavia, Croatia would immediately take the same course of action and that intervention by the United States and the international community might become necessary to preserve peace in the Balkans—revealed his anxiety that Croatia not be left alone to face a showdown with Serbia and the JNA. In spring 1991, the "Serbian question" had also begun to become a more sensitive issue in Bosnia-Hercegovina. But owing to the prevailing (albeit tenuous) triethnic formula for political management of the republic, ethnic conflicts temporarily remained nonviolent as the cautious Moslem and Croatian leadership in the republic avoided taking extreme positions in the federation-confederation debate.

During April and May, Yugoslavia's slide toward disintegration gathered momentum. After a summit meeting of interrepublican leaders on April 4, Milošević admitted that progress on negotiations up to that point had been only "microscopic."[25] The demonstrated inability of most republican leaders to transcend fixed positions or retreat from their maximum goals ensured that progress was equally insubstantial in similar summit meetings held later in April. Another bilateral meeting between Tudjman and Milošević on April 15 also failed to achieve a breakthrough, although the two leaders agreed that the country's problems should be resolved democratically and without resort to violence. Once again, however, rumors of a secret agreement swirled around the Tudjman-Milošević talks, this time focusing on an alleged deal by the two leaders to divide up Bosnia-Hercegovina between Croatia and Serbia.

The issue of Bosnia-Hercegovina also arose in relation to discussions concerning the best way to ascertain how the citizens of the country viewed their future. Although the republican leaders agreed that referenda would be a valid way to determine the sentiment of citizens in each republic, there was no consensus on how such a process should be conducted. Milošević endorsed the view that every major ethnic group in each republic should have a separate referendum, whereas most other leaders preferred that all citizens of a republic take part in a single process. Commenting on his strong difference of opinion with Milošević on the referendum, Alija Izetbegović warned that the Milošević formula would "cause an explosion that could blow Bosnia-Hercegovina to smithereens and that in the future people would be shooting at each other from windows...the people of Bosnia-Hercegovina are mixed up like corn and flour."[26]

Meanwhile, studiously avoiding entangling their own republic in the complexities of the "Serbian question," the leaders of Slovenia continued to methodically take further measures to enhance their republic's control over military and economic affairs. Because their republic had already voted for sovereignty and independence, the question of referenda on the future of Yugoslavia held little interest for Slovenian representatives in the interrepublican talks. Thus on April 11 the president of Slovenia's legislature told an interviewer that preparations for the republic's independence would be completed by the end of June, as envisioned by the plebiscite held in December 1990.[27] Warnings by federal officials that Slovenia should resume sending Slovenian recruits to the JNA, and should also revoke decisions to stop paying customs and other import duties to the federal treasury, were simply ignored in Ljubljana. In an address to the Federal Assembly on April 19, the completely frustrated federal prime minister evenhandedly laid blame for the country's severe difficulties on the incessant political and ethnic disputes—concerning "sovereignty, armament, borders, about the ambitions of 'big' and 'small' states"—which had served to "pauperize" all parts of the country and effectively deprive the federation of any power.[28]

As Ljubljana officials watched the JNA's widening involvement in Croatia's Krajina region in early May, Slovenia stepped up its control and coordination of republican Territorial Defense units. Demonstrations against the JNA by Croats in Bosnia-Hercegovina, and the killing in Split on May 26 of a Macedonian JNA conscript by Croatian demonstrators opposed to the presence of JNA forces in Croatia, were among the first indications that resistance to the federal armed forces had begun to assume the character of a popular rebellion. On the same day, Yugoslavia's defense minister announced that the country was in a virtual state of civil war, but Slovenian and Croatian representatives in a meeting of the federal presidency were able to block the proclamation of a state of emergency.

Slovenian representatives had warned only days earlier that the Supreme Command of the JNA had begun "distancing" itself from the presidency's control. Slovenia's Defense Minister Janša meanwhile claimed that the JNA had fallen under the control of General Adžić and Serbian extremists, and he predicted that in the event of an all-out civil war in the country the armed forces would fall apart.[29] During the month of May, the first group of Slovenian recruits was also directed to the republic's own barracks rather than to the facilities of the federal army for training. The seedbed of an independent Slovenian army was also beginning to take shape, as long predicted and feared by the federal military elite. It was a prediction that Janša was working hard to make come true.[30] At the same time, Croatia's President Tudjman observed that because the JNA was clearly siding with local Serbian militias in the Krajina, his government had taken steps to transform "political forces into national guard units" to "fight terrorism."[31]

As distrust and conflict among the republics deepened during April and May, and it became more probable that the leaders of Croatia and Slovenia would proceed with their previously announced plans to leave the existing federation, attention once again focused on the collective federal presidency. Although seriously discredited by its earlier failures to resolve the country's prolonged crisis and divisions, and particularly by the Jović resignation in mid-March, the presidency remained the highest level of formal authority in the state and also the civilian body technically responsible for directing the armed forces. With the likely disintegration of the country looming, Serbia and Montenegro feared that the officially scheduled rotation of Croatia's Stipe Mesić into the one-year term of president of the federal presidency on May 15 (and the departure of Serbia's Jović from that position) would radically alter the balance of political power in that body and immobilize its potential authority to take military action against seceding republics should such action become necessary. Although Mesić enjoyed the support of four republics in the eight-member presidency (Croatia, Slovenia, Bosnia-

Hercegovina, and Macedonia), his normal rotation into the post was blocked on May 15 when Serbia and its two provinces voted against his election and when Serbia's ally, Montenegro (whose representative was to become vice-president during the next year), abstained.

An attempt to break the deadlock the next day failed when Mesić's opponents in the presidency reneged on a previous informal agreement to support his election in return for Slovenia and Croatia dropping their previous objections to the Federal Assembly's endorsement of new representatives in the presidency from Serbia and its provinces. The Serbian leadership justified its obstruction of Mesić by claiming that he had disqualified himself from the presidency by previously announcing his intention to preside over the country's dissolution and by his alleged claim that he would be Yugoslavia's "last president." Mesić denied making any such statements, explaining to an interviewer that he had only urged the country to "change its present model" but that he did not necessarily mean "breaking up Yugoslavia."[32]

The four-to-four split stalemated the collective presidency and again placed the country in the bizarre and dangerous position of not having a head of state or an operational civilian body controlling the armed forces. In a hasty effort to fill the vacuum of formal authority, the rump collective presidency appointed a "coordinator" (Kosovo's Sejdo Bajramović, ironically the new Albanian representative in the federal presidency who was hand picked by Milošević back in March) to serve as acting president and to supervise the collective presidency's activities. Meanwhile, Yugoslav Prime Minister Marković—who made public the formation of his own "coordinating group" to keep the government functioning—suggested that the country was still under civilian control. As a result of the deadlocked and headless presidency, however, there was little doubt that the political autonomy of the top military elite, which had already been growing incrementally for several months, had considerably expanded.

The shabby treatment accorded to Croatia's Mesić probably served to add a few percentage points to the large majority of voters in Croatia who expressed support for the republic's independence in a referendum held on May 19, 1991. Turnout was 84 percent overall, and approximately 93 percent of those voting supported the creation of a "sovereign and independent" country that would guarantee cultural autonomy and the "rights of citizens to the Serbs and members of other nationalities in Croatia" and would enter into an alliance of sovereign states with other republics. Approximately 92 percent responded in the negative to another question asking whether Croatia should stay in a federal Yugoslav state.

Croatia's Krajina Serbs boycotted the republic's referendum, only one week earlier having held a separate vote in which 99.8 percent of those turning out supported the idea of their region's union with Serbia.

Buoyed by the overwhelming mandate in the republic-wide referendum, and dismissing the Krajina vote as an illegal act, Croatian officials announced that they would decide on the republic's future status by the end of June. Meanwhile, Slovenia's resolve to proceed with its own plans for independence became even more acute at the end of May following an incident in which members of the republic's Territorial Defense forces were kidnapped by the JNA and a JNA armored vehicle accidentally killed a Slovenian demonstrator. During the first week in June, Slovenian legislators debated the details of a law on independence that was scheduled to be proclaimed in June 26 and, in the absence of any other agreement among the republics, also announced the formation of Slovenia's own armed forces.

On June 3, in a last-ditch effort to head off the country's complete disintegration, Bosnia-Hercegovina's Izetbegović and Macedonia's Gligorov unveiled their joint proposal designed to combine the contending confederal and federal options. Under their proposal, a new "Community of Yugoslav Republics" would be created as a unified state with a common market as well as common institutions for defense and foreign policy. Rather contradictorily, the plan also provided that each republic should be entitled to maintain its own armed and diplomatic representation. It was envisioned that such an agreement would have a term of five or ten years and would be reviewed near the end of the century. Serbian politicians initially rejected the proposal, claiming it was just a cover-up for establishing a loose confederation. However, at the sixth interrepublican summit meeting in Sarajevo on June 6, they gave the proposal conditional support, probably as a result of mounting international pressure on Belgrade to soften its negotiating stance. Guarded optimism about the Izetbegović-Gligorov model was also expressed by Slovenian and Croatian summit participants, and it was agreed by all parties that the proposal should be the basis of a June 12 three-sided mini-summit including Tudjman, Milošević, and Izetbegović.

But the compromise plan had arrived too late. Although the Izetbegović-Gligorov model received some approval by all the negotiating parties, by this time each of the major republics was already deeply committed to its own particular strategies and timetables for dealing with Yugoslavia's future. Thus, Croatia and Slovenia had no intention of changing their planned independence declarations in order to open yet another round of negotiations that, even if successful, would unacceptably preserve many aspects of the existing federal structure. On June 12, Slovenian Prime Minister Peterle announced to the legislature of Slovenia that all the necessary preparations for the independence of the republic had been completed. Peterle was followed to the podium by visiting federal Prime Minister Marković, who pleaded for the preservation of the Yugoslav community, but by then his arguments fell largely on deaf ears.[33]

Indeed, on June 15 Slovenian and Croatian leaders held a meeting in Ljubljana in which they coordinated their plans to proclaim the independence of their two republics no later than June 26, 1991.[34] For Serbia, though, acceptance of the joint Bosnian-Macedonian plan meant acquiescence to the idea of a highly decentralized Yugoslavia, which also would permit the northwestern republics to push ahead with their plans for independent armed forces.[35] Moreover, by June the JNA forces present in Croatia were actively assisting the Krajina Serbs to maintain control over their local enclaves—a military posture that Milošević and the JNA top command hardly relished having to abandon because of a last-minute, and only partially acceptable, compromise agreement.

Thus at their June 12 summit in Split, Tudjman and Milošević, firmly committed as usual to their completely antithetical views, were reportedly less interested in discussing the promising, if somewhat delinquent, Bosnian-Macedonian compromise than they were in talking about how to divide Bosnia-Hercegovina into separate ethnic "cantons." Izetbegović at first denied that such a prospect was discussed at the meeting and warned that he would walk out of any talks convened to negotiate the division of his republic, although he later admitted that the notion was probably "in the air." As far as the broader question of Yugoslavia's future, Izetbegović claimed that he had tried unsuccessfully to keep "forcing" the topic of reconciling the notion of sovereignty for the republics with the idea of retaining a single "state community." Izetbegović's efforts, however, were to no avail.

Another meeting of the same three leaders on June 19 in Belgrade proved to be equally futile.[36] Commenting on the Bosnian-Macedonian plan, Tudjman told a Zagreb newspaper that "this hybrid does not satisfy Croatia and Slovenia, and Serbia is dissatisfied too."[37] After nearly six months of negotiations, the country's leaders had failed to reach a compromise on a mutually acceptable model for keeping the territorial units of the existing federation together in some sort of common state, or interstate, framework.

International Involvement:
An EC Offer and Baker's Mission Impossible

By mid-June 1991 the international community was becoming increasingly alarmed that the failure of Yugoslavia's republican leaders to achieve a compromise might lead to the violent disintegration of the Balkan state. Preferences regarding one or another model of Balkan cohesion varied considerably from one foreign capital to another. German, Austrian and Italian political leaders, for example, were generally more sympathetic to the views advanced by the governments of Slovenia and Croatia for a confederation of sovereign states, whereas Serbian advocacy of a remodeled federation—though not necessarily according to the highly centralized perspectives of Milošević—were received more sympathetically in London and Paris. In Moscow, where Gorbachev was still desperately trying to cobble together a "Union Treaty" among his country's increasingly nationalistic republics, official Soviet policy supported the notion of Yugoslav unity. In an interview during his April 1991 visit to Belgrade, Soviet Foreign Minister Bessmertnykh remarked that the territorial integrity of Yugoslavia was considered by Moscow to be "one of the essential preconditions for the stability of Europe."[38] Although the Kremlin adopted a relatively evenhanded and constructive approach to Yugoslavia's interethnic problems, the traditional Slavic and Eastern Orthodox religious ties between the Russians and the Serbs, and also the continued penchant for "socialist reform" by Gorbachev and Soviet conservatives, generally heartened conservative and Yugoslav-oriented socialist forces in Belgrade who felt that they could depend upon the USSR.[39]

Meanwhile the Bush administration, worrying that potential Yugoslav disintegration would have negative repercussions on Soviet cohesion, steadfastly supported the country's unity and the pragmatic reform policies of Prime Minister Marković. Washington's historic policy of supporting Yugoslav unity had been made even more explicit in late February 1990 when Deputy Secretary of State Lawrence Eagleburger was dispatched to Belgrade for a two-day visit. Eagleburger at that time had reconfirmed the U.S. view that Yugoslavia should remain united and that the Marković government was on the right track. Moreover, Eagleburger's experience in Yugoslavia—he had been ambassador to Belgrade during the early 1980s, and had extensive business ties with the country from 1984 to 1988—had convinced him that Yugoslavia would not ultimately disintegrate because, as he put it, the "Yugoslavs know well what would happen to them if they divided."[40] Eagleburger also had a longtime acquaintanceship—or what on a later occasion he called a "well-tested working relationship"—with Slobodan Milošević and believed the Serbian leader was a reasonable man with whom Washington could do business.[41] Persuaded that the Yugoslav leaders understood the gravity of the situation, the Bush administration throughout 1990 and the first half of 1991 continued to express its support for the unity of the Yugoslav federation, and also applauded the reform efforts of Prime Minister Marković.[42] Thus, American policy ignored the possibility that the preservation of the Yugoslav federation might no longer be tenable, and that emphasis should be placed on ensuring its peaceful breakup or reconfiguration into a confederation. Recognition that Yugoslavia might violently disintegrate was provided by the intelligence community—for example, a CIA warning in November 1990 that the Yugoslav "experiment" had failed and that the country would violently fall apart within eighteen months[43]—but Washington remained committed to the unity of the Yugoslav state.

It was only on the eve of the planned "disassociation" of Slovenia and Croatia in late June, however, that international attention regarding the Balkans noticeably escalated, though not necessarily in the thoughtfully crafted and coordinated manner that might have made a difference to the eventual outcome. On May 30 and 31, 1991 Jacques Santer, Chairman of the European Council of Ministers, and Jacques Delors, Chairman of the European Commission, flew to Belgrade for talks with Yugoslavia's federal and republican leaders. The EC officials suggested that if Yugoslavia's leaders resolved their constitutional difficulties the EC would be willing to intercede with international financial institutions, such as the IMF, to obtain further support for Yugoslav economic stabilization (e.g., strengthening of foreign currency reserves, support for the convertibility of the dinar, new investments, and so on), and also that the EC was prepared to start talks immediately on Yugoslavia's associate membership in the Community. EC financial support ranging between $4 and $5 billion would also be provided if a political settlement could be reached. During talks lasting eighteen hours, each of Yugoslavia's republican leaders reiterated the well-honed and inflexible positions they had been advancing for months in the stalemated constitutional negotiations. Serbia's Milošević, for example, expressed satisfaction that the EC strongly supported Yugoslavia's integrity, while Slovenia's Kučan warned that Slovenia would "probably have to" secede from Yugoslavia through "a unilateral act." Macedonia's Vasil Tupurkovski warned Santer and Delors that the absence of a unified European policy toward Yugoslavia was sending mixed signals to the different political forces in the country, and was resulting in various divergent reactions which were actually exacerbating the crisis.[44] In a press conference held before he left Belgrade, Santer observed that EC activity in recent years had been directed toward Eastern Europe, but that the twelve members of the Community had "not forgotten Yugoslavia." Santer stressed, however, that any model for cooperation among the Yugoslav republics would ultimately have to be reached by the leaders of Yugoslavia themselves, that is, exactly the same message the EC had conveyed in previous comments on the Yugoslav crisis.[45] The same point was reiterated by Yugoslavia's Prime Minister Marković who observed that despite the EC's generous financial incentives to foster the unity of the federation, "Europe is not prepared to pay us not to fight. Let's have no illusions about this. We must solve our own problems."

Only twenty days after the EC mission to Belgrade the international community made yet another hastily contrived effort to address the looming Yugoslav crisis. At a meeting of the 35-nation Conference on Security and Cooperation in Europe (CSCE), held in Berlin on June 19 and 20, U.S. Secretary of State James Baker received support from major European leaders to vigorously advocate Yugoslavia's continued territorial unity, democratization, and the reforms of the federal Marković government. Croatian efforts at Berlin to obtain support for the peaceful disassociation of the country were brushed aside by the United States.[46] On June 21, James Baker arrived in Belgrade for one day of talks with federal and republican leaders. Meeting with each of the republican leaders individually, Baker made it clear to the presidents of Slovenia and Croatia that the United States disapproved of any "preemptive unilateral actions" and would not recognize their planned declarations of independence. U.S. and CSCE support for continued dialogue and the importance of avoiding violence, were also the messages emphasized to the pro-Yugoslav socialist leaders of Serbia and Montenegro and also to the more flexible presidents of Macedonia and Bosnia-Hercegovina (whose compromise plan had been floated without much success over the previous two weeks). Although Baker emphasized that Washington wanted to see the problems of Yugoslavia resolved peacefully through negotiations, his strong opposition to "unilateral actions" by Slovenia and Croatia may have been deliberately misinterpreted by the JNA high command as a green light for taking military steps to forestall secessionism. It still remains unclear whether an ambiguous message from Baker actually contributed to subsequent orders by the JNA high command for military intervention, whether the JNA elite simply ignored a strict injunction from Baker against the use of the army to deal with the northwestern republics under any circumstances, or whether—in another plausible scenario that has been suggested—the top brass was given the nod by Baker behind the scenes to use force, but only if it became absolutely necessary.

Before leaving Belgrade, Baker admitted that what he had heard in his meetings was not encouraging. The republican leaders had simply repeated to Baker what they had been saying to each other, or rather saying past each other, for the previous six months. Attempting to demonstrate flexibility, the leaders of Serbia and Montenegro had told Baker of their willingness to support the Bosnian-Macedonian compromise formula discussed over the past two weeks. Montenegro's Bulatović conceded, however, that the six republican presidents were not very good negotiators and that they were all "captives" of their own policies.[47] The leaders of Slovenia and Croatia indicated their determination to move ahead with "disassociation" from the existing federation and were distressed that the U.S. Secretary of State lacked sympathy for their opposition to leave the fold of a united state governed from Belgrade. A top Croat leader later explained that "the owner of the biggest ranch in Wyoming" could not free himself from the "American tradition of demonizing the phenomenon of secession. He didn't have an ear for our proposal to establish a union of sovereign states."[48] Putting the best face possible on the stalemated situation, Baker claimed that at least all sides had supported the need for further dialogue, peaceful methods, and the legitimate interests of the international community in the outcome of negotiations.[49] In the final analysis, however, Baker emphasized that "it's really going to be up to the people of Yugoslavia" to reconcile their differences.[50]

On June 23, the members of the European Community (EC), echoing Baker's message, unanimously voted *not* to recognize the independence of Slovenia and Croatia if those republics unilaterally seceded from the Yugoslav federation. Two days later, according to their prearranged plans, Slovenia and Croatia ignored the signals from the United States and the European Community and declared their independence. Within 24 hours, JNA tanks rolled into action against units of the Slovenian Territorial Defense forces. General Adžić, the JNA chief of staff, claimed that the army had been "forced" into a "war for the defense of the country" and that he was stunned by the ferocity of Slovenian military moves against the JNA. He added that "having been brought up over decades in the Yugoslav spirit, we could not believe that so much evil and hatred could accumulate in one place and be expressed in such terrible forms."[51]

Slovenian leaders would later blame Prime Minister Marković for the JNA's military action in view of the fact that the army had based its activity on federal government decisions made between June 13 and 26 that were designed to prevent Yugoslavia's 67 border posts in Slovenia (along a 671-kilometer frontier) from falling into the hands of republican authorities. Marković would insist that the army had gone beyond his order to protect the country's external frontiers, and even high-ranking Croatian leaders would later support Marković's position.[52] Although the debate over who was to blame for initiating military action would continue, there was little disagreement that Yugoslavia's diverse peoples had entered a new and tragic chapter in their political development.

Notes

1. "Activities of the SFRY Presidency Relating to the Political Future of the Country," *Yugoslav Survey*, Vol. 32, No. 2 (1991), p. 14. Slovenian officials persistently objected that they were not planning to secede from Yugoslavia but rather to "disassociate" or "separate" through "consentaneous division," exercising their republic's right to self-determination "through a process of becoming independent." "It is not a question of avoiding terminology or of using recondite terms," observed Slovenia's President Kučan, but of using terms that under international law allow sovereign units of a federation to unilaterally become "equal successors" to an existing state in a "legal material sense, and in every other sense." In contrast to disassociation, observed Kučan, "secession is the recognition that a state remains, that one part secedes, and that the part that remains determines for the other the conditions under which it can secede, the obligations it may take with it, and finally the rights that may possibly be recognized by it." *FBIS-EEU*, March 19, 1991, p. 51.

2. *FBIS-EEU*, January 10, 1991, p. 40.

3. *Ibid.*; *FBIS-EEU*, January 14, 1991, p. 55.

4. *FBIS-EEU*, January 15, 1991, pp. 54-55.

5. *Politika: The International Weekly*, February 2, 1991, p. 1.

6. *FBIS-EEU*, March 12, 1991, p. 54.

7. *FBIS-EEU*, March 1, 1991, p. 38.

8. *FBIS-EEU*, March 15, 1991, p. 51.

9. *Borba*, February 8, 1991, p. 11; and *Danas*, February 12, 1991, p. 36. He expressed the same sentiment in early April. *Danas*, April 9, 1991, p. 30.

10. *Vreme*, February 18, 1991, p. 12.

11. *FBIS-EEU*, March 4, 1991, p. 47. On March 8, 1991, Slovenia's Prime Minister Peterle told an Austrian newspaper, reporter that Slovenia would be prepared by May 15 to take "several steps" toward independence if "wild events" take place and that after July 1, 1991, Yugoslavia would no longer exist

in its conventional form. He also claimed that the creation of a confederation looked unlikely but that Ljubljana officials had not totally abandoned their support for the idea. *FBIS-EEU*, March 11, 1991, pp. 59-60.

12. *FBIS-EEU*, March 8, 1991, p. 50.

13. *FBIS-EEU*, March 13, 1991, p. 72.

14. *FBIS-EEU*, March 24, 1991, pp. 32-34.

15. *FBIS-EEU*, March 18, 1991, p. 47.

16. *Vreme*, April 15, 1991, p. 66.

17. *FBIS-EEU*, March 14, 1991, p. 57. On political divisions in the military, see also *FBIS-EEU*, March 18, 1991, p. 40.

18. A communiqué issued after a discussion between Milošević and Tudjman on January 25, 1991, indicated that relations between Serbia and Croatia were "at their lowest point since the last war, and that there are major differences relating to the solution of national questions, the future of Yugoslavia, the Yugoslav Federation and its institutions and in particular the Yugoslav National Army." "Documents on the Future Regulation of Relations in Yugoslavia," *Yugoslav Survey*, Vol. 32, No. 1 (1991), p. 12.

19. Milan Andrejevich, "Retreating from the Brink of Collapse," *Report on Eastern Europe*, April 12, 1991, p. 29.

20. *FBIS-EEU*, March 28, 1991, p. 41.

21. *FBIS-EEU*, April 15, 1991, p. 47.

22. *Vreme*, April 15, 1991, p. 66.

23. Milton Viorst, "A Reporter at Large: The Yugoslav Idea," *New Yorker*, March 18, 1991, p. 74.

24. *FBIS-EEU*, April 5, 1991, p. 36.

25. *Ibid.*, p. 35.

26. *FBIS-EEU*, April 14, 1991, p. 43. At the end of April, Izetbegović observed that although the presidents of the republics had already negotiated for seventy hours, everything was roughly the way it was at their first meeting because nobody was prepared to move one step in the direction of the other or stay for five minutes "in the skin of the other." *FBIS-EEU*, April 30, 1991, p. 37.

27. *FBIS-EEU*, April 16, 1991, p. 42.

28. Address by the President of the Federal Executive Council, Mr. Ante Marković, at the Meeting of Both Houses of the Assembly of the SFRY, Belgrade, April 19, 1991, *Review of International Affairs*, No. 986 (May 5, 1991), p. 11.

29. *FBIS-EEU*, May 10, 1991, p. 27.

30. This is detailed by Janša in *Premiki: Nastajanje in obramba slovenske države 1988-1992* (Ljubljana: Mladinska knjiga, 1991).

31. *FBIS-EEU*, May 3, 1991, p. 40.

32. *Politika: The International Weekly*, No. 62 (May 25-May 3, 1991), p. 5; and *FBIS-EEU*, May 23, 1991, p. 20.

33. *Information from Slovenia*, June 20, 1992, p. 5.

34. Stipe Mesić, *Kako smo srušili Jugoslaviju: Politički memoari* (Zagreb: Globus International, 1992), p. 43.

35. *Borba*, June 4, 1991, p. 10.

36. *FBIS-EEU*, June 17, 1991, p. 45.

37. *FBIS-EEU*, June 20, 1991, p. 38.

38. *Politika: The International Weekly*, No. 56 (April 13-April 19, 1991), p. 2.

39. For various viewpoints on the Yugoslav crisis in the USSR, see Suzanne Crow, "Soviet Reaction to the Crisis in Yugoslavia," *Report on the USSR*, Vol. 3, No. 31 (August 2, 1991), pp. 9-12.

40. *FBIS-EEU*, March 6, 1990, pp. 74-75.

41. Describing his changing views about Yugoslavia, Eagleburger would later admit that he had "misjudged Milošević." *New York Times*, June 19, 1992, p. A4. See also, Roger Boyes, "America Gets Tough With the Serbs in Policy Switch," *Times*, April 23, 1992, p. 1.

42. In May 1991 the Bush administration underlined its strong support for Yugoslav unity, but suggested that it could only soften congressional prohibition on aid to Yugoslavia—the November 1990 Nickles Amendment giving Belgrade until May 6, 1991 to end repression against Albanians in Kosovo—if Yugoslav leaders resolved their constitutional crises. David Binder, "Bush Tells Belgrade That U.S. May Consider Restoring Aid," *New York Times*, May 22, 1991, p. A3.

43. *New York Times*, November 28, 1990, p. 7.

44. British Broadcasting Company, Summary of World Broadcasts [hereafter cited as BBCSWB], Part 2 (Eastern Europe), June 5, 1991, p. EE/1090/A1.

45. Commission of the European Communities, Press Conference, April 12, 1991.

46. Mesić, *Kako smo*, p. 35.

47. *FBIS-EEU*, June 24, 1991, p. 35.

48. Mesić, *Kako smo*, pp. 35, 37. See also *FBIS-EEU*, June 24, 1991, p. 39.

49. "U.S. Concern About the Future of Yugoslavia," *U.S. Department of State Dispatch*, July 1, 1991, pp. 1-2.

50. David Hoffman, "Baker Urges Yugoslavia to Keep Unity," *Washington Post*, June 22, 1991, p. AO1.

51. *Politika: The International Weekly*, Vol. 2, No. 68 (July 6-12, 1991), p. 1.

52. Mesić, *Kako smo*, p. 47.

8

The Dissolution of the Second Yugoslavia: Balkan Violence and the International Response

If we have to fight, well then we will fight. But I hope they are not going to be crazy enough to fight with us. For if we don't know how to work and produce that well, at least we will know how to fight well.

—Slobodan Milošević, President of Serbia (March 16, 1991)

There is a tradition of oral aggression in the Balkans. Someone will say "I'm going to kill him. I am going to kill him." But then they will add "please stop me before I kill him"....If the killing starts nobody will be able to stop it.

—Slaven Letica, Adviser to the President of Croatia (March 26, 1991)

The Wars in Slovenia and Croatia

THE DECISION BY Slovenia and Croatia to unilaterally proceed with their plans for establishing independence near the end of June 1991 opened an entirely new phase in the Yugoslav crisis. In the case of Slovenia, the republic's assertion of sovereignty from the Yugoslav federation precipitated a short but fierce war between Slovene forces and the JNA that ended in a debacle for the federal military forces. After ten days of fighting, a cease-fire was arranged by a negotiating team from the European Community, and by July 19, 1991, the JNA had withdrawn its invasion forces entirely from Slovenia.

Originally committed to the limited goal of securing control over Yugoslavia's borders as a means of demonstrating federal authority over the country, JNA troops in Slovenia had found themselves surprised and surrounded by the better-organized Slovene forces. The swift defeat of the JNA in Slovenia was due in large measure to the efficient preparation for hostilities by Slovenian officials and particularly by Slovene Minister of Defense Janez Janša, the long-time foe of the JNA who had reorganized the republic's defense forces during the previous year. As a key component of this reorganization, Janša and his team of advisers had clandestinely established a pro-Slovene military network of officers and conscripts within and alongside the republic's existing Territorial Defense forces, which were still formally under the supervision of federal military authorities. Janša and his colleagues also received valuable information on military matters from high-ranking Slovenian officers working for the JNA in Belgrade. These officers sympathized with the Ljubljana government's quest for independence and opposed JNA plans for military intervention in Slovenia (a tactic supported, however, by other Yugoslav-oriented JNA Slovenian officers). Well trained to oppose an invading foreign army using guerrilla methods, and fighting in defense of their own territory, the Slovenian forces exhibited very high morale and competence. Quickly mobilized to reassert federal control, the JNA forces were also plagued by low morale (Slovenia was not regarded as a crucial region by many Serbian conscripts and officers), exceptionally poor planning, and organization. These important factors, together with the Slovenian officers' superior knowledge of the local terrain, contributed to the Slovene victory in the short war.

Casualties in the Slovene-JNA war were relatively light on both sides. Only a dozen members of the Slovenian forces were killed and 144 were wounded; the equivalent figures for the JNA were 37 killed and 163 wounded. Over 3,200 JNA soldiers, however, were forced to surrender to the Slovenian side.[1] Slovenia's military success came as a surprise to both foreign and many domestic observers, particularly in view of the republic's modest military history and the commitment of so many opposition political organizations in the republic (both prior to and following the collapse of the communist regime in 1990) to the ideas of demilitarization and pacifism.[2] High-ranking JNA officers who had supported the military intervention in Slovenia developed their own rationale for the war's outcome. Near the end of the struggle in the republic, for example, JNA Chief of Staff Blagoje Adžić accused the Slovenian forces of fighting a "dirty and underhanded war," and he blamed federal civilian authorities for undermining the activities of his

JNA forces by negotiating a cessation of hostilities with the Slovenes.[3] Humiliated by the military success of the Slovenes, and under strong pressure from the European Community to agree to a truce, the JNA elite ordered a retreat from Yugoslavia's northernmost republic.[4] Despite this turn of events, many high-ranking JNA officers and troops remained bent on a future demonstration of their military prowess, and the restoration of their damaged prestige.

In contrast to the Slovenian case, the Croatian government's attempt to leave the Yugoslav federation, and its ensuing conflict with the JNA, proved to be an exceedingly difficult and protracted process.[5] For more than one year prior to Croatia's declaration of independence on June 25, 1991, the leadership of the republic's large Serbian minority in the Krajina region had stated unequivocally that they had no intention of accepting rule from an independent Croatian government in Zagreb. The Krajina Serbs also made it clear that they would not acquiesce in either the dismemberment of the Yugoslav federation or the fragmentation of the country's Serbian population into various new state units. Supplied in large part with arms provided either by military and political circles in Belgrade, or purchased on the black market, the Krajina Serbs, though relatively few in number, were emboldened to assert their autonomy from Croatian governmental control. Thus, Zagreb's decision to follow Slovenia out of the Yugoslav federation quickly precipitated an armed struggle between Croatian police and military forces on one side, and forces from both the Serbian-led JNA and local Croatia-based Serbian militia on the other.[6]

Originally divided over the issue of military intervention in Slovenia, the JNA elite appeared more united on taking a strong stand to obstruct Croatian sovereignty and independence. Between July and December 1991, JNA and Serbian paramilitary forces, working in close cooperation, consolidated their control over almost one-third of the Croatian state's territory in bitter warfare that resulted in high military and civilian casualties (over 10,000 people killed and approximately 30,000 wounded), savage atrocities, the dislocation of hundreds of thousands of people, and the widespread destruction of property and historic monuments. One of the most ferocious battles of the war—and what soon became a prominent symbol of the shattered relations between Serbs and Croats— was the struggle for the eastern Slavonian city of Vukovar, not far from the Croatian border in Serbia.

At the outset of hostilities, Vukovar was an urban center of mixed ethnic population—in 1991, 43.7 percent Croat, 37.4 percent Serb, and 7.3 percent Yugoslav, with a smattering of other nationalities. JNA and

Serbian militia forces laid siege to Vukovar and shelled the city incessantly for three months. Over 2,300 people were killed and thousands wounded in this assault alone, and both sides fighting for control of the city were alleged to have committed atrocities against their civilian and military rivals.[7] When the Croatian forces capitulated on November 18, 1991, thousands of Croats fled Vukovar or were driven from the area by the winning side. Following the city's surrender, some Croatian fighters and citizens were also killed by the Serbian forces. Describing the destroyed city and traumatized population, Serbian opposition leader Vuk Drašković aptly characterized the battle of Vukovar as the "Hiroshima of both Croatian and Serbian madness" that, he suggested, should stand as "a monument to insanity."[8] For radical Serbian ultranationalists, who were determined to prosecute the war against Croatia and other perceived enemies of Serbia by any means necessary, the "liberation" of Vukovar stood out as a kind of Golgotha in the struggle for Serbian unity.[9]

The protracted hostilities in Croatia and the complete breakdown of the already fragile Serbian-Croatian concord that had existed in the former Yugoslav federation also accelerated the transformation of the JNA into an essentially Serbian-run and Serbian-manned military force, which became almost completely autonomous from civilian and federal control. Indeed, as early as July 5, 1991, during the war in Slovenia, JNA General Adžić invited all "non-Yugoslav-oriented officers" to leave the JNA.[10] The departure of Slovenian and Croatian officers and the more gradual departure of other non-Serbian officers (especially Moslems and Macedonians) from the JNA leadership structure was followed by the growing desertion of non-Serb conscripts. As the war in Croatia intensified during the second half of 1991, and as more and more refugees fled from the war zone into adjacent areas of Croatia and Serbia, it became very difficult for the JNA to recruit Serbian troops. Although the top ranks of the military establishment had long been composed of a disproportionate number of Serbs and Montenegrins, the ethnic disintegration of the JNA removed one of the last and most important institutions that had maintained and symbolized Yugoslavia's multinational character.[11]

The war in Croatia also seriously intensified the rift between Ante Marković's Yugoslav-oriented federal government and the JNA high command, a development that hastened the complete marginalization and delegitimation of the federal government and finally led to its collapse near the end of 1991. In a dramatic meeting on September 20, 1991, Marković requested the resignation of JNA Defense Minister Kadijević and his deputy, General Adžić, accusing both officers of waging their own war in Croatia and of plotting a secret arms deal with conservative military leaders in the Soviet Union during their visit to Moscow in March 1991. Remarks by Prime Minister Marković at the meeting and by members of the military elite reflected the complete breakdown of authority in the country and at the top of the Yugoslav government.

Prime Minister Marković: I believe that some officials at the Secretariat for National Defense should be replaced...I am completely aware of the responsibility which goes with this decision. I am also aware of what it can mean for me personally, including physical danger....I have criss-crossed the entirety of Yugoslavia like Gandhi, half-naked and barefoot, I gave speeches, visited parliaments, I tried everything. I let them spit on me and tell me all kinds of things, and I endured it all with composure trying to save this country. But there's a war going on out there, towns are being razed. I've seen it with my own eyes. That must not be tolerated....

Stane Brovet, Deputy Secretary for Defense: It appears from your proposal that the Yugoslav National Army is to blame for the ongoing disintegration of Yugoslavia. It appears that the secession of Slovenia and Croatia was its doing and that it was the army that attacked their illegal military units first, and not vice versa....

Marković: The war obviously continues. Can we say we're not guilty and that we did this or didn't do that? Where's the way out? Is the way out an all-out civil war in this country? I don't want to take part in such a war.

Brovet: Neither do I, but nobody asked me. Those who want this war are forcing it on all of us, we should all understand that. We should point our finger at the one who wants the war.

Marković: There is more than one.

Brovet: All right point two fingers then, but don't pick on a third party because these two are at each other's throats.

Marković: They are at each other's throats, but you have taken one side in the civil war. One must be blind not to notice that.[12]

Kadijević and Adžić refused to step aside. Three weeks later, in early October, Marković was nearly killed when a federal air force plane bombed the presidential palace in Zagreb, at a moment when the federal prime minister was meeting with Croatia's President Tudjman and federal state President Mesić. Prime Minister Marković accused Kadijević of "attempted murder" and announced that he would not return to Belgrade until Kadijević was ousted.[13] Not long thereafter, on December 20, 1991,

Marković resigned as prime minister, claiming that he was unable to accept the new budget—86 percent of which was allotted to the JNA to support the war.[14]

Functioning essentially as an autonomous institutional sector, the JNA's actions alternatively seemed to reflect perspectives favored by its more Yugoslav-oriented officers (such as the half-Serb, half-Croat General Kadijević and the Slovenian Admiral Stane Brovet) or the views of more pro-Serb officers such as General Adžić. If the JNA high command ignored Marković's orders and plotted against him, the military elite was even more contemptuous of state President Mesić. Mesić, a Croat, was only allowed to formally assume his post as president of Yugoslavia's collective state presidency in July 1991 as a direct result of the EC-brokered cease-fire (the so-called Brioni Declaration). Politically committed to radically remodeling Yugoslavia into a confederal "state of states" when he had assumed the post of state president, the frustrated Mesić proved unable to assert control over the JNA elite or to stop the war in his native Croatia. By early December, after already having abandoned his post as Yugoslavia's last president, Mesić took what little credit he could extract from the unhappy situation and announced to the Croatian Assembly: "I have fulfilled my duty—Yugoslavia no longer exists."[15]

Besides destroying both the unity of the military organization as a politically accountable multiethnic institution and the dwindling authority of the non-Serb federal civilian leaders such as Marković and Mesić, the JNA-led wars against Slovenia and Croatia also contributed to the broader erosion of the few tenuous interelite and mass level interethnic bonds still remaining in the former country. Thus, whether the wars were perceived, as in Slovenia and Croatia, as conflicts of political ideologies and cultures (the "Bolshevik" southeasterners of the Balkans against the "democratic" northwesterners of European civilization) or as an ethnoreligious struggle, as most Serbs chose to view matters (the Catholic pro-German South Slavs supported by the Vatican against the Orthodox believers of Serbia and Montenegro), the military struggles on the territory of the disintegrated Yugoslav federation eviscerated any remaining support for Yugoslavism and the Yugoslav idea. Indeed, once the military attack on their territory began, the political leaders of Slovenia and Croatia completely abandoned their earlier support for a loose confederation of South Slav states that would include Serbia and Montenegro. As one Macedonian politician and social scientist, Vasil Tupurkovski, observed in early 1992: "Until the war broke out, we could think about various options, even about whether some Yugoslav idea could succeed. But when war came, it was clear to me that it was the end of it all."[16]

Internationalizing the Balkan Crisis: Improvisation and Mixed Signals

The violent disintegration of Yugoslavia occurred just as the Cold War was drawing to an end but before mechanisms for conflict management had been established to deal with a crisis of such proportions. As a result, the response of both the international community and multilateral organizations to the breakup of the Yugoslav federation was hastily contrived, incoherent, and frequently lacked a sophisticated grasp of the region's complexity. As previously discussed, signals from the European Community and the United States in June 1991 encouraging Yugoslavia's unity and strongly discouraging Slovenia's and Croatia's planned unilateral disassociation from the existing federation (owing to a fear it might set a dangerous precedent for the USSR) may have actually encouraged the Yugoslav federal government and the JNA to employ force against the country's two breakaway republics. Although the EC was unable to prevent the dissolution of the Yugoslav federation, it did successfully negotiate a general cease-fire agreement—the Brioni Declaration—shortly after hostilities began in Slovenia. Among other things, that agreement provided for a three-month moratorium on further moves toward independence by Croatia and Slovenia and for EC-sponsored negotiations among the republics regarding their future. For some Yugoslavs, such as Aleksander Mitrović, the Serbian deputy prime minister of the federal government, the EC had acquired a very large and unacceptable role in Yugoslavia's internal life. "Yugoslavia," Mitrović claimed, "has become a protectorate of the European Community."[17] In fact the role of the EC in Yugoslav affairs was far less substantial than met the eye. For example, when JNA forces subsequently retreated from Slovenia into Croatia a short time after the Brioni Declaration, the EC, lacking its own joint military forces and internally divided about the best method for handling the crisis, proved helpless to prevent an escalation of Serbian-Croatian conflict.

Divisions in the 12-member EC (a newly assertive and reunified Germany, for example, strongly supported the self-determination of Slovenia and Croatia and expanded EC involvement in peace-keeping, whereas Britain and France favored a continuation of some form of a united Yugoslavia and more limited EC engagement in the Balkans), sent mixed signals to the warring parties who exploited the international disagreements to pursue their respective and conflicting agendas. Brussels did establish the European Community Monitor Mission (ECMM) to assist the passage of JNA forces out of Slovenia and later to monitor hostilities in Croatia, but its relatively small force dressed in white and transported

in white vehicles—hence the popular appellation "the ice cream men"—
was neither mandated nor equipped to become involved in peace
enforcement. Other multilateral organizations also initially failed to provide
any meaningful assistance for managing the Yugoslav crisis: Under North
Atlantic Treaty Organization (NATO) rules, for example, the crisis was
initially an "out-of-area conflict"; the Conference on Security and
Cooperation in Europe (CSCE) was untested, lacked military forces, and
could take action only by consensus; and the West European Union
(WEU), perceived as a kind of EC security arm, had never undertaken a
major peace-keeping venture.

As military strife in Croatia intensified during summer 1991, and the
prospects for an EC-brokered peace waned, European public enthusiasm
for the preservation of a unified Yugoslav state rapidly eroded. Public
opinion surveys conducted in both Western and Eastern Europe in
September 1991 revealed (Table 8.1), for example, that a substantial
majority of citizens in most countries believed that respect for democratic
sentiments and recognition of the right of self-determination, including
independence for certain republics of the Yugoslav federation, were of
uppermost importance in the Balkans. European public opinion—on
both the elite and mass levels—was, however, by no means uniform on
the issue of the Yugoslav crisis. It is interesting to note that whereas
respondents in Germany exhibited slightly lower levels of support for
self-determination in the Balkans than did citizens of other EC states,
related surveys revealed that German managerial elites were exceptionally
strong advocates of the breaking up the Yugoslav federation, with only
15 percent of German managerial leaders supporting the preservation of
Yugoslavia.[18]

Sentiment for acknowledging self-determination of the individual
Yugoslav republics was the weakest in a number of countries bordering
on the disintegrating state. For example, in Romania and Greece, a
majority of citizens expressed support for the preservation of Yugoslavia's
territorial integrity, whereas in Bulgaria only 54 percent of those surveyed
favored self-determination for the Yugoslav republics. Romania's own
problems with ethnic relations in Transylvania and the concern of Greeks
and Bulgarians about the potential difficulty connected with Macedonian
independence probably played an important role in the survey results. In
contrast, friction between Yugoslavia's Serbian majority on the one side
and the federation's Hungarian and Albanian minorities on the other,
undoubtedly contributed to the strong support for self-determination in
Yugoslavia expressed by respondents in Albania and Hungary. High
levels of support for self-determination in the Balkans were also revealed

TABLE 8.1   Attitudes of European Citizens Toward Yugoslavia's Future Cohesion by Country, September 1991 (in percent)

Country of Respondents		Most Important Consideration			
		Preserve Yugoslavia's Territorial Integrity	Respect Democracy and Self-Determination (including possible independence for Republics)	Don't Know	Total
EC	Belgium	20	73	7	100
	Denmark	12	70	18	100
	Germany	18	63	19	100
	Spain	17	71	12	100
	France	20	73	7	100
	Ireland	13	74	13	100
	Luxembourg	19	69	12	100
	Netherlands	20	65	14	100
	Portugal	13	76	12	100
	United Kingdom	17	73	9	100
	Greece	39	36	25	100
	Italy	22	63	15	100
Yugoslavia's Neighbors	Romania	48	33	19	100
	Bulgaria	22	54	24	100
	Albania	4	85	11	100
	Hungary	16	72	13	100
Eastern European	Poland	22	61	17	100
	Estonia	16	68	15	100
	Latvia	13	72	15	100
	Lithuania	11	78	11	100
	Czechoslovakia	28	63	9	100
	European Russia	38	45	18	100
Total EC countries		19	68	13	100
Total Eastern European without European Russia		20	65	15	100

Source: "The Yugoslavian Crisis," Eurobarometer, No. 36 (December 1991), p. A41.

in the small Baltic states (which were in the midst of their own separation from the USSR), whereas citizens of European Russia (and also the increasingly fragile Czechoslovak federation) were less sanguine about the virtues of self-determination.

With European public opinion increasingly sympathetic to Croatian self-determination, and with Croatian forces hard pressed by the assault of superior Serbian-oriented JNA forces in fall 1991, the Tudjman government believed that immediate internationalization of the Yugoslav crisis was absolutely crucial. Indeed, the deployment of foreign troops in Croatia was seen in Zagreb as its best chance for survival as an independent state and as the only long-term strategy for reasserting Croatia's sovereignty over its war-torn multiethnic regions. The Serbian government, the JNA leadership, and local Serbian militias regarded the EC's immobility and limited engagement as a positive situation, providing their allies and forces with an opportunity to either quash Croatian independence or at least expand the territory under Serbian control. As the international community floundered in resolving the crisis, over a dozen EC negotiated cease-fire agreements collapsed in rapid succession, and the small number of EC cease-fire monitors stationed in the region were unable to control the spreading violence. Meanwhile, EC-hosted negotiations concerning Yugoslavia's future held at the Hague and later in Brussels—the much-touted Conference on Yugoslavia—also failed to achieve a peaceful model of disassociation and cooperation among the various parties.

On October 7, 1991 the three-month moratorium restricting moves by Slovenia and Croatia toward independence expired, and both republics reaffirmed their intention to leave the Yugoslav federation. By this point in time, it had become apparent to most observers that there was very little chance of restoring Yugoslavia's unity, even under confederal arrangements, and that the most urgent matters at hand were to end the fighting in Croatia and to prevent a further expansion of violence. At a meeting of the EC Conference on Yugoslavia at the Hague on October 4, Lord Carrington, the chairman of the conference, presented participants with an agenda for discussion that was premised on the assumption that Yugoslavia no longer existed and that future negotiations should focus on the establishment of peace and new arrangements among sovereign states. The representatives from Serbia were shocked that the EC had apparently made a political decision to dismember the Yugoslav federation, or what the Serbs still regarded as a legally extant state unit. The Serbs were even more disconcerted when the Carrington initiative was signed by all of the other republics, including Montenegro, Serbia's long-time ally in political-constitutional discussions.[19]

On October 18, Slobodan Milošević sternly told the EC conference that Serbia could not "accept the tendered proposal for resolving the Yugoslav crisis as it suspends the present constitutional order and abolishes Yugoslavia as a state which has been in existence for 70 years."[20] Choosing to ignore their own share of responsibility for the earlier breakdown of negotiations (January-June 1991) among republican leaders concerning the reorganization of the Yugoslav federation, Serbian leaders now viewed Carrington's political *fait accompli*, and particularly the strong German pressure in the EC that allegedly motivated him, as the crucial ingredient in Yugoslavia's collapse. General Kadijević, Yugoslavia's Minister of Defense, claimed that the EC initiatives at the Hague implied:

> the disappearance of Yugoslavia as a common state, and by implication, of all institutions of a Yugoslav character, including the Yugoslav People's Army...under the most serious threat are the unity and interests of the Serbian nation, whose considerable sections will be separated from each other, reduced to the status of a national minority, and exposed to the danger of being exterminated....Germany is about to attack our country for a third time this century...today it is relying on the strategy of indirect action and a whole spectrum of special war methods, while preparing first for an economic, and then a military onslaught.[21]

Meanwhile, any discussion of renewed cooperation among the former Yugoslav republics—except perhaps a loose custom's union—was viewed by leaders of Slovenia and Croatia as a threat to the recognition of their independence and as an invitation to further Serbian aggression. Croatian and Slovenian politicians were encouraged, on the other hand, by reassurance from Germany in October that Bonn would soon recognize their independence and that it was "only a matter of choosing the right moment and the right circumstances."[22] Against this background, further EC efforts at the Hague to develop a new model of organization among the former Yugoslav republics, and to press for a cessation of hostilities in Croatia through the adjournment of the peace conference and the imposition of sanctions against all parties in Yugoslavia, were to no avail.[23]

It was at this juncture in the late fall that Germany's political leaders, who had been maneuvering behind the scenes for Western recognition of Slovenia and Croatia since July, and were in close and sympathetic consultation with the governments in Zagreb and Ljubljana (Bonn had opened a consulate in Ljubljana on November 7), decided to break ranks with their colleagues in the EC and to advocate the immediate recognition of the sovereignty-seeking Balkan states. At a raucous nine-hour meeting of EC foreign ministers at Brussels which began on the evening of December 16, 1991 and ended on the morning of December 17, Germany announced that it would no longer go along with the prevailing EC consensus and would formally recognize Croatian and Slovenian independence no later than Christmas Day. Britain's foreign secretary and other EC members cautioned that this course of action could result in an escalation of the Balkan war. Britain and France in particular regarded the eventual recognition of Slovenia and Croatia as inevitable but also felt that the timing of the recognition should await an overall solution by the Hague Peace Conference of all major problems connected with Yugoslavia's disintegration. When Germany's Foreign Minister Genscher, under strong pressure from the pro-Croatia lobby in Germany, refused to back down and reminded the British of German support for their position on other matters at the important Mastricht meeting of the EC just a short time earlier, a compromise of sorts was reached.

Thus, it was agreed that recognition of the two Balkan states should not occur before January 15, 1992, and that to give the EC strategic *volte-face* a modicum of orderliness, a five-member EC judicial commission would be established to assess applications from those Yugoslav republics seeking independence and diplomatic recognition. Republics making application to the commission would be required to provide guarantees concerning the human rights of their citizens and to establish constitutional protections for ethnic minorities. Notwithstanding this agreement, however, Germany broke ranks yet a second time, recognizing the independence of Croatia and Slovenia on December 18, 1991. Fending off criticism for having acted so precipitously on the matter, Germany's Genscher would later claim that the EC compromise permitted each state to unilaterally schedule recognition.[24]

Although the EC had been prodded by Germany into coming to grips with the existence of successor states to Yugoslavia's collapsed federation, it was proving woefully unsuccessful at both its peace-making and peace-keeping efforts in Croatia. Indeed, the chairman of the EC Conference on Yugoslavia, Lord Carrington, would later admit that the German-initiated strategy of recognizing Croatian and Slovenian independence seriously weakened his leverage to work out a lasting cease-fire among the various parties.[25] The Serbian side in particular viewed the EC as having capitulated to the pro-Croatian views of Germany and therefore no longer able to serve in the role of a neutral arbitrator. Carrington also warned— prophetically, as matters would later turn out—that circumventing the admittedly deadlocked EC Conference on Yugoslavia at the Hague and promising the Yugoslav republics their imminent recognition as independent states would increase the probability of further hostilities in the Balkans. Looking ahead to the possible consequences of this action, Lord Carrington astutely asked: "What would happen in Bosnia? How do you get the JNA out of Croatia?"[26] UN special envoy Cyrus Vance, who in October 1991 had been appointed by the UN secretary-general to deal with the Yugoslav crisis, agreed with Carrington's assessment.[27] Moreover, Vance pointed out that the president of Bosnia-Hercegovina, whose republic was situated "in a very exposed position right next to the Croatian border," had also argued against early recognition of the Yugoslav republics.[28]

At the end of 1991, as fighting continued in Croatia, the EC temporarily turned its peace-keeping mandate in Yugoslavia over to the United Nations, which had remained on the sidelines owing to the organization's internal divisions about the propriety of intervention in a sovereign state's domestic disputes. On December 18, 1991, the UN sent twenty-one officials to Croatia to reconnoiter the possibilities for expanding a cease-fire agreement worked out at the Hague on November 23 into a comprehensive truce monitored by UN peace-keeping forces. On January 3, 1992, after further negotiations in Yugoslavia, Cyrus Vance concluded a peace accord that called for the establishment of a major peace-keeping force in Croatia. Despite the shooting down of an EC helicopter by the Yugoslav federal air force, which resulted in the death of four EC observers (an incident that was followed immediately by the resignation of Yugoslav Minister of Defense, Kadijević), planning for deployment of the force went forward. The helicopter incident and other violations of the cease-fire in Croatia did, however, contribute to Vance's natural cautiousness about placing UN troops in harm's way.[29] Such understandable prudence and UN organizational problems would delay the arrival of UN troops in Croatia until late March. A serious problem with Vance's plan for the deployment of UN troops was that it focused entirely on the conflict in Croatia, and did not address the looming interethnic confrontation in Bosnia. Even though the small headquarter's staff for the UN troops in Croatia was to be located in Bosnia's capital, Sarajevo, the developing crisis in Bosnia would soon explode into a major zone of violence and warfare.

Exhausted by the war, having already seized considerable territory in Croatia, and faced with imminent European recognition for the Zagreb government on January 15, 1992, both the Serbian authorities in Belgrade, and JNA leaders, viewed the Vance peace proposal as a tactical compromise.[30] Although leaders of the militant Serbian community in the Krajina felt betrayed by the Belgrade government's decision to end the hostilities and submit to the deployment of international troops in their region, Milošević rationalized his action by pointing to provisions of the agreement stipulating that Serbian enclaves in Croatia would remain outside the direct control of the Zagreb authorities. Moreover, notwithstanding their agreement with the UN-brokered cease-fire, Milošević and the remnants of the federal army had absolutely no intention of abandoning their efforts to settle the "Serbian question" on their own terms.

Thus, although the EC and its member states went ahead with the recognition of both Slovenian and Croatian independence on January 15[31] and fighting had temporarily ceased in the northwestern sections of the former federation, the violent consequences of Yugoslavia's disintegration were far from over. For the moment, however, the focus of activity by military and ultranationalist forces, both Serbian and non-Serbian, would simply be transferred from Croatia to Bosnia-Hercegovina.

The War in Bosnia-Hercegovina

Bosnia-Hercegovina, with its complicated mosaic of ethnoreligious communities (in 1991 it was 43.7 percent Moslem, 31.4 percent Serb, 17.3 percent Croat, and 5.5 percent Yugoslav), had long been recognized as the Balkan's most explosive powderkeg. Even though the violence in neighboring Croatia had temporarily wound down and plans for the deployment of UN forces in that newly recognized country were well under way, by early February 1992 relations among Bosnia's three major ethnic communities had significantly deteriorated. Ethnic leaders from the three communities had cooperated uneasily in the republic's tripartite governing coalition since 1990, but spillover from the violence and animosity between Croats and Serbs in Croatia and growing uncertainty about Bosnia's future status and governance had raised ethnic tensions to a high pitch.[32]

Ethnic relations had taken a turn for the worse in October 1991, when Moslem and Croatian legislators had approved documents—after Serbian deputies had walked out of a session of Bosnia's legislature—that provided a basis for the eventual secession of the republic from the disintegrating Yugoslav federation. Ignoring Serbian protests once again in December, the Bosnian government, under its Moslem President, Alija Izetbegović, formally applied to the EC for Bosnia-Hercegovina's recognition as an independent state. The anxiety of Bosnian Serb leaders concerning the future of their ethnic community in the republic was significantly heightened in February 1992, when Moslem and Croatian leaders announced their determination to go ahead with a referendum on Bosnia-Hercegovina's sovereignty and independence.[33]

In the referendum held at the end of February 1992, Moslems and Croats voted overwhelmingly for Bosnia-Hercegovina's independence. Approximately 64.4 percent of the eligible voters cast votes, and 99.7 percent of the valid votes favored an independent Bosnian state.[34] Fearing that they were about to be excluded from the governance of the area that they had long regarded as an integral part of Serbia's historical patrimony, the republic's Serbs abstained from voting. Bosnian Serb officials, working in close association with locally based JNA forces, proceeded to prepare for hostilities. JNA forces in Bosnia had been significantly enlarged following the arrival of troops and equipment that had been withdrawn from Slovenia, and which were now arriving from Croatia as a result of the temporary end of hostilities in that state.

In this already volatile context, interethnic violence was ignited on March 1, 1992, when unidentified gunmen fired on members of a festive Serbian wedding party who were waving Serbian flags in the mainly Moslem section of Sarajevo, killing the groom's father and wounding another guest. Within hours, barricades manned by armed Serbs had been erected in the city, and up to a dozen people were killed in fighting that soon spread to other regions of the republic. Faced with the real possibility that Bosnian Serbs—the former country's largest diasporic Serbian community—would become formally separated from Serbia proper, the Belgrade government, Serbs in Bosnia-Hercegovina, and JNA forces in the republic shared a common determination to use force as a means to forestall such an eventuality. As interethnic tension accelerated in Bosnia at an alarming rate, the international community—which had only recently reached a difficult consensus on the commitment of UN forces to address the Croatian situation—appeared unable to achieve a coherent strategy to extinguish the proliferating conflict.

At a conference held in Lisbon during late February, EC negotiators obtained initial agreement from all of Bosnia's three major parties for a promising draft constitutional agreement organizing Bosnia-Hercegovina into three territorial units and providing for Moslem-Serb-Croat power sharing. Unfortunately, disenchantment with the agreement on the Moslem side—because of implications for the ethnic division of the republic—forced Moslem leader Izetbegović to quickly abandon support for the deal. Serbian chagrin over the Moslem rejection of the Lisbon accord, followed by the Serbian boycott of the referendum, soured the atmosphere for a political settlement. The Serbian side remained adamant that Bosnia-Hercegovina should be divided into three ethnic cantons, a position viewed sympathetically by most Croatian leaders in Bosnia but vehemently rejected by the Moslem side. EC-sponsored talks in Sarajevo in mid-March resulted in another agreement in principle among the parties, but the details of the plan were again deferred and each side interpreted what had been decided in a different manner. By late March, Serbian leaders took further steps to institutionalize their own "Serbian Republic of Bosnia-Hercegovina" (which had taken initial shape in January), and acts of violence escalated among Bosnia's various ethnic communities.

Despite such major problems, the EC and the United States decided to recognize Bosnian independence. Mistakenly believing that diplomatic recognition of Slovenia and Croatia by the EC and the UN in January had been the crucial factor dampening hostilities in those republics, and still chafing from earlier criticism about its commitment to Yugoslav unity during the first half of 1991, the United States joined the EC's hasty recognition of Bosnia-Hercegovina in April 1992 (and finally also recognized Croatia and Slovenia). For the Serbs, the fact that EC recognition came precisely on April 6, 1992, the anniversary of the date in 1941 that the Germans had bombed Belgrade, added insult to injury. Ironically, although criticism may be warranted that Washington and Brussels contributed to the outbreak of hostilities in mid-1991 by their rather inflexible opposition to the secession of the Yugoslav republics— particularly at the time of the ineffectual Baker mission to Belgrade (see Chapter 7)—the lack of a political settlement among the major ethnic groups within Bosnia-Hercegovina actually justified postponing recognition of that republic as another new state in April 1992.

Thus, Western expectations that diplomatic recognition of Bosnia-Hercegovina would serve to calm matters, seriously underestimated the history of ethnoreligious violence in that republic,[35] the contending claims to the region by Serbs and Croats, and the very tenuous authority of Alija Izetbegović's Moslem-controlled Bosnian government located in Sarajevo. Moreover, despite the fact that Bosnia-Hercegovina's various ethnoreligious groups had coexisted nonviolently during the authoritarian Tito era, and that most inhabitants of the republic deplored the idea of intergroup strife, intense latent hatred and psychological distance existed among the various groups, a situation ripe for exploitation by ultranationalist leaders willing to employ force to further their extreme policies. As the astute and moderate Bosnian Moslem, Adil Zulfikarpašić, remarked: "Bosnia is the kind of country in which your neighbor may be your friend, but also a savage enemy, the boundaries of crime are close, the thread of peace is a thin one and there are problems that have to be handled carefully, and never played around with."[36] Moreover, assessments of ethnic relations in Bosnia-Hercegovina by the international community based on the cheerful atmosphere observed in Sarajevo during the 1984 Winter Olympic games, and other glib media claims that the area had been an oasis of intergroup harmony for hundreds of years, seriously misjudged the real situation of underlying interethnic animosities.

The bloody interethnic war that ensued in the newly independent state of Bosnia and Hercegovina in mid-1992 led to even more casualties than the previous struggle in Croatia.[37] To a large extent, many citizens of Bosnia-Hercegovina in 1992 and 1993, just as a half century earlier, were intent on "settling accounts of centuries of hatred."[38] Thus, terrified at the prospect of once again being dominated by a Croatian-Moslem alliance (together constituting 61 percent of Bosnia-Hercegovina's population) strongly supported by Germany,[39] Serbian forces endeavored to alter the demographic structure of Bosnia by brutally employing their superior military strength to forcibly oust Croat and Moslem inhabitants from Serbian-controlled territory—the notorious and internationally condemned strategy of "ethnic cleansing." Croatian and Moslem paramilitary forces often defended and advanced their own interests with equal brutality, re-creating a pattern of ethnoreligious violence and atrocities against innocent civilians that was all too familiar in the region.

Public awareness about the Bosnian conflict was significantly heightened and condemnation was justifiably directed at certain segments of the Serbian military forces in Bosnia as the world watched the relentless bombardment of Sarajevo by the Serbian military and learned about the network of Serbian detention camps for interning Moslems and Croats, as well as other vicious atrocities linked to ethnic cleansing.[40] Knowledge of similar, albeit fewer, Moslem and Croatian camps to detain Serbs also became available, but only added to the international outrage at the repression and suffering experienced in the region. Explaining such behavior remains a task for systematic psychological research, but sheer terror and hatred toward other ethnoreligious groups were undoubtedly key factors setting neighbor upon neighbor and friend against friend. The basis for such intense feeling can be traced to the intergenerational socialization of negative stereotypes regarding the history and behavior of other groups.[41] Thus, although barbaric acts of individual pathology were reported in Bosnia, a general outpouring of pent-up intergroup hatred was also clearly at work in the unrelenting and savage pattern of violence.

The ferocity of the struggle in Bosnia was intensified by the important role played in the conflict by various external actors. The Serbs of Bosnia benefited the most in this respect, although the Croats and Moslems of the new state were also the recipients of outside assistance. Despite considerable evidence to the contrary, Serbian officials in Belgrade consistently maintained that they had no control over the fighting in Bosnia and that Serbian forces in the former Yugoslav republic were conducting their own struggle. Justification for such claims was enhanced, in the Serbian view, after the reorganization of the Yugoslav army, which occurred following the establishment in mid-April 1992 of the new "third" Yugoslavia, composed of the former republics of Serbia and Montenegro.[42] According to the argument made in Belgrade, Serbian conscripts in Bosnia were no longer under the direct control of the new Yugoslav army, and therefore Belgrade authorities had no responsibility for their activities.

Extremely close connections continued, however, between Belgrade's top political and military circles, and Serbian leadership groups in Bosnia-Hercegovina. Moreover, several extreme ultranationalist paramilitary groups based in Serbia (some closely linked to Belgrade official circles) were directly engaged in the fighting in Bosnia.[43] One of the most notorious examples of such externally orchestrated Serbian paramilitary activity in Bosnia involved the Belgrade underworld figure and aspiring warlord Željko Ražnjatović, widely known by his *nom de guerre*, Arkan. It was a group of Arkan's irregular troops, the so-called "Tigers," who helped fuel the onset of hostilities between Serbs and Moslems in Bosnia during April 1992, when they moved from Serbia across the Drina River into Bosnia to forcibly "liberate" the small and predominantly Moslem town of Bijeljina.

Very substantial Croatian forces—some directly in the service of the Tudjman government and some directed by the more ultranationalist Croatian Party of Right (led by Dobroslav Paraga)—were also committed on the side of the local Bosnian Croats and operated most extensively in the Croatian region of Western Hercegovina, or "Herceg-Bosna," as it became known. Indeed in late July the governments of Croatia and Bosnia would sign an agreement on "Friendship and Cooperation" which condemned the aggression of Serbian and Montenegrin forces in Bosnia, and provided a framework for "broad cooperation" in the military sphere against such aggression. Although Moslem forces were the most modestly equipped and internationally isolated at the beginning of the struggle in Bosnia, they eventually received some assistance from Islamic "volunteers" arriving from Iran, Afghanistan, and other Middle Eastern countries.[44]

Despite Serbian-Croatian hostility in Bosnia however, both sides also exhibited a common interest in carving up the fledgling state at the expense of the Moslems. For example, in early May 1992, as the military struggle accelerated, two major leaders of Bosnia-Hercegovina's Serbian and Croatian communities—Radovan Karadžić, of the Serbian Democratic Party, and Mate Boban, the deputy head of the local Croatian Democratic Alliance—met in Graz, Austria and signed an agreement to divide the new state between their forces. Although there was no evidence that Serbia's Milošević and Croatia's Tudjman had orchestrated the Graz meeting, and even though both Presidents continued to publicly reject the notion of Bosnia's partition, it was widely believed that they had discussed the idea at their meetings in 1991 and still viewed the idea of partition as a distinct possibility. Indeed, Croatian political commentator Jelena Lovrić has argued that the mutual goal of Tudjman and Milošević to divide the territory of Bosnia-Hercegovina between Croatia and Serbia helped to provoke efforts at creating ethnically compact zones of control throughout the state (see Map 8.1), and also the attendant brutal "shifting" of populations.[45]

Condemning the connection of the Belgrade authorities to the Bosnian Serb onslaught against Croats and Moslems in Bosnia-Hercegovina, the UN and the EC imposed harsh economic sanctions against Serbia in May 1992. As unrelenting violence with tragic consequences for the civilian population continued throughout the summer and into the fall, however, the absence of an established international security force, and political differences among members of the international community regarding how to resolve such crises, hampered both peace-making and peace-keeping efforts. Even the small 12-person European Community Monitor Mission which had been posted in Bosnia since late 1991 was forced to withdraw from the republic in mid-May 1992 because of the outbreak of heavy fighting (thereafter its monitoring was conducted by telephone and short visits).[46] Thus except for a small number of officers already posted in Sarajevo (as headquarters staff for the UN peace-keeping forces in Croatia), international forces were not deployed in Bosnia-Hercegovina until hostilities there were well under way, and then only a small force was utilized to open the airport in Sarajevo.[47]

As the fighting in Bosnia escalated, NATO and the WEU would alter their traditional roles so that their organizations would be able to provide military assistance to other multilateral organizations carrying out nonmilitary activities outside of Western and Central Europe (which led to the July deployment of Western naval forces in the Adriatic to monitor the implementation of sanctions against Serbia). Despite this assistance, most leading members of the international community were extremely reluctant to become deeply enmeshed in the exceptionally complex and bloody Balkan struggle. By July 1992, a dispute had even emerged between the UN's Security Council and the UN's Secretary-General Butros Butros-Ghali about whether further resources should be expended on the Yugoslav case when so many other international conflicts and humanitarian crises deserved attention. Butros-Ghali claimed that compared to other deserving areas of UN concern, such as Somalia, the situation in Yugoslavia was a "rich man's war." The secretary-general also observed that his rationale was to do as much as he could to contain UN intervention in Yugoslavia. Otherwise, he argued, "it would be a kind of Vietnam for the United Nations."[48]

As the violent consequences of Yugoslavia's disintegration continued unabated in Bosnia-Hercegovina during the summer of 1992, the

MAP 8.1   Military Control in Croatia and Bosnia-Hercegovina:
             September 1992

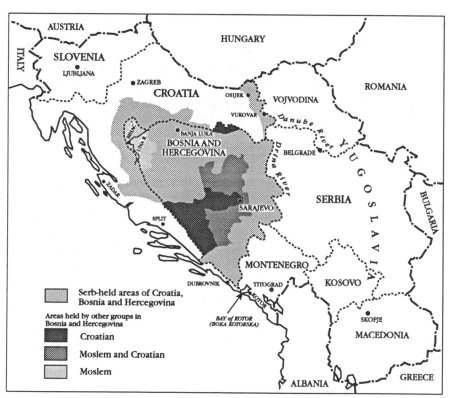

international community continued its clumsy, albeit well-meaning, improvisation of new "security architecture" for the post-Cold War period. Although increasingly worried that the war in Bosnia would spill over into other regions of the former federation—the long-troubled and predominantly ethnic Albanian province of Kosovo, which had been under Belgrade's tight control for several years, seemed the next most likely flashpoint—most foreign governments continued to hope that a continuation of diplomatic pressure and economic sanctions against Serbia would eventually yield a solution. In late August 1992, at a meeting in London sponsored by the UN and the EC, both foreign states and the warring sides in Bosnia created a permanent "Working Group" in Geneva to deal with Bosnia-Hercegovina as part of a new "International Conference on the Former Yugoslavia" (replacing the EC "Conference on Yugoslavia"), but promising agreements reached to end the fighting were never implemented.[49] The UN subsequently expelled the new Yugoslavia[50] (composed of Serbia and Montenegro), authorized sending additional troops to Bosnia-Hercegovina, and created a War Crimes Commission to investigate reported atrocities, but hostilities and "ethnic cleansing" nonetheless continued.[51] As the winter of 1992-1993 approached, many feared that the trickle of humanitarian aid reaching Bosnia would be insufficient to avoid a heavy loss of civilian life.

The Geneva Negotiations on Bosnia-Hercegovina

In late October 1992, as international economic and diplomatic pressure failed to end the war and the rising toll of human hardship in Bosnia, the co-chairmen of the Geneva-based EC-UN International Conference on the Former Yugoslavia, Cyrus Vance and Lord Owen (the former British foreign secretary had succeeded Lord Carrington in August), formulated a draft plan for the political organization of Bosnia and Hercegovina. The plan was based on work done by the Conference's Bosnia-Hercegovina Working Group which had been engaged in extensive meetings with all sides to the conflict since late August. As a concession to concerns advanced by the Moslem-led Bosnian government of Alija Izetbegović, the Vance-Owen plan called for the "regionalization" of Bosnia rather than its "cantonization" along strictly ethnic lines. Moreover, although each of the seven to ten proposed regions would have considerable power, a viable central government would be based in Sarajevo and composed of regional representatives. Under the Vance-Owen constitutional proposal, however, the central government would be considerably weaker than under the model favored by Izetbegović and his colleagues.

Serbian leaders from Bosnia strongly opposed provisions that vested political sovereignty in a central Bosnian governmental authority and that would prevent the political association and territorial linkage of various areas under Serbian control—which since mid-August had been organized into the so-called "Serbian Republic" (*Republika Srpska*)—by treating them as distinct administrative units. In view of their success on the battlefield, and the consequences of the ethnic cleansing policy employed in much of the area under their control (the forced outmigration of Moslems), Serbian leaders felt that they were in a strong position to oppose ideas put forward by the predominantly Moslem Sarajevo government, which exercised authority over only a relatively small portion of Bosnia-Hercegovina. Bosnian Serb leader Radovan Karadžić claimed that the plan "sounds unacceptable to the Serbs" because of the fragmentation of areas under Serbian control. "What we want," Karadžić argued, "is to preserve our people's unity....The Serbs do not want to accept being broken apart. Enough of breaking the Serbs apart! The Serbs have been broken apart in the Balkans, and now they should be broken apart in Bosnia-Hercegovina itself. We cannot accept that."[52]

Once again, as after the Lisbon agreement which had been formulated in February 1992, the position of Croatian political leaders regarding Bosnia's future constitutional architecture was rather ambivalent. The views of some Croats were similar to the Serbian notion concerning the tripartite cantonization of Bosnia along ethnic lines, whereas others preferred a more unitary state with several semiautonomous administrative regions. Croatian views were undoubtedly shaped by the fact that Croat forces already maintained a tight grip on the predominantly ethnic Croatian regions of Western Hercegovina adjacent to Croatia. For most Moslem leaders, meanwhile, the Vance-Owen plan, albeit imperfect from their perspective, did provide an opportunity to regain territory that was temporarily under both Serbian and Croatian control. Although cooperating closely in the struggle against the Bosnian Serbs, and ostensibly united in their aversion to the partition of Bosnia-Hercegovina along ethnic lines, Moslem and Croat forces frequently clashed when it came to the question of who should exercise control over specific pieces of real estate.

Complaining of Moslem attacks on Croat forces, Mate Boban, the leader of the Croatian community in Hercegovina (Herceg-Bosna), observed: "It is simply incomprehensible and difficult to understand that those who have survived thanks to the Croatian people and the Croatian units...those who have gained their strength their breath of life, thanks to Croats—have now turned against the Croats." Boban rejected the constitutional division of Bosnia along ethnic lines but still claimed that "within it the Croatian people are to have their own rights in a cultural, economic, political, and any other sense, so they can be a people with all those trappings of sovereignty that every people have."[53] Thus, although Boban's views could be contrasted with Serbian demands for Bosnia-Hercegovina's cantonization, confederalization, or partition, both Serbian and Croatian leaders in the region were strongly committed to their respective ethnic group's constitutionally acknowledged sovereignty.

In early January 1993, Vance and Owen, after having held discussions separately with each of the major ethnic leaders from Bosnia on several different occasions, convened a meeting in Geneva at which all of the principal actors were present. In view of the strong resistance from the Moslem led Bosnian government to the prospect of direct negotiations with the Serbian leadership—whom the Moslems labeled as war criminals—the organization of such a meeting was no mean feat in its own right. Vance and Owen also invited the presidents of both Croatia and Yugoslavia, Franjo Tudjman and Dobrica Ćosić, to attend the meeting, as important outside parties who could play a potentially crucial role in the resolution of the crisis. Tudjman and Ćosić had met on two earlier occasions under UN auspices near the end of 1992, and had reached agreement on some matters of common interest to their two states.[54]

At Geneva, Vance and Owen presented the conference participants with a ten-point plan that built upon their earlier initiatives and discussions. The plan called for the establishment of a highly "decentralized state" in which the three major ethnic groups would be recognized as the "constituent units" of Bosnia and Hercegovina (a group of "others" was also recognized in order to accommodate the presence of smaller nationalities). However, Bosnia would be organized administratively into ten provinces (see Map 8.2) in an ambitious attempt to avoid the appearance of establishing three ethnically pure territorial spheres of influence.[55] Each of the provinces would have a mixture of the different ethnic groups, although nine of the provinces would also contain a dominant majority from one particular group. Sarajevo, the tenth province, was specially designated as "mixed," but it would also be multiethnic with the Moslems being in the majority. Seeking to quickly extinguish the bloodletting in Bosnia, Owen and Vance studiously ignored the contradiction between the constitutional entrenchment of three ethnic groups as the state's governing actors and the administrative fragmentation of the state into ten multiethnic provinces. For the moment, little thought was devoted to how the three constituent ethnic "units," most probably headquartered in the provinces where they had the largest majority status, would avoid the temptation to enlarge their territorial control through the exploitation of the multiple irredentisms created under the plan.

MAP 8.2   The Division of Bosnia and Hercegovina into 10 Provinces According to the Vance-Owen Plan (January 1993)*

*The map indicates which ethnic group would likely dominate in each province. Moslems would also be the majority in the "mixed" province of Sarajevo.

Under the Vance-Owen model, a central government, operating from the "mixed" province of Sarajevo, would be responsible for foreign policy, international commerce, citizenship rights, defense and taxation. Most governmental functions would be carried out, however, by the provinces, and the provinces would have a determining role in selecting the personnel serving in the central government. A civil service would also be constituted on the principle of "group balance."[56] It was anticipated that the state would eventually be demilitarized, the current forces of the various belligerents demobilized, and most security matters presumably transferred to provincial police. Issues of "vital concern" addressed in the constitution would be altered only by consensus of all three constituent units, but routine governmental business undertaken by legislative, executive, and judicial bodies would not be subject to veto. Under the plan, the international community would assume a very prominent role in Bosnia's affairs. For example, members of international bodies, including the International Conference on the Former Yugoslavia, the UN, the EC, and the CSCE, would be directly involved at least temporarily in selected aspects of Bosnia's institutional development, such as its constitutional court, election process, agencies for the protection of human rights (e.g., an ombudsman and human rights court), as well as in the formation of an ethnically "integrated" Bosnian army and provincial police forces.

Predictably, the most difficult obstacle which arose during the Geneva negotiations in early 1993 focused upon the degree of autonomy which would be granted to Bosnia's respective ethnic communities. The Serbs, who held the bulk of the territory, particularly resisted the idea of being subjected to what they viewed as potential Moslem-Croat "domination" from a unitary Bosnian state governed from Sarajevo. The map of the proposed ten provinces was particularly disconcerting to the Bosnian Serbs for three reasons: (1) it divided the Serbian-controlled territory into several administrative jurisdictions, (2) it required the Serbs to relinquish control over a considerable amount of the territory they presently controlled, and (3) it cut off the land corridor linking much of the existing Serbian zone of control to the Serbian republic in the Third Yugoslavia. Countering the Vance-Owen plan, Bosnian Serb leaders advanced initiatives for a "confederal" Bosnia or a "community of cantons" that they argued would preserve the unity of the region's Serbian communities and the Serbs' territorial conquests on the battlefield and would also ensure a territorial link to the new Serbo-Montenegrin Yugoslavia.

The Moslem side rejected the Serbian plan as nothing but a "state within a state" or a fig leaf for a three-way division of the region. At the same time, having already lost political control over most of Bosnia and having suffered terribly as the principal target of the ethnic cleansing strategy, Moslem leaders and members of Izetbegović's Bosnian government found little to be enthusiastic about in the Vance-Owen plan. In the Moslem view, the plan offered very little prospect for the creation of a viable centrally governed Bosnian state along "civic" rather than ethnic lines, or for addressing the forced migration and mistreatment of the Moslem population. However, having unsuccessfully lobbied the international community to either militarily intervene in Bosnia or lift the arms embargo so that the Moslem side could acquire heavy weapons, Moslem leaders also weighed the political advantages of accepting a flawed plan. Thus the division of Bosnia into ten provinces would ostensibly prevent the formation of ethnic "para-states" frequently advocated by both Serbian and Croatian leaders.[57] Moreover, if the plan was rejected by the Serbian side, who viewed it as even more unacceptable than did the Moslems, the onus of international disapproval would likely fall on the Serbs. After all, Vance and Owen made it quite clear that whoever was perceived to be responsible for obstructing an agreement at Geneva would suffer the full consequences of international chagrin and the likely foreign military intervention that would soon follow.

Initially, only the Croatians agreed to the Vance-Owen plan. Indeed, the leaders of the Croatian community in Hercegovina were elated that the proposed map of provincial boundaries granted them control not only of areas they currently occupied but also of additional territory where Moslems had been in the majority. Moreover, in view of their *de facto* sovereignty over most of Western Hercegovina, the Croats had already established close links with Zagreb, so it mattered very little for the moment whether Bosnia was regionalized into ten provinces or was the subject of a three-way cantonization. Croatia's President Tudjman also encouraged a rapid conclusion of the war in Bosnia owing to his primary concern with the continued Serbian occupation of Croatian territory, a problem that had not been reversed by the provisions of the Vance peace plan negotiated in January 1992 and had not been ameliorated by the presence of UN peace-keeping forces throughout Croatia. Thus by January 1993, Tudjman already had the sphere of influence he had always sought in Western Hercegovina—uncontested by the Bosnian Serbs—and was ready to turn his attention to other important issues that were outstanding within Croatia.

After obtaining Croatian agreement to the Bosnian peace settlement, and with the expectation that the Moslems would eventually accept the plan (in lieu of any other immediate options or in the hope of irritating the Serbs), Vance and Owen turned to the more difficult problem of obtaining Serbian acquiescence to their proposals. From August to December 1992, as Vance and Owen had made preparations for the Geneva meeting, they had hoped, along with most Western leaders, for the emergence of a more flexible and moderate government in Belgrade. Considerable speculation existed that such a government might encourage a peaceful resolution of both the Bosnian and the broader Balkan crisis and also end Serbia's moral and material support for Bosnia's militant Serbian leadership. Optimism centered on Milan Panić, the Serbia-born American citizen and businessman who was selected as the prime minister of the new Yugoslavia in July 1992. Feisty, and claiming he wanted to establish real democracy and end Serbia's international isolation, Panić soon became embroiled in a bureaucratic power struggle with Milošević over who would guide the destiny of the new Serbo-Montenegrin Yugoslavia.[58] In Western capitals, Panić's decision to challenge Slobodan Milošević in the December 1992 contest to become president of Serbia, seemed to hold out the prospect of a breakthrough in resolving the horrific and seemingly endless Balkan struggle.[59]

Hopes for leadership change in Belgrade were dashed, however, with the electoral victory of Slobodan Milošević on December 20, 1992. Confronted by strong opposition to their plan by the Serbian leadership in Bosnia, Vance and Owen decided in early January 1993 to deal with the realities at hand in Belgrade and to solicit Milošević's political assistance. Although Milošević was generally blamed for encouraging and materially assisting the Serbian struggle in Bosnia over the previous nine months, Vance had developed a good working relationship with the Serbian president after having secured his support to arrange a cease-fire in Croatia one year earlier. Dobrica Ćosić, the writer-president of Yugoslavia who had astutely sat on the fence during the Milošević-Panić electoral contest, also had come to realize the urgency of securing peace in Bosnia if Serbia was to avoid further isolation and a military struggle with the West and was therefore also prepared to assist Vance and Owen in making overtures to Milošević.[60]

For his part, Milošević had become more flexible concerning the Bosnian struggle for a number of reasons. Most important, although he had won the election for the presidency of Serbia, Milošević's political position was considerably weaker than two years earlier following Serbia's first multiparty elections. For example, the number of seats in the Serbian Assembly won by his Socialist Party had slipped considerably, and his margin of victory over Panić, though substantial, was not as impressive as his showing in 1990. Even more significant, the Serbian economy was in deep trouble as a result of the international sanctions imposed on the new Yugoslavia (see Chapter 9), and matters seemed likely to worsen owing to the Western view that Serbia was responsible for the ongoing war in Bosnia. Many Serbs, perhaps the majority, still felt very strongly that Serbia should not capitulate to Western pressure—as evidenced by the electoral success of Milošević and a surge of support for the even more radical nationalists headed by Vojislav Šešelj of the Serbian Radical Party—but there was also growing fatigue, anxiety, and anger in Serbia (and Montenegro) concerning the new Yugoslavia's isolation and the seemingly open-ended military struggle in the Balkans.

Indeed, by January 1993 the Serbian military situation in Bosnia had become even more precarious than it had been a few months earlier, and Moslem and Croatian forces were becoming both stronger and bolder. Milošević was also well aware that the soon-to-be installed Clinton administration in Washington was very likely to take a more activist military stance against Serbia than its predecessors in the White House.[61] For all of these reasons, and others (Milošević also may have been stunned by having been branded a war criminal,[62] and he wished to deal with other problems closer to home such as Kosovo), Serbia's president seemed prepared to adopt a flexible view when Owen and Vance flew to Belgrade during the first week of January 1993 and approached him for help with the Geneva negotiations.

As events were to unfold at Geneva, Milošević's assistance proved to be crucial in obtaining support from the Bosnian Serbs for the Vance-Owen agreement. Indeed, momentum for the entire Vance plan nearly collapsed on January 8 when a Bosnian Serb shot and killed Bosnia's deputy prime minister, a Moslem, while he was riding in a UN convoy from the Sarajevo airport to the city's center. In an ironic and possibly useful coincidence for the Moslem side, news of the killing reached Bosnia's President Izetbegović while he was meeting in Washington, D.C., with several of President-elect Bill Clinton's foreign policy advisers. The assassination occurred only one day after Izetbegović had accepted the Vance-Owen plan in principle as a basis for further negotiations. The negotiations in Geneva got back on track only after a hasty, but partial, Serbian explanation for the incident. However, Bosnian Serb objections to the Vance-Owen proposal continued.

By the weekend of January 9-10, it appeared that failure was again at hand. As Serbian representatives from Bosnia and Belgrade arrived in Geneva for further discussions, President Izetbegović flew off to Senegal— in a plane provided by Turkey's President Turgut Ozal—to lobby Islamic countries to provide arms to the Moslem side in the Bosnian struggle.

The UN-EC negotiators announced that Izetbegović had not officially left the Geneva talks but would return in two days, and they turned their attention to getting the Serbs on side. On Monday, January 11, Vance and Owen gave Serbian leader Radovan Karadžić a deadline of 10:00 a.m. the following day to accept or reject their ten-point plan on Bosnia's future. That night, Owen and Vance met privately with Karadžić to exert pressure on him, and they brought along Milošević, Ćosić, and the president of Montenegro, Momir Bulatović, to a meeting that lasted until 2:00 in the morning. Lord Owen, in particular, made Karadžić and the assembled group aware of the "brutal truths" regarding what might happen—presumably Western military intervention—should the peace plan be rejected.[63]

In spite of such extensive and anxious discussions, Karadžić returned to the conference table on Tuesday morning and again stubbornly indicated his reasons for opposition to the plan. During a pause in the meeting, Lord Owen spoke of a "breakdown" in the talks. A small glimmer of hope, however, still remained with Cyrus Vance who reported that although "Mr. Karadžić said no, Mr. Ćosić and Mr. Milošević said yes." The EC-UN negotiators now called a temporary adjournment of the meeting, requesting that Karadžić reconsider matters. It was at this crucial juncture in the talks that Karadžić was pressured by Milošević, Ćosić, and Bulatović into reversing his position. According to some observers, Milošević bluntly informed Karadžić that if the Bosnian Serbs were prepared to fight the whole world they could not count on Serbia to provide supplies.[64] Vance and Owen provided some assistance to the search for consensus by agreeing to reorder provisions of the agreement in order to give enhanced priority to the section characterizing Bosnia as a state with three constituent nations. According to spokesmen for Vance and Owen, this change gave "higher visibility" to the notion of "ethnic identity" in the agreement, an alteration that was very important to the Serbian side.

Finally overwhelmed by the pressure of the extended discussions, Karadžić signed the agreement, and although insisting that the plan would have to be ratified by the Serbian parliament of Bosnia-Hercegovina, he maintained that he was willing to argue for ratification and to resign his position if the agreement was rejected. Karadžić later claimed that his decision to sign was based on looking at the agreement from a new vantage point: "I decided to look at in a different way—to stop looking at what the Serbs weren't getting and look instead at what the Moslems weren't getting. I realized that they were not getting very much, so I decided to go along with it."[65] Meanwhile, the European Community announced that the Serbs in Bosnia had seven days to decide on their acceptance of the Vance-Owen plan and threatened that if the agreement was rejected the consequences would be dire. On January 20, the same day Bill Clinton was inaugurated as president of the United States, the Bosnian Serbs legally ratified the agreement, 55 to 15. Characteristically obstreperous, Serbian leader Karadžić also announced, however, that Bosnian Serb leaders had no intention of relinquishing any territory or of abandoning their important corridor between Sarajevo and Serbia.

Still angered over the assassination of their colleague, and dissatisfied with the plan's emphasis on a decentralized state, Moslem leaders rationalized that their tentative acceptance of the Vance-Owen model would serve as a basis for the eventual *integration* of Bosnia-Hercegovina and as a means of regaining influence consistent with their group's relative majority in Bosnia prior to the war's onset. The Serbs, in contrast, rationalized their signature on the agreement as the beginning of a *separation* from the Moslems and Croats of Bosnia and as their eventual integration with other Serbs from the former Yugoslavia. Justifying his decision to sign the agreement, Serb leader Karadžić claimed that his ethnic constituency would never again tolerate being "mixed" with the Moslems or subjected to a central government that would impose "Moslem domination": "I don't think we can live with each other, but we can live beside each other...we are like oil and water. When you shake us we mix, when we are left alone we separate. This is natural....[In the past] we have been squeezed together by declarations. We felt terrible all of us."[66]

Anticipated discussions in late January at which the three ethnic delegations would work on military disengagement and finalize maps of the provincial boundaries, were viewed by Karadžić as a mechanism for the Serbs "to separate in a democratic way."[67] Meanwhile, even before discussions on the details of the modalities could resume in Geneva, Tudjman's Croatian forces accelerated their own agenda, which led to clashes with both Moslem forces in Bosnia, and a major offensive against Serbian forces in Croatia. Once again, as so often had happened in the Balkan crisis of the early 1990s, a peace plan had been accepted, but peace remained elusive. Whether the Vance-Owen plan—clearly flawed in many respects—would be the precursor to the end of hostilities, a fig leaf for the Serbs to avoid outside military intervention and allow the international community to postpone other alternatives in resolving the Bosnian crisis, or just another twist in the bewildering saga of Balkan chaos still remained very unclear.[68]

As fighting intensified in Bosnia and Croatia at the end of January, both the Serbs and Moslems balked at going through with various final steps necessary for acceptance of the Geneva peace plan.[69] Having once again failed to hammer out a resolution to the crisis, negotiators Vance and Owen flew to New York to discuss matters with the UN Security Council and the new U.S. administration. Stopping in London on his way to the United States, Owen admitted that his greatest fear was that the Moslems, who had suffered the greatest setbacks in the Bosnian war, would refuse to sign the agreement and would look instead to Washington for military assistance: "There is a belief in the government of Bosnia-Hercegovina, the Moslem delegation effectively, that all they have to do is go on appealing to President Clinton—and that the U.S. cavalry is going to run in and help them, save them, and intervene!" Owen remained optimistic, however, adding that he did not expect the Clinton administration to authorize sending ground forces to Bosnia without a peace agreement and that the idea of lifting the UN arms embargo to assist the Moslems would simply be "quite crazy."[70]

By February 1993 the new Clinton administration had engaged the United States more actively in efforts to establish peace in the Balkans.[71] Externally engineered efforts to transform war-ravaged Bosnia and Hercegovina into a "durable state," remained, however, a highly problematic enterprise that seemed likely to cause continued suffering to the area's inhabitants, and tremendous difficulties and costs to the international community. Thus the Vance-Owen peace proposal and the potential deployment of up to 75,000 foreign troops to carry out cease-fire enforcement duties held out the prospect of producing a temporary lull in hostilities, and the formal acceptance of a ten province constitutional model by the warring sides in Bosnia. But the chance of the area's three major ethnic groups peacefully cohabiting in a single state for any sustained period of time—without the presence of such an international military force to maintain order—was highly unlikely.

Notes

1. See, *War in Slovenia: From First "Attacks" on YPA to Final Victory Over the Yugoslav Army* (Ljubljana: Ljubljana International Press Center, August 1991), p. 108; and Stanoje Jovanović, *The Truth About the Armed Struggle in Slovenia* (Belgrade: Narodna Armija, 1991), pp. 23-24.

2. For the background concerning this dimension, see Zvone Filipović, *Demilitarizacija Slovenije in nacionalna varnost* (Ljubljana: Znantveno in publicistično središče, 1991).

3. Robert Fox and Michael Montgomery, "Yugoslav Army Declares War," *Daily Telegraph*, July 3, 1991, p. 1.

4. All JNA forces were not fully withdrawn from Slovenia until October.

5. Speaking in early August 1991 about Croatia's particular difficulties, President Tudjman sought to explain why the policy of the Slovenian leaders appeared to be more "resolute" and "decisive" in their efforts to obtain independence than the Zagreb authorities and why Slovenia had not been subjected to as much pressure as Croatia: "First is [Slovenia's] geographical position. Second they do not have the problems we have with the Serbs in Croatia. Third Slovenia was given the go-ahead by the overall Serbian policy, and by a sector of the Yugoslav army top command allowing it to leave Yugoslavia, in fact to leave it as soon as possible. In these circumstances it was in fact the Federal Executive Council which provoked the army intervention [in Slovenia] after it was revealed that a section of the army was in favor of that intervention, but a majority was not in favor of that intervention, and so the adventure ended the way it did." *FBIS-EEU*, August 2, 1991, p. 46.

6. James Gow has provided a useful inventory of paramilitary forces involved in the war in Croatia. On the Serbian side such irregular forces included the Serbian Guard, the Serbian Volunteer Guard, the Serbian Chetnik Movement, the Martićevci (later the Knindže), Dušan Silni, and the Beli Orli; Croatian paramilitary included the Zebras, Black Legion, Wolves of Vukovar (a renegade unit of the Croatian National Guard), and the forces of the Croatian Defense Union (HOS). "Military-Political Affiliation in the Yugoslav Conflict," *RFE/RL Research Report*, Vol. 1, No. 2 (May 15, 1992), pp. 16-25.

7. In January 1993, a UN sponsored team unearthed a mass grave near Vukovar containing several hundred bodies. Investigators believe that the grave contains the remains of civilians and wounded Croatian soldiers killed by Serbian forces after the capitulation of Vukovar. *Independent*, January 23, 1993, p. 9.

8. *FBIS-EEU*, March 13, 1992, p. 29.

9. Marcus Tanner, "Macabre Rite to Celebrate a Serb Conquest," *Independent*, November 19, 1992, p. 10.

10. *War in Slovenia*, p. 96.

11. In an interview near the end of 1992, General Života Panić, the Chief of the General Staff of the Armed Forces of Yugoslavia (Serbia-Montenegro) remarked that: "The JNA is now very different to the multi-ethnic Armed Forces of the former SFRY, and now the biggest part of the Armed Forces is made up of Serbs and Montenegrins. And the fighting morale of the JNA is no longer based on the old communist values. Now it is based on patriotism, the very best war traditions of Serbs and Montenegrins, on professionalism and loyalty to the new state." *Defense and Foreign Affairs Strategic Policy*, Vol. 20, No. 12 (December 31, 1992), pp. 11-12.

12. *Politika: The International Weekly*, September 28-October 4, 1991, p. 7.

13. Christopher Walker, "Missile Strike into the Heart of Zagreb," *Times*, October 8, 1991, p. 1.

14. During 1992, Marković participated in the formation of a social democratic party in his native Croatia and then moved to Graz, Austria in mid-1992 where he established his own company dealing with international affairs.

15. *BBCSWB*, December 7, 1991, Part 2 (Eastern Europe), p. EE/1249/C1/1. In November, Mesić told a Hungarian interviewer that he had remained at his post in order to freeze Yugoslav funds abroad and not let the money "get into Serb hands." *BBCSWB*, November 20, 1991, Part 2 (Eastern Europe), p. EE/1234/C1/1.

16. *FBIS-EEU*, February 5, 1992, p. 47.

17. *Politika: The International Weekly*, No. 69, July 13-19, 1991, p. 5.

18. "The Yugoslavian Crisis," *Eurobarometer*, No. 36 (December 1991), p. 41.

19. For information on the response of Serbian representatives at the Hague, see Miodrag Jovičić (ed.), *Pravo u senci politika: kako Evropska zajednica rastura Jugoslaviju* (Belgrade: Srpska Akademija nauka i umetnosti, 1992); and "Naša zalaganja u evropskoj zajednici," *Srbija danas*, Vol. 1 (November 11, 1992), Special Edition. See also Predrag Simić, "Europe and the Yugoslav Issue," and Mirko Ostojić, "Foreign Factor in the Breaking Up of Yugoslavia," *Review of International Affairs*, Vol. 43, No. 1001 (February 5, 1992), pp. 1-7.

20. "Meeting at the Hague Discusses Yugoslav Crisis, Address of Serbian Prime Minister Milošević," *Review of International Affairs*, Vol. 42, Nos. 995-997 (October 5-November 5, 1991), p. 32.

21. *FBIS-EEU*, October 23, 1991, p. 43.

22. A spokesman for the Slovenian Ministry of Foreign Affairs, following President Kučan's visit to Germany in early October. *FBIS-EEU*, October 10, 1991, p. 35.

23. At a meeting in Moscow in mid-October, Mikhail Gorbachev was able to convince Tudjman and Milošević to sign yet another cease-fire agreement but it failed to dampen hostilities in the Balkans.

24. John Newhouse, "The Diplomatic Round: Dodging the Problem," *New Yorker*, August 24, 1992, p. 66.

25. *Ibid.*

26. *MacNeil/Lehrer Newshour* (December 17, 1991), Show 4227, transcript by "Strictly Business," p. 3.

27. Newhouse, "The Diplomatic Round," p. 66.

28. *MacNeil/Lehrer Newshour*, p. 3.

29. On September 30, 1992, two officers of the JNA were sentenced, in absentia, to twenty years imprisonment for downing the helicopter. *FBIS-EEU*, October 1, 1992, p. 36.

30. Colonel General Života Panić of the JNA argued—shortly before becoming chief of staff of the newly reorganized Yugoslav armed forces in early 1992—that EC pressure on the JNA not only ended the hostilities in Slovenia but also was decisive in settling the war in Croatia. Panić cited in James Gow, "The Use of Coercion in the Yugoslav Crisis," *World Today* (November 1992), p. 200.

Gow, relying heavily on Panić's remarks, probably exaggerates the significance of EC pressure in bringing about a peace settlement in Croatia.

31. The EC Arbitration Commission, established to consider the status of the former Yugoslav republics, recommended on January 15 that Slovenia, Macedonia and Croatia be recognized by the EC, although in the latter case the Zagreb government was asked to improve its legislation concerning its treatment of minorities. "Report of the European Community Arbitration Committee," *Yugoslav Survey*, No. 1 (1992), pp. 121-134. The Arbitration Commission later found that Croatian laws largely took account of the "reservation" expressed in January and that although Croatian constitutional provisions regarding the status of its minorities "sometimes fall short of the obligations assumed by Croatia...it nonetheless satisfies the requirements of general international law regarding the protection of minorities." "Conference for Peace in Yugoslavia, Arbitration Commission (July 4, 1992)." *International Legal Materials*, Vol. 31, No. 6 (November 1992), pp. 1505-1507.

32. The political polarization of Bosnia-Hercegovina was apparent in a November 1991 survey of students in the republic. From the 900 students surveyed, 86 percent of the students of Croatian ethnic affiliation expressed a positive attitude toward Bosnia's secession from the Yugoslav federation, while the equivalent figures were 55 percent for Moslem students and 43 percent for Serbian students. Regarding the possible existence of Bosnia-Hercegovina *without* membership in the Yugoslav federation, Croatian and Moslem students supported the idea at the level of 71 percent and 61 percent respectively, while only 8 percent of the Serbian students polled felt the same way. The survey is discussed in Vladimir Goati, "Politički život Bosne i Hercegovine 1989-1992," in Srdjan Bogosavljević, Vladimir Goati, Zdravko Grebo, *et al.*, *Bosna i Hercegovina izmedju rata i mira* (Belgrade and Sarajevo: Forum za etničke odnose, 1992), pp. 51-52.

33. Izetbegović would later speculate that the violence which eventually engulfed Bosnia might have been avoided if the Bosnian government had not decided to leave the Yugoslav state. But he also claimed that once Croatia had become an independent state—and Bosnia could no longer function as a "balancing factor" at "equal distance" from both Croatia and Serbia in a united federation—the Bosnians felt that they had no alternative other than independence for their own republic. *BBCSWB*, February 17, 1993, Part 2 (Eastern Europe), C.1 Special Supplement, p. EE/1615/C1.

34. *The Referendum on Independence on Bosnia-Hercegovina, February 29-March 1, 1992* (Washington, D.C.: Commission on Security and Cooperation on Europe, 1992), p. 23.

35. See Yeshayahu A. Jelinik, "Bosnia-Hercegovina at War: Relations Between Moslems and Non-Moslems," *Holocaust and Genocide Studies*, Vol. 5, No. 3 (1990), pp. 275-292.

36. *FBIS-EEU*, October 9, 1992, p. 18.

37. On January 23, 1992, the medical authorities of Bosnia-Hercegovina reported that 130,782 people had been killed, had died from cold and hunger,

or had been missing from the beginning of the war. Over 8,000 of those deaths had occurred in Sarajevo. Over 138,000 people had also been wounded in the war. Western press reports of casualties were significantly lower, whereas statements from Bosnian Moslem politicians were somewhat higher. *BBCSWB*, January 26, 1993, Part 2 (Eastern Europe) C.1 Special Supplement, p. EE/1596/C1.

38. Vladimir Dedijer, *The Beloved Land* (New York: Simon and Schuster, 1961), p. 317.

39. In April 1990, Tudjman told one German interviewer: "Croatians and Serbs do not only have different historic characteristics: they also belong to different cultures. Therefore any attempt to create a unitary Yugoslavia is doomed to fail. The future new federation of states must guarantee a high degree of independence both for the Serbs and the Croatians....According to our tradition we are closely linked with central Europe and with Germany....Croatia will have closer ties with Germany than with any other country." *FBIS-EEU*, April 26, 1990, p. 81.

40. For this aspect of the war in Bosnia, see *The Ethnic Cleansing of Bosnia: A Staff Report to the Committee on Foreign Relations United States Senate* (Washington, D.C.: U.S. Government Printing Office, 1992); *War Crimes in Bosnia-Hercegovina* (New York: Helsinki Watch Report, August 1992); *Bosnia-Hercegovina: Gross Abuses of Basic Human Rights* (New York: Amnesty International U.S.A., October 1992); and, *Report of the CSCE Mission to Bosnia-Hercegovina 29 August to 4 September*, (Presented to the Sixteenth Meeting of the Committee of Senior Officials of the Conference on Security and Cooperation in Europe, September 16-18, 1992). The European Community and various international groups estimated that up to 20,000 women may have been raped during the war in Bosnia, mostly Moslems attacked by Serbian military and paramilitary personnel. Generally such reports also noted that many Serbian women were also the victims of rape by Moslems and Croats. Serbian officials in Bosnia characterized allegations against their side as either totally erroneous or wildly inflated and claimed that any violations of discipline and crimes by their forces were under investigation. Some international groups have noted that reports concerning the number of rapes in the former Yugoslavia may be exaggerated because of the political interests of the various sides and also because of distortions resulting from the repetition of the same information. See, for example, Jeri Laber, "Bosnia: Questions About Rape," *New York Review of Books*, Vol. 40, No. 6 (March 25, 1993), pp. 3-6.

The Serbian journalist Snežana Bogavac observed that "in spite of the unreliability of various sources two things need not be doubted: rape is a mass occurrence in Bosnia-Hercegovina and it is more frequently practiced by the Serbian side, which is militarily superior to the other two and holds more territory. Foreign media make distinctions according to which the Serbian side 'rapes systematically,' while the others do so 'sporadically.' Statements made by raped woman from all sides do not offer evidence of any difference among the rapists from any of the sides. All are aware that rape is an 'ideal' method of ethnic cleansing....Consciously or unconsciously, rape in Bosnia has another more subtle dimension: to estrange women and destroy the germ of renewing neighborly life." "War and Rape," *Vreme News Digest Agency*, No. 67 (Vreme No. 115), January 4, 1993, p. 9.

41. Survey research of Serbian and Croatian secondary school children at the end of the 1980s revealed an increase in ethnic distance between the two groups, with each group having highly negative stereotypes about the other. For example, by and large, Croatian children described their own group as proud, democratic, and peace-loving, but perceived Serbs as domineering, antagonistic toward others, aggressive, and perfidious. Serbian students saw themselves as proud, hospitable, brave, and lively, but viewed Croats as perfidious, antagonistic toward others, conceited, chauvinistic, and envious. Aleksander Ćirić, "Zastrašujući pogled na druge," *Vreme*, April 29, 1991, pp. 18 and 20.

42. Although the new federal republic of Yugoslavia (FRY) was allegedly established to ensure the continuity of the Yugoslav idea and the former federation, Milošević made it clear that the Third "Yugoslavia has not created Serbia, just as the previous one has not done so....Therefore, such a Yugoslavia created out of Serbia and Montenegro must function in the interests of the Republics of Serbia and Montenegro, of course." *FBIS-EEU*, October 13, 1992, p. 35. Following the formation of the FRY, a widespread purge was undertaken of all non-Serb personnel in top positions of the Yugoslav People's Army. *FBIS-EEU*, October 1, 1992, p. 37.

43. Philip Sherwell, "Serbia's Warlords Walk Tall in Beknighted Bosnia," *Sunday Telegraph*, April 26, 1992, p. 16; Tim Judah, "Kaleidoscope of Militias Fights Over Bosnia," *Times*, May 30, 1992, p. 1; and Roger Boyes, "Belgrade Gangland Killing Unveils Link to the Death Squads," *Times*, November 26, 1992, p. 1.

44. Askold Krushelnycky and T.K. Korsak, "How Iran Is Arming Bosnia's Moslems," and Askold Krushelnycky, "The Arms Trail," *European*, January 24-31, 1993, pp. 1 and 6.

45. "The Knife Over Bosnia," *Independent*, August 3, 1992, p. 17. By late summer 1992 almost all of Bosnia-Hercegovina's territory had fallen under the control of either Serbian or Croatian forces. Spokesmen for the Bosnian government and the Moslem population (who although a majority in the new state had become either unhappy junior partners of the Croats or brutalized victims of the local Serbian authorities) pleaded for international military intervention and arms. Calls for such measures also increased from outside the Balkans—including dissident voices inside the Bush administration—as more information became available during August concerning atrocities and violence in Bosnia-Hercegovina.

46. British Information Services, "Work of the EC Monitor Mission in Former Yugoslavia," *Briefing Notes Former Yugoslavia*, Issue 1/92 (1992).

47. Major General Lewis MacKenzie, who was named in March 1992 as UN field commander in Bosnia-Hercegovina, would later observe that the UN

diplomats and officials who drafted the original plans for the peace-keeping mission in Croatia and Bosnia did a "lousy" job and that there was "no command and control after 5:00 p.m. New York time." He also claimed that hundreds of civilian logistical support personnel that he was promised never arrived in the Balkans but went instead to Cambodia because the per diem payments were higher. Jeff Sallot, "MacKenzie Opens Fire on the UN," *Globe and Mail*, January 29, 1993, pp. 1-2.

48. Harvey Morris, "UN Chief Gives Warning of a Vietnam in Yugoslavia," *Independent*, August 3, 1992, p. 1.

49. Patrick Moore, "The London Conference on the Bosnian Crisis," *RFE/RL Research Report*, Vol. 1, No. 36 (September 11, 1992), pp. 1-6.

50. The Belgrade government was informed that it could reapply to join the United Nations as a new member state but that its acceptance would be contingent on the new Yugoslavia's policies and particularly its compliance with initiatives to resolve the crisis in Bosnia.

51. Beyond humanitarian aid and negotiations, the principal UN/EC initiative in October 1992 to deal with the Bosnian war was the adoption of a resolution (No. 781) calling for a "no-fly zone" over the region to curtail the use of air power by the Serbian forces.

52. *FBIS-EEU*, October 30, 1992, p. 20. In a November submission to the Peace Conference on the Former Yugoslavia the delegation of the Serbian Republic of Bosnia-Hercegovina suggested that a "common life" for the three peoples of the region had become "impossible, and morally untenable. One must say that up to now the three peoples, Serbs, Croats, and Moslems lived 'voluntarily' together only under foreign occupation...and under dictatorship. Throughout history, as soon as one of these two factors ceased to exist, there began a settling of longtime accounts usually at the expense of the Serbs." *Prijedlog uredjenja Bosne i Hercegovine* (Geneva: Republika Srpska, November 1992), p. 2.

53. *FBIS-EEU*, October 27, 1992, p. 26.

54. For example, in early October 1992, Ćosić and Tudjman agreed to the UN monitored demilitarization of the Prevlaka peninsula in the far south of Croatia, and the removal of heavy weapons form neighboring areas of Montenegro and Croatia. The Prevlaka peninsula's strategic value derives from its command over entry to Kotor Bay in Montenegro, the Third Yugoslavia's only naval base.

55. In an October 1992 report outlining the basis of their plan, Vance and Owen explained why they had rejected proposals (principally from the Serbian side) for creating a confederation of "three territorially-distinct states based on ethnic or confessional principles. Any plan to do so would involve incorporating a very large number of members of the other ethnic/confessional group. Such a plan could achieve homogeneity and coherent boundaries only by a process of enforced population transfer—which has already been condemned by the International Conference, as well as by the [UN] General Assembly.... Furthermore, a confederation formed of three such States would be inherently unstable, for at least two would surely forge immediate and stronger connections

with neighbouring States of the former Yugoslavia than they would with the other two units of Bosnia and Herzegovina." *Report of the Co-Chairmen on Progress in Developing a Constitution for Bosnia and Herzegovina* (Geneva: International Conference on the Former Yugoslavia, October 27, 1992), Document STC/2/2, pp. 4-5.

56. It was left open whether the word balance meant "equal" or "proportional" representation. "Annex VII: Proposed Constitutional Structure for Bosnia and Herzegovina," *International Legal Materials*, Vol. 31, No. 6 (November 1992), pp. 1588 and 1591.

57. "Our goal during the negotiations," Izetbegović later remarked, "was, to put it bluntly, to kill the para-states, to eliminate the para-states, so we do not have states within a state. That is why we went toward this compromise with the provinces...even though we do not like the provinces—to tell you the truth." *BBCSWB*, February 17, 1993, Part 2 (Eastern Europe), C.1 Special Supplement, p. EE/1615/C1.

58. One of Panić's ambitious initiatives in mid-October was to open talks with Albanian leaders in Kosovo, though little came of the effort because of opposition from Milošević.

59. Speaking to the European Parliament's Committee on Foreign Affairs and Security in November 1992, Panić described the December 20 elections as crucial for reaching a decision "between peace and an endless tragic conflict" in the Balkans. When asked by Simone Viel whether Bosnia was in danger of disappearing as a state, Panić remarked, "the less I know about the history of the Balkans, the better I feel....Just like you I too abhor what is happening in Bosnia-Hercegovina. If I succeed in introducing democracy in Yugoslavia, Bosnia-Hercegovina will not disappear. For me, it is another country, and we will recognize it." *"Europe,"* No. 5853 (New Series) (November 7, 1992), p. 4.

60. In a somber televised speech to the Serbian people on January 6, 1993, Ćosić emphasized the urgency of reaching a peace settlement in Bosnia: "The outcome of the Geneva conference will condition the final decision on military intervention on a war of the USA and EC against the Serbian nation in Bosnia-Hercegovina, but Serbia and Montenegro are also threatened by the same horror....The outcome of the Geneva talks will have a direct influence on the lifting or tightening of sanctions...a fateful impact on the political recovery of the entire territory of the former Yugoslavia and the Balkans....Serbs are therefore faced with a terrible dilemma: political and military capitulation or an assault by the world's most powerful forces." *BBCSWB*, Part 2 (Eastern Europe), C.1 Special Supplement, p. EE/1582/C1.

61. For example, in October 1992, Clinton told an interviewer: "I support a strong American role in the UN and with the EC to end Serbian aggression and provide a peaceful solution to this tragic conflict. I have supported the use of multi-lateral military force, if necessary, to ensure that UN relief efforts are protected. We cannot ignore the human agony of what has been taking place in the very heart of modern Europe." "Bush and Clinton Speak Out," *Europe* (October 1992), p. 7.

62. Just days before the December 20 Serbian election, U.S. Secretary of State, Lawrence Eagleburger, named Milošević, along with several other Serbian and Croatian military and political leaders as possible war criminals. *New York Times*, December 17, 1992, pp. 1, 10. The American who managed Panić's campaign later claimed that Eagleburger's decision to brand Milošević a potential war criminal actually helped the Serbian leader to garner more votes in the election. Douglas E. Schoen, "How Milošević Stole the Election," *New York Times Magazine*, February 14, 1993, p. 40. After leaving office, Eagleburger was asked if he had indeed indirectly helped Milošević to win: "Yeah, of course I did, and I don't give a hoot...I'm sure it helped....I think he would have won anyway, but yes, I think I gave him some more votes." *Crossfire*, CNN Transcripts 775, February 23, 1993, p. 8.

63. Michael Sheridan, "Medicine Man Casts a Spell on Karadžić," *Independent*, January 17, 1993, p. 4.

64. Alan Philips, "Karadžić Forced into Submission," *Daily Telegraph*, January 13, 1993, p. 11.

65. *European*, January 24, 1993, p. 1. In an interview of January 17, 1993, an adviser to Yugoslavia's President Ćosić claimed that Milošević and Ćosić were most responsible for getting Karadžić to agree to support the Vance-Owen plan and that military pressure from the international community, or alleged pressure from Moscow, played no role in the Karadžić decision. *BBCSWB*, January 19, 1993, Part 2 (Eastern Europe), C.1 Special Supplement, p. EE/1590/C1.

66. John Burns, "Holding Lead Serbs in Bosnia Look to End Fighting," *New York Times*, January 17, 1993, p. 6.

67. *BBCSWB*, January 22, 1993, Part 2 (Eastern Europe), C.1 Special Supplement, p. EE/1593/C1.

68. On the eve of Clinton's inauguration, the Security Council prepared the text of a resolution to permit military actions for the enforcement of an air exclusion zone over Bosnia that had been adopted in October. Serious British and French reservations to the adoption of such a resolution, however, still remained.

69. The Serbian and Croatian delegations accepted the military agreement to end hostilities that was proposed by Vance and Owen, but only the Croats accepted the maps on the borders among the provinces.

70. Report on National Public Radio, January 30, 1993.

71. Statements made by Bill Clinton during the presidential campaign encouraged the Moslem-led Bosnian government to expect a more activist posture by Washington in the Balkans if President Bush was defeated. However, though the new Clinton administration expressed various reservations about the Vance-Owen plan—particularly that it rewarded advances made by the Serbian side at the expense of the Moslems—Secretary of State Warren Christopher quickly eschewed any direct U.S. military action to roll-back Serbian gains in Bosnia. Thus on February 10, 1993 he announced that Washington supported the general approach of the Vance-Owen plan (although differences between U.S. and UN-EC views on the plan's details continued behind the

scenes), and would continue the embargo on arms shipments to the Balkan region (lifting the arms embargo was a key Moslem request in lieu of international military intervention). Christopher also announced that the Clinton administration would expand humanitarian aid to Bosnia, tighten the sanctions against Serbia, appoint a special U.S. representative to the Bosnian negotiations (Reginald Bartholomew), and solicit the involvement of the Russian government in the negotiations. The U.S. Secretary of Defense, Les Aspin, explained on March 7 that: "The current policy is to use heavy diplomatic pressure. We want the Germans to talk to the Croatians, the Russians to talk to the Serbs—whoever anybody has some influence with—marshall the opinion.... That's kind of at the core of the policy at the moment, and we ought to give that a chance to see whether it would work...to use non-military means to try and put pressures on all of the parties. And it's not just the Serbs, although the Serbs are the particular problem at this moment....You always want to be extraordinarily careful about committing any kind of forces in these things, because, once you're in, you're there." *ABC News This Week With David Brinkley*, March 7, 1993, Transcript 593, pp. 6-7.

Washington's new policy led to air-drops of humanitarian aid to eastern Bosnia in late February and March. But parallel efforts at the United Nations to obtain Moslem and Serb agreement on a revised map of the Vance-Owen ten province model for Bosnia proved extremely difficult. The Bosnian Serbs were particularly concerned that they would be forced to forfeit control of territory— from approximately 70 percent of Bosnia to about 42 percent—and worried that provisions of the plan previously signed in Geneva might be altered (the Serbs were especially adamant that they retain control over their heavy weapons). Meanwhile, the Moslem-led authorities in Sarajevo were unhappy with the provincial boundaries of the Vance-Owen map: they wanted the plan to include a strengthened central government and stronger assurances regarding international enforcement. By mid-March only the Croats had agreed to all three elements of the Vance-Owen plan, namely, the constitutional principles, the military arrangements, and the map of the ten provinces. Despite such difficulties, U.S. Ambassador Batholomew claimed on March 8 that "the active and direct engagement of the United States" in the process had assisted in persuading the Moslems to join the Croats and Serbs in signing the military accord portion of the agreement. He also indicated that it was Washington's intention to "create and help maintain a durable Bosnian state," and any side within Bosnia that proved to be "recalcitrant" about reaching a "fair and workable settlement," would be subjected to sanctions and a kind of "formal diplomatic isolation the world hasn't seen." *MacNeil/Lehrer Newshour*, March 8, 1993, Transcript 4579, pp. 10-11. Although President Clinton continued to regard U.S.-Russian cooperation as essential in finding a settlement to the Bosnian crisis, serious internal difficulties in Russia limited the Kremlin's ability to influence events. Meanwhile, at a meeting in Paris, French President Mitterand attempted to exert pressure on Serbia's Milošević to assist in obtaining full Bosnian Serb agreement to the Vance-Owen proposal. However the French government, always cautious about enhanced U.S. influence in Europe and opposed to placing their troops under the overall command of a British General who was proposed to head the international force, provided less cooperation to NATO's contingency planning for enforcement of a future peace plan for Bosnia. Once again, as throughout the tragic Balkan crisis of 1991-1993, the intransigence of the region's leaders and political divisions among foreign states obstructed efforts to reach a solution.

On March 25, 1993 the Bosnian Moslems, after receiving U.S. assurances that the international community would seriously implement cease-fire enforcement measures should a peace plan be concluded, finally agreed to all the terms of the Vance-Owen proposal (including a revised map of the ten provinces enlarging Moslem control in the province of Sarajevo, which also received the renewed support of the Bosnian Croats). Immense diplomatic pressure—or what President Clinton termed a "full-court press"—was now directed at the Serbian side to acquiesce in the Vance-Owen plan.

On April 2, a majority in the Bosnian Serb legislature rejected the revised Vance-Owen ten province map. U.S. Secretary of State Warren Christopher, commenting on the move at the Russian-American summit in Vancouver, Canada, called the rejection "regrettable," but emphasized that the Serbs had left the door open to further negotiations. Christopher also suggested that "tougher and tighter" sanctions by the international community would be forthcoming. Meanwhile, American hopes of obtaining President Yeltsin's support for stronger sanctions against Serbia remained contingent on the outcome of the power struggle in Moscow. What steps Washington would ultimately adopt in the event that the Bosnian Serbs maintained their resistance to a ten province peace accord depended upon the outcome of ongoing policy disputes within the Clinton administration between advocates of continued political-economic measures to address the Bosnian crisis and those favoring some sort of external military intervention.

9

Yugoslavism's Failure and Future

I want to see my parents again....I love everybody: Serbs, Moslems, Croats, they are all my brothers. This is what my parents taught me. Why were they killed?

—Nermina Gusö, 13-year-old Moslem resident of Sarajevo

My imagination does not go far enough to see Serbs, Moslems, and Croats co-existing again for as long as the children and people who can remember this terrible Bosnian war are alive.

—Dobrica Ćosić, President of Yugoslavia (Serbia-Montenegro)

Yugoslavia's Violent Collapse in the "Prism of History"

TWO IMPORTANT AND complex issues have troubled observers in relation to the catastrophic events that unfolded in the Balkans during the early 1990s. First, and perhaps the less difficult of the two issues, is the matter of why the "Second Yugoslavia" (1945-1991) collapsed. Second, there is the related and perplexing question as to why the disintegration of the federation generated so much violence and suffering. In addressing the first issue, this book has focused primarily on the failure of political leaders—newly elected or reelected to power during the "pluralist revolution" of 1990—to agree upon a revised model of political and economic coexistence that could have preserved some form of state unity among the peoples of Yugoslavia but would also have permitted expanded sovereignty for the former federation's constituent territorial and ethnic groups. Serious difficulties stemming from interelite mistrust and elite-led ethnic nationalism, or what was referred to earlier as "the politics of intransigence," did not begin with the disintegration of the League of Communist's monopoly in early 1990. Once multiparty pluralism and competitive elections emerged, however, issues related to transcending disagreements among regional elites became far more complex and serious. Not only did the number of centrist parties— mainly reconfigured communist-nationalists and noncommunist nationalists—multiply but a large number of ultranationalist parties and movements also emerged on the scene.

Most of the country's major civilian and military leaders recognized the danger of impending state disintegration and political violence if they failed to reach agreement on a new constitutional model, but they proved woefully inept in finding a way out of the looming disaster. After months of elite posturing and stalemate in the negotiations regarding the intractable federation-confederation dispute, saber rattling by all sides, and leadership mishandling or outright manipulation of the explosive "Serbian question," it became impossible to sustain the cohesion of a perennially fragile country afflicted with a history of deep ethnic and regional enmities. External factors—particularly German and Austrian support for the secessionist goals of Slovenia and Croatia, and the "pasted together diplomacy"[1] exhibited by the United States and EC when handling Yugoslav affairs—certainly played an important role in the collapse of the federation but the major responsibility rests with the quarrelsome nationalist leaders of Yugoslavia's republics.[2]

Explanations for the collapse of the Yugoslav federation are closely linked but are still separate from the second issue raised here, namely, why state disintegration spawned such widespread, protracted, and barbarous violence. Three closely related factors raised in earlier chapters are particularly significant for understanding the intense violence associated with the dissolution of the Yugoslav federation: first, the persistence and intensification of deep-seated animosities among the country's diverse ethnic and religious groups, who lived together rather uneasily in the Balkan region for centuries but who shared membership in a common state from only 1918 to 1991; second, the desire of many Yugoslav citizens to redress grievances arising from the violent bloodletting among ethnic groups during World War II; and, finally, the failure of the communist regime's nationality policy and modernization programs to resolve outstanding, albeit temporarily submerged, interethnic grievances and to engender a substantial basis for long-term interethnic tolerance. The combined impact of the preceding three factors not only contributed substantially to the elite intransigence that led to the demise of the Second Yugoslavia, but in the particular circumstances and traditions endemic to the Balkans, also unleashed extremely violent interethnic strife.

Consideration of the policies and strategies conducted by successive political regimes is crucial to an understanding of the deep intergroup antagonisms in Balkan society. Indeed, throughout much of Balkan history the region's intrinsic heterogeneity was nurtured and utilized as a basis for maintaining authoritarian political rule. For example, the contending Ottoman and Hapsburg empires, which asserted hegemony over the various South Slav ethnic groups between the late fourteenth and early sixteenth centuries, maintained political control of their multiconfessional and multiethnic Balkan domains up to the early twentieth century by means of various divide-and-rule strategies, including the segmentation of religious communities.[3] Although some members of the nonruling intelligentsia did endeavor to forge closer ties among different ethnically related communities—for example, the "Yugoslav idea," elaborated in Croatian elite circles during the first part of the nineteenth century (see Chapter 1)—such notions enjoyed only shallow and uneven support from the region's ethnically and religiously divided population.[4]

Notwithstanding its limited popular support, a unified Yugoslav state was created in 1918, bringing together several South Slavic and non-Slavic ethnic groups within a single territorial framework. Although the new state's Belgrade-based political regimes largely abandoned earlier imperial policies of group segmentation, their various attempts to induce a pan-ethnic "Yugoslav" consciousness during most of the next 73 years, though contrasting with the policies of their imperial predecessors, tended to aggravate the general pattern of ethnic antagonisms. Thus the imperatives of central political rule once again constrained the free expression of ethnic and religious differences. Whether under the Serbian-dominated unitary state between the two world wars or under the more ethnically balanced but oppositionless communist federation established by Tito, ethnic grievances continued to accumulate and fester into potential sources of political instability.

Short-lived periods of political contestation or liberalization—such as the fragmented multiparty system of the 1920s, and the factionalized one-party socialist pluralism reluctantly permitted by Tito in the second part of the 1960s—proved to be episodes of chaotic ethnopolitical rivalry that offered little opportunity for the sustained reconciliation of intergroup animosities. Thus although precommunist and communist political elites in Belgrade did manage to constrain the outbreak of widespread ethnic conflict for substantial periods of time, as did earlier rulers in Constantinople, Vienna, and Budapest, deep-seated ethnic resentments persisted as a vital latent force, simmering beneath the facade of contrived stability and cohesion.

Historically, the potential for ethnically and religiously based violence in the Balkans was most evident during periods of regime crisis and breakdown (e.g., the last phase of Ottoman control which led to the Balkan Wars; the final throes of Hapsburg rule just before and during World War I; the collapse and dismemberment of the Yugoslav state in 1941). Indeed, perceptive observers of Balkan society have frequently noted the close relationship between regime breakdown, historically based ethnoreligious antagonisms, and intense violence. Discussing his native Bosnian society in the period just before World War I, Nobel-Prize-winning author Ivo Andrić brilliantly captured how seemingly tranquil intergroup relations have traditionally exploded into an orgy of mutual bloodletting.[5] In an illustrative case, Andrić describes the "Sarajevo frenzy of hate" that erupted among Moslems, Roman Catholics, and Orthodox believers following the assassination on June 28, 1914, of Archduke Franz Ferdinand in Sarajevo:

> Adherents of the three main faiths, they hate one another from birth to death, senselessly and profoundly...often, they spent their entire lives without finding an opportunity to express that hatred in all its facets and horror; but whenever the established order of things is shaken by some important event, and reason and law are suspended for a few hours or days, then this mob or rather a section of it, finding at last an adequate motive, overflows into the town...and, like a flame which has sought and has at last found fuel, these long-kept hatreds and hidden desires for destruction and violence take over the town, lapping, sputtering, and swallowing everything, until some force larger than themselves suppresses them, or until they burn themselves out and tire of their own rage.[6]

Vera St. Erlich, a Zagreb sociologist, also emphasized the Balkan tradition of violent interethnic struggle, particularly in areas such as Bosnia-Hercegovina and other regions that have been under Turkish rule, when attempting to explain how a "determination to fight" was so quickly "revived" following the dismemberment of the Yugoslav state in 1941. In St. Erlich's view, the protracted resistance struggle waged by the South Slavs against Ottoman tutelage fashioned a "heroic value orientation," imprinting the collective conviction "that no force in the world can conquer fighters."

> Generations of Yugoslavs from the fourteenth century until today grew up with this value orientation. Their character was formed through

loyalty to resistance movements and not through conformity to an established culture and institutions....As the old authorities collapse under enemy attack and invasion, the unity of society ceases to exist. From then on factions raise their claims, and the people divide into hostile camps, the individual is compelled to make his choice.[7]

The dismemberment of the "First Yugoslavia" (1918-1941), and the collapse of authority in that state, precipitated savage interethnic violence during World War II, which resulted in the death of approximately one-tenth of the country's population. Wartime atrocities and radically heightened political polarization left a pattern of emotional scars that were only superficially masked by the communist system's promising slogans (e.g., "Brotherhood and Unity," "Equality of Nations"), pan-ethnic strategies, and artificial political uniformity.

Although broad-ranging generalizations, such as those made by Andrić and St. Erlich, often neglect the important differences within and among particular ethnic groups and regions, they do serve to draw attention to the important historical factors that have conditioned Balkan and South Slav political life. The impact of historical factors on current Balkan development has also been recognized in more recent sociological research relating to the intensification of ethnic conflict in Yugoslavia during the 1980s and 1990s. For example, a comprehensive review by the Serbia-based sociologist Sergej Flere of various theoretical approaches seeking to explain the upsurge of ethnic antagonism in post-Tito Yugoslavia identified the historical perspective as the most convincing.[8] Flere conceded that as recently as the late 1980s it appeared to most observers that modernization had largely eroded religious divisions and had contributed to Yugoslavia's "emancipation from tradition." By 1990 however, Flere argued, the role of traditional religions in generating ethnic conflicts—including resentments derived from the history of religious warfare and forced religious conversion in the Balkans—was already very pronounced.

Flere acknowledged, as many other analysts so often had in past years, the considerable changes in Yugoslav society during the post-World War II period and the existence of various potentially integrative factors (e.g., intermarriage by individuals belonging to different ethnic groups, substantial numbers of citizens self-identified as "Yugoslavs"), but he emphasized that socialist Yugoslavia remained "substantially unintegrated" and "retained a basically segmented quality."[9] Buffeted and alienated by the severe economic crisis of the 1980s, the subsequent breakdown of the socialist federation, and lacking a strong sense of common identity and reciprocal trust, Yugoslavia's citizens—in both the economically developed and disadvantaged regions of the country—sought refuge in their only superficially or partially eradicated traditional ethnoreligious beliefs and resentments.[10] Thus viewed in historical perspective, particularly in the context of the Balkan region's traditional proclivity for ethnoreligiously based violence at times of regime breakdown, an explosion of intercommunal hatred and savagery was not at all surprising when ethnic elites proved tragically inept at peacefully resolving their differences.

Post-Yugoslavia:
The Successor States in Transition

By mid-1992, the political map of the Balkan peninsula had already been profoundly altered (see Map 9.1). Three of the republics in the former federation—Croatia, Slovenia, and Bosnia-Hercegovina— established their independence through unilateral "disassociation" from the Yugoslav state, and despite armed struggles that ensued on their territories, they were soon recognized by the international community. A fourth republic, Macedonia, also proclaimed independence[11] but its recognition was postponed pending the resolution of complaints from Greece that a sovereign state with that name would have territorial aspirations to Greece's northern province of Macedonia.

International acceptance also eluded the "Third Yugoslavia"—a remodeled two-unit federation composed of Serbia and Montenegro— which endeavored to inherit the mantle of the former Yugoslav state.[12] This new Yugoslavia temporarily failed to obtain legitimacy from the international community owing to the widely held judgment that Serbian president Slobodan Milošević had masterminded military aggression first against Croatia and then against Bosnia-Hercegovina. Milošević's cooperation had been solicited by Cyrus Vance and Lord Owen in their well-meaning, but highly controversial effort to bring peace to Bosnia in early 1993 but the Serbian leader still remained a pariah to most of the international community. Indeed, many observers saw the Vance-Owen plan as unworkable, and for others it was a highly inappropriate act of appeasement and desperation in view of Milošević's record of activities.[13]

As the fierce fighting and carnage continued through the first months of 1993, and hostilities resumed between Serbs and Croats in Croatia, the development of a coordinated and consistent international response to Yugoslavia's collapse remained beyond the grasp of the international community. Apart from the crucial and immediate problem of containing the bloodletting and human tragedy, however, other significant issues would also need to be addressed if any long-term resolution of the so-called Yugoslav crisis might be reached. For example, within each of the new Balkan states, disruption, warfare, and political violence relating to the former Yugoslavia's disintegration had seriously complicated—either directly or indirectly—the resolution of many pressing internal problems. Most significant in this regard were the obstacles to political democratization and economic transformation, or the two principal sectors of regime transition that have preoccupied all the former authoritarian communist regimes in Eastern Europe.

The most serious threat to the institutionalization of democratic rule in each of the successor states to the former Yugoslav federation has been the salience of nationalism and ultranationalism in Balkan political life. The role of patriotic and nationalist sentiments in relation to democratic political change cannot, of course, be characterized as entirely

MAP 9.1   New Balkan States After 1991

○ National capitals

⊛ Yugoslav republic capitals

● Yugoslav autonomous regions capitals

• Other cities

regressive. Thus, nationalism had significantly contributed to the initial pressure for ending one-party monopoly in each of the republics during the twilight of the communist regime and also in the first phase of pluralist development during the 1990 elections. The onset of warfare during 1991 and 1992, however, and the consolidation of control by powerful nationalist parties and elites in each of the principal frontline successor states (Croatia, Bosnia-Hercegovina, and Serbia-Montenegro) tended to undermine the fuller development of stable competitive politics. In Bosnia intense ethnonationalist warfare completely precluded any pursuit of democratic development, and the politics of violent nationalism also helped retard democratic political development in both Croatia and Serbia. For example, although the nationalist leaders of those two states, Franjo Tudjman and Slobodan Milošević, both had to contend with opposition parties in their respective legislatures, and also in the elections held during 1992, the style of leadership and the authoritarian cast of the various measures they employed to intimidate their critics (particularly in the media) frequently smacked of the prepluralist environment in which both men had been politically socialized and had made their early careers.

Generally speaking, the Croatian political opposition that emerged following the collapse of the one-party regime in 1990 was stronger and less fragmented than its counterpart in Serbia. However, the imperatives of the ongoing war being waged on Croatian soil from July 1991 to January 1992, followed by a fragile truce and the active involvement of Croatian forces in Bosnia, tended to militarize societal and political life. In view of the war the Zagreb government felt justified, for example, in taking legal action against selected members of the media and opposition who were either critical of the ruling authorities or were regarded as a threat to the constitutional order. Such measures, although understandable in the circumstances of warfare and fledgling democracy, seriously chilled the atmosphere for free political interplay. Commenting on a pattern that has characterized many postcommunist regimes, Tudjman's former adviser, Slaven Letica, described the result of such problems on Croatian political life:

> The culture or evil spirit of a single-party system is again present in Croatia. It is the spirit of "conformism" which holds that any critical opinion has no objective justification, that it is a subjective fallacy, or even high treason ("opposition from within" and "enemies from without")....The new political elite has inherited and extended the system of the abuse of power...the same people are being rotated from post to post, from one ministry to another, and there is no professional logic

behind these shifts, just like there was none in the old regime....The public is given virtually no explanation as to why somebody is appointed to a post or removed from it.[14]

In August 1992, Tudjman and his party won their second victory in a competitive election, but the overall situation in the new state could hardly be described as normal. As Tudjman's major competitor for the post of president later observed:

I dreamed of a different Croatia...our country today is a sad sight, but nevertheless we have an independent and internationally recognized state....But this political form in which it has been realized—for now truncated borders, rudimentary democracy, a low level of political culture, devastated cities and towns, social indigence—is only a transitory form of the Croatian state. Today's Croatia is not the only possible Croatia.[15]

In Serbia, the negative impact of nationalism and ultranationalism on democratic political life during the early 1990s simply continued a trend that had been instigated by Milošević during the twilight of the one-party regime. Thus, mobilizing support for the Serbs of Croatia and Bosnia, and exploiting the anxiety of the citizens of Serbia regarding their isolation and condemnation by the international community, the Milošević regime appealed for "patriotic unity" and the "ethnic loyalty" of the Serbian population. Such tactics were extremely effective in mounting a campaign against Serbia's highly fragmented and weak opposition parties—many of which were cross-pressured between their liberal democratic principles and a need to appear as strong advocates of Serbian national interests.[16] Milošević had a tremendous advantage over the squabbling opposition parties in light of the ruling socialist leadership's organizational experience, its access to Serbian governmental resources, and particularly its control over both the state media and the local power structures outside of Belgrade. As one Serbian opposition leader put it in October 1992:

Our party system is not even a true party system...and with respect to the opposition political parties, I think that parties do not exist here in the real meaning of the word...elementary conditions for the work of political parties have not been ensured. We are not living in normal political circumstances, and we do not have regular public life. There was a mistaken assumption that the path from an authoritarian regime to a democratic one was something that was very simple and something that was self-evident. The transition from an authoritarian regime to democracy does not necessarily have to result in democracy. Different forms of undemocratic regimes can arise.[17]

Following his victory over Milan Panić in the important 1992 Serbian election, Milošević and his allies began a widespread purge of oppositionists from the state-controlled television and radio network. As in Croatia, where Tudjman's regime had earlier purged most Serbian personnel from the media, Milošević also used his victory in the election to carry out an ethnic purge of remaining Moslem and Croat employees. In a throwback to the practices of the collapsed single-party system, the regimes in both Belgrade and Zagreb viewed unconventional expression and any strong criticism of the ruling authorities as an abuse of democracy rather than as a crucial pillar of democratic development.[18]

Democratic change in both Serbia and Croatia has also been seriously obstructed by intolerant regime sponsored policies and practices regarding ethnic minorities in both of the new states. For example, the decision by the authorities in Belgrade to curtail the political autonomy of Serbia's province of Kosovo and to effectively quash Albanian opposition through military and police rule prompted the Albanian population to boycott the political process in both Serbia and the new Yugoslav state during the 1990s. Employing a policy of passive resistance and noncooperation with the Serbian authorities, the Albanians of Kosovo established a parallel or alternative state and societal structure, complete with schools, colleges, hospitals, and political institutions. "We are organizing a separate life outside the Serbian system," observed Albanian leader Ibrahim Rugova. "This is our way. We do not want a violent confrontation with Serbia and we will not accept Serbian rule."[19]

Although Serbian authorities claimed that the Albanian population enjoyed full civil liberties and human rights, Milošević's brand of populist nationalism remained intolerant of the accommodations necessary to peacefully satisfy the large concentrated Albanian minority in Kosovo. Thus, Belgrade's policy created an explosive ethnic conflict within the borders of Serbia and also an island of blatant authoritarianism that forced Albanian leaders to seek full self-determination or independence for their constituents. For his part, Milošević viewed the aspirations of Kosovo's Albanians for sovereignty as completely "out of the question" because, in his opinion, such a development would conflict with the self-determination rights of the Serbian "majority," that is, the Serbs of the republic and its two provinces (considered as a single unit).[20]

The same official attitude toward minority demands for self-determination was prevalent in Croatia. Thus for President Tudjman and the ruling HDZ party in Zagreb, the sovereignty of the Croatian state was viewed as an expression of the Croatian nation's collective will. When sovereignty is conceived of in this "collectivistic" manner (rather than as an outgrowth of the sovereignty of individuals) it is generally considered as entirely legitimate and appropriate for those that interpret the collective will—often a person or individuals with authoritarian pretensions—to accord the dominant ethnic group a privileged status in society.[21] This mindset, that has aptly been described as "constitutional nationalism" when it becomes the basis for fashioning fundamental laws and policies,[22] views the aspirations of minorities for special representation and self-government as secondary and even seditious. Actions taken to entrench the sovereignty of the dominant nation within this context naturally tend to seriously alienate large minorities seeking constitutional recognition and political influence.

The most deleterious consequences of such constitutional nationalism were manifest in the violent collision between the Croatian majority and the Serbian minority in Croatia following the immediate postcommunist period—a pattern that, not surprisingly, resurfaced in early 1993 after a year-long stand off. President Tudjman made it very clear that his opposition to Serbian self-determination was related to the activities of those he often referred to as "Serbian rebels" in Croatia, not to the new Yugoslavia engineered by Slobodan Milošević:

> From the Croatian point of view, we cannot deny to Serbia and Montenegro the right to unite in some kind of community, a Yugoslav community...it is a reality despite the fact that it is not recognized. Croatia as well, the Independent Republic of Croatia, was a reality even before it was recognized....Concerning certain Serbian extremists who would like to gain the right to some kind of self-determination...no minority in any country, including the independent sovereign Croatia has the right to any kind of self-determination.[23]

Frustrated by the inability of the UN peace-keeping forces to facilitate the re-establishment of the Zagreb government's authority over the predominantly Serbian Krajina and the return to the area of Croatian residents who had been forced to flee during the fighting in 1991, Tudjman launched a military initiative in early 1993 to retake Croatian territory and to bring Serbian resistance in Croatia to an end.[24] Unfortunately, the new round of hostilities seemed likely to further complicate majority-minority relations in Croatia and to exacerbate the militarization of political life in the new state.

As of early 1993, Slovenia appeared to be the most successful of all the successor states in implementing the difficult transition from authoritarianism to democratic rule. This transition was not, however, without its problems. The most apparent defects of Slovenian politics appeared to be a pattern of chaotic decisionmaking and endless parliamentary disputes, and what was described at one point as "real civil war at the institutional level" between different branches of the government and among various political parties.[25] A certain personalization of politics in Slovenia, which was connected to an absence of deep-seated support for specific parties and party platforms, also was a factor in the state's democratic development. "This is a legacy from the former one-party system in which nobody weighed up the programs, but rather the persons executing them," observed one Slovene editorial commentator. "We have a multiparty system, but we are behaving as in a one-party system. If you do not believe this, reflect on how often you can hear that (as a small nation, etc.) we should unite."[26]

Moreover, even the small Alpine republic was not immune from the deleterious effects of politicized nationalism. In this regard, many Slovenian commentators have remarked on the amusing and petty side of the postcommunist emphasis on the "Slovene essence," which includes references to "Slovene chickens," "Slovene soil," and "Slovenian descent" of families. Other observers, however, have pointed to the potential dangers of calls for the banning of all that is multicultural and non-Slovene and also "the animation of a militant patriotic consciousness,"[27] especially by those who take excessive pride in the recent accomplishments of Slovenia's popular Minister of Defense, Janez Janša. Despite such difficulties, the three major political forces which came to dominate the multiparty system of Slovenia at the end of 1992—Liberal Democrats, Christian Democrats, and Social Democrats—seemed to be cooperating in order to achieve a relatively stable and competent government.

The difficulty of managing a smooth transition from authoritarianism to democracy in the Balkans, while avoiding the negative side of nationalist politics has been seriously complicated by the disastrous economic consequences of the recent ethnic conflict and warfare in the region. In a vicious circle, violent ultranationalism has wrecked the economy in most regions, and in turn, economic failures have fueled ultranationalism. For example, in August 1992 President Tudjman estimated the cost of the direct material damage from the war in Croatia at over US$20 billion.[28] As a result of the wars in Croatia and later in Bosnia, the Zagreb government was also burdened with the cost of caring for hundreds of thousands of refugees.[29] In August 1992 Tudjman estimated that Croatia was spending US$3 million per day for the care of those refugees. The costs of the military struggle, and also the severe disruption of Croatian industry and tourism, completely derailed the postcommunist regime's plan for economic transformation and marketization, thereby severing the positive link between economic development and political pluralism, which can prove so crucial in the emergence of democratic stability. In this regard, one Croatian minister observed that "[the 1991] war destroyed production, transport and communications networks. We have no tourists, no foreign investment, our markets in old Yugoslavia are gone."[30] It was also estimated that Croatia's gross national product had shrunk 50 percent from 1990 to 1993, and production capacity had slipped 40 percent during the same period. Because the Zagreb government was forced to print Croatian dinars to pay for military expenses, refugees, and privatization and welfare costs, inflation was approximately 1,000 percent in 1992.

In Serbia and Montenegro the severe pattern of deterioration was traceable in large part to the international community's economic sanctions, the general disruption of the traditional economic links among regions of the former Yugoslav federation, and also the costs associated with Serbo-Montenegrin humanitarian and military support for the Serbian communities in Bosnia and Croatia. Serbia's gross domestic product dropped by nearly 45 percent between 1989 and 1992. Exports in 1992 dropped 46 percent from 1991 levels, and imports were down by one-third. Business closures and a steep drop in production also led to a massive increase in the number of people who were unemployed, on welfare, or on paid leave. In 1992, a hyperinflation of over 20,000 percent exceeded traditional Latin American levels of price fluctuation, which had earlier held the global record. Such depressed conditions in Serbia contributed to rampant currency speculation by powerful money brokers and shady private banks that temporarily offered beleaguered Serbian citizens inflated monthly rates on their dinar accounts. Compounding this situation was the proliferation of private businessmen, war profiteers, and sanction-busting smugglers, who manipulated the rapidly growing black market and often acquired a certain celebrity status and political influence in Serbia's vortex of competing nationalist and ultranationalist political groups. Indeed, some Serbian economists believed that the sanctions had intensified the growth of a so-called "Columbian syndrome" in Serbia that began with the sharp drop in the standard of living during the last years of the former communist regime, and was characterized by a fusion between political power and various forms of economic underworld activity.[31]

Endeavoring to turn the economically debilitating sanctions to his benefit by urging the Serbian population to assert their "patriotic conscience" in the face of unyielding international pressure against

Belgrade, Milošević was forced to admit that the sanctions had created the basis for various kinds of "economic pathology" that "have undermined the entire legal system."[32] The Serbian leader could not, however, simply explain away the tangible consequences of sanctions on his fellow citizens by merely bemoaning the growth of economic crime and the general impairment of the rule-of-law. In his successful bid for reelection in December 1992, for example, Milošević used slick television ads to distract attention from the war, the breakdown of order, and the sanctions. The ads focused voter attention on the remaining facets of security and happiness in their midst, such as Serbia's natural beauty. Pictures of the Serbian landscape accompanied by the Socialist Party label and the slogan "Tako treba" ("That's the way") were combined to elicit reassurance that a vote for Milošević would preserve the things that really mattered in life. Such a campaign strategy, together with a reservoir of nationalist supporters who still believed in him and with some practiced electoral chicanery by his Socialist Party stalwarts,[33] combined to give Milošević another electoral victory, though by a slimmer margin than in 1990.

Interestingly, a large number of the voters who chose to leave the Milošević fold switched their support to his more ultranationalist ally, Vojislav Šešelj, the head of the Serbian Radical Party. The strong support for Šešelj and his party—which was very likely attributable to a strong feeling on the part of the Serbian population that it was unfairly under siege by both other Balkan ethnic groups and the international community—was a dangerous omen for Serbian democratic development and perhaps also for Slobodan Milošević's future ability to politically exploit Serbian nationalist concerns.[34] Although Milošević and Šešelj maintained an informal alliance in the wake of the elections—cooperating to oust Milan Panić from the prime ministership of Yugoslavia in January 1993—it was unclear how long their working relationship would survive.

By early 1993, the impact of the sanctions together with other factors (see Chapter 8) had prodded Milošević into adopting a more flexible position in the negotiations on resolving the war in Bosnia, but the Serbian economy had sustained major damage that probably would not be reversed for several decades. "If the West's intention was to destroy our economy as a punishment for our political leadership," observed one Serbian economist, "then the sanctions are a success. But if they were designed to bring about multiparty centrist democracy, the sanctions are counter-productive. The election [of December 20, 1992] showed that with the sanctions everything shifted to the far right."[35] Although some Serbian observers urged the lifting of international sanctions as a means to weaken Milošević's appeal for Serbian unity and his manipulation of anti-foreign and particularly anti-Western feeling, there was also a real chance that Milošević would take credit for ending sanctions and Serbia's isolation. Tarred in most of the Western media with epithets such as "bully" or "butcher of the Balkans," and also more vigorously challenged by domestic competitors, Milošević was bowed but by no means beaten or willing to step aside. "I'm not as confident as I used to be, but I will not resign," Milošević defiantly claimed seven days after being reelected president of Serbia.[36]

The war-related sanctions had the severest impact on the economies of Croatia, Bosnia-Hercegovina, Serbia, and Montenegro, but economic development in Macedonia and Slovenia also suffered from the general disruption of trade patterns in the wake of the former Yugoslavia's collapse. Thus Macedonia, positioned adjacent to Serbia, suffered serious collateral economic damage from the international sanctions against Belgrade and was also subjected to an oil embargo by Greece arising from Athens' opposition to Macedonian independence. By the end of 1992, the Macedonian economy was reeling from massive foreign debt and unemployment, hyperinflation, and plunging economic production. Such economic difficulties contributed to renewed internal tensions, particularly between the ethnic Macedonians and the large Albanian minority, which threatened the political stability of the still internationally unrecognized Balkan state and potentially also the states in the surrounding regions.

Slovenia—the former Yugoslavia's most economically developed republic—also had its share of economic difficulties that tended to fuel political extremism and nationalism. For example, as many observers had warned prior to Ljubljana's declaration of independence, the new state no longer enjoyed its traditional "Yugoslav" sources of raw materials or the markets for its finished goods. The wrenching post-Yugoslav and postcommunist economic reorientation, and the cost of reconstruction from the short war with the JNA, led to an economic depression and a slump in Slovenia's standard of living during the second half of 1991 and the first half of 1992. The situation seemed to be slowly improving near the end of 1992, particularly relative to the problems faced by the other successor states, as international banks (including the International Monetary Fund) and markets slowly opened for the Slovenes, foreign trade was balanced, and the exchange rate of the new state's currency, the *tolar*, was stabilized. The cost of caring for refugees fleeing from the turmoil in Croatia and Bosnia, however, proved troubling to the Slovenian economy and also added to traces of xenophobia and nationalism at the fringe of the political spectrum. For example, tapping the anxiety of extreme right-oriented voters who worried that foreign immigrants to Slovenia—some of whom were granted Slovenian citizenship—would become a financial burden and take away Slovenian jobs, the chauvinist Slovene National Party (SNS) won 12 percent of the seats in the new state's legislature in the election held in December 1992. The SNS was excluded from the state's new coalition government, but it constituted the fourth largest party in the legislature, and surveys revealed that its controversial leader was quite popular.[37]

As of early 1993, the regimes in most of the successor states—Slovenia being the most notable exception—included significant undemocratic features and might best be described as troubled protodemocratic regimes. Whether these regimes become an "assemblage of little fascisms," as one Serbian author has described them,[38] or establish stronger democratic institutions and more viable pluralist politics, depends in large measure on their internal management of ultranationalist forces and also on their successful economic recovery. Of course, resolution of both these preceding problems is contingent on the much broader issue of achieving peace and coexistence among the newly independent Balkan states and their diverse ethnic populations. For the moment, the ideological or philosophical basis for such coexistence remains elusive. Thus "Yugoslavism," or the "Yugoslav idea"—as conceived in any of its various earlier emanations (prior to 1918 and also during the royalist and communist periods)—is currently a notion that is dormant or held in wide disrepute and therefore incapable of stimulating closer bonds among the Balkan peoples.

This is not to say that certain groups and individuals desirous of establishing peace in the region and encouraging a spirit supportive of cooperation among the South Slavic peoples and their neighbors are totally absent in the region. "Yugoslavist" and cooperative tendencies are evidenced in various circles, such as among the partners and offspring of the thousands of ethnically mixed marriages who refuse to be divided or to endorse the prevailing ultranationalism, members of fledgling peace groups that have been founded throughout the Balkans, leaders of nonnationalist parties and movements in every region, moderate clergy from all of the major religions, and professionals in many occupations who seek to work together with others in their special areas of concern and expertise irrespective of ethnic origins. Such individuals and groups still harbor hopes for the restoration of interethnic tolerance and perhaps even the encouragement of commitments to some overarching identity on the territory of the former Yugoslav federation that can supersede ethnic and religious divisions. There are also many thousands of others in all regions of the former Yugoslavia who are less actively or consciously committed to cross-ethnic interdependence but who have suffered from the strains of the present war and bloodletting which they did nothing to encourage; they simply yearn for peace and are willing to live with their diverse neighbors to achieve that goal.

Unfortunately, calls for cross-ethnic cooperation, or some kind of renewed pan-ethnic identification, have been temporarily drowned out by the ascendancy of shrill and violent ultranationalism in most regions of the former Yugoslavia. At the onset of 1993, modes of ethnic segregation and intense ethnic conflict dominated the scene throughout Bosnia and in much of Croatia. In Kosovo, where semimilitary rule has produced a tenuous truce between Albanians and Serbs, interdependence and mingling among different ethnic groups have been supplanted by a "semiofficial apartheid system," which can be observed in various aspects of Kosovo's societal life. For example, in Priština, the capital of the province of Kosovo, Albanians and Serbs take separate evening strolls, the "corso," with the Serbs in the center of town and the Albanians taking to the side streets. The major leader of the Kosovo Albanians observed during mid-1992 that he had not taken a walk in the city center for two years. "And if we organized a public protest in the city center there would be a massacre."[39] Elsewhere, such as in parts of Vojvodina, Macedonia, and Serbia proper (without the provinces), where violence remains episodic and ethnic differentiation is less intense, interethnic tensions have been growing steadily. As the Croatian opposition figure Ivan Čičak has observed, in the former Yugoslavia "one can reach out and touch the hatred."[40]

As the turmoil wrought by the Second Yugoslavia's collapse dragged on through 1992 and into 1993 the interelite mistrust and mutual disdain which had helped to instigate the orgy of interethnic bloodletting remained in ample evidence. President Tudjman, for example, reminded an interviewer in June 1992 that for two years he had been alerting observers that:

> There is not just a difference of national identity between the Croatians and Serbs. They are separated by their civilizations. Whether royalist, socialist, or liberal, the Serbs will continue to kill each other. Whether or not Slobodan Milošević is overthrown, whether he succeeds or fails, there is no indication that there will be truly democratic forces to take over. It will still be Balkan-style democracy.[41]

Serbian leaders at the helm of the Third Yugoslavia (Serbia-Montenegro) were equally blunt in describing their Croatian neighbors. For example, while the new Yugoslavia's President Ćosić was willing to negotiate with Croatia's Tudjman on the future relations between their two states, he minced no words when describing the character of Croatian nationalism:

> The foundation of their nationalism has been religion, ever since the mid-nineteenth century. So the Croatian is a Catholic even more than a nationalist. Catholicism in Croatia has the role of an outright constitutional principle. Hence the Croat's profound hostility toward the Serb, guilty in his eyes of two capital sins—both an Orthodox or an atheist and a communist!...And behind Croatian nationalism there lies...hatred of diversity. This ideology subsequently became part of the Serbian people's unconscious, exacerbating antagonism and antipathy, to the extent of mutual hatred and the desire to fight. The tragedy of Serbia and Croatia is exactly that of Cain and Abel.[42]

Beyond the current pattern of ethnic distance, warfare, and general societal disruption in early 1993, it remained unclear whether the various successor states to the Second Yugoslavia, and their ethnically diverse populations, would be able to successfully resuscitate the extensive economic linkages that previously existed among the republics and regions of the disintegrated federation. The imperatives of economic survival and reconstruction, as well as geographic proximity and other earlier interdependencies, suggested that such cooperation would eventually resume despite the recent episodes of terrible ethnic, religious, and political violence. However, unless the war in Bosnia could be brought to an end—and by the spring of 1993 there was still no assurance of such an outcome—it seemed likely that perennial strife in the Balkans would result in the long-term interruption of the region's various "infrastructural links" (e.g., roads, railways, air transport, and telecommunications).[43]

Developing new strategies for overcoming the present violence and establishing routine forms of interstate and interethnic association remain the great challenges for the next generation of Balkan leaders. The fact that the citizens of the Balkan successor states, and particularly the younger generation, have been so deeply affected, alienated, and perhaps even psychologically damaged by the appalling warfare of the early 1990s, only increases the burden confronting those who will assume positions of political leadership. In view of their role in generating or tolerating the events that led to the disintegration of the former Yugoslav state, and also the turbulence and carnage that followed in the wake of that state's collapse, it is highly unlikely that the incumbent political leaders can or will serve as the architects of peace and coexistence.

Political forces in Serbia, Croatia, and Bosnia in particular, but in the other regions as well, must urgently advance new leaders capable of transcending both the politics of narrow nationalism and the discredited pattern of elite intransigence. International assistance can help facilitate the search for Balkan rapprochement, but in the long-term even carefully designed modes of diplomatic, humanitarian, and military intervention by the international community cannot take the place of cooperation among the region's constituent peoples and decisionmakers. Lacking the will and wisdom to overcome their own difficulties, the leaders and citizens of the Balkan region will remain mired in the current "frenzy of hate," or forever chained to its roots and consequences.

Notes

1. The phrase is Lawrence Eagleburger's description of how diplomats have related to the "non-Cold War world." Elaine Sciolino, "A Lame Duck Diplomat Wrestles With a World in Flux," *New York Times*, December 20, 1992, p. 3.

2. The leaders involved, of course, tend to see the matter quite differently. For example, in early 1993 Slobodan Milošević told a *Pravda* interviewer that the dissolution of the former Yugoslav federation was "in the German-Catholic alliances' interest...it all began with the unification of Germany. As soon as that happened, Germany began punishing the victors in the Second World War....Yugoslavia had to be destroyed. Yugoslavia was the first casualty of the policy of revanchism." *BBCSWB*, February 25, 1993, Part 2 (Eastern Europe), C.1 Special Supplement, p. EE/1622/C1. A Serb who served as the former Deputy Federal Secretary for Foreign Affairs in the Marković government has observed that only after the Yugoslav Socialist Federation was unable to control "its own destiny and when, through our own activities, it opened itself to foreign influences, the international community witnessed a sudden revival of the ambition of certain countries, especially the losers in World War One and Two....However these countries were not able to organize the disintegration of Yugoslavia, rather they made use of the opportunity that we ourselves presented them with." Milivoje Maksić, "The 'Foreign Conspiracy' Hype," *Review of International Affairs*, Vol. 43, Nos. 1009-1011 (October 1-December 1, 1992), p. 14.

3. For Austro-Hungarian and Ottoman models of governance see Robin Okey, "State, Church and Nation in the Serbo-Croat speaking Lands of the Hapsburg Monarchy, 1850-1914," in Donal A. Kerr (ed.), *Religion, State and Ethnic Groups* (New York: New York University Press, 1992), pp. 51-78; and Wayne S. Vucinich, "The Nature of Balkan Society Under Ottoman Rule," *Slavic Review*, Vol. 21, No. 4 (December 1962), pp. 597-616.

4. Milorad Ekmečić, *Stvaranje Jugoslavije 1790-1918, Volume II* (Belgrade: Prosveta, 1989), pp. 829-832.

5. Ethnoreligious divisions in Bosnia-Hercegovina intensified during the late nineteenth and early twentieth centuries, creating an "explosive" atmosphere for the ruling authorities. Robert J. Donia, *Islam Under the Double Eagle: The Muslims of Bosnia and Hercegovina, 1878-1914* (New York: Columbia University Press, 1981), pp. 27-29, 187-190.

6. Ivo Andrić, *Gospodjica* (Zagreb: Mladost, 1961), p. 77. On June 19, 1914 a correspondent for the *Times* of London reported that "the town of Serajevo *[sic]* presents such racial and religious excesses that it has been necessary to proclaim a state of siege. The disorders began last night with a demonstration by Catholic Croats, who manifested their horror at the assassination and loyalty to the throne by parading the streets singing the Austrian National Anthem. They were joined by large numbers of Moslem young men…and then proceeded to break the windows of the principal hotels, which are owned by Orthodox Serbs.…Catholics, Moslems, and Tsiganes [Gypsies] of the lowest classes, together with students, marched through the town sacking shops, private houses, and institutions belonging to Orthodox Serbs. The police appeared to remain helpless when finally the troops were called in to preserve order. At Agram [Zagreb], too, anti-Serb demonstrations are taking place. Last night large crowds of Catholic Croats marched through the streets shouting, 'Down with the Serbian murders! Down with the Serbo-Croat Coalition!' After which they broke the windows of Serb houses and of the offices of the principal Serb newspapers." *Times*, June 30, 1914, p. 8. For the interethnic and foreign factors which contributed to a "state of latent revolution" in Bosnia before World War I, see also R.W. Seton-Watson, *The Role of Bosnia in International Politics (1875-1914)* (London: Proceedings of the British Academy, 1931).

7. "Value Orientation and Culture Contact: The Yugoslav Example," *International Journal of Sociology*, Vol. 1, No. 1 (Spring 1971), pp. 20-21.

8. "Explaining Ethnic Antagonism in Yugoslavia," *European Sociological Review*, Vol. 7, No. 3 (December 1991), pp. 183-193.

9. Despite its innovative institutions and "revolutionary" origins, Stevan Pavlowitch has argued that the Tito regime "fell short on imagination perhaps even more than the previous one, for it was essentially interested in power. It claimed to have solved the national question by removing the old order, but it prevented all integrative developments that fell outside its ideological control…or democratic forces, or even the timid yet real flowering of Christian ecumenism in the 1960s." *Tito: Yugoslavia's Great Dictator, A Reassessment* (London: C. Hurst and Company, 1992), p. 100.

10. "Explaining Ethnic Antagonism in Yugoslavia," *European Sociological Review*, Vol. 7, No. 3 (December 1991), p. 192. Public opinion surveys conducted in 1990 convinced researchers in Yugoslavia that the country as a whole, and particularly its multiethnic communities, were "at the edge of national and religious war." Ljiljana Baćević *et al.*, *Jugoslavija na kriznoj prekretnici* (Belgrade: Institut društvenih nauka, 1991), p. 320. The percentage of individuals

identifying themselves by the pan-ethnic designation of "Yugoslav" dropped from 5.4 percent in the 1981 census to 3.0 percent in the 1991 census. In Croatia, the figures were 8.2 percent and 2.2 percent respectively.

11. In a referendum in September 1991, 95 percent of those voting in Macedonia supported independence, though members of the large Albanian minority (20-30 percent of the republic) boycotted the vote.

12. The new Federal Republic of Yugoslavia (FRY) has approximately 10.5 million inhabitants, with Serbs constituting 62 percent of the total population, Albanians 16.6 percent, Montenegrins 5 percent, Hungarians 3.3 percent, "Yugoslavs" 3.2 percent, Moslems 3.1 percent, and all others combined 6.3 percent.

13. See, for example, Zbigniew Brzezinski, "Bombs and Blather: A Strategy Deficit; Can Clinton Find America's Missing Foreign Policy?" *Washington Post*, January 17, 1993, p. C1. For a related view, see Zalmay Khalilzad, "Stop Negotiating With Serbia," *New York Times*, January 7, 1993, p. A15. Cyrus Vance referred to such charges as "mindless criticism...in Bosnia there is no viable alternative to a negotiated settlement...it's nonsense to say that we are appeasers for talking to people who can make a difference in our pursuit of a lasting settlement." David Binder, "Criticized as Appeaser, Vance Defends Balkans Peace Role," *New York Times*, January 19, 1993, p. A6.

14. *Obećana zemlja: politički antimemoari* (Zagreb: Globus International, 1992), p. 491. Commenting on the Tudjman regime's punitive measures against dissident journalists another Croatian observer was even more critical: "Tudjman is a Bolshevik general who became a nationalist leader. Now he talks about democracy. What can you expect. The war is being used as an excuse for everything. If you are a political opponent, you are a traitor. I think that the war will live on in the Croatian media for 20 years while democracy and human rights are ignored." Cited in Philip Sherwell, *Globe and Mail*, August 15, 1992, p. 7. Some critical journalists in neighboring Slovenia have been even sharper in their assessments of the Franjo Tudjman regime, referring to it as "Balkan-style Francoism" or "Franjoism." Vlado Mihelak, "Franjoism and Slovenian-Croatian Relations," *IN*, No. 35 (September 11, 1992), p. 1.

15. Interview with Dražen Budiša, translated in *FBIS-EEU*, September 15, 1992, p. 30. Another presidential candidate, Marko Veselica, put it this way: "The Croatian political crystallization did not occur under the normal conditions of post-communism as was the case in other Eastern countries...a certain nationalistic euphoria occurred which then became an obstacle to democratic development...the war was used as an instrument for forging democracy. People are thus fighting over the methodology of unity. Unity cannot be achieved by parrot-like rituals without critical assessment. We, for example, cannot defend Tudjman's concept of defense if we cannot discuss it at all or influence it in any way." *FBIS-EEU*, April 8, 1992, p. 31. In February 1993, Tudjman's party also won elections for the upper house of Croatia's legislature by a sizeable margin.

16. The major opposition parties boycotted the first election to the newly organized federal Assembly of Yugoslavia at the beginning of June 1992. Of the 106 seats allotted to Serbia in the Chamber of Citizens, Milošević's SPS won 73 seats, while the ultranationalist Serbian Radical Party (SRS) won 30 seats (2 seats went to a Hungarian minority party, and 1 to small citizen's group). Overall turnout in the election was approximately 56 percent (16 percent less than in the 1990 election), but in the Kosovo electoral district of Priština, where Albanian citizens and parties boycotted the election, the turnout was only 24 percent. The number of invalid ballots cast was 7 percent, indicating a high level of dissatisfaction and a pattern reminiscent of the noncompetitive elections under the single-party regime.

17. Interview with Vojislav Koštunica, translated in *FBIS-EEU*, October 29, 1992, p. 50. For additional analysis of limitations on democratic development in Milošević's Serbia see Lenard J. Cohen, "Regime Transition in a Disintegrating Yugoslavia: The Law-of-Rule vs. the Rule-of-Law," *Carl Beck Papers in Russian and East European Studies*, No. 908 (April 1992).

18. In early 1993, there was also evidence that political purges in Serbia were expanding from the media and political jobs in state institutions to include nonpolitical jobs in the arts, medicine, and the educational system. Marcus Tanner, "Serbia is Swept by 'Political Cleansing'," *Independent*, February 5, 1993, p. 10.

19. Marcus Tanner, "Albanians in Kosovo Set Up a Shadow State," *Independent*, July 20, 1992, p. 10.

20. *FBIS-EEU*, October 13, 1992, p. 40. See also, Prvoslav Ralić, *Minority Rights in Serbia* (Belgrade: The Ministry of Information of the Republic of Serbia, 1992).

21. For an excellent discussion of the differences between individualistic-libertarian nationalism and collectivistic-authoritarian nationalism, see Liah Greenfield, *Nationalism: Five Roads to Modernity* (Cambridge: Harvard University Press, 1992), pp. 10-12. On the complex relationship between nationalism and democracy, see also G. Nodie, "Nationalism and Democracy," *Journal of Democracy*, Vol. 3, No. 4 (October 1992), pp. 3-23; and Francis Fukuyama, *The End of History and the Last Man* (New York: Free Press, 1992), pp. 266-275.

22. Robert Hayden, "Yugoslavia Where Self-Determination Meets Ethnic Cleansing," *New Perspectives Quarterly*, Vol. 9, No. 4 (Fall 1992), pp. 41-46.

23. *FBIS-EEU*, October 6, 1992, pp. 31-32. See also, Dušan Bilandžić, *et al.* (eds.), *Croatia Between War and Independence* (Zagreb: University of Zagreb, 1991).

24. The Croatian military's initial success against the Serbs probably helped Tudjman's HDZ in winning approximately two-thirds of the vote in the February 7, 1993 election for the upper house of the Croatian legislature.

25. Darko Štrajn, "How Democracy Creates Itself," *IN*, Nos. 30-31 (July 31, 1992), p. 1.

26. "Quasi-Government," *IN*, No. 85 (November 11, 1991), p. 1.

27. Igor Zagar, "A 'New' Slovene Essence of Being Slovene," *IN*, No. 36 (September 18, 1992), p. 1, and "Slovenianness," *IN*, No. 29 (July 24, 1992), p. 1.

28. *BBCSWB*, August 29, 1992, Part 2 (Eastern Europe: London Conference on Former Yugoslavia), p. EE/1472/C2/1.

29. By mid-December 1992, the Croatian government's Office Displaced Persons and Refugees registered 268,526 persons displaced from their homes in Croatia and 426,852 refugees from Bosnia-Hercegovina who had come to Croatia. *Glasnik ureda za prognanike i izbjeglice*, Vol. 1, No. 20 (December 16, 1992).

30. *Reuters*, January 15, 1992.

31. Nenad Stefanović, "Crime and the Authorities," *Vreme News Digest Agency*, No. 74 (February 22, 1993), p. 24. The flight from Yugoslavia in March 1993 of one of Belgrade's major private bankers, Ježdimir Vasiljević, threatened the savings of thousands of Serbs who had hoped to benefit from the high interest rates offered by his bank (Jugoskandik). American officials saw the Vasiljević affair and a rash of other financial scandals in Belgrade as evidence that international economic sanctions against Serbia were having their intended effect, and that popular opposition to the Milošević regime was one likely result of the situation. *New York Times*, March 21, 1993, p. 6. There was also evidence, however, that the sanctions against Serbia were backfiring into support for the war among those segments of the Serbian population who saw a "plot against the nation." *New York Times*, March 27, 1993, p. 4.

32. *FBIS-EEU*, October 8, 1992, p. 37.

33. Election observers, including this author, from the CSCE countries who assessed the December 20, 1992 election in Serbia, concluded that this voting process was "seriously flawed" but nonetheless a competitive exercise.

34. Interviewed in August 1991, Šešelj claimed that he was a "warlord" awarded the title by the "oldest living Chetnik leader" in California. He specified his notion of Serbia's appropriate borders as including "the current Serbia, including the provinces of Vojvodina and Kosovo...the republics of Bosnia-Hercegovina, Macedonia and Montenegro, and the Serbian parts of Croatia." When asked if he was Milošević's henchman, he remarked: "If I come to power, I will probably arrest Milošević. As long as the Americans try to overthrow Milošević...however, I will help Milošević." *FBIS-EEU*, August 5, 1991, p. 53. During early 1993, human rights groups in Belgrade reported that some Milošević supporters and right-wing paramilitary groups in Serbia were intimidating and harassing political opponents suspected of being anti-Serbian. Louise Branson, "Milošević Imposes a Reign of Terror in Belgrade," *Sunday Times*, February 14, 1993, p. 1.

35. Cited in Robert Block, "Serbs Fail to Hide Pain of UN Sanctions," *Independent*, January 4, 1993, p. 6.

36. Dragan Bujošević, "The Time of Unstable Government," *Politika: The International Weekly*, Nos. 146-147, January 2-15, 1993, p. 1.

37. Leon Magdalenc, "Weekly Politics, Popular Slovenians," *IN*, January 22, 1993, p. 7.

38. Stojan Cerović, as translated in *FBIS-EEU*, October 6, 1992, p. 40.

39. Marcus Tanner, "Albanians in Kosovo Set Up a Shadow State," *Independent*, July 20, 1992, p. 10.

40. Interview with Ivan Čičak, translated in *FBIS-EEU*, June 11, 1992, p. 42.

41. *FBIS-EEU*, June 26, 1992, p. 19.

42. *FBIS-EEU*, September 15, 1992, p. 35.

43. Zoran Medved, "Statistical Truths," *IN*, February 12, 1993, p. 1.

About the Book and Author

Struggling against high odds, Yugoslavia managed to survive from its inception in 1918 until the early 1990s. But now, tragic ethnic and regional conflicts have irrevocably fragmented the country. In his timely book, Lenard Cohen explores the original conception and motives underlying the "Yugoslav idea," looking at the state's major problems, achievements, and failures during its short and troubled history.

Cohen answers a broad range of questions concerning contemporary Yugoslavia: How did the state plunge from its position as a positive model to an essentially negative case of socialist reform? What measures for recovery were proposed by the country's ethnically and regionally segmented one-party elite? What were the reasons for the eventual abandonment of reform socialism, the elimination of the single party's monopoly, and the rapid delegitimation of the country's federal political institutions? What programs have been offered by the noncommunist and "born-again" communist leaders elected to power during the revival of multiparty pluralism in 1990? How did their efforts to achieve regional and ethnic sovereignty place the country in such a precarious and ultimately fatal position?

The book concludes with an analysis of the causes and horrifying consequences of the civil war, a discussion of the impotent efforts at peace-keeping and an overview of the problems faced by Yugoslavia's successor states, and the future viability of the Yugoslav idea.

Lenard J. Cohen is a professor of political science at Simon Fraser University, British Columbia, Canada. His two earlier books on Yugoslavia are *Political Cohesion in a Fragile Mosaic: The Yugoslav Experience* (Boulder, Colo.: Westview Press, 1983), and *The Socialist Pyramid: Elites and Power in Yugoslavia* (Oakville, Ontario: Mosaic Press, 1989).

Index